Y0-BEK-517

Public Policy and Economic Theory

RENEWALS 458-4574
DATE DUE

WITHDRAWN
UTSA LIBRARIES

Previous titles in this series:

Public Policy and Economic Theory

Edited by
Torben M. Andersen
and
Karl O. Moene

Copyright © Scandinavian Journal of Economics 1998

First published 1998

Blackwell Publishers
108 Cowley Road, Oxford OX4 1JF, UK
and
350 Main Street,
Malden, MA 02148, USA

All rights reserved. Except for the quotation of short passages for the purposes of criticism and review, no part of this publication may be reproduced, stored in a retrieval system, or transmitted, in any form or by any means, electronic, mechanical, photocopying, recording or otherwise, without the prior permission of the publisher.

Except in the United States of America, this book is sold subject to the condition that it shall not, by way of trade or otherwise, be lent, re-sold, hired out, or otherwise circulated without the publisher's prior consent in any form of binding or cover other than that in which it is published and without a similar condition including this condition being imposed on the subsequent purchaser.

British Library Cataloguing in Publication Data applied for

Library of Congress Cataloguing in Publication Data applied for

ISBN 0-631-20943-3

Library
University of Texas
at San Antonio

Printed in Great Britain by Page Bros, Norwich

Contents

Editors' Preface

The relevance of theoretical and empirical methods for public policy issues has been among the core interests of *The Scandinavian Journal of Economics* (*SJE*) since the first volume was published as *Ekonomisk Tidskrift* in 1899. It is in keeping with this tradition that our anniversary volume is devoted to the interlinkages between economic theory, econometrics and economic policy. This book is based on papers presented at a conference organized by the *SJE* at Lysebu/Oslo, January 30–February 1, 1997, to celebrate the 100th anniversary of the journal. The invited contributors were asked to highlight important links between public policy and theoretical advances within their own field of expertise in economics. To broaden the perspective, each paper is followed by two discussions. The resulting papers provide fresh insights on policy implications as well as on how challenges in policymaking have been addressed by different subdisciplines. We are proud to publish the contributions of so many prominent scholars.

Neither the symposium nor the publication of these proceedings could have taken place without external financial support, and we would like to take this opportunity to thank the Central Banks of Denmark, Finland, Iceland, Norway and Sweden, the Norwegian Research Council, Oslo, and the Yrjö Jahnsson Foundation, Helsinki, for their generosity.

Torben M. Andersen and Karl O. Moene

Scand. J. of Economics 100(1), 1–9, 1998

The First Century of *The Scandinavian Journal of Economics*

Mats Persson

IIES, Stockholm University, S-106 91 Stockholm, Sweden

Abstract

This paper surveys the history of *The Scandinavian Journal of Economics* and the early contributions of e.g. Davidson, Wicksell, Cassel, Heckscher, Ohlin, Myrdal and Lindahl. It also analyses the population dynamics of economics journals. Finally, it addresses some issues concerning the publishing and editing of professional journals, raised by the emergence of new electronic media, internet publication, etc.

I. The History

The Scandinavian Journal of Economics first appeared, under the name of *Ekonomisk Tidskrift* ("Economic Journal"), in 1899. It was the brainchild of David Davidson (1854–1942), Professor of Economics at Uppsala University.[1] The first volume contained 22 articles, of which Davidson himself had written seven, but he had also secured contributions by some of Sweden's most distinguished economists, including four articles by Gustav Cassel, and two by Knut Wicksell. Reading the contributions by the latter two personalities, one can sense the competitive tension between them even at this early date; they simply cannot avoid pecking at each other, and the combat evolves in subsequent volumes. Sweden just doesn't seem large enough for both of them.

In the 1899 volume, there were also 16 short notes, three of which were signed by Davidson and five unsigned — but probably written by the diligent editor himself. Finally, there were 17 book reviews, one of which was Davidson's respectful but cautiously noncommittal review of Wicksell's *Geldzinz und Güterpreise*, which had been published the previous year.[2]

The intricate principal/agent problem of journal editing had been solved in an elegant manner which is well worth considering by today's editors: Davidson himself provided the funding, he was the owner as well as the editor. He then ran the journal basically as a one-man operation, being

---

[1] On Davidson, see Uhr (1975, 1989) and Heckscher (1952).
[2] I would like to say many nice things about Davidson, but in this case I must admit that he had not fully understood the work of his junior colleague.

editorial secretary and referee as well (this part of the deal is not recommended to today's editors), sometimes using Wicksell as a complementary referee. When he retired at the age of 85, in 1939, he was succeeded by the joint editorship of Erik Lundberg and Ingvar Svennilson.

Browsing today through the old volumes makes for some fascinating reading. During those early years the journal is quantitatively dominated by Davidson (250 signed articles and an unknown number of unsigned ones), followed by Wicksell (80 articles), Heckscher (60) and Cassel (30) — but all Swedish economists of any importance in those days are amply represented. For the historian, the journal provides a rich and untapped source of knowledge of the ongoing scholarly debate. In fact, apart from the Davidson portrait by Heckscher (1952) and occasional references by Uhr (1975), the history of the journal still remains to be written.

It contains, however, many interesting contributions. In the second volume, for example, there is an article where Wicksell (1900) uses the constant-returns-to-scale production function $y = k^{\alpha} \cdot \ell^{1-\alpha}$, which the Anglo-Saxon world attributes to Messrs. Cobb & Douglas, who employed it almost three decades later. Subsequent volumes include such classics as Heckscher's first statement of what was later to be called the Heckscher–Ohlin theory of international trade[3] (1919, Part II) and Lindahl's wonderfully sharp analysis (1929) of intertemporal general equilibrium, with rational expectations and all.[4] Another influential piece is Myrdal's lengthy paper (1931) containing the seeds of the *ex ante* and *ex post* analysis (although he does not explicitly use those terms in the paper) which was later to appear as a cornerstone of his 1939 book on *Monetary Equilibrium*.

The book reviews are particularly interesting in retrospect. Nowadays, when we know so much more about what books turned out to be important and what books did not, it is sometimes rather moving to see the contemporary reviewers struggling with the material and trying to find a proper context for it. By reading, for example, Davidson's review of Keynes's *A Tract on Monetary Reform* (1924) and Palander's of *The General Theory* (which needed several years of digestion and did not appear until 1942), or Dickson's review of Hick's *Value and Capital* (1941), we can get an interesting perspective on the dissemination of new ideas in the academic community.

To do justice to all these contributions, substantial space and scholarship are required. Being equipped with neither, I just want to delve into one piquant item: Wicksell's 32-page review of Cassel's *Theoretische Sozialökonomie* in the 1919 volume. This may well be the most malicious review of

---

[3] English translation in Heckscher and Ohlin (1991).
[4] A slightly revised English translation in Lindahl (1939).

a major work ever written in the history of economics; apart from its importance for those who study the history of doctrines, it is of considerable psychological interest. Grossly unfair, but nevertheless with a grain of truth, Wicksell deprives Cassel of all dignity and respectability, both as a man and a scientist, concluding with the ominous verdict:[5]

> "Macaulay mentions as a characteristic of James II that when a member of his court dared to contradict him and humbly warn him against the consequences of his explicit avowals, he used to repeat what he had said in identically the same way and then believed that *he had sufficiently refuted all objections*. Such a method may be all very well for kings in difficulties, although, as the example shows, it has its dangers even for them. For laymen who have not yet become the acknowledged monarchs of their subject it is decidedly not to be recommended. Professor Cassel must learn — unless it is indeed too late — to use his critical faculties on himself as well as on others, to give as well as to take — otherwise his life-work will not survive critcism."

In the beginning, all papers were written in Swedish. The first paper in English, Jan Tinbergen's "The Use of Correlation Analysis in Economnic Research", appeared in 1947, and then the number of English papers increased steadily. In 1965, the journal switched entirely into English under the new name of *The Swedish Journal of Economics*. After a decade, it was maintained that Sweden alone could not support such a large venture as an international scholarly journal. It was thus transformed into an inter-Nordic undertaking, with financial and human capital provided by all the Nordic countries, and the name was consequently changed into the present one in 1976.

II. The International Environment

It is interesting to note that only twenty years ago, the joint efforts of the Nordic countries were barely sufficient to run this journal. Today our profession has grown so much that two more economics journals aimed at the international research community are thriving in this remote corner of Europe: the *Finnish Economic Papers* (esatablished in 1988), and the *Swedish Economic Policy Review* (established in 1993).

Let us widen the geographical scope. Today, the number of international scholarly journals is really staggering, and it seems to increase every month. It is, of course, difficult to decide what constitutes a "scholarly" journal; let us for simplicity accept the listing by Miller and Punsalan (1988). They cover 214 international journals that were in the market in 1984. Of these, 13 were established before 1900 — although some of them are perhaps rather marginal to the economics profession today. If we limit

---

[5] English translation in Wicksell (1934).

ourselves to the Top 100 economics journals,[6] only a handful were established before 1900:

> *Journal of the Royal Statistical Society, Series A* (1838)
> *The Quarterly Journal of Economics* (1886)
> *The Economic Journal* (1981)
> *Yale Law Journal* (1891)
> *Journal of Political Economy* (1892)
> *The Scandinavian Journal of Economics* (1899)

Our journal thus belongs to a rather exclusive sisterhood. After 1900, things changed quickly. By arranging the 214 journals of Miller and Punsalan (1988) in order of first appearance, Figure 1 provides us with a vivid picture of the great publication boom of the last two or three decades.

The Miller and Punsalan data set obviously suffers from what is called *survivorship bias* in the financial literature; it includes only those of the older journals that had survived in 1984. But with detailed data on the age distribution of the existing stock at a given point in time, we can correct for such a bias and obtain interesting information about the journal populaton dynamics. Assume a population where each individual is subject to the

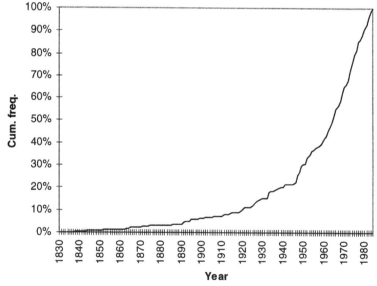

Fig. 1. Cumulative distribution over time of the dates of first appearance of the 214 economics journals listed in Miller and Punsalan (1988)

---

[6] Ranking according to Laband and Piette (1994).

same death probability, δ, which does not change over the individual's lifetime. Assume further that there is a constant birth rate β such that, at each time t, the size of the population is S_t, while in the next period βS_t individuals will be born and δS_t individuals will die. It is then straightforward to show that at any time t, the fraction of individuals of age n, i.e., the fraction of individuals who were born at time $(t-n)$, in the population is given by

$$f_n = \frac{\beta}{1+\beta-\delta} \left(\frac{1-\delta}{1+\beta-\delta} \right)^n.$$

Given observations of the age distribution, the parameters of this equation can in principle be estimated. This is not a straightforward procedure, however; it is considerably simpler if we can obtain an estimate of one of the parameters from some other data source. I have therefore used EconLit, the electronic database of the American Economic Association, to estimate $\hat{\delta}$. That database now (early 1997) covers 539 journals. Backtracking, it covers 192 journals from 1969. This would imply an annual growth rate of 7.2%, but such a figure is an overestimation due to the "inclusion bias": the number of journals in EconLit increases not only because the number of existing journals grows, but also because a larger fraction of the existing journals successively gets included in the database. This objection does not apply to the use of EconLit for estimating the death rate. The disappearance of a journal from the database could be due either to actual discontinuation of the journal or to a decision by the managers of the database to delete it because it does not belong there any longer — and both contingencies could be said to correspond to the "death" of a scholarly journal. Of the original 192 journals, 137 are still in the database in 1997. This implies an annual death rate of 2.2%.

With this information, we can easily estimate the above nonlinear relationship between f_n and n to obtain estimates of the birth rate $\hat{\beta}$ and the growth rate $\hat{g} \equiv \hat{\beta} - \hat{\delta}$. Running the regression for three different subperiods,[7] I have obtained the estimates in Table 1.

Since the estimates are surprisingly constant over the subperiods, our assumption of constant birth and death probabilities is perhaps not entirely unrealistic — even if the low $\bar{R}^2$ and Durbin–Watson statistics seem to indicate that there are substantial short-run movements around the long-run exponential trend. Using the estimates for the latest subperiod of Table 1 above to extrapolate the 214 Miller and Punsalan journals into 1997, we obtain an estimate of today's stock of journals: there are 245 of

---

[7] The subperiod 1952–1984 was chosen because 1951 is the last year with an observed f value equal to zero.

Table 1. *Estimates of birth and growth rates of the number of economics journals, 1838–1984*

Period	$\hat{\beta}$	$\hat{g}$	$\bar{R}^2$	DW
1838–1984	0.0297	0.0077	0.6383	1.6408
1952–1984	0.0309	0.0089	0.0902	1.3820
1970–1984	0.0294	0.0074	−0.1981	1.5196

them.[8] With a birth rate of 2.97%, this means that there are 7 new journals appearing every year, or one new journal every 50 days.[9]

It was a relatively simple task to be one of the Top 10 journals in 1900, but it is probably much more difficult to be in the Top 100 league in 2000. If the death rate is constant, our journal may not be handicapped by its high age. But one may still ask the question: is there room for *The Scandinavian Journal of Economics* in the twenty-first century?

III. The Next Century

As an economist, I should try to avoid making forecasts of the future, since this is an area where we definitely do not have a good track record. Still, it might be said that since there is obviously room for so many new journals, there will be room for our journal, too — provided, of course, that we can stay competitive. There is one issue, however, which raises the much broader question of whether there will be any room for traditional journals at all in the twenty-first century. This is the issue of electronic networks and Internet publication.[10] Many people think that these new distribution channels will revolutionize the world of journal publishing. I do not share that view. Of course, any technological change will affect market structure — the number of firms, the size distribution of firms, and the welfare of the consumers — but I think this particular change will not have substantially greater impact than other technological advances in the history of journal publishing.

According to a common view, a journal is a device for making papers available to readers If this were true, all journals, with their painstakingly long publication lags and expensive distribution technology, should of course be replaced by electronic bulletin boards; as soon as a scholar has

---

[8] This could be compared to the 539 journals in EconLit. Obviously, the two databases have different criteria for inclusion. There is no reason to believe that the birth and death rates are substantially different, however,

[9] If we instead use the 539 journals in EconLit, and apply a birth rate of 2.97%, we find that there are 16 new journals every year, or one new journal every 23 days.

[10] See Jacob (1996) and Goffe and Parks (1997) and the references cited therein.

completed a paper, it will then be immediately made available to the entire economics community.

The view of *the journal as a bulletin board*, however, can be challenged by the view of *the journal as a filter*. According to the latter, a professional journal is a device not for making all papers immediately available to everyone, but a device for disseminating knowledge. This means publishing papers as well as rejecting papers. When the new electronic media make it economically possible for anyone to post his or her own journal, the role of the journal as a filter becomes even more important.

In technical jargon, a journal editor can make two types of errors:

Type 1 error: To reject a good paper[11]
Type 2 error: To accept a bad paper.

Examples of *Type 1 errors* are abundant and often have a high entertainment value; see for example Gans and Shepherd (1994) and Shepherd (1995). An author who has been subject to a *Type 2 error* does not have a similar incentive to make his case known to the profession, and therefore such stories are considerably less frequent.

The above-mentioned view of the journal as a bulletin board implies that the probability of *Type 1 errors* is reduced to zero, while the probability of *Type 2 errors* is increased to unity. Whatever the optimal tradeoff between these two errors, it is hardly likely that it corresponds to such an extreme point on the probability–possibility frontier. This means that the view of the journal as a filter remains valid, and thus the role of the traditional journal — although maybe distributed both as an electronic file and as a paper copy — remains.

This in turn means that publication lags cannot be reduced as dramatically as is sometimes claimed. With electronic publishing, we can save the time it takes to typeset the traditional journal and distribute the paper copies.[12] For the average journal of today, this procedure takes a few months — but anyone who has served as editor knows that this is not a major part of the publication lag. Since it is hard to see why electronically

---

[11] For the sake of brevity, I will avoid the philosophical question of what ultimately constitutes a "good" paper. Note, however, that the history of science provides many examples of scientific works that were considered "good" by the general public, or by the contemporary academic establishment — but that have nevertheless been unfavourably judged by posterity.

[12] We sometimes hear the argument that e-mail will make Internet publishing even more time efficient than traditional publishing, since editors can then communicate faster with authors and referees. This argument relies, however, on a misconception of the basis for comparison. Even traditional paper-copy journals can use e-mail or fax to communicate with authors and referees, and thus these new communication channels do not affect the relative position of Internet publishing.

submitted manuscripts would make it easier for an editor to find willing and reliable referees, and would induce those referees to do a quicker job than they do today, it is also hard to see why electronic publication will result in any major reduction of the publication lag.

What will probably happen is that electronic bulletin boards will assume the role of today's (non-refereed) working paper series. Refereed journals, on the other hand, will play essentially the same role as they do today — whether as electronic channels or paper copies or both. By bestowing their *imprimatur* on a subset of the articles found in working paper series, these journals will signal a certain level of quality (which could, of course, be subject to the *Type 2 error* mentioned above). Like in all markets where signaling is important, it is difficult to say anything specific about the uniqueness or the optimality of equilibrium — but this problem is basically the same for paper-copy journals as for electronic ones.

Things have really changed since the days when David Davidson struggled with ink-blotted manuscripts in Uppsala, now and then dispatching them to Wicksell in Lund for occasional refereeing. With increased specialization and a more extensive use of referees, our journal has perhaps become more efficient than it was in those days, in the sense that we might have been able to reduce the probability of *Type 2 errors* without simultaneously increasing the probability of *Type 1 errors*. We are thus closer to the probability–possiblity frontier.

There is, however, no reason to believe that Internet publishing *per se* will result in any major efficiency gains of that kind.[13] We will be able to save some time in the actual production process, and that's about all. There is perhaps a slight chance that the publication lags in some favorable cases will be brought down to what they were in David Davidson's days, when the editorial process took maybe a month (including one or two revisions) and when the printer delivered the final product after just another month. Twenty-first century technology helping us to attain nineteenth century publication lags is, of course, a good thing — but that could hardly be called a revolution.

References

Gans, Joshua S. and Shepherd, George B.: How are the mighty fallen: Rejected classic articles by leading economists. *Journal of Economic Perspectives 8*, 165–179, 1994.
Goffe, W. L. and Parks, R. P.: The future information infrastructure in economics. *Journal of Economic Perspectives 11*, 75–94, 1997.

---

[13] There are some factors that might lead to productivity increases in research in general, in the sense that *Type 2 errors*, once made, will be revealed more quickly. For example, with electronic publications, data sets and programs used in published articles could be more easily available for replication.

Heckscher, Eli F.: David Davidson. *International Economic Papers 2*, 111–135, 1952; first published in Swedish in *Ekonomisk Tidskrift 53*, 127–160, 1951.

Heckscher, Eli F. and Ohlin, Bertil: *Heckscher–Ohlin Trade Theory*. MIT Press, Cambridge, MA, 1991.

Jacob, Herbert: The future is electronic. *Social Science Quarterly 77*, 204–209, 1996.

Laband, David N. and Piette, Michael J.: The relative impact of economics journals: 1970–1990. *Journal of Economic Literature 32*, 640–666, 1994.

Lindahl, Erik: *Studies in the Theory of Money and Capital*. George Allen & Unwin, London, 1939.

Miller, A. Carolyn and Punsalan, Victoria J. (compilers): *Refereed and Nonrefereed Economic Journals. A Guide to Publishing Opportunities*. Greenwood Press, Westport, CT and London, 1988.

Shepherd, George B. (ed.): *Rejected. Leading Economists Ponder the Publication Process*. Horton and Daughters, Sun Lakes, AZ, 1995.

Uhr, Carl G.: *Economic Doctrines of David Davidson*. Uppsala, 1975.

Uhr, Carl G.: David Davidson. *Ekonomisk Debatt 17*, 283–290, 1989.

Wicksell, Knut: Om gränsproduktiviteten såsom grundval för den nationalekonomiska fördelningen (On marginal productivity as the foundation of economic distribution). *Ekonomisk Tidskrift 2*, 305 37, 1900.

Wicksell, Knut: *Lectures on Political Economy. Vol. 1: General Theory*. Routledge, London, 1934.

Scand. J. of Economics 100(1), 11–32, 1998

Efficiency with Non-Convexities: Extending the "Scandinavian Consensus" Approaches*

Peter J. Hammond

Department of Economics, Stanford University, CA 94305–6072, USA

Antonio Villar

Department of Economics, University of Alicante and I.V.I.E., E-03080 Alicante, Spain

Abstract

There are two distinct "Scandinavian consensus" approaches to public good supply, both based on agents' willingness to pay. A Wicksell–Foley public competitive equilibrium arises from a negative consensus in which no change of public environment, together with associated taxes and subsidies which finance it, will be unanimously approved. Alternatively, in a Lindahl or valuation equilibrium, charges for the public environment induce a positive consensus. To allow general non-convexities to be regarded as aspects of the public environment, we extend recent generalizations of these equilibrium notions and prove counterparts to both the usual fundamental efficiency theorems of welfare economics.

I. Introduction and Outline

Non-Convexities and the Public Environment

A modern mixed economy can be regarded as combining a private market sector with a public non-market sector. In the private market sector, individual economic agents make decisions within their private feasible sets. These private agents take as given certain important variables which are determined outside the market mechanism, often as a result of deliberate public policy decisions. Examples of such non-market variables include prevailing social rules like the legal system and especially the assignment of property rights. They also include private goods provided by the public

---

* We are particularly grateful to the discussants at the symposium, Agnar Sandmo and Jean-Charles Rochet, for their insightful remarks which have led to several improvements. For encouraging and helpful comments on earlier versions of different parts of this work, thanks are also due to an anonymous referee, to the editors of this Journal, to Joaquim Silvestre and Kotaro Suzumura, as well as to Luis Corchón, Ignacio Ortuño-Ortin, Jim Mirrlees, Karl Shell, David Starrett, and other members of seminar audiences at Cambridge, Essex, Hitotsubashi and Stanford Universities, and at the European University Institute. We also wish to acknowledge the financial support provided by the Spanish DGICYT (Dirección General de Investigación Científica y Técnica) under project PB92-0342 which, in particular, has facilitated our collaboration.

sector, such as many transport, health and education services. Often, what matters here is the quality rather than the quantity of these services. Other non-market variables can be used to describe the regulation of private economic activity through quotas, quality standards, legislation affecting health and safety at work, etc. The working of the tax and benefit system in the economy is yet another kind of non-market variable. Finally, many externalities and environmental concerns involve non-market variables, even if the rights or duties to create externalities are allocated through the price mechanism — e.g., through a market for pollution licences, or allocating the contract for providing an unprofitable but socially desirable bus or rail service to whichever private firm demands the lowest subsidy.

All such non-market variables constitute what we choose to call the *public environment*, or simply the *environment*. This is a very broad concept allowing many different economic problems to be treated within one unified framework. The environment in this sense will be treated as a public good, that is as a collection of variables which are common to all agents. Needless to say, the environment may in turn affect agents' feasible sets and objectives. Devising a good procedure which determines each aspect of the public environment, together with the taxes needed to finance that environment, is obviously one of the key tasks of economic policy makers.

In order to ecompass many different situations, our mathematical framework follows Mas-Colell (1980) in allowing the vector z of variables describing the environment to range over an abstract set Z with no special structure. In particular, Z need not be convex. This framework allows us to discuss, in principle, not only non-convexities in public sector decisions, but also issues such as whether to allow production by private firms with fixed set-up costs. The idea of treating what may be private non-convexities in this way appears to be due to Malinvaud (1969, 1972) and to an unpublished Ph. D. thesis due to Beato; see also Dierker (1986) and Laffont (1988).

Readers may recall that classical writers like Say (1826), Dupuit (1844), or Hotelling (1938) discussed large projects such as those involving roads, bridges, canals, or railways. Whether or not the constructor and/or the operator is privately owned, such projects inevitably have many of the features of a public good. In part, this is because they create pecuniary externalities in the form of modifications to the price system as a whole, especially in the geographical vicinity of any such project. For this reason, a major issue of public policy is to create guidelines for determining the criteria under which each such potential project is to be accepted or rejected, and how the project is to be financed if it is accepted. In fact, whether a private firm should incur significant set-up costs is virtually always a public policy issue, even if it is usually not recognized as such. This is because it shares the key features of a decision affecting public goods or the public environment in some more conventional sense.

With this background in mind, the main concern of the paper is to characterize Pareto efficient allocations in such a mixed economy, when for each given public environment, including variables describing non-convexities, agents trade private goods competitively. In order to do so we shall look for equilibrium concepts for which both the efficiency theorems of welfare economics are true — that is, any equilibrium allocation should be Pareto efficient, and conversely (under suitable assumptions). In this respect, the much discussed marginal cost pricing rules fail because, without suitable lump-sum redistribution of initial wealth, marginal cost pricing equilibria need not be Pareto efficient — see, for example, the recent discussions by Guesnerie (1989), Quinzii (1992) and Villar (1994, 1996). Our characterization will involve suitably revised versions of both the Wicksell (1896) and the Lindahl (1919) approaches to the efficient provision of public goods. More specifically, we shall consider appropriate revisions of the equilibrium notions which more modern economic theorists have created in order to capture their ideas. These notions may be regarded as further extensions of the "Scandinavian consensus" — to use the evocative term due to Bergstrom (1970), who analysed consumption externalities using a development of Lindahl's approach.

Two Kinds of Consensus

In fact, the literature on public goods presents us with two main approaches to the problem of achieving a Pareto efficient allocation. The first harks back to Wicksell (1896), but was originally formalized in modern mathematical terms by Foley (1967). This approach tends to regard the choice of public goods z as an essentially political matter, about which the economist has little to say. This is the kind of allocation which Foley called "publicly competitive", and which Malinvaud (1969, 1972) called, perhaps more appropriately, a "politico-economic" equilibrium. The Wicksell–Foley idea is to have either the community of agents, or its representatives in government, draw up proposals for both public good production and taxes to finance this production. These are "public sector proposals." Then any public sector proposal can be amended if and only if each consumer in the economy, and each producer, favours the amendment. A consumer will favour the amendment if, taking present prices for private goods as given, the change in the public goods which are provided gives a net benefit exceeding the net cost of any extra taxes that have to be paid. A firm will favour the amendment if the change in the public goods which are provided, including those which it might be called on to produce, allows it to cover the (net) cost of any extra taxes it has to pay from the extra net profit it makes at fixed prices. An equilibrium results from a negative consensus, in which agents are unable to agree unanimously on how to change the public environment.

The second main approach to the problem of achieving Pareto efficiency with public goods is named after Lindahl (1919). It requires all consumers and private producers to pay a "Lindahl price" for each public good according to the marginal benefits which they receive from it. Each public good is produced so that the total marginal benefit to all private consumers and producers is equal to the marginal cost of providing it. In equilibrium the Lindahl prices must be chosen so as to reach a positive consensus, in which all agents agree that the same public environment is optimal, given their budget constraints or profit functions.

When non-convexities are involved, however, setting prices equal to marginal benefits is clearly going to be insufficient, in general. So we adapt an idea due to Mas-Colell (1980) and allow a valuation scheme with non-linear Lindahl pricing — see also Vega-Redondo (1987), as well as Diamantaras and Gilles (1996), Diamantaras, Gilles and Scotchmer (1996). This leads us to consider what Mas-Colell calls a *valuation equilibrium*, which is defined as a price vector, a tax system, a feasible allocation, and a public environment such that: (a) each consumer's equilibrium combination of a private net trade vector together with the public environment is weakly preferred to any other such combination which is affordable, given the non-linear tax system; (b) each firm's combination of a net output vector for private goods together with the public environment is chosen to maximize profit over its production set, given the non-linear tax system; and (c) aggregate net tax payments (i.e., taxes less subsidies) are zero.[1]

Outline of Paper

In the rest of the paper, Section II describes our model. It is a "conditionally convex" economy in the sense that, for each fixed public environment $z \in Z$, there is a standard Arrow–Debreu private good economy satisfying the usual convexity and continuity conditions.

Thereafter, Section III considers publicly competitive equilibria, using an extension of Foley's definition. In Foley's formulation, private agents

---

[1] In a private economy where some production sets may be non-convex, Brown and Heal (1980) consider interesting decentralizations of Pareto efficient alocations by means of non-linear "value functions". These functions, however, are restricted to be homogeneous of degree one, which only makes sense when the domain is a linear space. In addition, their equilibria need not be Pareto efficient, so their equilibrium concept does not characterize efficient allocations.

are implicitly assumed to be "myopic" in the sense that they ignore how the equilibrium prices of private goods depend on the choice of public environment. This is an instance of price-taking behaviour in which agents neglect the influence of even collective decisions upon private good prices. Of course, when there is only one private good, as in Mas-Colell (1980) and many other papers, this is not an issue. Also, in the absence of non-convexities, one can usually disregard the effect of any marginal change in the public environment on the equilibrium prices of private goods.

By contrast, we assume that all agents see how the change in public environment passes an appropriate cost–benefit test when one considers a suitable new conditional equilibrium price vector. In this sense, agents are assumed to be "far-sighted." This plays an important role in finding counterparts to the usual efficiency theorems of welfare economics when there are many private goods and also non-convexities associated with the public environment.

Section IV turns towards the Lindahl approach, and — like Diamantaras and Gilles (1996), Diamantaras, Gilles and Scotchmer (1996) — looks for a simple generalization to economies with many private goods of those results due to Mas-Colell (1980) which characterize Pareto efficient allocations as valuation equilibria.[2] Unlike previous writers, however, we allow the non-linear valuation of the public environment to depend also on prices for private commodities. This allows Mas-Colell's results to be extended to economies with many private commodities under somewhat less restrictive conditions than those imposed by Diamantaras *et al.*

Finally, Section V summarizes the main results. It also contains a brief concluding discussion of iterative adjustment procedures and of incentive constraints.

II. A Conditionally Convex Economy

Assumptions

Consider an economy with a finite set G of private commodities, a finite set I of individual consumers, and a finite set J of producers. In addition, suppose there is an abstract set Z whose members are vectors of those variables which define the *environment*. Each agent's feasible set and objectives may be affected by the values taken by the vector $z \in Z$. No particular structure will be postulated on the set Z, though it may be thought of as a subset of $\mathbb{R}^k$, for some k. We assume that some kind of public agency or *public sector* determines these variables. We also assume

---

[2] Attempts to generalize results on the core and on adjustment procedures are left for later work; see also Diamantaras and Gilles (1996).

that the public sector may affect consumers' budget sets and firms' profit functions via taxes and subsidies. Even though the tax system itself can be thought of as part of the environment, we find it more convenient to treat these variables separately.

We assume that the economy is *conditionally convex*, meaning that the public environment $z \in Z$ is able to capture all the relevant non-convexities in the economy, in the following sense. Each individual $i \in I$ is assumed to have:

(1) a feasible set $\tilde{X}^i \subset \mathbb{R}^G \times Z$ such that, for each $z \in Z$, the *conditionally feasible set*

$$X^i(z) := \{x^i \in \mathbb{R}^G \mid (x^i, z) \in \tilde{X}^i\}$$

of private good net trade vectors is convex and closed; it will be assumed in addition that $X^i(z)$ is bounded below by a vector $\underline{x}^i(z)$ with the property that $x \in X^i(z)$ implies $x \geq \underline{x}^i(z)$;

(2) a (complete and transitive) preference ordering R^i on $\tilde{X}^i$ such that, for each $z \in Z$, the *conditional preference ordering* $R^i(z)$ defined by

$$\forall x^i, \bar{x}^i \in X^i(z) : x^i R^i(z) \bar{x}^i \Leftrightarrow (x^i, z) R^i(\bar{x}^i, z)$$

is convex, continuous, and locally non-satiated.

In addition, each producer $j \in J$ is assumed to have:

(3) a production set $\tilde{Y}^j \subset \mathbb{R}^G \times Z$ such that, for each $z \in Z$, the *conditional production set*

$$Y^j(z) := \{y^j \in \mathbb{R}^G \mid (y^j, z) \in \tilde{Y}^j\}$$

is convex and closed.

Essentially the above axioms say that, for any given value of the environmental variables, the resulting conditional economy is standard. Observe that these axioms involve no restriction on the set Z, which may therefore contain all kinds of variables. So our formulation allows many different kinds of non-convexity.

Next, for each individual $i \in I$, for each pair $(\hat{x}^i, \hat{z}) \in \tilde{X}^i$, and any alternative public environment $z \in Z$, define the two sets

$$P^i(\hat{x}^i, \hat{z}; z) := \{x^i \in X^i(z) \mid (x^i, z) P^i(\hat{x}^i, \hat{z})\}$$

$$R^i(\hat{x}^i, \hat{z}; z) := \{x^i \in X^i(z) \mid (x^i, z) R^i(\hat{x}^i, \hat{z})\}$$

Both are upper preference sets in $\mathbb{R}^G$. Because preferences are locally non-satiated in private goods, note that $P^i(\hat{x}^i, z; z)$ is non-empty whenever $R^i(\hat{x}^i, \hat{z}; z)$ is.

In the following, let $X^I(z)$ and $Y^J(z)$ denote the Cartesian products $\Pi_{i \in I} X^i(z)$ and $\Pi_{j \in J} Y^j(z)$, respectively.

This paper is concerned with conditions under which a particular feasible allocation $(\hat{x}^I, \hat{y}^J, \hat{z})$ is an equilibrium. When considering alternative public environments, it will lose no generality to restrict attention to the subset $\hat{Z}$ of Z whose members satisfy the requirement that, for each $i \in I$, the conditional weak preference set $R^i(\hat{x}^i, \hat{z}; z)$ is non-empty. This excludes those public environments z which are so bad for some individual $i \in I$ that no choice of net trade vector could possibly compensate i for upsetting the *status quo* $(\hat{x}^i, \hat{z}) \in \tilde{X}^i$. Because of local non-satiation, the corresponding conditional strict preference set $P^i(\hat{x}^i, \hat{z}; z)$ must also be non-empty for each $i \in I$. Note that $\hat{Z}$ consists precisely of those $z \in Z$ which would allow consumers to reach a weakly Pareto superior allocation provided that the economy were sufficiently productive.

Restricted Profit and Compensation Functions

For every price vector $p \neq 0$ and every public environment z, define the (restricted) profit function of each private producer $j \in J$ in the obvious way by

$$\pi^j(p, z) := \sup_{y} \{py | y \in Y^j(z)\}$$

Note that $+\infty$ is admitted as a possible value of a profit function, but this causes no difficulty.

This paper will consider conditions for particular allocations $(\hat{x}^I, \hat{y}^J, \hat{z})$ to be decentralizable equilibria of various kinds. These conditions will involve measures of anticipated consumer and producer benefit associated with deviations from the equilibrium allocation. To this end, given the particular allocation $(\hat{x}^I, \hat{y}^J, z)$ and any pair (p, z) with $p \neq 0$ and $z \in Z$, it is useful to introduce the notation

$$\hat{e}^i(p, z) := \min_{x^i} \{px^i | x^i \in R^i(\hat{x}^i, \hat{z}; z)\}$$

for each consumer i's *compensation function*. This is the minimum expenditure on private goods needed to ensure that individual i is no worse off than at $(\hat{x}^i, \hat{z})$, given the price vector p and the alternative public environment z. The assumptions of the preceding subsection imply that $\hat{e}^i(p, z)$ is well-defined and finite whenever $p > 0$ and $R^i(\hat{x}^i, \hat{z}; z)$ is non-empty, as it must be whenever $z \in \hat{Z}$. Provided that $R^i(\hat{x}^i, \hat{z}; z)$ is non-empty, we assume that $\hat{e}^i(p, z)$ is well defined, even when $p \not> 0$. Finally, define

$$\hat{S}(p, z) := \sum_{j \in J} \pi^j(p, z) - \sum_{i \in I} \hat{e}^i(p, z)$$

This *aggregate net benefit function* measures the surplus by which aggregate profit exceeds the minimum aggregate wealth needed to ensure that no consumer i is worse off than with $(\hat{x}^i, \hat{z})$. When $\hat{S}(p, z) > 0$, then moving to the new public environment z effectively passes a cost–benefit test indicating a potential Pareto improvement — provided that, after this move combined with suitable lump-sum wealth redistribution, private good markets will clear at the price vector p.

Private Good Competitive Allocations

The allocation $(\hat{x}^i, \hat{y}^j, \hat{z})$ is said to be *private good competitive* at the non-zero price vector $p \in \mathbb{R}^G \backslash \{0\}$ provided that:

(1) for all $i \in I$, the net trade vector $\hat{x}^i$ maximizes $R^i(\hat{z})$ subject to $x^i \in X^i(\hat{z})$ and $px^i \leq p\hat{x}^i$;

(2) for all $j \in J$, the net output vector $\hat{y}^j$ maximizes py^j subject to $y^j \in Y^j(\hat{z})$;

(3) $\sum_{i \in I} \hat{x}^i = \sum_{j \in J} \hat{y}^j$.

Thus, all agents treat the public environment $\hat{z}$ as fixed. Also, each consumer $i \in I$ maximizes the conditional preference ordering $R^i(\hat{z})$ given the budget constraint $px^i \leq w^i$, where $w^i := p\hat{x}^i$ is a level of wealth just large enough for i to afford $\hat{x}^i$. And each firm $j \in J$ maximizes profits py^j over its conditional production set $Y^j(\hat{z})$. Finally, (3) is the resource balance constraint, which obviously entails the budget balance constraint $\sum_{i \in I} p\hat{x}^i = \sum_{j \in J} p\hat{y}^j$. The r.h.s. of this equation includes the aggregate net profits from the net output of private goods used in creating public goods. Such net profits are typically negative, of course. So (3) and the associated budget equation allow for the need to finance the inputs used in creating the public environment, as well as representing the distribution to individual consumers of the profits arising from producing private goods.

Say also that the allocation $(\hat{x}^i, \hat{y}^j, \hat{z})$ is *private good compensated competitive* at the price vector $p \neq 0$ provided that (1) above is replaced by:

(1′)   for all $i \in I$, the net trade vector $\hat{x}^i$ minimizes px^i subject to $x^i \in X^i(\hat{z})$ and $x^i R^i(\hat{z})\hat{x}^i$;

whereas (2) and (3) are satisfied as before.

When preferences for private goods are locally non-satiated, such a private good competitive allocation will be *Pareto efficient given z* in the sense that there is no Pareto superior allocation $(\hat{x}^i, \hat{y}^j, \hat{z})$ with the same public environment. Conversely, given the standard assumptions set out above, any allocation $(\hat{x}^i, \hat{y}^j, \hat{z})$ which is Pareto efficient given $\hat{z}$ will also be private good compensated competitive at some price vector $p \neq 0$.

The Cheaper Point Lemma

As with the classical second efficiency theorem, it will only be shown here that a Pareto efficient allocation is some kind of *compensated* equilibrium. Additional assumptions such as those set out in Hammond (1993, 1998) are required to ensure that this compensated equilibrium is an uncompensated equilibrium. Indeed, the following result is a simple adaptation of one that is familiar in classical economic environments.

Cheaper Point Lemma. *Suppose that the price vector $p \neq 0$ is such that, whenever $(x^i, z) \in \tilde{X}^i$ satisfies $(x^i, z) R^i(\hat{x}^i, \hat{z})$, then $px^i \geq w^i$. Suppose too that there exists a "cheaper point" $\underline{x}^i \in X^i(z)$ with $p\underline{x}^i < w^i$. Then any $(x^i, z) \in \tilde{X}^i$ with $(x^i, z) P^i(\hat{x}^i, \hat{z})$ must satisfy $px^i > w^i$.*

Proof: Suppose that $(x^i, z) \in \tilde{X}^i$ with $(x^i, z) P^i(\hat{x}^i, \hat{z})$. The assumptions of Section II imply that $X^i(z)$ is convex and $R^i(z)$ is continuous. Accordingly, there must exist some small λ with $0 < \lambda < 1$ such that the point $x^i(\lambda)$ $:= x^i + \lambda(\underline{x}^i - x^i) \in X^i(z)$ and also $(x^i(\lambda), z) P^i(\hat{x}^i, \hat{z})$. Then $(x^i(\lambda), z) \in \tilde{X}^i$ and $(x^i(\lambda), z) R^i(\hat{x}^i, \hat{z})$, of course. So the hypothesis of the Lemma implies that

$$px^i(\lambda) = p[x^i + \lambda(\underline{x}^i - x^i)] \geq w^i$$

This is equivalent to

$$(1 - \lambda)px^i \geq w^i - \lambda p\underline{x}^i > (1 - \lambda)w^i$$

where the last strict inequality follows because $\lambda > 0$ and $p\underline{x}^i < w^i$. But then, dividing by $1 - \lambda$ which is also positive, we obtain $px^i > w^i$. ∎

III. Far-Sighted Public Competitive Equilibrium

Generalized Public Sector Proposals

Following Wicksell's (1896) original insight, Foley (1967) considered public sector proposals in the form of a revised vector of public goods, together with taxes on consumers in order to finance the inputs needed to produce those public goods. Implicitly, however, his definition has private agents who are "myopic" in the sense that they treat the price vector p for private goods as independent of the public environment $z \in Z$. Also, he does not allow private producers. Greenberg (1975) has one aggregate private producer and allows more complex tax systems, but still has myopic agents.

As an obvious extension of the Wicksell–Foley approach, suppose that each consumer $i \in I$ faces a net tax $t^i(p)$ and each producer $j \in J$ faces a net subsidy $s^j(p)$, all of which depend on the price vector $p \neq 0$. Thus, there is a *tax/subsidy system* $(\mathbf{t}^I(p), \mathbf{s}^J(p)) := (\langle t^i(p) \rangle_{i \in I}, \langle s^j(p) \rangle_{j \in J})$. Moreover, suppose that each consumer i's net wealth is also a function $w^i(p)$ of p, and let $\mathbf{w}^I(p):=\langle w^i(p)\rangle_{i\in I}$ denote the economy's *wealth distribution rule*. Then a *generalized public sector proposal* is defined as a collection $(z, \mathbf{w}^I(p), \mathbf{t}^I(p), \mathbf{s}^J(p))$ satisfying the following conditions:

(a) all the functions $w^i(p)$, $t^i(p)$ and $s^j(p)$ are both continuous and homogeneous of degree 1;
(b) $\sum_{i\in I} w^i(p) = \sum_{j\in J}[\pi^j(p, z) + s^j(p)]$;
(c) $\sum_{i\in I} t^i(p) = \sum_{j\in J} s^j(p)$;
(d) for all $i\in I$ and $p\neq 0$, one has $w^i(p) - t^i(p) > \hat{e}^i(p, z)$ whenever $\hat{S}(p, z) > 0$.

Of these conditions, (a) is intended to help ensure existence of competitive equilibrium in an obvious way. Evidently (b) and (c) require, respectively, the wealth distribution rule and the tax/subsidy system to be balanced.

Finally, whenever $\hat{S}(p, z) > 0$ and so the economy can afford to allow each consumer to spend more than $\hat{e}^i(p, z)$ on a private good net trade vector, condition (d) requires that they be allowed to do so. This will ensure that whenever p is a compensated equilibrium price vector in the conditional economy given z and this equilibrium p satisfies $\sum_{j\in J}\pi^j(p, z) > \sum_{i\in I}\hat{e}^i(p, z)$, then every consumer has a "cheaper point" in the conditionally feasible set $X^i(z)$ that lies below the budget hyperplane $px^i + t^i(p) = w^i(p)$. By the Cheaper Point Lemma at the end of Section II, it follows that the compensated equilibrium will be an ordinary or "uncompensated" equilibrium. Furthermore, because consumers maximize preferences in such an equilibrium and can find a $\tilde{x}^i$ with $(\tilde{x}^i, z)R^i(\hat{x}^i, \hat{z})$ such that $p\tilde{x}^i + t^i(p) < w^i(p)$, it must be true that each consumer's equilibrium net trade vector x^i satisfies $(x^i, z)P^i(\hat{x}^i, \hat{z})$. Essentially, condition (d) requires the wealth distribution rule, when combined with the tax rule, to convert potential Pareto improvements into actual ones, as in Grandmont and McFadden (1972).

Definitions

After these necessary preliminaries, consider the feasible allocation $(\hat{\mathbf{x}}^I, \hat{\mathbf{y}}^J, \hat{z})$ together with a price vector $\hat{p} \neq 0$. This combination is said to be a *far-sighted public competitive equilibrium* (or FSPCE) if:

(i) $(\hat{\mathbf{x}}^I, \hat{\mathbf{y}}^J, \hat{z})$ is private good competitive at prices $\hat{p}$;
(ii) there is no generalized public sector proposal $(z, \mathbf{w}^I(p), \mathbf{t}^I(p), \mathbf{s}^J(p))$ permitting the existence of an associated feasible allocation $(\mathbf{x}^I, \mathbf{y}^J, z)$ which is private good competitive at a price vector $p^* \neq 0$ satisfying $p^*\hat{x}^i = w^i(p^*)$ for all $i\in I$, as well as passing the cost–benefit test $\hat{S}(p^*, z) > 0$.

According to (ii), therefore, there can be no alternative generalized public sector proposal, including the taxes needed to finance the altered public environment z, which allows the economy to reach an equilibrium at a price vector $p^* \neq 0$ for which the cost–benefit test $\hat{S}(p^*, z) > 0$ is passed.[3]

As Foley (1967) in particular admits, any such definition fails to specify what political process underlies the choice among the many public sector proposals which might satisfy condition (ii) when the economy is not at an FSPCE. The only assumption is that amendments will be made repeatedly until no further amendment which everybody favours can be found.

The combination $(\hat{\mathbf{x}}^I, \hat{\mathbf{y}}^J, \hat{z}, \hat{p})$ is a *compensated* FSPCE when condition (i) above is weakened to:

(i′) $(\hat{\mathbf{x}}^I, \hat{\mathbf{y}}^J, \hat{z})$ is private good compensated competitive at prices $\hat{p}$;

but (ii) remains the same as before.

Suppose that $(z, \mathbf{w}^I(p), \mathbf{t}^I(p), \mathbf{s}^J(p))$ is a generalized public sector proposal for which $(\mathbf{x}^I, \mathbf{y}^J, p^*)$ is a private good compensated competitive equilibrium satisfying $\hat{S}(p^*, z) > 0$. Then condition (d) of the previous definition implies that the Cheaper Point Lemma is applicable. It follows that $(\mathbf{x}^I, \mathbf{y}^J, p^*)$ must be a private good (uncompensated) competitive equilibrium, and that $(x^i, z) P^i(\hat{x}^i, \hat{z})$ for all $i \in I$.

First Efficiency Theorem

First, add the plausible assumption that for each $z \in Z$, there is an upper bound $\bar{y}(z)$ for the set J of producers as a whole with the property that, whenever $y^j \in Y^j(z)$ satisfies $\sum_{j \in J} y^j \geq \sum_{i \in I} \underline{x}^i(z)$, then $\sum_{j \in J} y^j \leq \bar{y}(z)$. Essentially, this is the standard requirement that bounded inputs cannot generate unbounded outputs. In fact, given any public environment $z \in Z$, the combination of this extra assumption with those set out in Section II is sufficient to ensure compactness of the attainable set

$$A(z) := \left\{ (\mathbf{x}^i, y) \in \mathbf{X}^i(z) \times \sum_{j \in J} Y^j(z) \,\middle|\, \sum_{i \in I} x^i = y \right\}$$

---

[3] An alternative equilibrium concept would modify (ii) to exclude directly any proposal allowing a private good competitive equilibrium in which all consumers attain preferred allocations within their respective budget sets, while each private firm makes no less profit after adjusting the net subsidy. That is, the public sector proposal cannot be amended in a way which is unanimously approved by all consumers and producers. Such an alternative concept may actually capture the idea of a negative consensus rather better. In any case, this modification would make the two efficiency results Theorems 1 and 2 below hold almost trivially.

of all conditionally feasible combinations of consumer net trade vectors with an aggregate net output vector.

Consider any *status quo* feasible allocation $(\hat{\mathbf{x}}^I, \hat{\mathbf{y}}^J, \hat{z})$. Recall that the definitions and assumptions at the beginning of Section II already imply that, for all $i \in I$ and $z \in \hat{Z}$, the conditional strict preference set $P^i(\hat{x}^i, \hat{z}; z)$ must be a non-empty subset of $X^i(z)$. But here we go further and assume as well that each $P^i(\hat{x}^i, \hat{z}; z)$ is a subset of the interior of $X^i(z)$. Hence, the indifference curve which bounds this strict preference set is precluded from meeting the boundary of $X^i(z)$. Without this admittedly unsatisfactory additional interiority requirement, it is hard to see how to guarantee that any FSPCE is even weakly Pareto efficient.

These two extra assumptions enable the following natural counterpart of the usual first efficiency theorem of welfare economics to be proved:

Theorem 1. *Any FSPCE is weakly Pareto efficient.*

Proof: Let $(\hat{\mathbf{x}}^I, \hat{\mathbf{y}}^J, \hat{z})$ be any feasible allocation. Suppose that the feasible allocation $(\mathbf{x}^I, \mathbf{y}^J, z)$ is strictly Pareto superior — i.e., that $(x^i, z)P^i(\hat{x}^i, \hat{z})$ for all $i \in I$. Because $A(z)$ is compact, it loses no generality to assume that $(\mathbf{x}^I, \mathbf{y}^J)$ is (constrained) Pareto efficient in the conditional economy given z. By the standard assumptions set out in Section II, there must exist a price vector $p^* \neq 0$ at which the allocation $(\mathbf{x}^I, \mathbf{y}^J, z)$ is private good compensated competitive. Because $(x^i, z)P^i(\hat{x}^i, \hat{z})$, the extra assumption set out above implies that x^i is an interior point of $X^i(z)$. Because preferences are continuous, there must exist $\tilde{x}^i \in X^i(z)$ such that $p^*\tilde{x}^i < p^*x^i$ and $(\tilde{x}^i, z)P^i(\hat{x}^i, \hat{z})$. It follows that $p^*x^i > e^i(p^*, z)$ for all $i \in I$. Therefore

$$\sum_{j \in J} \pi^j(p^*, z) = \sum_{j \in J} p^*y^j = \sum_{i \in I} p^*x^i > \sum_{i \in I} e^i(p^*, z)$$

implying that $\hat{S}(p^*, z) > 0$. Now construct $\mathbf{w}^I(p)$ and $\mathbf{t}^I(p)$ to satisfy

$$w^i(p) - t^i(p) = \hat{e}^i(p, z) + \theta^i \hat{S}(p^*, z)$$

for all $i \in I$ and $p \neq 0$ where, in order to ensure that $w^i(p^*) - t^i(p^*) = p^*x^i$, one chooses

$$\theta^i := [p^*x^i - \hat{e}^i(p^*, z)]/\hat{S}(p^*, z) > 0$$

Then $\sum_{i \in I} \theta^i = 1$, of course. Also, construct $s^j(p) := \pi^j(\hat{p}, \hat{z}) - \pi^j(p, z)$ for all $j \in J$ and $p \neq 0$.

These constructions make $(z, \mathbf{w}^I(p), \mathbf{t}^I(p), \mathbf{s}^J(p))$ a generalized public sector proposal which violates part (ii) of the definition of an FSPCE. This implies that $(\hat{\mathbf{x}}^I, \hat{\mathbf{y}}^J, \hat{z})$ cannot be an FSPCE allocation at any price vector $\hat{p} \neq 0$.

On the other hand, when $(\hat{\mathbf{x}}^I, \hat{\mathbf{y}}^J, \hat{z}, \hat{p})$ is an FSPCE, it follows that the allocation $(\hat{\mathbf{x}}^I, \hat{\mathbf{y}}^J, \hat{z})$ must be Pareto efficient. ∎

Second Efficiency Theorem

The following counterpart of the usual second efficiency theorem is true without any additional assumptions:

Theorem 2. *Suppose* $(\hat{\mathbf{x}}^I, \hat{\mathbf{y}}^J, \hat{z})$ *is a weakly Pareto efficient allocation. Then there is a price vector* $\hat{p} \neq 0$ *such that* $(\hat{\mathbf{x}}^I, \hat{\mathbf{y}}^J, \hat{z}, \hat{p})$ *is a compensated FSPCE.*

Proof: Let $(\hat{\mathbf{x}}^I, \hat{\mathbf{y}}^J, \hat{z})$ be any feasible allocation. Suppose there is a generalized public sector proposal $(z, \mathbf{w}^i(p), \mathbf{t}^i(p), \mathbf{s}^j(p))$ with an associated allocation $(\mathbf{x}^i, \mathbf{y}^j)$ which is private good competitive at a price vector p^* satisfying $\hat{S}(p^*, z) > 0$. Then condition (d) ensures that the Cheaper Point Lemma applies, and also that the allocation $(\mathbf{x}^i, \mathbf{y}^j, z)$ is both feasible and Pareto superior.

Conversely, if $(\hat{\mathbf{x}}^I, \hat{\mathbf{y}}^J, \hat{z})$ is weakly Pareto efficient, there can be no such generalized public sector proposal. Moreover, by the usual second efficiency theorem of welfare economics, there must exist a price vector $\hat{p} \neq 0$ at which the Pareto efficient allocation is private good compensated competitive. The above definitions imply that $(\hat{\mathbf{x}}^I, \hat{\mathbf{y}}^J, \hat{z}, \hat{p})$ is a compensated FSPCE. ∎

IV. Valuation Equilibrium

Self-Financing and Balanced Valuation Schemes

In the tradition of Lindahl's pioneering work, it will now be assumed that the environment z is determined by unanimous choice as a result of some pricing scheme. Like Mas-Colell (1980), this pricing scheme will typically be non-linear. But as in the recent work by Diamantaras *et al.*, we extend the pricing scheme to accommodate many private goods. In fact we go beyond their work by allowing the valuation scheme for the public environment z to depend on the price vector p for private goods, since agents may not know this in advance.

In fact, let the unit sphere $P := \{p \in \mathbb{R}^G | \Sigma_{g \in G} p_g^2 = 1\}$ be the private good normalized price domain. Then each individual $i \in I$ will be required to pay a net amount $\tau^i(p, z)$, as a function of (p, z) defined on some domain $D \subset P \times Z$. In addition, each firm $j \in J$ will receive a net subsidy $\sigma^j(p, z)$, also defined on D. A *valuation scheme* is defined as a collection (τ^I, σ^J) consisting of one complete profile $\langle \tau^i(p, z) \rangle_{i \in I}$ of consumer tax or payment functions, together with a second complete profile $\langle \sigma^j(p, z) \rangle_{j \in J}$ of producer subsidy or revenue functions.

Say that the valuation scheme is *self-financing* if $\Sigma_{j \in J} \sigma^j(p, z) \leq \Sigma_{i \in I} \tau^i(p, z)$ for all $(p, z) \in D$. This simply requires the valuation scheme to earn a non-negative profit because aggregate net subsidies paid to producers do not exceed aggregate net payments by consumers. On the other hand, the valuation scheme is *balanced at* $(p, z) \in D$ if $\sum_{i \in I} \tau^i(p, z) = \sum_{j \in J} \sigma^j(p, z)$. Thus, balance requires aggregate net payments by consumers to equal aggregate net subsidies to firms — as they do in cost-sharing mechanisms, for example. In particular, the degenerate valuation scheme satisfying $\sigma^j(p, z) = \tau^i(p, z) = 0$ for all i, j and all $(p, z) \in P \times Z$ is balanced everywhere. Trivially, any scheme that is balanced everywhere must be self-financing, though the reverse is obviously not true.

Valuation Equilibria

The following definition is reminiscent of the generalization of Lindahl equilibrium due to Mas-Colell, Diamantaras, and others. It also extends to many private goods Kaneko's (1977) concept of ratio equilibrium — see also Mas-Colell and Silvestre (1989, 1991). Relative to a valuation scheme $\tau^I(p, z)$, $\sigma^J(p, z)$, a *valuation equilibrium with lump-sum transfers* (or VELT) is a collection $(\hat{\mathbf{x}}^I, \hat{\mathbf{y}}^J, \hat{z}, \hat{p})$ of conditionally feasible individual plans $(\hat{\mathbf{x}}^I, \hat{\mathbf{y}}^J) \in \mathbf{X}^I(\hat{z}) \times \mathbf{Y}^J(\hat{z})$ for consumers and producers, together with a public environment $\hat{z}$ and a private good price vector $\hat{p}$, such that:

(i)   the valuation scheme is defined at $(\hat{p}, \hat{z})$;
(ii) $\sum_{i \in I} \hat{x}^i = \sum_{j \in J} \hat{y}^j$;
(iii) for all $j \in J$ and $(p, z) \in D$, if $y^j \in Y^j(z)$ then $py^j + \sigma^j(p, z) \leq \hat{p}\hat{y}^j + \sigma^j(\hat{p}, \hat{z})$;
(iv) for all $i \in I$ and $(p, z) \in D$, if $(x^i, z)P^i(\hat{x}^i, \hat{z})$ then $px^i + \tau^i(p, z) > \hat{p}\hat{x}^i + \tau^i(\hat{p}, \hat{z})$.

Note that many producers have replaced the single producer who appears in the work of Mas-Colell, Diamantaras, *et al.* Like consumers, producers are also faced with non-linear Lindahl prices. In valuation equilibrium, no agent can deviate to a better alternative allocation. As in the usual formulation of Lindahl equilibrium, the valuation scheme provides incentives that result in the equilibrium public environment $\hat{z}$ being chosen unanimously.

In fact, producers could be entirely disregarded when seeing if there is a consensus. Instead, they could simply be commanded to do their part in bringing about $\hat{z}$. After all, the net subsidies which firms receive are merely passed on to consumers. However, we follow normal first-best theory in requiring a firm to receive compensation for any public goods it produces, and also if its set-up costs are too large to be covered when prices are set equal to marginal cost.

A *compensated valuation equilibrium* is defined similarly, the only difference being that condition (iv) is replaced by:

(iv′) for all $i \in I$ and $(p, z) \in D$, if $(x^i, z)R^i(\hat{x}^i, \hat{z})$ then $px^i + \tau^i(p, z) \geq \hat{p}\hat{x}^i + \tau^i(\hat{p}, \hat{z})$.

The Cheaper Point Lemma of Section II provides sufficient conditions for a compensated valuation equilibrium to be a valuation equilibrium.

Proper Valuation Schemes and the First Efficiency Theorem

Recall the definition of $\hat{Z}$ as the subset of Z consisting of those z for which each consumer i's conditional weak preference set $R^i(\hat{x}^i, \hat{z}; z)$ is non-empty. Say that the valuation scheme $\tau^I(p, z)$, $\sigma^J(p, z)$ is *proper* provided that, for each $z \in \hat{Z}$, there exists at least one $p \in P$ such that $(p, z) \in D$ and the scheme is balanced at (p, z).

Diamantaras and Gilles (1986) consider a valuation scheme which is both defined and balanced on a domain $D \subset P \times Z$ satisfying the property that, for each $z \in Z$, there exists a single price vector $p(z)$ for which $(p(z), z) \in D$. They suggest that $p(z)$ be interpreted as a common conjecture concerning what price vector will emerge from a change in the public environment. A special case would be if agents were far-sighted in the sense of Section III. Clearly, any such valuation scheme is proper according to the definition we have just given. But our definition is more general, allowing agents to contemplate multiple possible price vectors in each public environment.

Like the usual first fundamental efficiency theorem of welfare economics, the first main result says that a valuation equilibrium is Pareto efficient. Generally, however, it is only valid if the valuation scheme is proper.

Theorem 3. *If* $(\hat{x}^I, \hat{y}^J, \hat{z}, \hat{p})$ *is a VELT relative to a proper valuation scheme* $\tau^I(p, z)$, $\sigma^J(p, z)$, *then the allocation* $(\hat{x}^I, \hat{y}^J, \hat{z})$ *is Pareto efficient.*

Proof: Suppose that $(x^i, z)R^i(\hat{x}^i, \hat{z})$ for all $i \in I$, with $(x^h, z)P^h(\hat{x}^h, \hat{z})$ for some $h \in I$. Suppose too that $y^j \in Y^j(z)$ for all $j \in J$. Because $z \in \hat{Z}$, there must exist $p \in P$ such that the proper valuation scheme is defined and balanced at (p, z). Then the above definitions and local non-satiation of consumers' preferences together imply that $\hat{p}\hat{y}^j + \sigma^j(\hat{p}, \hat{z}) \geq py^j + \sigma^j(p, z)$ for all $j \in J$, and that $px^i + \tau^i(p, z) \geq \hat{p}\hat{x}^i + \tau^i(\hat{p}, \hat{z})$ for all $i \in I$, with strict inequality when $h = i$. It follows that

$$\sum_{i \in I} [px^i + \tau^i(p, z)] > \sum_{i \in I} [\hat{p}\hat{x}^i + \tau^i(\hat{p}, \hat{z})]$$

$$= \sum_{j \in J} [\hat{p}\hat{y}^j + \sigma^j(\hat{p}, \hat{z})] \geq \sum_{j \in J} [py^j + \sigma^j(p, z)]$$

Hence

$$p\left(\sum_{i\in I}x^i-\sum_{j\in J}y^j\right)>\sum_{j\in J}\sigma^j(p,z)-\sum_{i\in I}\tau^i(p,z)=0$$

where the last equality follows because the valuation scheme is balanced at (p, z). It follows that there can be no Pareto superior allocation $(\mathbf{x}', \mathbf{y}', z)$ satisfying the feasibility constraint $\sum_{i\in I}x^i = \sum_{j\in J}y^j$.   ∎

Observe that a valuation equilibrium allocation could be inefficient if there were some $z\in\hat{Z}$ such that for all $p\in P$ the valuation scheme were undefined or else lacked balance. For example, one or more firms could be encouraged to incur unnecessary extra costs through subsidies that need to be financed by unnecessarily large charges on consumers.

Regular Valuation Schemes and the Second Efficiency Theorem

The second result corresponds to the second fundamental efficiency theorem by establishing that any Pareto efficient allocation can be decentralized as a compensated valuation equilibrium relative to a suitable proper valuation scheme. But in fact a stronger result is possible, because the valuation scheme can be made to satisfy a stricter "regularity" condition.

Recall the definition of $\hat{S}(p,z):= \sum_{j\in J}\pi^j(p,z)-\sum_{i\in I}\hat{e}^i(p,z)$ as the surplus of aggregate maximum profit at (p, z) over the minimum total expenditure needed to make consumers no worse off than in the *status quo*, and the use of the inequality $\hat{S}(p, z)>0$ as a cost–benefit test indicating that changing the public environment to z would be a potential Pareto improvement if p could emerge as an equilibrium price vector. Say that the valuation scheme $\tau^i(p, z)$, $\sigma^j(p, z)$ is *regular* if it is self-financing and, for each $z\in\hat{Z}$, there exists at least one $p\in P$ satisfying the following two properties simultaneously:

(i) $(p, z)\in D$ and the valuation scheme is balanced at (p, z);
(ii) either $\hat{S}(p, z)\leq 0$ or alternatively, if $\hat{S}(p, z)>0$, then in the conditional private good economy given z there must be a feasible allocation $(\mathbf{x}', \mathbf{y}')$ which is competitive at a price vector $p\neq 0$ satisfying $px^i>\hat{e}^i(p, z)$ for all $i\in I$.

Because of (i), a regular valuation scheme is proper. But it must also be self-financing. Then the extra requirement (ii) imposes a significant further strengthening, especially when z passes the test $\hat{S}(p, z)>0$; for all $p\in P$. In this case, given z, there must be balance for at least one price vector that could emerge from a private good Walrasian equilibrium relative to a distribution rule specifying the wealth $w^i(p)$ of each consumer $i\in I$ as a function of p satisfying $\sum_{i\in I}w^i(p) = \sum_{j\in J}\pi^j(p,z)$ and also $w^i(p)>\hat{e}^i(p, z)$ for all $p\in P$. Because preferences are locally non-satiated, the allocation

$(\mathbf{x}^I, \mathbf{y}^J)$ resulting from any such equilibrium evidently satisfies $(x^i, z)P^i(\hat{x}^i, \hat{z})$ for all $i \in I$. In fact, when $\hat{S}(p, z) > 0$, property (ii) is similar to the test used in Section III when defining a far-sighted public competitive equilibrium.

Theorem 4. *Let $(\hat{\mathbf{x}}^I, \hat{\mathbf{y}}^J, \hat{z})$ be a weakly Pareto efficient allocation. Then, under the assumptions of Section II, there exists a price vector $\hat{p} \in P$ and a regular valuation scheme $\tau^I(p, z)$, $\sigma^J(p, z)$ defined on the whole domain $D = P \times Z$ relative to which the allocation is a compensated VELT at the price vector $\hat{p}$.*

Proof: For each $z \in \hat{Z}$, define

$$B^i(z) := \{x^i \in X^i(z) | (x^i, z)P^i(\hat{x}^i, \hat{z})\}$$

as the (non-empty) set of net trade vectors allowing i to be better off than at $(\hat{x}^i, \hat{z})$, but in the public environment z instead of $\hat{z}$. Because $(\hat{\mathbf{x}}^I, \hat{\mathbf{y}}^J, \hat{z})$ is weakly Pareto efficient, the two non-empty convex sets $\sum_{i \in I} B^i(z)$ and $\sum_{j \in J} Y^j(z)$ are disjoint. So there is a non-empty set $\Pi(z)$ of price vectors $p \in P$ which each determine a separating hyperplane $px = \alpha$ such that, whenever $x \in \sum_{i \in I} B^i(z)$ and $y \in \sum_{j \in J} Y^j(z)$, then $px \geq \alpha \geq py$. In particular, because there exists x^i in the closure of each $B^i(z)$ such that $px^i = \hat{e}^i(p, z)$, and also there exists y^j in each Y^j such that $py^j = \pi^j(p, z)$, it follows that

$$\sum_{i \in I} \hat{e}^i(p, z) \geq \alpha \geq \sum_{j \in J} \pi^j(p, z) \qquad (*)$$

This implies that $\hat{S}(p, z) \leq 0$ for all $p \in \Pi(z)$.

Because $\hat{z} \in \hat{Z}$, one can choose $\hat{p} \in P$ as any member of the non-empty set $\Pi(\hat{z})$. But $\hat{p}\hat{x}^i \geq \hat{e}^i(\hat{p}, \hat{z})$ for all $i \in I$ and $\hat{p}\hat{y}^j \leq \pi^j(\hat{p}, \hat{z})$ for all $j \in J$. Also, because $(*)$ applies when $(p, z) = (\hat{p}, \hat{z})$, it follows that

$$\sum_{i \in I} \hat{p}\hat{x}^i \geq \sum_{i \in I} \hat{e}^i(\hat{p}, \hat{z}) \geq \alpha \geq \sum_{j \in J} \pi^j(\hat{p}, \hat{z}) \geq \sum_{j \in J} \hat{p}\hat{y}^j$$

Now, because of local non-satiation, the aggregate net trade vector $\sum_{i \in I} \hat{x}^i = \sum_{j \in J} \hat{y}^j$ belongs to the intersection of $\sum_{j \in J} Y^j(\hat{z})$ with the closure of $\sum_{i \in I} B^i(\hat{z})$. So the hyperplane $\hat{p}x = \alpha$ must pass through this point of the intersection, implying that $\sum_{i \in I} \hat{p}\hat{x}^i = \sum_{j \in J} \hat{p}\hat{y}^j = \alpha$. It follows that $\hat{p}\hat{x}^i = \hat{e}^i(\hat{p}, \hat{z})$ for each $i \in I$ and that $\hat{p}\hat{y}^j = \pi^j(\hat{p}, \hat{z})$ for each $j \in J$.

Next, let $\hat{\sigma}^J$ and $\hat{\tau}^I$ be profiles of arbitrary constants satisfying $\sum_{j \in J} \hat{\sigma}^j = \sum_{i \in I} \hat{\tau}^i$. Let $\langle \alpha^j \rangle_{j \in J}$ be any profile of positive marginal profit shares that are paid as subsidies to firms, with $\sum_{j \in J} \alpha^j = 1$. Consider the valuation scheme defined on the whole of $P \times Z$ by

$$\sigma^j(p, z) := \hat{p}\hat{y}^j + \hat{\sigma}^j - \pi^j(p, z) + \alpha^j \min \{0, \hat{S}(p, z)\} \text{ (all } j \in J)$$

and

$\tau^i(p, z) := \hat{p}\hat{x}^i + \hat{\tau}^i - \hat{e}^i(p, z)$ (all $i \in I$)

Then the conclusion of the previous paragraph implies that $\tau^i(\hat{p}, \hat{z}) = \hat{\tau}^i$ for each $i \in I$ and that $\sigma^j(\hat{p}, \hat{z}) = \hat{\sigma}^j$ for each $j \in J$.

Now, feasibility of the allocation $(\hat{x}^i, \hat{y}^j, \hat{z})$ implies that $\sum_{i \in I} \hat{x}^i = \sum_{j \in J} \hat{y}^j$. Also, we assumed that $\sum_{i \in I} \hat{\tau}^i = \sum_{j \in J} \hat{\sigma}^j$. Therefore,

$$\sum_{i \in I} \tau^i(p, z) - \sum_{j \in J} \sigma^j(p, z)$$

$$= \sum_{j \in J} [\pi^j(p, z) - \alpha^j \min \{0, \hat{S}(p, z)\}] - \sum_{i \in I} \hat{e}^i(p, z)$$

$$= \hat{S}(p, z) - \min \{\hat{S}(p, z), 0\} = \max \{0, \hat{S}(p, z)\} \geq 0$$

with equality if and only if $\hat{S}(p, z) \leq 0$. Hence, the valuation scheme is always self-financing, and is balanced whenever $\hat{S}(p, z) \leq 0$. Because $\Pi(z)$ is non-empty for each $z \in \hat{Z}$ and $\hat{S}(p, z) \leq 0$ for all $p \in \Pi(z)$, it follows that this valuation scheme is regular.

Our construction implies that for all $j \in J$ and $(p, z) \in D$, whenever $y^j \in Y^j(z)$ then

$$py^j + \sigma^j(p, z) \leq \pi^j(p, z) + \sigma^j(p, z) \leq \hat{p}\hat{y}^j + \hat{\sigma}^j = \hat{p}\hat{y}^j + \sigma^j(\hat{p}, \hat{z})$$

Similarly, for all $i \in I$ and $(p, z) \in D$, whenever $(x^i, z)R^i(\hat{x}^i, \hat{z})$ then

$$px^i + \tau^i(p, z) \geq \hat{e}^i(p, z) + \tau^i(p, z) = \hat{p}\hat{x}^i + \hat{\tau}^i = \hat{p}\hat{x}^i + \tau^i(\hat{p}, \hat{z})$$

It has been verified that all four parts (i), (ii), (iii), and (iv′) of the above definition of a compensated VELT are satisfied. ∎

In proving Theorem 4, the valuation scheme has been given an explicit form with an easy and sensible interpretation. Each $\sigma^j(p, z)$ consists of four terms, of which the first three make the change in net subsidy exactly offset the firm's net decrease in profits. As for the last term that is always non-positive, whenever the net benefit $\hat{S}(p, z)$ is negative, it represents firm j's share of the total contribution $-\hat{S}(p, z)$ needed to finance this negative amount; otherwise the last term is zero. On the other hand, the extra payment $\tau^i(p, z) - \hat{\tau}^i$ demanded from consumer i is equal to the Hicksian compensating variation associated with the change from $(\hat{p}, \hat{z})$ to (p, z).

V. Concluding Remarks

Assessment

The Wicksell–Foley approach to determining the public environment involves a notion of politico-economic equilibrium where there is a negative consensus in the sense that no alternative public proposal is unanimously preferred. Section III set out to demonstrate the two efficiency theorems using this notion of equilibrium. When the public environment involves non-convexities, it seems that agents must foresee the pecuniary externalities that arise because changing the public environment alters prices for private goods. This permits acceptable results, though the first theorem of the text relies on a somewhat restrictive assumption.

The usual efficiency theorems of welfare economics concern Walrasian equilibria in economies with only private goods, or Lindahl equilibria in economies with both public and private goods, or "Lindahl–Pigou" equilibria in economies with externalities as well as both public and private goods — see Hammond (1998) for a recent exposition. When the public environment involves non-convexities, Mas-Colell (1980) introduced the concept of a valuation equilibrium for economies with only one private good. A valuation equilibrium is like a Lindahl equilibrium, but with non-linear pricing of the public environment. In this special framework, he was able to derive convincing versions of the usual efficiency theorems of welfare economics, as well as a version of core equivalence.

Section IV turned to this Lindahl approach, involving a positive consensus regarding what public environment should be chosen. Mas-Colell's versions of the efficiency theorems were generalized for an economy with many private goods, with assumptions that are somewhat less restrictive than those invoked by Diamantaras *et al*. Our results require a "proper" valuation scheme that is financially balanced on a suitable regular domain whose members are pairs consisting of a price vector together with a public environment. If agents ignore the dependence of prices on the public environment, however, generally it is impossible to have a proper valuation scheme. Hence, our results require agents to recognize how private good prices may depend on the public environment. Of course, when there is only one private good, this dependence does not matter and our definition reduces to that of Mas-Colell.

Adjustment to Equilibrium

The classical Walrasian theory of general competitive equilibrium invokes an auctioneer whose task it is to steer the economy toward an equilibrium price vector through a *tâtonnement* process. Because a Lindahl equilibrium is merely a Walrasian equilibrium for an economy in which there is a separate copy of the public environment for each individual agent, the Walrasian auctioneer could also be used to reach a Lindahl equilibrium.

Nevertheless, it is more intuitive to regard the public environment, together with the means of financing it, as emerging from a political process. Indeed, this view is made quite explicit in the Wicksell–Foley definition of a public competitive equilibrium. Perhaps with this in mind, Malinvaud (1971, 1972) together with Drèze and de la Vallée Poussin (1971) suggested what generally came to be known as the MDP procedure.

In Malinvaud's approach, prices adjust to excess demands as in a Walrasian *tâtonnement*, while quantities of public goods adjust to the difference between total marginal willingness to pay and the marginal cost of producing those public goods. On the other hand, Drèze and de la Vallée Poussin (1971) adjust quantities even of private goods. For the case when public goods are subject to non-convexities and there is only one private good, Mas-Colell (1980) proposed a "global version" of the MDP procedure. Of course, when there is only one private good, there is no need for the *tâtonnement* part of the MDP procedure. In future work, it remains to be seen whether when there are many private goods, one can re-introduce the *tâtonnement* part of the MDP procedure in order to reach a Pareto efficient allocation, as Malinvaud (1972) does for convex economies. Or whether a quantity guided procedure is needed even for private goods. Or whether, as suggested by the results in Section III especially, it will be necessary to allow the procedure first to converge to some kind of equilibrium in the private good economy given the public environment z, before applying a cost–benefit test which decides whether it is worth moving to z.

Incentive Constraints and the Second Best

A major limitation of our results so far is the neglect of private information. This is especially acute when one considers the public environment for which, as is well known, individuals typically have incentives to misreport their true willingness to pay. Of course, similar concerns apply to the MDP procedure itself, as many have recognized. It is all but impossible to avoid manipulation by agents who focus on the allocation to which the procedure eventually converges, rather than myopically on the direction of movement.

Nevertheless, the results reported in Hammond (1979, 1987) on mechanisms for economies with public goods and a continuum of agents may still be helpful. Under appropriate smoothness assumptions concerning private goods, these results show that the only hope of reaching a first-best Pareto efficient allocation using a strategy proof mechanism is to make the market value of the private goods allocated to each consumer independent of their preferences for the public environment, or of any other private information. In particular this suggests that public goods have to be financed by "poll taxes" which are levied regardless of individual circumstances.

Of course, even poll taxes are manipulable if some agents can plausibly plead an inability to pay them. Private information, therefore, is likely to lead in general to binding incentive constraints which make it impossible to achieve any first-best Pareto efficient allocation at all. Public goods, the public environment, and firms' set-up costs all have to be financed by distortionary taxes or by prices that exceed marginal cost. These are distortions which, by the way, can only arise in an economy with many private goods[4].

However, in the case of production with set-up costs or other non-convexities, this view may be unduly pessimistic. Often these non-convexities apply to the production of intermediate goods, like aircraft which are bought only by airlines, or microprocessors which are bought only by computer manufacturers. Then, instead of consumers' demands for public goods, it is other producers' derived demands that are relevant. To the extent that these depend on observable technology, such demands may well be less subject to manipulation.

In any case, this is another issue which has to be left for later work. Our main conclusion remains — namely, the need to think of any "lumpy" decision in the economy as likely to give rise to pecuniary externalities. These imbue such decisions with many of the essential features of decisions affecting public goods or the public environment.

References

Arrow, K. J. and Scitovsky, T.: *Readings in Welfare Economics*. American Economic Association, Homewood, 1969.

Bergstrom, T. C.: A "Scandinavian consensus" solution for efficient income distribution among non-malevolent consumers. *Journal of Economic Theory 2*, 383–398, 1970.

Brown, D. J. and Heal, G.: Two part tariffs, marginal cost pricing and increasing returns in a general equilibrium model. *Journal of Public Economics 13*, 25–49, 1980.

Diamantaras, D. and Gilles, R. P.: The pure theory of public goods: Efficiency, decentralization, and the core. *International Economic Review 37*, 851–860, 1996.

Diamantaras, D., Gilles, R. P. and Scotchmer, S.: Decentralization of Pareto optima in economies with public projects, nonessential private goods and convex costs. *Economic Theory 8*, 555–564, 1996.

Dierker, E.: When does marginal cost pricing lead to Pareto efficiency? *Journal of Economics/Zeitschrift für Nationalökonomie Suppl. 5*, 41–66, 1986.

Drèze, J. H. and de la Vallée Poussin, D.: A tâtonnement process for public goods. *Review of Economic Studies 38*, 133–150, 1971.

Dupuit, J.: De la mesure de l'utilité des travaux publics. *Annales des Ponts et Chaussées, 2nd series, 8*, 1844; translated in *International Economic Papers 2*, 83–110, 1952; reprinted in Arrow and Scitovsky (1969).

Foley, D. K.: Resource allocation and the public sector. *Yale Economic Essays 7*, 45–98, 1967.

Grandmont, J.-M. and McFadden, D.: A technical note on classical gains from trade. *Journal of International Economics 2*, 109–25, 1972.

Greenberg, J.: Efficiency of tax systems financing public goods in general equilibrium analysis. *Journal of Economic Theory 11*, 168–195, 1975.

---

[4] We owe this important point to Agnar Sandmo.

Guesnerie, R.: First-best allocation of resources with nonconvexities in production. In B. Cornet and H. Tulkens (eds.) *Contributions to Operations Research and Economics*. M.I.T. Press, Cambridge MA, 1989.

Hammond, P. J.: Straightforward individual incentive compatibility in large economies. *Review of Economic Studies 46*, 263–282, 1979.

Hammond, P. J.: Markets as constraints: Multilateral incentive compatibility in continuum economies. *Review of Economic Studies 54*, 399–412, 1987.

Hammond, P. J.: Irreducibility, resource relatedness, and survival in equilibrium with individual non-convexities. In R. Becker, M. Boldrin, R. Jones, and W. Thomson (eds.) *General Equilibrium, Growth, and Trade II: The Legacy of Lionel W. McKenzie*. Academic Press, San Diego, 1993.

Hammond, P. J.: Efficiency and market failure. In A. P. Kirman (ed.), *Elements of General Equilibrium Analysis*. Basil Blackwell, Oxford, to appear 1998.

Hotelling, H. S.: The general welfare in relation to problems of taxation and of railway and utility rates. *Econometrica 6*, 242–269, 1938. Reprinted in Arrow and Scitovsky (1969).

Kaneko, M.: The ratio equilibrium and a voting game in a public goods economy. *Journal of Economic Theory 16*, 123–136.

Laffont, J.-J.: *Fundamentals of Public Economics*. M.I.T. Press, Cambridge MA, 1988.

Lindahl, E.: *Die Gerechtigkeit der Besteuerung: Eine Analyse der Steuerprinzipien auf der Grundlage der Grenznutzentheorie*. Gleerup and H. Ohlsson, Lund, 1919. Ch. 4 ("Positive Lösung") translated as: Just taxation — a positive solution. In Musgrave and Peacock (1958, pp. 168–176).

Malinvaud, E.: *Leçons de théorie microéconomique*. Dunod, Paris, 1969. Translated as *Lectures on Microeconomic Theory*. North-Holland, Amsterdam, 1972.

Malinvaud, E.: A planning approach to the public good problem. *Swedish Journal of Economics 11*, 96–112, 1971.

Malinvaud, E.: Prices for individual consumption, quantity indicators for collective consumption. *Review of Economic Studies 39*, 385–405, 1972.

Mas-Colell, A.: Efficiency and decentralization in the pure theory of public goods. *Quarterly Journal of Economics 94*, 625–641, 1980.

Mas-Colell, A. and Silvestre, J.: Cost-share equilibria: A Lindahlian approach. *Journal of Economic Theory 47*, 239–256, 1989.

Mas-Colell, A. and Silvestre, J.: A note on cost-share equilibrium and owner-consumers. *Journal of Economic Theory 54*, 204–214, 1991.

Musgrave, R. A. and Peacock, A. T. (eds.): *Classics in the Theory of Public Finance*. Macmillan, London, 1958.

Quinzii, M.: *Increasing Returns and Efficiency*. Oxford University Press, New York, 1992.

Say, J.-B.: *Traité d'Economie Politique, 5th. edn.* Chez Rapilly, Paris, 1826.

Vega-Redondo, F.: Efficiency and nonlinear pricing in nonconvex environments with externalities: A generalization of the Lindahl equilibrium concept. *Journal of Economic Theory 41*, 54–67, 1987.

Villar, A.: Existence and efficiency of equilibrium in economies with increasing returns to scale: An exposition. *Investigaciones Económicas 18*, 205–243, 1994.

Villar, A.: *General Equilibrium with Increasing Returns*. Springer, Berlin, 1996.

Wicksell, K.: Ein neues Prinzip der gerechten Besteuerung. *Finanztheoretische Untersuchungen*. iv–vi, 76–87 and 101–159, 1896. Extracts translated as: A new principle of just taxation. In Musgrave and Peacock (1958, pp. 72–118).

Scand. J. Economics 100(1), 33–36, 1998

Comment on P. J. Hammond and A. Villar, "Efficiency with Non-Convexities: Extending the 'Scandinavian Consensus' Approaches"

Jean-Charles Rochet

Université des Sciences Sociales, F-31042 Toulouse, France

This discussion is organized as follows. I start with a series of comments on the paper itself. Then I try to put it into a more general perspective, and answer the question: what has gone wrong with the welfare state and the Scandinavian consensus?

Comments on the Paper

This paper clearly belongs in a domain to which Scandinavian economists have contributed a great deal, namely second best economics. The starting point is the idea that in a mixed economy, all decisions concerning the non-market sector (what Hammond and Villar call the environment) have to be made collectively and, if possible, reach a consensus among agents. The question examined is: can this collective decision be organized in such a way that the two fundamental welfare theorems are preserved?

The first approach followed by the authors was initiated by Wicksell, and later formalized by Foley. An allocation is publicly competitive relative to a tax/subsidy system if and only if it corresponds to a competitive equilibrium of the private sector and if there is no alternative public sector proposal (i.e., an environment z and a tax-subsidy schedule) that is both feasible and Pareto superior. A crucial distinction is whether consumers are shortsighted (i.e., do not anticipate the impact of changes in public sector proposals on private sector prices) as in Foley's original contribution, or not, as in Hammond and Villar assume. In both cases the first welfare theorem holds. However, while the second welfare theorem always holds if consumers are farsighted, an additional convexity assumption is needed when they are shortsighted.

Mas-Colell and Vega-Redondo have generalized this idea by allowing non-linear Lindahl prices, so as to deal with non-convexities. This works well when there is a unique private good. Hammond and Villar try to extend it to the case of several private goods and find that it does not work very well when agents are shortsighted. More specifically, they use Mas-Colell's notion of *valuation equilibrium* (essentially a Lindahl equilibrium with non-linear tax and subsidy schedules). They find that the first welfare theorem is true if the tax schedule is balanced, but that the second holds only if balancedness is replaced by the much weaker notion of viability of the tax schedule, which means that a waste of resources by the public sector is allowed.

However, when agents are farsighted, Hammond and Villar are able to show that the two fundamental theorems of welfare economics extend to this non-convex context.

This is clearly an important contribution, but I must say (and this will be my main criticism) that I have difficulty with the valuation equilibrium concept and, more specifically, with the fact that firms seem to vote on the choice of the environmental variable z. What exactly are the political institutions that are implicit behind this concept? In the classical general equilibrium model, firms are presented as independent economic agents that maximize profits. This is perfectly justified by the fact that it is the stockholders who decide, the crucial point being that they are unanimously in favor of profit maximization. In the Lindahl equilibrium concept, this is somewhat less clear but it works if the public good is produced by competitive private firms. Here, the ownership structure is not specified, and the authors use the abstract notion of wealth distribution rules for splitting the profit of the private sector among consumers. If these rules are specified further and replace the usual private ownership of shares, then consumers will in general not be unanimous about the choice of the environmental variable z. So the decision problems both within the firms and concerning the environment are not clearly founded.

The Welfare State and the Scandinavian Consensus

Let me now adopt a more general perspective and try to answer the question: *what has gone wrong with the welfare state and the Scandinavian consensus?* Why is it that 30 years ago, in most parts of western Europe at least, it was a generally accepted view that the government had an active role to play in the country's economy (direct control of public firms, active welfare programs, redistributive taxation and, of course, interventionist macroeconomic policy). Today, quite the opposite view prevails in most countries: public firms are privatized; flat tax schemes are implemented; welfare programs are cut; and budget deficits are fought ... Why is this so?

A first possible explanation is that this is just a cycle. Politicians have gone too far in their active interventions in the economy and have thus been punished by electors who have selected other politicians with a symmetric bias. Then these politicians themselves will go too far in the other direction, leading to another cycle. These ideas have been used in the positive political economy models – *à la* Buchanan, in which politicians select the economic policy that maximizes the utility of the interest group they represent. In fact, these views can be traced back to Wicksell's ideas, where the ideal constitution of a country is regarded as a "just procedure" under which politicians and voters will act in their own interest. This is opposed to the notion of "just outcomes" often adopted in normative public economics.

A second possible explanation for the failure of the Scandinavian consensus is that the world has changed. Three directions of change seem particularly important:

(i) new technologies have fundamentally altered the market value of human capital and its repartition across individuals;
(ii) the inequality of the distribution of (before-tax) incomes has dramatically increased in most developed countries;
(iii) on average, our societies have become much richer than 20 years ago, and it seems well established that richer people tend to care less about others.

The third (and perhaps more reasonable) explanation for the dismantlement of the welfare state is that the recommendations of normative public economics have been much too naive. The paradigm of an omnipotent, omniscient, benevolent policymaker traces back of the utopists of market socialism. Of course, relaxation of the first two assumptions (omnipotent and omniscient) has led to an important body of literature: second best theory (to which the paper by Hammond and Villar is a valuable contribution), but also incentives theory (with, in particular, the work of Vickrey, Mirrlees and Stiglitz). It may in fact be the third assumption (benevolence) that most needs to be relaxed.

It is true that the public choice school has already offered a (somewhat extreme) description of what can happen when civil servants and politicians are eager to be corrupted. More generally, American economists have rightly drawn our attention to some questions that had essentially been neglected by European public economists:

(i) the possibility of capture of regulators by interest groups;
(ii) the commitment problem of the government in macroeconomic policy; and
(iii) the need for central bank independence.

However, the prevalent school in political economy seems to hold simplistic views on the behavior of public organizations. Without too much exaggeration, one can say that politicians are essentially regarded as thieves, who are prepared to do anything (and, in particular, to buy as many votes as possible) to get elected and, once in power, to steal as much public money as they can. We clearly need a more reasonable story. For example, politicians can be considered as particular agents to whom their fellow citizens delegate the power of deciding on public issues. This resembles the very interesting line of research pursued by Tim Besley and Steve Coate (1995) in their economic model of representative democracy). Another interesting theory under development is transaction cost politics, as a parallel drawn by Avinash Dixit (1995) with transaction cost economics.

Finally, I would like to conclude this discussion by giving an example of an important question that cannot be addressed within the standard framework of public economics but could hopefully be studied within these new paradigms. This question is the choice of ownership structure for a natural monopoly, studied e.g. by Laffont and Tirole (1991).

A first possibility is a publicly owned monopoly. In this case, the government is supposed to find an optimal tradeoff between the interests of consumers (low prices, good quality of products and services) and the interests of taxpayers (high profits or, if impossible, low deficits). With opportunistic politicians (and/or civil servants), we are in a context of a multitask principal-agent relationship – à la Holmström and Milgrom (1991), where only low-powered incentives schemes can be used. Moreover, it is not clear that majority voting (given the heterogeneity of voters) will even lead to such a second-best incentive scheme for the government.

The alternative system is a private monopoly, submitted to the control of a regulatory agency. This separation has the advantage of giving clear objectives to the two groups of stakeholders: stockholders provide incentives for the manager to maximize profits, while consumers' interests are represented by the regulatory agency. More highly powered incentive schemes can be used, but the cost is a multiprincipal externality – à la Martimort (1996).

References

Besley, T. and Coate, S.: An economic model of representative democracy. CARESS DP, University of Pennsylvania, 1995.

Dixit, A.: The making of economic policy: A transaction cost politics perspective. DP, Princeton University, 1995.

Holmström, B. and Milgrom, P.: Multitask principal-agent analysis: Incentive contracts, asset ownership and job design. *Journal of Law, Economics, and Organization 7*, 24–51, 1991.

Laffont, J.-J. and Tirole, J.: Privatization and incentives. *Journal of Law, Economics and Organization 7*, 84–105, 1991.

Martimort, D.: Exclusive dealing, common agency and multiprincipal incentive theory. *Rand Journal of Economics 27* (1), 1–31, 1996.

Scand. J. Economics 100(1), 37–40, 1998

Comment on P. J. Hammond and A. Villar, "Efficiency with Non-Convexities: Extending the 'Scandinavian Consensus' Approaches"

Agnar Sandmo

Norwegian School of Economics and Business Administration, N-5035 Bergen-Sandviken, Norway

This paper is an excellent beginning for the 100th anniversary symposium of the *Scandinavian Journal of Economics*. In considering fundamental issues in the theory of taxation and public goods, it goes straight to the core of the theory — perhaps I should say the pure theory — of economic policy. It also only just misses the 100th anniversary of the publication of Knut Wicksell's doctoral dissertation, *Finanztheoretische Untersuchungen* (1896), which is an important milestone in the research tradition to which the paper belongs. As it also relates to Erik Lindahl's work, it is safe to say that the topic of the paper is very appropriate for the occasion, particularly when one keeps in mind that the journal was originally a Swedish, not a Scandinavian or Nordic publication.

The way I think about the valuation equilibria that Hammond and Villar study is as follows. In the standard competitive model we can think of the equilbrium as being the final outcome of the work of a Walrasian auctioneer, who announces a price vector and then revises it until there is a balance between supply and demand in all markets. In this extended equilibrium model, one could think of the auctioneer as having been joined by a social planner who announces a vector of public goods and an associated tax-subsidy scheme, and then revises it until the proposed allocation has the unanimous support of all agents. There is consensus in the same sense in which there is consensus in the standard competitive model; resources are efficiently allocated relative to the distribution of income between agents. Thus, consensus does not mean that there are no conflicting interests among agents, but these are only due to conflicts of interest over the distribution of income or resources. The equilibrium is one of benefit taxation, so that the results seem to vindicate those nineteenth century economists who thought of benefit taxation as an analogue of the market mechanism for private goods. But one has to bear in mind that the paper does not really tackle the problem of agents' individual incentives to reveal their preferences for public goods, so that Samuelson's (1969) criticism of the benefit principle as an equilibrium concept still applies.

The paper by Hammond and Villar is in certain respects a generalization of the analysis in Mas-Colell (1980). Max-Colell has the same idea about a valuation equilibrium, but he assumes that there is only one private good, which is to be thought of as a Hicksian composite commodity. This assumption requires that all relative prices within the set of goods making up the composite commodity remain constant in the process of analysis. This is, of course, almost always unrealistic, although for a number of applications it is of little importance. But when one makes this assumption, it has strong implications for the kinds of taxes that one can accommodate in the analysis; since relative price changes are ruled out by assumption, taxes must be non-distortionary. With many private goods, the analysis can be generalized in this respect, but this is actually not the way Hammond and Villar proceed. Taxes here are payments for public goods, denominated in units of the *numéraire* and bearing no direct relation to consumers' factor supplies or commodity demands; thus, they are lump-sum, or poll taxes, the payments of which do not vary with individuals' income, consumption or wealth. Private goods prices may change as a result of changes in the public environment, but they always sustain an efficient allocation of private goods. It would be interesting to learn something about possible extensions of the analysis to the case of distortionary taxes. The individualized lump-sum taxes of the present paper are ideal for achieving consensus. The more restrictions that one imposes on the admissible tax system, the harder it presumably becomes to achieve consensus. I imagine that results could be derived about incomplete consensus that would be relative to the tax system. The difficulty with such a concept is that one would then also like to think of the tax system itself as determined by some sort of political equilibrium, so that the development of a more realistic approach is far from easy. In any case, future efforts to extend the framework of analysis to the case of income and commodity taxation will have to build on the foundations established by this paper.

As usual in general equilibrium theory, the paper distinguishes between two types of agents, consumers and producers. However, in the standard version of welfare economics, the notions of Pareto optimality and Pareto improvements are related solely to the preferences of consumers. In contrast, unanimous approval of a proposed change in the public environment in this paper requires the approval of all consumers *as well as of all producers*. Usually one thinks of producers as firms which are privately owned, and consumer interest in the firms is derived from the profit generated by production. An increase in the supply of a public good might benefit the individual as a consumer and harm him as a producer (as is often the case with environmental protection), but what counts is the total effect of the policy change on his welfare. Here it seems that the producers have an existence of their own, separate from the set of consumers in the economy, and I have had some difficulties with the interpretation of this. It seems worthwhile to elaborate a little on this point.

This is a paper about equilibrium, not about welfare. Therefore, the possible objection that only consumer preferences should count for welfare evaluation, misses the point. The issue is not whether or not the assumption satisfies our ethical notions of economic welfare, but whether it is realistic in terms of the political process leading to the Scandinavian consensus. As Hammond and Villar themselves admit, however, they have little to say about the nature of this process; the only assumption made about it is that "amendments will be made repeatedly until no further amendment which everybody favours can be found". Whatever the process is, something more is clearly implied than regular parliamentary and local elections. If no more than elections had been involved, the assumptions made about firms as separate political agents would clearly have been objectionable, since firms as such have no votes in elections. But in a broader view of the political process, this might be different.

If the process leading to consensus is regarded as one in which the government collects viewpoints from many sources in society, e.g. by following the public debate in the media, eliciting the opinions of voluntary organizations and local communities, etc., private firms might be one of its sources of information and opinion. For example, if the government proposes to regulate a river for hydroelectric development, it might collect the views of individual consumers, particularly those living in the area, as well as those of private firms. Now it seems clear that even if the owners and employees of a particular firm consisted entirely of people living in the area, the viewpoint expressed by the firm as such, reflecting an aggregate or compromise of the views of the individuals connected with it, might not coincide with the majority view among individuals, nor indeed with the view of any single individual. If this were a purely technical point related to the well-known difficulties of preference aggregation, it would presumably be of little interest, and in any case it would beg the question of why the government would want to know the views of private firms in the first place. But it may well be that individuals have good reason to take a somewhat different position on a particular issue as a single consumer and as an employee of a firm or a member of a voluntary organization. When expressing a political opinion in public, individuals know that the context in which their statement is made will make a difference for the chance it has of influencing the political outcome. Governments, knowing this, might therefore wish to obtain a consensus that encompasses both individual consumers and firms. In fact, it is not clear that firms in the usual sense are the only organizations to impose constraints on a consensus-seeking government, and I would like to suggest that economists start thinking more seriously about incorporating *voluntary organizations* into models of policy formation.One need only consider the important role that environmentalist organizations have had for policy formation to realize that this might be a significant step forward in terms of descriptive realism.

When one looks at the statistics of public spending and taxation in the Scandinavian countries one is struck by the fact that only about half of gross spending is on goods and services, while the rest is on subsidies and transfer payments to the private sector. Much of this is social security which is to some extent a substitute for private insurance; this could explain why individuals would support a redistributive system of taxation and social security, even though it might appear to go against their own short-run interests. But a good deal of it is genuine redistribution among consumers, and even in this area there seems to be a good deal of consensus; thus, hardly any political party in the Scandinavian countries opposes some form of progressive taxation. If this is to be explained in a convincing way, it will presumbly be necessary to introduce a richer set of assumptions concerning individual preferences.

Hammond and Villar have several interesting observations related to non-convexities in the production of private goods. They note that a decision about output capacity, involving significant set-up costs, frequently becomes a matter of public policy "even if it is usually not recognized as such". The remark is interesting because it reminds us that there is often a case for arguing that the *availability* of a certain private good is a concept that has much in common with a public good. But I believe it is worth pointing out that the non-recognition of this as a policy issue may be more typical of economists than of the population at large. Local governments often spend a good deal of their taxpayers' money to ensure the availability of a wide range of consumer goods and services in the community, in spite of the fact that the view in most economics textbooks, at least by implication, would be that these are decisions that had best be left to the market.

References

Max-Colell, A.: Efficiency and decentralization in the pure theory of public goods. *Quarterly Journal of Economics 94*, 625–641.

Samuelson, P. A.: Pure theory of public expenditure and taxation. In J. Margolis and H. Guitton (eds.), *Public Economics*, Macmillan, London, 1969; reprinted as Chapter 172 in R. C. Merton (ed.), *The Collected Scientific Papers of Paul A. Samuelson, Vol. III*, MIT Press, Cambridge, MA, 1972.

Scand. J. of Economics 100(1), 41–68, 1998

The Economics of Poverty in Poor Countries

Partha Dasgupta*

University of Cambridge, Cambridge CB3 9DD, England and Beijer International Institute of Ecological Economics, S-104 05 Stockholm, Sweden

Abstract

This paper examines the links that have recently been studied between poverty, high fertility and undernourishment, on the one hand, and degradation of the local environmental-resource base and civic disconnection, on the other, in poor countries. An account is offered of a number of pathways involving positive feedbacks that create poverty traps, in which certain identifiable groups of people in an economy can get caught even when the economy in the aggregate experiences economic growth. The relevant policy implications are noted.

I. Orthodox Dichotomies and Their Limitations

Development economics has traditionally been as much concerned with the study of resource allocation mechanisms harbouring large-scale poverty, as it has been with seeking to alter such mechanisms in ways that would enable people to lift themselves out of poverty. If public policy has loomed large in the subject, so has positive analysis of poverty. Unhappily though, the social and ecological context in which such analyses have most frequently been undertaken were, until recently, inappropriate. Thus, in particular, the links connecting poverty, high fertility and undernourishment, on the one hand, and degradation of the local environmental-resource base and civic disconnection, on the other, remained unexplored.[1] It should come as no surprise that as a group, development economists have come under periodic criticism from anthropologists, demographers, ecologists, nutritionists, and political scientists.

I have a reason for pointing to this particular weakness in development economics: much of my own work in recent years has been an attempt to understand the links that bind these routine features of the lives of the poor in poor countries.[2] So if the account I sketch below of recent developments in the subject seems biased, this is because it *is* biased. My aim is not

---

* For their comments I am most grateful to Kaushik Basu, Thorvaldur Gylfason, and Assar Lindbeck.
[1] The survey article on development economics by Stern (1989) reflects this neglect.
[2] Dasgupta (1982, 1990, 1993, 1995a,b, 1996, 1997a,b,c), Dasgupta and Ray (1986, 1987), and Dasgupta and Mäler (1991).

to survey development economics, rather, it is to try to present a unified treatment of a set of interrelated problems that are faced by the poorest in poor countries.[3]

The literature on macroeconomic growth has been much concerned with the question whether in recent years nations have shown signs of convergence in their living standards, and if they have not, then why not. The theme I elaborate upon here bears a faint resemblance: we ask if an economy can harbour poverty traps even when in the aggregate it grows, and we identify an overarching mechanism by which it can. Much recent development economics has quantified poverty and identified the poor. In contrast, the findings I report here concern pathways by which people become poor and remain poor.

I have another motive for presenting developments in development economics in the way I do here. In recent years modern economics has come under regular attack from both within, e.g. Heilbroner and Milberg (1995), and without, e.g. Cassidy (1996). I want to defend modern economics here, because it is eminently defendable. So I also use this occasion to demonstrate that the economist's lens has enriched our understanding of the lives of the poor, in particular, it has enabled us to identify connections among observed phenomena that earlier went unexamined.

To take an example, orthodox discussions of economic institutions, e.g. Heilbroner (1993), are conducted in the context of a markets-versus-State dichotomy. This is so restrictive as to be misleading. Societies throughout the world have fashioned intermediate, often criss-crossing institutions, such as the household, extended-family and kinship networks; civic, commercial, and religious associations; charities; production units; and various layers of what is known as government. Each serves functions at which the others are not so good. They differ not only in terms of the emotional bonds that connect members, but also in regard to the information channels that serve them, the kinds of agreements that bind them, and the investment outlays and severence costs that help sustain them. Their elucidation, in particular our increased understanding of their strengths and weaknesses, has been one of the most compelling achievements of economics over the past twenty-five years or so.

In a similar vein, orthodox discussions of property rights, e.g. Heilbroner (1993) cling to a private-versus-public dichotomy. As we will see, this too is misleading: societies throughout the world have allowed people to hold assets in other forms of ownership, for example, ownership among members of local communities. So when development economists today

---

[3] The exposition here borrows freely from the works cited above. Space forbids that I offer extensive references; for them, see Dasgupta (1993).

talk of the need for institutional reforms and reforms in the structure of property rights, they include in it the need for strengthening those institutions that complement the pairs that define the orthodox dichotomies.

There is another dichotomy that has been the cause of mischief. Some, e.g. World Bank (1986) have located the cause of poverty and hunger at production failure owing to a suppression of markets, while others have identified it with distributional failure, e.g. UNDP (1994). Among the economic policies that suggest themselves from this dichotomy are, on the one hand, measures that widen markets and reduce traditional distortions, and a variety of "social security" measures, on the other. But these two extreme viewpoints encourage us to regard future well-being and an equitable distribution of current well-being as necessarily consonant with each other. If conducted with care, certain policies that encourage economic growth (e.g. the provision of basic infrastructure) can indeed improve the distribution of well-being. Similarly, certain policies that improve the distribution of well-being (e.g. primary education) do improve overall economic performance. Both theory and empirics testify to them. But the two social goals are not invariably consonant with each other. In those circumstance where they are not, citizens face a tradeoff between them, and a choice has to be made over the combinations that are available.

Much of the evidence and analysis I offer in this article bears on sub-Saharan Africa and the Indian sub-continent. They are currently the two poorest regions, comprising nearly 2 billion people. Moreover, approximately 75 percent of the poor in sub-Saharan Africa and the Indian sub-continent are rural people, obtaining their livelihood directly from the environmental-resource base, most especially agriculture. So it pays to study the rural poor.[4]

The plan of the paper is as follows:

Section II contains a summary of evidence on the magnitude and incidence of world poverty. Sections III–VI explore various pathways by which people become poor, remain poor, and take actions to cope with poverty. Specifically, in Section III we study the connection between undernourishment and a person's capacity to work and show that it forms one pathway by which poverty traps are created. In Sections IV–V we look at the dependence of the rural poor in poor countries on common-property resources and see how the very process of economic growth (conventionally measured) can result in the breakdown of communitarian arrangements, making certain sections of the population (viz. women, children, and the old) especially vulnerable to economic shocks. Sections VI–VII

---

[4] I will not discuss urban poverty because I am inexpert on the matter. World Bank (1991, 1994) contain excellent analyses of the main problems there.

focus on fertility behaviour. I suggest that the links between poverty, high fertility, and environmental deterioration may well constitute yet another pathway by which people can get trapped in poverty.

For each of the problems under study, public policies suggest themselves and we take note of them at appropriate places. But policies need to be evaluated. So one needs an evaluation criterion. Conventional indices (e.g. gross national product) are known to be very deficient. In response to this, environmental economists have extended the concept of net national product (NNP) to include resource depletion and environmental deterioration. Section VIII reviews this idea. I argue that if environmental and population problems have been much neglected by mainstream development economists, it may well be because they have been studying wrong economic indices.

Finally, in Section IX, I make a few remarks about certain wider issues in political economy.

II. The Magnitude of World Hunger

Visitors to the Indian sub-continent routinely observe emaciated beggars on the streets of large cities. They are the economically disenfranchised. I do not know their proportion in today's populations, but we do know that, at a conservative estimate, over 600 million people in Asia, Africa and Latin America are undernourished. Table 1 offers two estimates of the magnitude of world poverty, based on two alternative criteria for poverty. The "extreme poor" (annual income less than 275 international dollars in the mid-1980s) were some 630 million in number, comprising 18 percent of the total population of poor countries. The "poor" (annual income less than 370 international dollars in the mid-1980s) were 1,110 million in number, comprising a third of the total population of poor countries.

Table 1 also provides estimates of *poverty gaps* in various regions of the poor world. Notice that even in South Asia and sub-Saharan Africa a mere 4 percent growth in income, if it were distributed efficiently among the poor, would eliminate extreme poverty.

There are other estimates of world poverty, based on income, but they are not dissimilar. For example, IFPRI (1995) suggests that 800 million people, comprising 20 percent of the poor world's population, currently suffer from food insecurity. Of course, the idea of a poverty line, whether or not it is based on income, can be criticised. But the practical advantages of thinking in terms of a line that divides the "poor" from those who are "not poor" are considerable. So the concept is used widely.

The deficiencies of income-based concepts of poverty are, however, not so easy to ignore; see Morris (1979), Sen (1983). For this reason other

Table 1. *Magnitude of poverty (1985)*

Region	Extremely poor[a]			Poor[a]		
	Number (m)	HI (%)	PG (%)	Number (m)	HI (%)	PG (%)
Sub-Saharan Africa	120	30	4	180	47	11
East Asia	120	9	0.4	280	20	1
China	(80)	8	1	(210)	20	3
South Asia	300	29	3	520	51	10
India	(250)	33	4	(420)	55	12
Middle East and North Africa	40	21	1	60	31	2
Latin America and the Caribbean	50	12	1	70	19	1
All developing countries	630	18	1	1,110	33	3

HI — Headcount Index (%).
PG — Poverty Gap (%).
[a] The poverty line in 1985 PPP dollars is $275 *per capita* a year for the extremely poor, and $370 *per capita* a year for the poor.
Source: World Bank (1990, Table 2.1).

indicators of poverty have frequently been advocated. What is striking, though, is that estimates of the magnitude of world poverty are similar even when such other criteria are put to work. For example, FAO (1992) have calculated that some 785 million people (of whom approximately 530 million are in South and East Asia, and 170 million are in sub-Saharan Africa) suffer from dietary energy deficiency. About 1 billion people in poor countries have no access to modern health services, and about 1.3 billion people do not drink potable water. Moreover, estimates based on anthropometric indicators are not dissimilar; see James *et al.* (1992). Approximately 185 million children under six years are currently thought to be seriously underweight. Deficiencies in micro-nutrients are even more pervasive. Approximately 1.2 billion people (and more than half the number of pregnant women in poor countries) suffer from anemia; 600 million suffer from iodine deficiency disorders, and 125 million preschool children suffer from vitamin-A deficiency.

Eradication of micro-nutrient deficiencies would not demand much resources. Rough calculations indicate that less than 0.3 percent of world income is all that would be required on an annual basis. A problem of far greater magnitude is the availability of dietary energy. The general consensus among nutritionists is that, barring diets that build on root and tuber crops, those that contain adequate energy are adequate also in their protein content. Among the world's poor, cereals (viz. wheat, rice, maize, and barley) as food are the main sources of nutrition, accounting for more than 50 percent of their energy intake. So when people worry about food prospects in, say, the year 2020 or 2050, they typically worry about the availability of cereals.[5]

III. Undernourishment and Poverty Traps

Rural households in poor countries are vastly more circumscribed in their ability to do things than their counterparts are in rich countries. By this I do not only mean that they have less incomes, but that they also face more stringent constraints in their ability to engage in economic transactions. There is, for example, an extreme paucity of infrastructure, such as roads and other means of communication. Villages resemble enclaves; they are often not integrated with the rest of the economy.[6] This in turn means that both insurance and credit facilities for the rural poor are greatly circumscribed. Formally, it is to say that correlations among environmental risks within villages can be "large" and, so, the scope for pooling risks "small", which is another way of saying that both insurance and credit markets can be relatively thin. As always, even within poor societies the poor are less able to insure themselves against adverse circumstances than the rich. They are also less able to obtain credit: they own less in the way of collateral.

The link between household poverty and an inability to obtain insurance and credit is one pathway by which people can fall into a poverty trap. The link creates a positive feedback — Myrdal (1944) called such feedbacks *cumulative causation* — one which enables those who have assets to move further ahead, even while it prevents those who do not have assets to be trapped in poverty; see Braverman and Stiglitz (1989).

But there are more fundamental issues in the economics of food deficiency and poverty traps. Modern nutrition science has shown that undernourishment is not necessarily the immediate cause of death. Relatively low mortality rates can co-exist with a high incidence of undernutrition, morbidity and, thus, low capacity for work.[7] For this reason the classical notion of "subsistence wage" finds little resonance in the modern literature. Undernutrition is not the same as starvation. So the economics of undernutrition is not the same as the economics of famines. Famines are disequilibrium phenomena. They cannot persist, for the reason that their victims do not survive. In contrast, even a widespread incidence of undernourishment can persist indefinitely: people are capable of living and breeding in circumstances of extreme poverty. But if over an extended

---

[5] I have gone into these issues in greater detail in Dasgupta (1997b).
[6] Rudra (1984) and Platteau and Hayami (1997) offer brisk substantiations of this.
[7] Spurr (1988, 1990) contain authoritative statements on the matter. The modern classic on childhood malnutrition is Waterlow (1992).

period of time people are to convert potential labour power into actual labour power of any specified, physiologically admissible amount, they require among other things nutrition of a corresponding quality and magnitude over that period. Dasgupta and Ray (1986, 1987) showed that the link between nutritional status and the capacity to work creates a particularly menacing pathway by which poor households can get trapped in poverty.[8] The undernourished are at a severe disadvantage in their ability to obtain food: the quality of work they are able to offer is inadequate for obtaining the food they require if they are to improve their nutritional status. Thus, over time undernourishment (more generally, ill-health) can be both a cause and consequence of someone falling into a poverty trap. Moreover, such poverty can be dynastic: once a household falls into a poverty trap, it can prove especially hard for descendents to emerge out of it, even if the economy in the aggregate were to experience growth in output for a while.

Dasgupta and Ray (1986, 1987) also showed that if the distribution of assets (e.g. land) is highly unequal in an economy that is poor, certain patterns of egalitarian redistribution of assets can enhance economic growth. Analyses of international cross-section data offer support for this finding: initial inequality of assets, as measured by the distribution of land, has been found to exert a significant negative impact on subsequent growth; Deininger and Squire (1997).

The source of such positive feedbacks and poverty traps as I have described is the large "maintenance requirement" of living. As is well known, something like 60–75 percent of the energy intake of someone in nutrition balance goes toward maintenance; the much smaller 40–25 percent is spent on "discretionary" activities, such as work and play; see e.g. WHO (1985). Large maintenance requirements are a reason why, in poor societies, we would expect to see the emergence of inequality among people who may have, to begin with, been very similar. In short, a society's poverty could in itself be a cause of stark inequality.

Notice the unusual causal direction being identified here. It is a commonplace to say that poverty among households is a reflection (even a consequence) of economic inequality. I am talking of a possible reverse causality: from poverty to inequality.

There are, of course, implicit qualifications in the account of poverty traps I am offering here. I have confined myself to central tendencies. The cycle of poverty is not inevitable. Luck can play a role, and even the poorest of households have been known to pull themselves out of the mire. But the nutrition-based theory of poverty traps has explanatory power. It offers an

---

[8] The theory is developed more fully in Dasgupta (1993, 1997a).

explanation of the modern incidence of poverty and undernutrition amidst plenty; and it explains how and why, despite the secular growth in income and food production that the world as a whole has enjoyed since the end of the Second World War, 15–20 percent of the world's population currently suffers from food deficiency.[9]

But there are problems within problems in the economics of poverty. Economic growth within a society can impose additional pressures, enabling poverty traps to have an even greater stranglehold over the lives of the poor in that society. This can come about because of a shift from cereal to meat in the dietary habits of those whose incomes rise. Table 2 provides an indication of food-feed shares of cereals in 40 poor countries and 26 industrial market economies in the mid-1980s. In 1980, consumption of cereals in the former group was 208 million metric tons, whereas cereals as feed amounted to only 5 million tons. In contrast, the corresponding figures in the latter group were 104 and 288 million tons. As the table also shows, income elasticities of demand for cereals as food and feed in the poorest countries are 0.23 and 0.75, respectively, and in industrial market economies they are 0.03 and 0.14. All this is in accordance with what one would expect.

However, as is well known, animal metabolism (especially that of cattle) is not very efficient in the conversion of plant food. Thus, growth in average

Table 2. *Competition between food and feed*

(1) Aggregate cereal demand (million metric tons)		
Food	208	104
Feed	5	288
(2) Rate of growth of demand for cereals (1966–80)		
Food	2.9	1.0
Feed	3.8	1.3
(3) Rate of growth of *per capita* demand for cereals (1966–80)		
Food	0.4	0.1
Feed	1.3	0.4
(4) Income elasticity of demand for cereals		
Food	0.23	0.03
Feed	0.75	0.14

Source: Yotopoulos (1985, Tables 1–2).

----

[9] Fogel (1994) has also offered such an account as this, but to explain why beggars constituted as much as a fifth of the populations of *ancien regimes* in late eighteenth century France. The picture of begging our analysis draws contains both physiological and behavioral adaptation with vengeance. It tells us that emaciated beggars are not lazy: they have to husband their precarious hold on energy.

income generates an incentive for farmers to shift land away from the production of food-grain toward that of cereals as feed-grain and toward grazing grounds. In terms of calories, the shift is disproportionate because of the inefficient conversion process. This goes to impoverish the poor further because, among other things, grain prices rise to equilibrate the market. As an example of how sensitive to availability grain prices can be, one should recall that the world food crisis of 1972–74 involved a 3 percent shortfall in grain production, accompanied by a 250 percent price increase. Yotopoulos (1985) has made the point that increases in the number of middle-income people exacerbate the incidence of malnutrition among those without assets, because the composition of demand shifts in an adverse way. There are indications that this is a potent force. For example, the annual rate of growth of cereal consumption in the poorest countries during 1966–80 was 2.9 percent, whereas that of feed was 3.8 percent. These are not comforting statistics.

IV. Communal Rights and the Local Commons

The foregoing analysis suggests why a form of asset ownership of particular significance to the rural poor is communal. Hardin's (1968) famous observation on the fate of common-property resources, that they erode because people free-ride on others, was telling for such globally mobile resources as the atmosphere and the open seas. However, the "tragedy of the commons" is not necessarily an apt metaphor for geographically localized common-property resources, such as irrigation water, woodlands and local forests, threshing grounds, grazing fields, inland and coastal fisheries, and swidden fallows. For it has been discovered that, typically, the local commons are not open for use to all. They are not "open access" resources; in most cases they are open only to those having customary rights, through kinship ties, community membership, and so forth. Social capital, viewed as a complex of interpersonal networks by e.g. Coleman (1990) and Putnam (1993), is telling in this context: it hints at the basis upon which cooperation has traditionally been built. Thus, from the theory of games, we have known for some time that the local commons can in principle be managed efficiently by the users themselves: there is no obvious need for some agency external to the community of users (e.g. the State) to assume a regulatory role, nor is there an obvious need for privatising the assets. A large body of recent evidence confirms the theory's prediction, in that members of local communities have often cooperated in protecting their commons from excessive use.[10]

---

[10]There is now a large empirical literature recording both the successes and failures of common-property resource management. Feeny *et al.* (1990), Ostrom (1990), and Baland and Platteau (1996, Chs. 10–13) offer good reviews of the findings.

Why should we expect such a marked difference between the fates of local and global common'property resources? One reason is that individual use is more easily observable by others when the resource is not spread out spatially; which means that it is easier to prevent people from free-riding on the local commons. (Contrast the use of a village tube-well with the littering of streets in a metropolis; or cattle-grazing in the village commons with deforestation on mountainous terrains). However, bargaining, enforcement, and information costs also play a role in the relative efficacy of the various rules that can in principle be invoked for sharing the benefits and burdens associated with an efficient use of common-property resources. Thus, it matters whether the users know one another (contrast a village grazing ground with ocean fisheries); it matters whether increased mobility makes future encounters among group members more uncertain (contrast a traditional village with a modern metropolis); and it matters whether population pressure makes transaction costs exceed the benefits of cooperation. The confirmation of theory by current evidence on the fate of different categories of common-property resources has been one of the most pleasing features of modern economic analysis.

Are common-property resources extensive in poor countries? As a proportion of total assets, their presence ranges widely across ecological zones. In India they appear to be most prominent in arid regions, mountain regions, and unirrigated areas; they are least prominent in humid regions and river valleys. There is, of course, an economic rationale for this, based on the common human desire to pool risks. An almost immediate empirical corollary is that income inequalities are less where common-property resources are more prominent. However, aggregate income is a different matter, and it is the arid and mountain regions and unirrigated areas that are the poorest. This needs to be borne in mind when government policy is devised. As may be expected, even within dry regions, dependence on common-property resources declines with increasing wealth across households.

Jodha (1986, 1995) used data from over 80 villages in 21 dry districts from six tropical states in India to estimate that, among poor families, the proportion of income based directly on the local commons is for the most part in the range 15–25 percent. Moreover, as sources of income, they are often complementary to private-property resources. Common-property resources also provide the rural poor with partial protection in times of unusual economic stress. For landless people they may be the only non-human asset at their disposal. A number of resources (such as fuelwood and water, berries and nuts, medicinal herbs, resin and gum) are the responsibility of women and children.

A similar picture emerges from Hecht, Anderson and May (1988), who describe in rich detail the importance of the extraction of babassu products among the landless (and most especially, the women among them) in the Brazilian state of Maranhão. These products are an important source of cash income in the period between agricultural-crop harvests.[11]

So studies have confirmed that the local commons are quite prevalent in rural areas of poor countries. Empirical studies have also confirmed that resource users in many instances cooperate, on occasion through not undemocratic means, so as to ensure that the resource base is not eroded. Attempts have also been made by social scientists to explain observed asymmetries in the distribution of benefits and burdens of cooperation in terms of underlying differences in the circumstances of the various parties. For example, in her study of collectively-managed irrigation systems in Nepal, Ostrom (1996) has explained observed differences in benefits and burdens among users (e.g. who gets how much water from the canal system and who is responsible for which maintenance task) in terms of such facts as that some farmers are headenders, while others are tailenders. Ostrom (1990) has also tried to explain why cooperation has failed to get off ground where it did not get established.

Wade (1988) has conducted an empirical investigation of community-based allocation rules over water and the use of grazing land in a sample of 41 South Indian villages. He found that downstream villages (i.e., those facing especial water scarcity) had an elaborate set of rules, enforced by fines, for regulating the use of water from irrigation canals. Most villages had similar arrangements for the use of grazing land. In an earlier work on the Kuna tribe in the Panama, Howe (1986) described the intricate set of social sanctions that are imposed upon those who violate norms of behaviour designed to protect their source of fresh water.

Behaviour dictated by social norms could seem incongruent with the democratic ideal, but the theory of repeated games has shown that there can be a close connection between the two. Social norms can be viewed as self-enforcing behavioural strategies. Even if a resource allocation rule among members of a community were chosen democratically, there would be a problem of enforcement. Norms are a way the rule could be enforced without the community having to rely on the coercive powers of a higher authority (e.g. the State).

This said, it is important to caution against romanticising communitarian arrangements over the use of the local commons. For example, McKean (1992) has noted that in common-property systems almost everywhere, entitlements to the products have mostly been based on private holdings. They have thus reproduced the inequality in private wealth. Beteille (1983) contains examples of how access is often restricted to the

---

[11] For a similar picture in the West African forest zone, see Falconer (1990).

privileged (e.g. caste Hindus in India). Rampant inequities exist in rural community practices. I am laying stress upon the fact that the local commons are often not unmanaged; I am not suggesting that they are invariably managed efficiently, nor that they are necessarily managed democratically, nor that they are inevitably managed in ways that involve an equitable distribution of benefits and burdens. Good management of the commons requires more than mere local participation; it needs enlightened government engagement as well.

Not surprisingly, information about the ecology of the local commons is usually in the hands of those who, customarily, have made use of them. This means that as a general rule decisions concerning the local commons ought to be left in the hands of the users themselves. It forms one reason why it is so important that local democracy be encouraged to flourish in rural communities of poor countries. The local commons will almost certainly remain the single source of vital complementary and insurance goods for poor people for a long time to come. We may conclude from this that a duty of the State is to help develop rural infrastructure and markets for credit and insurance, each of which could be expected to lessen the community's reliance on the commons. However, there is little case for centralized command and control over the use of the commons; quite the contrary, there is a case for helping the growth of local democracy. As women are often the ones to work on the commons, they would be expected to know more than others about the ecological processes upon which their communities depend. So a task of the State is to help women participate in the democratic process. More generally, the State should be obliged to ensure that local decision-making is made in an open way. It would help prevent the economically powerful among rural communities from usurping control over such decisions. This tension — the simultaneous need for increased decentralization of rural decision-making, and for State involvement in ensuring that the seat of local decisions is not usurped by the powerful — poses a central dilemma in the political economy of rural poverty. Local democracy, income security, and environmental protection would appear to be tied to each other.

V. Institutional Failure: Poverty and Degradation of the Environmental-Resource Base

But much else has not gone well: case studies undertaken both in the Indian sub-continent and in sub-Saharan Africa have revealed deteriorations in the environmental-resource base in the poorest regions. Why and how have they happened?

A recent intellectual tradition argues that the reason the poor today degrade their environmental-resource base is that their poverty forces them to discount future incomes at unusually high rates; see, for example, Bardhan (1996). I do not know of much evidence in support of this. In any event, the argument would apply to the poor of the past as well. If it were valid, they would hardly have invested in their resource bases to the extent they appear to have done, the fruits of which we enjoy today. In what follows I identify a less parsimonious, but hopefully more persuasive, explanation for contemporary resource depletion: low rates of return on private investment in the resource base owing to institutional failure.

There are a number of systematic features of institutional failure in poor countries that have been easy enough to detect. Governments in many poor countries, most especially those in sub-Saharan Africa, have for long discriminated against agriculture, creating strong disincentives for farmers to invest in it. Export quotas, over-valued exchange rates, and state marketing boards that purchase agricultural produce at artificially low prices have ensured that something like 50 percent of the agricultural income of poor countries has been transferred to the rest of their economies through the years.[12]

Peasants' property rights to the agricultural-resource base have also been insecure in many poor countries (e.g. China). This has created further disincentives for farmers to invest in the land they till. Over the past 10 years, grain production per head in China has reached a plateau. China's grain imports have risen with her income, and a natural question, "who will feed China", now appears routinely in publications; see e.g. Brown (1995). Prosterman, Hanstad and Li (1996) trace China's faltered agricultural performance to the weaknesses in the structure of property-rights in agricultural land. Chinese farmers' rights to the land they till even now do not extend beyond some 15 years. So they have little incentive to engage in long-term agricultural investment.

There is another type of institutional failure that disenfranchises the poor from an economy even while in the aggregate the society of which they are members enjoys economic growth: breakdown of communitarian norms. The point is that if you are steeped in social norms of behaviour and understand community obligations, you do not calculate every five minutes how you should behave. You follow the norms. This saves on costs all round, not only for you as an "actor", but also for you as "policeman" and

---

[12] See Krueger, Schiff and Valdes (1988). The classic on the errors of state marketing boards is Bauer and Yamey (1968). Pinstrup-Andersen (1994) contains an excellent summary of the current food situation in the world. There are other, systemic reasons, having to do with the structure of social life, why there is little scope for individual initiative to be rewarded in sub-Saharan Africa's rural economies. Platteau and Hayami (1997) offer an account of them and argue that they in large measure explain the economic decline of that region over the past twenty-five years.

"judge". It is also the natural thing for you to do if you have internalized the norms. But this is sustainable so long as the background environment remains approximately constant. It will not be sustainable if the social environment changes suddenly and trust is broken. You may even be destroyed. It is this heightened vulnerability, often more real than perceived, which is the cause of some of the greatest tragedies in contemporary society.

There are other, related sources that trigger the process of resource degradation and economic disenfranchisement among the poor. For example, an erosion of the local commons can come in the wake of shifting populations accompanying the development process itself. As economic opportunities outside the village improve, those with lesser ties (e.g. young men) are more likely to take advantage of them and make a break with customary obligations. If they were to anticipate this, they would be more likely to behave opportunistically even in advance. Likewise, those with greater attachments (e.g. women) would perceive that those with greater outside opportunities are not to be trusted. They would thereby discount at a higher rate the benefits that could be expected from complying with agreements. Either way, norms of reciprocity could be expected to break down, making certain groups of people (e.g. women) worse off.

But an erosion of the local commons can also come about in the wake of technological change, an increase in population (and the consequent pressure on these resources), unreflective public policies, and more directly, predatory governments and thieving aristocracies. There is now an accumulation of evidence on this range of causes. In what follows, I present a sketch of four sets of studies, covering three continents.

1. In his work on a sample of villages in the drylands of India, Jodha (1986, 1995) noted that over a twenty-year period, starting in the early 1960s, there had been a 25–60 percent decline in the area covered by the commons. This was in part due to the privatization of land, a good deal of which in his sample had been awarded to the rural non-poor. In an earlier work, Jodha (1980) identified the rise in the profitability of land from cropping and grazing as a central reason for increased desertification in the northern state of Rajasthan. Jodha argued that, ironically, it was government land reform programmes in this area, unaccompanied by investment in improving the productive base, that had triggered the process.

2. Ensminger's (1990) study of the privatization of common grazing lands among the Orma in northeastern Kenya showed that the transformation took place with the consent of the elders of the tribe. She attributes this willingness to changing transaction costs brought about by cheaper transportation and widening markets. The elders were, quite naturally, from the stronger families, and it does not go unnoted by Ensminger that privatization has accentuated inequalities.

3. In an earlier work on the Amazon basin, Feder (1977) described how massive private investment in the expansion of beef-cattle production in fragile ecological conditions had been supported by domestic governments in the form of tax concessions and provision of infrastructure, and loans from international agencies such as the World Bank. The degradation of vast tracts of forests was accompanied by the disenfranchisement of large numbers of small farmers and agricultural labourers from the economy. At best it made destitutes of traditional forest dwellers; at worst it simply eliminated them.[13] The evidence suggests that during the decades of the 1960s and 1970s protein intake by the rural poor declined even while the production of beef increased dramatically. Some of the beef was destined for exports, for use by fast-food chains.

This said, I am not advocating a mono-causal explanation of the depletion of the Amazon forests. In a wider discussion of the conversion of forests into ranches in the Amazon basin, Schneider (1995) has demonstrated that the construction of roads through the forests (an instance of integration with outside markets) has been a potent force. The construction of roads greatly reduced transport costs between outside markets and the resource base in the Amazon. This in turn vastly increased individual incentives for opportunistic behaviour in a world with unsettled property rights.

4. In a summary of research findings on local irrigation in Nepal, Ostrom (1996) notes that systems that had been improved by the construction of permanent headworks were in worse repair, delivered substantially less water to the tail-end than to the head-end of the systems, and had lower agricultural productivity than the temporary, stone-trees-and-mud headworks that had been constructed and managed by the farmers themselves.

Ostrom has an explanation for this. She suggests that, unless it is accompanied by counter-measures, the construction of permanent headworks alters the relative bargaining positions of the head- and tail-enders, resulting in so reduced a flow of benefits to the latter group that they have little incentive to help repair and maintain the headworks, something the head-enders on their own cannot do. Head-enders gain from the permanent structures, but the tail-enders lose disproportionately. Ostrom (1996) also notes that traditional farm-managed systems sustained greater equality in the allocation of water than modern systems managed by such external agencies as the government and foreign donors.

The sources that were identified in the first three sets of studies as having transformed common-property resources into private resources differed

---

[13] See also Hecht (1985).

considerably. Therefore, the pathways by which the transformation affected those with customary rights were different. Since the impact of these pathways to privatization on the poorest of the poor are confirmed by economic theory, the findings of these case studies are almost certainly not unrepresentative. Many of the studies suggest that privatization of village commons and forest lands, while hallowed at the altar of economic efficiency, can have disastrous distributional consequences, disenfranchising entire classes of people. The point is a simple one: unless an appropriate fraction of the rents earned from the resource-base subsequent to privatization are given to the customary users, they become worse off. Ironically, case studies also show that public ownership of such resources as forest lands is by no means necessarily a good basis for a resource allocation mechanism. Decision-makers are in these cases usually far removed from site (living as they do in imperial capitals), they have little knowledge of the ecology of such matters, their time horizons are often short, and they are in many instances overly influenced by interest groups far removed from the resource in question.

All this is not to suggest that rural development is to be avoided. It is to say that resource allocation mechanisms that do not take advantage of dispersed information, that are insensitive to hidden (and often not-so-hidden) economic and ecological interactions, that do not take the long view, and that do not give a sufficiently large weight to the claims of the poorest within rural populations (particularly the women and children and the old in these populations) are going to prove environmentally disastrous. It appears that, during the process of economic development there is a close link between environmental protection and the well-being of the poor. Elaboration of this link has been a compelling achievement at the interface of anthropology, economics and nutrition science.

VI. Fertility Behaviour and the Structure of Households

Since the Second World War both the Indian sub-continent and sub-Saharan Africa have experienced unprecedented growth in population (since the early 1960s, the annual percentage rate of growth of population in the two regions have been 2.3 and 2.9, respectively). But there have been substantial differences in the experiences of the two regions (see Table 3). What account can we provide for each of the two features?

Economic demographers in recent years have identified gender inequalities as an important component of the population problem in poor countries. In this regard, the focal point of the United Nations Conference on Population and Development in Cairo in September 1994, namely, women's reproductive rights and the means by which they could be

protected and promoted (e.g. investing in women's education), is consonant with this new perspective. But the Cairo Conference came very near
to treating the problems as identical. This was unfortunate, because it may
have lulled many into thinking that there is a single cause for pro-natalist
behaviour in the two regions. As with other phenomena in social life, there
is more than one cause behind this one. Indeed, differences in women's
educational attainments cannot explain the sharp differences in fertility
rates between the Indian sub-continent and sub-Saharan Africa. There is
more to the population problem.

This will come as no surprise to historical demographers. In his famous
analysis of fertility differences between seventeenth- and eighteenth-
century Northwest Europe on the one hand and modern pre-industrial
societies on the other, Hajnal (1982) drew upon the distinction between
"nuclear" and "joint" household systems. He observed that in Northwest
Europe marriage normally meant establishing a new household, which
implied that the couple had to have, by saving or transfer, sufficient
resources to establish and equip the new household. This requirement in
turn led to late marriages. It also meant that parents bore the cost of
rearing their children. Indeed, fertility rates in France dropped before
mortality rates registered a decline, before modern family-planning techniques became available, and before women became literate; see Coale
(1969). Hajnal contrasted this with the Asiatic pattern of household formation, which he saw as joint units consisting of more than one couple and
their children.

Table 3 displays the broad regional differences in fertility behaviour in
the contemporary world. I am not sure if Hajnal's taxonomy is adequate
here. For example, it can be argued that the rules of inheritance are a
critical factor governing interpersonal relations, and that differences in
inheritance rules may provide some explanation for why households in
sub-Saharan Africa are strikingly dissimilar to the "joint" household
system that has for long been taken to be the hallmark of the Asiatic form.
Of course, inheritance rules themselves require explanation, and it is
tempting to search for this in the mode and technology of agricultural

Table 3. *Total fertility rates in the late 1980s*

	Total fertility rate
Sub-Saharan Africa	6–8
India	4.2
China	2.3
Japan, and Western industrial democracies	1.5–1.9

Source: World Bank (1990).

production (viz. hoe versus the plough), and thereby in ecological factors (e.g. soil quality, population density, rainfall, and availability of domesticatable animals). These are delicate matters of historical analysis, and the causal links are not well understood. But Hajnal's account offers hints that have rightly been at the centre of what is often called the new household economics: it is to focus on the relative costs and benefits of procreation to various parties.[14]

One prominent motive for having children arises from their being an end.[15] This motive has been much studied in economic demography; see Becker (1981). Other motives involve viewing children as productive assets. For example, in rural economies where the avenues for saving are highly restricted, or where public support for the elderly are weak, parents value children as a source of security in their old age; see Cain (1981). In poor countries children are also useful as sources of current income. This provides households in these parts with another motive for procreation. It has possible consequences that have only recently been explored in theoretical analyses. Let us see what they are.

There are several pathways by which reasoned fertility decisions at the level of every household (whether the decision is based on the desire to have children because they are ends, or because they are productive assets) could lead to an unsatisfactory outcome from the perspectives of all households. One such pathway arises from the fact that traditional practice is often perpetuated by conformism, or imitative behaviour. Procreation in closely-knit communities is not only a private matter; it is also a social activity, influenced by the cultural milieu. In many societies there are practices encouraging high fertility rates which no household desires unilaterally to break. Such practice may well have had a rationale in the past, but not necessarily any more. It can then be that, so long as all others follow the practice and aim at large family sizes, no household on its own will wish to deviate from the practice; however, if all other households were to restrict their fertility rates, each would desire to restrict its fertility rate as well. In short, there can be multiple equilibria, and a society may get stuck in a self-sustaining mode of behaviour that is characterized by high fertility and low educational attainment, even when in principle this "same" society could have sustained a mode of behaviour characterized by low fertility and high educational attainment.

This does not mean that society will be stuck with it forever. As always, people differ in the extent of their absorption of traditional practice. There are inevitably those who, for one reason or another, experiment, take risks,

---

[14] Much work is currently being undertaken on how best to model the household; see, for example, Alderman *et al.* (1995).

[15] Vulgarly put, children are a durable consumption good.

and refrain from joining the crowd. They are the tradition-breakers, and they often lead the way. A concerted social effort (for example, a massive literacy and employment drive) can help dislodge such a society from the rapacious hold of high fertility rates to another equilibrium mode of behaviour where fertility is low. Exposure to other ways of living, through the media of radio and television, have also been found to be effective; see Freedman (1995).

But there are other pathways that lead to pro-natalist behaviour. Parental costs of procreation are "low" when the cost of rearing the child is shared among the kinship. In sub-Saharan Africa, "fosterage" within the kinship is a commonplace: children are not raised solely by their parents, the responsibility is more diffuse within the kinship group; see Goody (1982) and Bledsoe (1990). Fosterage in the African context is not adoption. It is not intended to, nor does it in fact, break ties between parents and children. The institution affords a form of mutual insurance protection in semi-arid regions. There is some evidence that, as savings opportunities are few in the low-productivity agricultural regions of sub-Saharan Africa, fosterage also enables households to smoothen their consumption across time.[16] In parts of West Africa up to half the children have been found to be living with their kin at any given time. Nephews and nieces have the same rights of accomodation and support as do biological offspring. There is a sense in which children are seen as common responsibility. However, the arrangement creates yet another free-rider problem if the parents' share of the benefits from having children exceeds their share of the costs. From the point of view of the parents, taken as a collective, too many children would be produced in these circumstances.

Related to this is a phenomenon that has been observed by Guyer (1994) in a Yaruba area of Nigeria. In the face of deteriorating economic circumstances, some women are bearing children by different men so as to create immediate lateral links with them. Polyandrous motherhood enables women to have access to more than one resource network.

In sub-Saharan Africa, communal land tenure of the lineage social structure offers yet another inducement for men to procreate. In addition, as conjugal bonds are weak, fathers often do not bear the costs of siring a child. Anthropologists have observed that the unit of African society is a woman and her children, rather than parents and their children. Often, there is no common budget for the man and woman. Descent in sub-Saharan Africa is, for the most part, patrilineal and residence is patrilocal (an exception are the Akan people of Ghana). Patrilineality, weak conjugal bonds, communal land tenure, and a strong kinship support system of

---

[16] This latter motivation has been explored by Serra (1996).

children, taken together, are a broad characteristic of the region; see Caldwell (1991). In principle they provide a powerful stimulus to fertility. Admittedly, patrilinearity and patrilocality are features of the northern parts of the Indian sub-continent also. But conjugal bonds are substantially greater there. Moreover, as agricultural land is not communally held, large family sizes lead to fragmentation of landholdings. In contrast, large families in sub-Saharan Africa are (or, at least were, until recently) rewarded by a greater share of land belonging to the lineage or clan.

VII. Population, Poverty and the Local Environment

The poorest countries are in great part biomass-based subsistence economies. Production throughput is low. Much labour is needed even for simple tasks. Moreover, households there do not have access to the sources of domestic energy available to households in advanced industrial countries. Nor do they have water on tap. In semi-arid and arid regions, water supply is often not even close at hand. Nor is fuel-wood near at hand when the forests recede. This means that the relative prices of alternative sources of energy and water faced by rural households in poor countries are quite different from those faced by households elsewhere. In addition to cultivating crops, caring for livestock, cooking food and producing simple marketable products, members of a household may have to spend as much as five to six hours a day fetching water and collecting fodder and wood. These are complementary activities. They have to be undertaken on a daily basis if the household is to survive. Each is time-consuming. Labour productivity is low not only because capital is scarce, but also because environmental resources are scarce. From about the age of 6 years, children in poor households in poor countries mind their siblings and domestic animals, fetch water, and collect fuelwood, dung, and fodder. Children are then needed as workers by their parents, even when the parents are in their prime. To give a sense of the order of magnitude, in their study of work allocation among rural households in the foothills of the Himalayas, the (Indian) Centre for Science and Environment, C.S.E (1990), recorded that children between 10 and 15 years work one-and-a-half times the number of hours adult males do.

Indeed, children can add so much to household income that, in some places, they are costless to rear by the time they reach adolescence. Cain (1977) studied data from the village Char Gopalpur in Bangladesh. He estimated that male children become net producers at as early an age as 12 years, and work as many hours a day as an adult. Using a zero (calorie) rate of interest, he calculated that male children compensate for their own cumulative consumption by the age of 15. This is almost certainly not typical in Bangladesh today. I cite it, nevertheless, to show the vast difference in the motivation for having children between households in rich countries and poor households in poor countries. The latter would appear to need many hands, and it can be that the overall usefulness of each additional hand increases with declining resource availability, at least over some range.

The need for many hands can lead to a destructive situation, especially when parents do not have to pay the full price of rearing their children, but share those costs with their community. In Section V it was noted that in recent years mores that once regulated local resources have changed. We noted also that the very process of economic development can erode traditional methods of control, say, by way of increased urbanization and mobility. Social norms are also endangered by civil strife and by the usurpation of resources by landowners or the state. As norms degrade, parents pass some of the costs of children on to the community by over-exploiting the commons. Indeed, even a marginal decline in compliance in agreements can trigger a process of cumulative causation. Over time the effect could be large. If access to shared resources continues, parents produce too many children, which leads to greater crowding and susceptibility to disease as well as to more pressure on the local resource base. This is an instance of the demographic free-rider problem.

The perception of both low costs and high benefits of procreation in sub-Saharan Africa induces "couples" to produce too many children. Theoretical considerations suggest that in certain circumstances a disastrous process can thereby begin. As the community's natural resources are depleted, more hands are needed to gather fuel and water for daily use. More children are then produced, further damaging the local resource base and in turn providing the "household" with an incentive to enlarge. When this happens, poverty, fertility, and environmental degradation reinforce one another in an escalating spiral. By the time some countervailing set of factors - whether public policy or diminished benefits from having further children due, say, to a scarcity of land - stops the spiral, millions of lives may have suffered through worsening poverty.[17]

Cleaver and Schreiber (1994) provide evidence for this thesis in the context of rural sub-Saharan Africa, and Filmer and Pritchett (1996) for the Sindh region in Pakistan. They report positive correlations between fertility and deterioration of the local environmental-resource base. Such data cannot reveal causal connections, but they are not inconsistent with the idea of a positive-feedback mechanism such as I have described. Over time, the spiral would be expected to have large effects, as manifested by

---

[17]Nerlove and Meyer (1997) have provided a formal analysis of such positive feedback processes.

battles for resources; see Homer-Dixon, Boutwell and Rathjens (1993). Civic disconnection, a powerful destroyer of property rights, can vastly reduce the rate of return on private investment in the local environmental-resource base. We should not be surprised, therefore, that it too is associated with degradation of the resource-base; see Deacon (1994).

Families with greater access to resources would, however, be in a position to limit their size and propel themselves into still higher income levels. I have not been able to locate published data on the matter, but my impression is that among the urban middle classes in north India the transition to a low fertility rate has already been achieved. As we observed in Section III, this does not mean there is an inexorable poverty trap. People from the poorest of backgrounds have been known to lift themselves out of the mire. Nevertheless, there are these additional forces at work which pull households away from one another in terms of their living standards.

In this background, it is hard to make sense of the oft-expressed suggestion that there are cumulative benefits to be enjoyed from increases in population size even in poor countries; that human beings are a valuable resource. To be sure, they are potentially valuable as doers of things and originators of ideas, but for this they require the means for personal development. Moreover, historical evidence on the way pressure of population led to changes in the organization of production, property rights, and ways of doing things, which is what Boserup (1981) studied in her far-reaching work, also does not seem to speak to the population problem as it exists today in sub-Saharan Africa and the northern parts of the Indian sub-continent.

VIII. Living Standards Indices

World food production has on average more than kept pace with world population since the end of the Second World War. This has been accompanied by improvements in a number of indicators of human well-being, such as the infant survival rate, life expectancy at birth, and literacy. It is possible such statistics as these have given economists and demographers a license to ignore ecology. The problem is that these conventional indicators of the standard of living pertain to commodity production, not to the environmental-resource base upon which all production ultimately depends. They do not say if, for example, increases in gross national product (GNP) per head are not being realized by means of a depletion of natural capital; in particular, if increases in agricultural production are not being achieved by a "mining" of the soil and water tables. By concentrating on GNP (and other current-welfare measures, such as life expectancy at birth), rather than net national product (NNP), we wrongly bypass these concerns.

In what is now an extensive literature, it has been shown that if NNP is to function effectively as an index of social well-being, it ought to be estimated by deducting from GNP not only the depreciation of physical and human capital, but also the depreciation of natural capital and the social losses incurred because of increases in stocks of environmental pollution. But then it is possible for GNP per head to increase for an extended period even while NNP per head is declining. We should be in a position to say if this has been happening in poor countries; or, for that matter, if it has been happening in rich countries. But the practice of national-income accounting has lagged so far behind its theory, that we have little idea of what the facts have been. The problem is not that we do not know what items NNP should ideally contain; rather, it is that we do not have adequate estimates of the prices of environmental resources with which to measure the value of changes in resource stocks. Estimation of the accounting prices of environmental resources should now be high on the agenda of research in development economics.

Current estimates of NNP are biased because a biased set of prices is in use: prices imputed to environmental resources on site are usually zero, and this amounts to regarding the depreciation of environmental capital as zero. But this in turn means that profits attributed to investment projects that degrade the environment are higher than their social profits. A consequence is that wrong sets of projects get selected, in both the private and public sectors.

One can go further: the bias extends to the prior stage of research and development. When environmental resources are underpriced, there is little incentive on anyone's part to develop technologies that economise on their use. The extent of the distortion created by this underpricing will vary from country to country. Poor countries inevitably have to rely on the flow of new knowledge produced in advanced industrial economies. Nevertheless, poor countries need to have the capability for basic research. The structure of accounting prices there is likely to be different from those in advanced industrial countries, most especially for non-traded goods and services. Even when it is publicly available, basic knowledge is not necessarily usable by scientists and technologists, unless they themselves have a feel for basic research. Often enough, ideas developed in foreign lands are merely transplanted to the local economy; whereas, they ought instead to be modified to suit local ecological conditions before being adopted. This is where the use of accounting prices is of help. It creates the right set of incentives, both among developers and users of technologies. Adaptation is itself a creative exercise. Unhappily, as matters stand, it is often bypassed. There is loss in this.

IX. Conclusions

This paper has been about the links that have recently been uncovered between poverty, high fertility and undernourishment, on the one hand, and degradation of the local environmental-resource base and civic disconnection, on the other, in poor countries. We have noted that while some of the policy implications of this new perspective are commonplace enough (e.g. the need for secure property rights), others are not so, at least they were not a commonplace until recently (e.g. the need for strengthening local democracy, and that direct measures for poverty alleviation are not incongruent with measures that enhance aggregate economic performance).

The new perspective takes high fertility rates in sub-Saharan Africa and the Indian sub-continent seriously and links it to environmental deterioration. It suggests that the most potent avenue open for bringing down fertility rates in the semi-arid regions of these continental masses involves the simultaneous deployment of a number of policies, not a single panacea, and that the relative importance of the various prongs would depend on the community in question. Thus, while family-planning services (especially when allied to public-health services) and measures that empower women (through both education and improved employment opportunities) are certainly desirable policies, there are others, such as those that involve the provision of infrastructural goods (e.g. cheap sources of household fuel and potable water), and measures that directly increase the economic security of the poor. The aim should not be to force people to change their reproductive behaviour; rather, it should be to identify policies that would so change the options men and women face that their reasoned choices would involve a lowering of their fertility rates to replacement levels and a sustainable use of their resource base.

While I have laid stress on the importance today of local democracy for the protection of the local environmental-resource base, evidence also suggests that even at the national level, political and civil liberties are positively correlated with improvements in income per head, life expectancy at birth, and the infant survival rate, and are negatively correlated with fertility rates.[18] We are, therefore, encouraged to think that political and civil liberties have instrumental value, even in poor countries; they are not merely desirable ends. But each of the prescriptions offered by the new perspective is desirable in itself, and commends itself even when we do not have the population problem or environmental degradation in mind. It seems to me this consonance of means and ends is a most agreeable fact.

---

[18] See Dasgupta (1990), Przeworski and Limongi (1995), and Barro (1996).

References

Alderman, H. *et al.*: Unitary versus collective models of the household: is it time to shift the burden of proof? *World Bank Research Observer 10* (1), 1–20, 1995.

Baland, J.-M. and Platteau, J.-P.: *Halting Degradation of Natural Resources: Is There a Role for Rural Communities?* Clarendon Press, Oxford, 1996.

Bardhan, P.: Research on poverty and development twenty years after *Redistribution with Growth*. *Proceedings of the Annual World Bank Conference on Development Economics, 1995* (Supplement to the *World Bank Economic Review* and the *World Bank Research Observer*), 59–72, 1996.

Barro, R. J.: Democracy and growth, *Journal of Economic Growth* 1(1), 1–27, 1996.

Bauer, P. and Yamey, B.: *Markets, Market Control and Marketing Reform*. Weidenfeld & Nicolson, London, 1968.

Becker, G.: *A Treatise on the Family*. Harvard University Press, Cambridge, MA, 1981.

Beteille, A. (ed.): *Equality and Inequality: Theory and Practice*. Oxford University Press, Delhi, 1983.

Bledsoe, C.: "The politics of children: fosterage and the social management of fertility among the Mende of Sierra Leone. In W. Penn Handwerker (ed.), *Births and Power: social change and the politics of reproduction*. Westview Press, London, 1990.

Boserup, E.: *Population Growth and Technological Change*. Chicago University Press, Chicago, 1981.

Braverman, A. and Stiglitz, J. E.: Credit rationing, tenancy, productivity, and the dynamics of inequality. In P. Bardhan (ed.), *The Economic Theory of Agrarian Institutions*. Oxford University Press, Oxford, 1989.

Brown, L.R.: *Who Will Feed China? Wake-Up Call for a Small Planet*. W.W. Norton, New York, 1995.

Cain, M.: The economic activities of children in a village in Bangladesh. *Population and Development Review* 3, 201–227, 1977.

Cain, M.: Risk and insurance: perspectives on fertility and agrarian change in India and Bangladesh. *Population and Development Review* 7, 435–474, 1981.

Caldwell, J.: The soft underbelly of development: demographic transition in conditions of limited economic change. *Proceedings of the Annual Bank Conference on Development Economics 1990* (Supplement to the *World Bank Economic Review* and the *World Bank Research Observer*), 207–54, 1991.

Cassidy, J.: The decline of economics. *New Yorker*, 50–64, December 2, 1996.

Cleaver, K. M. and Schreiber, G. A.: *Reversing the Spiral: the population, agriculture, and environment nexus in sub-Saharan Africa*. World Bank, Washington, D.C., 1994.

Coale, A. J.: The decline of fertility in Europe from the French Revolution to World War II. In J. Behrman, L. Corsa and R. Freedman (ed.), *Fertility and Family Planning: a world view*. University of Michigan Press, Ann Arbor, Michigan, 1969.

Coleman, J.: *Foundations of Social Theory*. Harvard University Press, Cambridge, MA, 1990.

C.S.E.: *Human-Nature Interactions in a Central Himalayan Village: a case study of village Bemru*. Centre for Science and Environment, New Delhi, 1990.

Dasgupta, P.: *The Control of Resources*. Harvard University Press, Cambridge, MA, 1982.

Dasgupta, P.: Well-Being and the extent of its realization in poor countries. *Economic Journal* 100 (Supplement), 1–32, 1990.

Dasgupta, P.: *An Inquiry into Well-Being and Destitution*. Clarendon Press, Oxford, 1993.

Dasgupta, P.: Population, poverty, and the local environment. *Scientific American* 272(2), 40–45, 1995(a).

Dasgupta, P.: The population problem: theory and evidence. *Journal of Economic Literature*

33(4), 1879–1902, 1995(b).

Dasgupta, P.: The economics of the environment. *Environment and Development Economics* 1(4), 387–421, 1996.

Dasgupta, P.: Nutritional status, the capacity for work and poverty traps. *Journal of Econometrics* 77(1), 5–37, 1997(a).

Dasgupta, P.: The economics of food. Mimeo. Faculty of Economics, University of Cambridge, 1997(b). In J. C. Waterlow, D. G. Armstrong, L. Fowden and R. Riley (ed.), *Feeding a World Population of More than Eight Billion People: A Challenge to Science.* Oxford University Press, New York, forthcoming 1998.

Dasgupta, P.: Economic development and the idea of social capital. Mimeo., Faculty of Economics, University of Cambridge, 1997(c).

Dasgupta, P. and Mäler, K.-G.: The environment and emerging development issues. *Proceedings of the Annual World Bank Conference on Development Economics, 1990* (Supplement to the *World Bank Economic Review* and the *World Bank Research Observer*, 101–132, 1991.

Dasgupta, P. and Ray, D.: Inequality as a determinant of malnutrition and unemployment: theory. *Economic Journal 96* (4), 1011–1034, 1986.

Dasgupta, P. and Ray, D.: Inequality as a determinant of malnutrition and unemployment: policy. *Economic Journal 97* (1), 177–188, 1987.

Deacon, R. T.: Deforestation and the rule of law in a cross section of countries. *Land Economics 70* (4), 414–430, 1994.

Deininger, K. and Squire, L.: Economic growth and income inequality: reexamining the links. *Finance and Development 34* (1), 38–41, 1997.

Ensminger, J.: Co-opting the elders: the political economy of State incorporation in Africa. *American Anthropologist* 92, 662–75, 1990.

Falconer, J.: *The Major Significance of "Minor" Forest Products.* Food and Agriculture Organization, Rome, 1990.

FAO: *World Food Supplies and Prevalence of Chronic Undernutrition in Developing Regions as Assessed in 1992.* Document ESS/MISC/1/92, Food and Agriculture Organization, Rome, 1992.

Feder, E.: Agribusiness and the elimination of Latin America's rural proletariat. *World Development* 5(5–7), 559–571, 1977.

Feeny, D. *et al.*: The tragedy of the commons: twenty-two years later. *Human Ecology* 18(1), 1–19, 1990.

Filmer, D. and Pritchett, L.: Environmental degradation and the demand for children. Research Project on Social and Environmental Consequences of Growth-Oriented Policies, Working Paper No. 2, World Bank, Washington, D.C., 1996.

Fogel, R. W.: Economic growth, population theory, and physiology: the bearing of long-term processes on the making of economic policy. *American Economic Review* 84(3), 369-395, 1994.

Freedman, R.: Asia's Recent Fertility Decline and Prospects of Future Demographic Change. Asia-Pacific Population Research Report No. 1, East–West Center, Honolulu, 1995.

Goody, E.: *Parenthood and Social Reproduction: Fostering and Occupational Roles in West Africa.* Cambridge University Press, Cambridge, 1982.

Guyer, J. L.: Lineal identities and lateral networks: the logic of polyandrous motherhood. In C. Bledsoe and G. Pison (ed.), *Nupitality in Sub-Saharan Africa: contemporary anthropological and demographic perspectives.* Clarendon Press, Oxford, 1994.

Hajnal, J.: Two kinds of preindustrial household formation systems. *Population and Development Review* 8(3), 449–94, 1982.

Hardin, G.: The tragedy of the commons. *Science* 162, 1243–48, (1968).

Hecht, S.: Environment, development, and politics: capital accumulation and the livestock sector in Eastern Amazonia. *World Development* 13(6), 663–684, 1985.

Hecht, S., Anderson, A. B. and May, P.: The subsidy from nature: shifting cultivation, successional palm forests and rural development. *Human Organization* 47(1), 25-35, 1988.

Heilbroner, R.: *21st Century Capitalism*. W. W. Norton, New York, 1993.

Heilbroner, R. and Milberg, W.: *The Crisis of Vision in Modern Economics*. Cambridge University Press, Cambridge, 1995.

Homer-Dixon, T, Boutwell, J., and Rathjens, G.: Environmental change and violent conflict. *Scientific American 268* (2), 16–23, 1993.

Howe, J.: *The Kuna Gathering*. University of Texas Press, Austin, Texas, 1986.

IFPRI: *A 2020 Vision for Food, Agriculture, and the Environment*. International Food Policy Research Institute, Washington, D.C., 1995.

James, W. F. T. *et al.*: *Body Mass Index: An Objective Measure of Chronic Energy Deficiency in Adults*. Food and Agriculture Organization, Rome, 1992.

Jodha, N. S.: The process of desertification and the choice of interventions. *Economic and Political Weekly 15* (32), 1351–56, 1980.

Jodha, N. S.: Common property resources and the rural poor. *Economic and Political Weekly* 21(27), 1169-81, 1986.

Jodha, N. S.: Common property resources and the environmental context: role of biophysical versus social stress. *Economic and Political Weekly 30* (51), 3278–83, 1995.

Krueger, A. O., Schiff, M. and Valdes, A.: Agricultural incentives in developing countries: measuring the effect of sectoral and economywide Policy. *World Bank Economic Review* 2(3), 255–272, 1988.

McKean, M.: Success on the commons: a comparative examination of institutions for common property resource management. *Journal of Theoretical Politics* 4, 256–68, 1992.

Morris, M. D.: *Measuring the Condition of the World's Poor: The Physical Quality of Life Index*. Pergamon, Oxford, 1979.

Myrdal, G.: *An American Dilemma: The Negro Problem and Modern Democracy*. Harper & Row, New York, 1944.

Nerlove, M. and Meyer, A.: Endogenous fertility and the environment: a parable of firewood. In P. Dasgupta and K.-G. Mäler (ed.), *The Environment and Emerging Development Issues, Vol. 1*. Clarendon Press, Oxford, 1997.

Ostrom, E.: *Governing the Commons: The Evolution of Institutions for Collective Action*. Cambridge University Press, Cambridge, 1990.

Ostrom, E.: Incentives, rules of the game, and development. *Proceedings of the Annual World Bank Conference on Development Economics, 1995* (Supplement to the *World Bank Economic Review* and the *World Bank Research Observer*), 207–34, 1996.

Pinstrup-Andersen, P.: World food trends and future food security. Food Policy Report, International Food Policy Research Institute, Washington, D.C., 1994.

Platteau, J.-P. and Hayami, Y.: Resource endowments and agricultural development: Africa vs. Asia. Mimeo., University of Namur, 1997. In M. Aoki and Y. Hayami (ed.), *The Institutional Foundation of Economic Development in East Asia*. Macmillan, London, forthcoming, 1998.

Prosterman, R. L., Hanstad, T. and Li Ping: Can China feed itself? *Scientific American* 275(5), 70-77, 1996.

Przeworski, A. and Limingo, F.: Democracy and development. Working Paper #7, Chicago Center on Democracy, University of Chicago, 1995.

Putnam, R. D., with Leonardi, R. and Nanetti, R. Y.: *Making Democracy Work: Civic Traditions in Modern Italy*. Princeton University Press, Princeton, NJ, 1993.

Rudra, A.: Local power and farm-level decision-making. In M. Desai, S. H. Rudolph and A.

Rudra (eds.), *Agrarian Power and Agricultural Productivity in South Asia*, University of California Press, Berkeley, 1984.

Schneider, R.: Government and the economy on the Amazon frontier. World Bank Environment Paper No. 11, World Bank, Washington, DC, 1995.

Sen, A.: Development: which way now?. *Economic Journal 93*(4), 745–62, 1983.

Serra, R.: *An Economic Analysis of Child Fostering in West Africa*. Ph.D. Dissertation, Faculty of Economics, University of Cambridge, 1996.

Spurr, G. B.: Marginal malnutrition in childhood: Implications for adult work capacity and productivity. In K. J. Collins and D. F. Roberts (eds.), *Capacity for Work in the Tropics*, Cambridge University Press, Cambridge, 1988.

Spurr, G. B.: The impact of chronic undernutrition on physical work capacity and daily energy expenditure. In G. A. Harrison and J. C. Waterlow (eds.), *Diet and Disease in Traditional and Developing Countries*. Cambridge University Press, Cambridge, 1990.

Stern, N.: The economics of development: A survey. *Economic Journal 99* (5), 597–685, 1989.

UNDP: *Human Development Report*. Oxford University Press, New York, 1994.

Wade, R.: *Village Republics: Economic Conditions for Collective Action in South India*. Cambridge University Press, Cambridge, 1988.

Waterlow, J. C.: *Protein Energy Malnutrition*. Edward Arnold, Sevenoaks, Kent, 1992.

WHO: *Energy and Protein Requirements*. World Health Organization, Geneva, 1985.

World Bank: *World Development Report*. (Published annually), Oxford University Press, Oxford, 1986, 1990, 1991, 1994.

Yotopoulos, P.: Middle-income classes and food crises: The 'new' food-feed competition. *Economic Development and Cultural Change 33* (3), 463–484, 1985.

Scand. J. Economics 100(1), 69–72, 1998

Comment on P. Dasgupta, "The Economics of Poverty in Poor Countries"

Kaushik Basu

Cornell University, Ithaca, NY 14853, USA

Underdevelopment as Trap

I.

The distinguished Indian economist, the late Professor V. M. Dandekar, once told me how, when he was a young man attending a seminar by a pompous "senior" economist, he spotted a simple mathematical mistake on the blackboard and pointed it out. The senior economist glared at him, and said, "Young man, we are not talking about the efficient, smooth economy of an industrialized nation; but about the chaos and clutter of underdevelopment … ". Development economics has come a long way since. Nowadays it has analytical rigor and empirical foundation; the attitude of "anything goes" has gone. This is true of the many sub-themes within development — the study of agrarian organization, distribution and growth, poverty and famines, and more. In addition, this analytical rigor is combined with a commendable openness to advances in other social sciences, such as anthropology, sociology and politics.

In this paper Partha Dasgupta demonstrates the power of this new method by lucidly describing and exploring analytically the linkages between the seemingly disparate themes of undernutrition, environmental deterioration and high fertility. He draws on the existing literature in anthropology, nutritional science and economics, including his own important work in the latter, to shed light on the interconnections. Though he does not go into formalism in this paper, he has done so in his earlier work, and also between the words and the lines one can see the outlines of models and mathematics.

There are two general claims around which Dasgupta pegs his discourse. These are: first, that the poor in a poor country tend to get caught in a trap involving, among other things, undernutrition and local environmental degradation; and, second, even when a poor country finally begins to grow it has a way of bypassing a lot of the poor, at times actually leaving them worse off than they were when the whole economy was stagnant.

The first claim is driven home very skillfully. There is a large literature, beginning with the work of Rosenstein-Rodan and Nurkse, which has now been formalized in different ways by several authors and, I believe, considerably deepens our understanding of economy-wide stagnation. But that is not the direction Dasgupta pursues. Instead, his focus is more on micro-economic causation, involving nutrition and a person's ability to work, which is an area where he did important original work in Dasgupta and Ray (1986) and which is elaborated very nicely in Dasgupta (1997).

The discussion of the second claim about economy-wide growth and enclaves of poverty could be elaborated further, however; and for this reason I restrict my comments mainly to this claim.

II.

Dasgupta first notes, by citing studies from different parts of the globe, that the rural poor derive a substantial part of their income (in some cases as much as 25%) from the local commons. Next he observes that, unlike in the case of global commons, local commons are not as susceptible to free-riding (and therefore over-use) as textbook economics would have us predict. The reason is that small communities develop norms and methods of monitoring one another and also of keeping outsiders from tapping into their common resources. When a country begins to grow, a necessary concomitant of this growth — so argues Dasgupta — is the breakdown and alteration in many long-standing institutions. This is often accompanied by increased discrimination against agriculture and the breakdown of the very social norms that allowed the management of local commons. So with economy-wide growth, the share of consumption that used to come from common resources shrinks; the result is destitution and the disenfranchise-ment of the poor from economic citizenship.

There is evidence that something like this does often happen. The growing urban slums in Mumbai and Delhi are not just a consequence of economic growth and prosperity in the cities, but also a commentary on the breakdown of the rural equilibrium so that large segments of people have no option but to migrate to the squalor of cities.

In recent years archaeologists and anthropologists have turned up some dramatic examples of whole civilizations perishing because of their own growth and subsequent environmental damage. There are several myster-ies of great civilizations having vanished without signs of war or sudden natural disasters, such as volcanic eruptions or earthquakes. For example, recent evidence suggests that the dissolution of the Maya civilization in the central areas — mainly northern Guatemala — during the late eighth and early ninth centuries AD can be attributed to its unsustainable economic growth. New excavations have made it clear that the Mayan population had increased to unsustainable levels by the late eighth century. As Coe (1993, p. 128) observes: "By the end of the eighth century, the Classic Maya population of the southern lowlands had probably increased beyond the carrying capacity of the land, no matter what system of agriculture was in use." From 790 to 830 AD the death rate outstripped the birth rate and by 830 AD new construction had virtually come to an end. People abandoned the cities and scattered far and wide. Agricultural productivity dropped because of soil fatigue and labor also got diverted "to the elite centres to satisfy the cultural demands of the burgeoning upper class" [Coe (1993, p. 128)]. This is so close to processes which Dasgupta describes that one cannot help feeling there is a great deal to be learned from studying this new archaeological evidence, since this is one case where the depletion of resources was played out till the very end, that is to the point of obliteration of a society.

What Dasgupta describes seems to be empirically well founded. However, I have two comments. First, there are some routes through which the poor can get left behind, which are distinct from those discussed by Dasgupta, but may, nevertheless, be empirically important. For instance, Atkinson (1995), in formalizing the concepts of capability and entitlement due to Sen (1981), has shown how the poor can become excluded from the market, depending on the extent of inequality in society and the market structure. Atkinson's model can be extended to show that the growth in income of some people may exacerbate the problem of exclusion from the market for others. Dasgupta does not deny these kinds of causation are possible; I bring this up simply as a suggestion of an avenue which, in my opinion, is worth exploring in the future.

Second, he bases much of his analysis on social norms. But what exactly *are* social norms? He says that norms are equilibrium strategies in repeated games. There is a large game-theoretic literature that takes this view of norms. But are all norms like this? Probably not and, moreover, Dasgupta himself refers to norms that do not fit this equilibrium-selection view.

In addition, for some of his analysis, the reference to norms seems unnecessary. He contends, for instance, that human beings are creatures of habit. So if they live in an unchanging environment long enough, they get habituated to a particular kind of behavior, which is optimal for that environment. If then, for external reasons, the environment changes, they may get "caught" with a habit which is no longer optimal, and so become impoverished. He motivates this reasoning by saying: "If you are steeped in social norms of behavior [...], you do not calculate every five minutes how you should behave." This is true, but it would be true even if you were not steeped in social norms. At least for *this* argument, the reference to equilibrium-selection norms seems unnecessary.

If this is a matter of norms at all, then it is so in a different sense. This "norm" is much closer to Schelling's (1985) "rules for oneself". The way I interpret Schelling's work is in terms of categories which are popular among moral philosophers. They distinguish between "act" and "rule" utilitarianism. Schelling's work suggests that there should be a similar distinction between what may be called "act optimization" and "rule optimization". What Dasgupta is doing here is equating a "norm" with "rule optimization", that is, optimization where you do not evaluate each *act* separately but follow *rules* which maximize utility. While this is all right — it is after all no more than a matter of definition — it suggests the need to acknowledge the varied nature of norms.

Nowadays there is work where norms take the form of simply affecting human preferences, making them dependent on what *others* are doing; see Lindbeck, Nyberg and Weibull (1997). Another kind of norm, distinct from Dasgupta's, but rooted in evolutionary game theory, has been used by Sethi and Somanathan (1996) to address a research agenda very similar to Dasgupta's. They use it to show how in the Kumaon hill region in India, forests were rapidly depleted when the colonial government interfered with the common property regime, resulting in the disruption of local norms. These are just two examples but suggestive enough for us to be on the lookout for more.

References

Atkinson, A. B.: Capabilities, exclusion and the supply of goods. In K. Basu, P. K. Pattanaik and K. Suzumura (eds.), *Choice, Welfare and Development*, Clarendon Press, Oxford, 1995.

Coe, M. D.: *The Maya*. Fifth edition, Thames and Hudson, New York, 1993 (first edition, 1966).

Dasgupta, P. S.: Nutritional status, the capacity for work, and poverty traps. *Journal of Econometrics 77*, 5–37, 1997.

Dasgupta, P. S. and Ray, D.: Inequality as a determinant of malnutrition and unemployment. *Economic Journal 97*, 177–88, 1986.

Lindbeck, A., Nyberg, S. and Weibull, J. W.: Social norms and economic incentives in the welfare state. WP 476, Research Institute of Industrial Economics, Stockholm, 1997.

Schelling, T. C.: Enforcing rules on oneself. *Journal of Law, Economics and Organization 1*, 357–74, 1985.

Sen, A.: *Poverty and Famines*. Clarendon Press, Oxford, 1981.

Sethi, R. and Somanathan, E.: The evolution of social norms in common property resource use. *American Economic Review 86*, 766–88, 1996.

Scand. J. Economics 100(1), 73–77, 1998

Comment on P. Dasgupta, "The Economics of Poverty in Poor Countries"

Thorvaldur Gylfason

University of Iceland, IS-101 Reykjavik, Iceland and SNS, S-114 86 Stockholm, Sweden

I think it is probably safe to say that development economics has by now, at last, entered the mainstream of economics, at least as far as macro-economics is concerned. By this I mean that the same principles of macro-economics are now routinely applied in developing and developed countries alike and there is no longer perceived to be a general need to tailor macroeconomic policy prescriptions to the special characteristics of poor countries. For example, the most effective remedies against inflation are basically the same everywhere — and always were, of course. What is new, however, is that over the past generation the rapid economic growth of East Asia,[1] in particular, has provided strong grounds for believing that the best ways to stimulate growth in the long run and hence also to lift poor countries out of poverty — namely, through increased saving and effi-ciency, including education — are most likely essentially the same, inde-pendently of the level of development of the country in question. Further, the idea that central planning is good for growth in developing countries is basically dead. Hence, market-friendly reforms (liberalization, privatiza-tion, stabilization, etc.) that are good for growth in Eastern Europe and East Asia are almost surely no less good for growth in India and Africa. Therein lies the hope that even the poorest countries can expect to experi-ence a revolution in their living standards in the twenty-first century. This hope, which rests on recent advances in the theory of economic growth as well as on experience with economic reforms in different parts of the world, is, to my mind, realistic.

Its entry into the mainstream of economics does not, however, dislodge development economics as an important, independent branch of economics. As Dasgupta's paper demonstrates, many aspects of economic development, not least persistent poverty in poor countries, cry out for independent study. It is important, then, that the whole body of relevant economic knowledge be brought to bear on such studies rather than merely a special subset tailored to the perceived special circumstances of poor countries. For example, in the section on communal rights and the

---

[1] See Asian Development Bank (1997).

local commons, Dasgupta emphasizes that "there is no obvious need for some agency external to the community of users (e.g. the State) to assume a regulatory role ... ". This applies when the local commons in question can be effectively closed to new entrants. Even so, there are many instances where government involvement in one form or another, local or central, remains the most effective way to ensure optimal exploitation of many common property resources, e.g. fisheries, through a clear demarcation of property rights, Pigovian fees, and free trade. There is no reason why the most efficient methods of fisheries management or, more generally, the principles of political economy, should not apply to rich and poor countries alike.

It is frequently maintained that empirical studies of economic problems and policies in developing countries differ substantially in method and scope from studies of industrial countries, in two main ways. First, it has often been said, quite correctly, that adequate and reliable data are usually not available in many developing countries, so that econometric research is effectively ruled out. This explains, for instance, why fully fledged macro-econometric modelling has been almost exclusively confined to industrial countries. But this is changing: there is a rapidly growing micro- and macroeconometric literature on poor countries. In the second place, it is often claimed that the standard paradigms of economic analysis are not really applicable to many developing countries, because their institutions and incentive structures are fundamentally different from those of industrial countries. In extreme form, this claim implies that econometric model-building would not really make much sense in developing countries, even if adequate data were available. Here I disagree. In many instances, standard economic paradigms have been adapted quite successfully to the institutional characteristics of different types of economies. The recent econometric literature on economic growth, which is based on large data sets covering up to 170 countries, most of them with low incomes, is a case in point. Another example is provided by the rapidly advancing empirical research on various development issues, including demography, as discussed by Dasgupta, and household expenditure patterns, as studied extensively by Angus Deaton, among others.

To my mind, therefore, what sets poor and rich countries apart as far as econometric research is concerned is primarily the availability of good data. This problem restricts the options of empirically inclined developments economists. As far as I can see, they have essentially three options. First, they can concentrate their efforts on those areas where reasonably good data do exist. This is, indeed, what many have chosen to do. This is why money demand and import demand equations have been estimated extensively in many developing countries, but disaggregated investment equations and full-fledged macroeconometric models have not. However, this strategy is undeniably a little bit like looking for a lost key under a lamppost because that is where the light is. Further, the problem is sometimes not only dearth of data, but rather that econometric methods for some reason do not produce the results that we expect to find, a problem that is not confined to developing countries. It is, for example, notoriously difficult to find or produce good statistical estimates of price elasticities of supply in agriculture and elsewhere, but that does not really shake our belief in upward-sloping supply schedules, nor should it, if we think we understand why supply elasticities are hard to identify.

The second option is to try to utilize the limited data that are available and somehow fill the gaps. Consider the following example. Suppose we need to estimate the effect of devaluation on the current account of the balance of payments in Bangladesh, and that we do not have the data necessary to estimate a fully specified econometric model of the Bangladeshi balance of payments. What can we do? One method which I find appealing is to build an analytical model of the main channels through which devaluation affects the current account; this model may be geared to the special circumstances of the Bangladeshi economy, or it may be a model which we could use to study the same problem in other comparable countries. The model ultimately produces a formula showing the effect of devaluation on the current account as a function of a large number of structural parameters. Some of these parameters such as, for example, the share of imports in GDP or the ratio of foreign debt service to exports, may be readily available from national or international statistical sources. Other parameters such as, for instance, price elasticities of exports and imports or the elasticity of substitution in production, may not be available, and may be impossible to estimate. What we can do instead is to assume a range of reasonable values for the missing parameters (or borrow estimates of these parameters from studies of other comparable counties), use them to compute the effect of devaluation on the Bangladeshi current account, and then test the sensitivity of the result to variations in the guesstimates involved. That way a combination of actual data, estimation, and informed guesswork can lead to potentially valuable empirical results. A weakness of this calibration strategy, however, is that it does not permit tests of the statistical significance of the results.

The third option is to try to compensate for the lack of data for each country by including several countries in the sample. This is the essence of comparative studies. Here the idea is to get around the data problem by comparing the experience of a coutnry in a given period with the experience of other countries in the same period, rather than with its own experience in earlier periods for which no data may be available: one simply substitutes cross-section data for missing time series and proceeds to estimate models or test hypotheses. If, on the other hand, cross-section data are not available either, one can try to compensate by collecting impressions from experience in the field, organizing these impressions within a reasonable analytical framework, and telling convincing stories about them. Until recently, much of what we knew, or thought we knew, about economic development was based on informal non-econometric investigation of this kind. This changed with the new empirical growth literature. Even so, analytical economic history as described above has served us reasonably well in the past. We would want to pursue this line of inquiry further, even if we did not have data problems; we would then, I think, want to combine analytical economic history with rigorous econometric investigation. Diversification is desirable in empirical research. Therefore, analytical economic history should not be viewed as a substitute for econometrics, but rather as a complement, just as economic history is a complement to, and not a substitute for, economic theory and empirical discrimination among competing theories by econometric methods.

I have stressed how development economics has gained strength from its fusion with other areas of economics. The benefit is mutual. Some of the issues that arise in development economics can be gainfully imported into the economic analysis of industrial countries. For example, the distinction between GNP and NNP, as Dasgupta discusses, has gained currency primarily among development and resource economists, and is now being put into practice at the World Bank and the United Nations. Nevertheless, it can also be of considerable relevance to high-income countries. The successful integration of human and natural capital accumulation and environmental degradation into our national income accounts will probably provide us with more reliable measures of the wealth of nations and how they compare.

Recent empirical evidence, based on cross-country data from both poor and rich countries, appears to indicate that natural resources may have been overrated as a source of wealth around the world. Specifically, recent studies seem to show that economic growth is inversely related to measures of natural resource abundance; see Sachs and Warner (forthcoming) and Gylfason *et al.* (forthcoming). One possible explanation is that primary production, especially agriculture, tends to be less human-capital intensive than industry, trade, and services. Thus, the preponderance of primary production may, through that channel, hamper economic growth. This problem may be compounded by the Dutch disease: primary production, such as oil production for export, tends to crowd out non-oil exports, and thereby changes the composition of exports away from human-capital intensive industries that confer positive spillover benefits on the rest of the economy. If these arguments withstand further empirical scrutiny, they may have important implications. They may entail that the best way for poor countries to grow rich is not through more effective agriculture and other primary production, but rather through the successful devolution of agriculture and other natural-resource intensive activity in favor of more human-capital intensive employment. After all, this is how Europe became rich over the past 50 years.

References

Asian Development Bank: *Emerging Asia, Changes and Challenges*. Manila, 1997.

Gylfason, Thorvaldur, Herbertsson, Tryggvi T. and Zoega, Gylfi: A mixed blessing: Natural resources and economic growth. Forthcoming in *Macroeconomic Dynamics*.

Sachs, Jeffrey D. and Warner, Andrew M.: Natural resource abundance and economic growth. Forthcoming in *Quarterly Journal of Economics*.

Scand. J. of Economics 100(1), 79–104, 1998

Emission Taxes versus Other Environmental Policies

Michael Hoel*

University of Oslo, N-0317 Oslo, Norway

Abstract

In the environmental policy of most countries, various forms of quotas and direct regulation are more important than environmental taxes. This paper addresses four arguments which are often given against the use of emission taxes. The three arguments related to information asymmetries and non-convexities are valid in the sense that they point to complications in the use of environmental taxes. The fourth argument is related to the employment effects of different types of environmental policies in economies with unemployment. Although this argument is frequently used by politicians, the analysis provides no justification for it. On the contrary: in the model used, employment is higher with environmental taxes than with non-revenue-raising environmental policies.

I. Introduction

In this paper I consider the classical type of environmental problem where environmentally harmful emissions occur as a by-product of a production process. There obviously exist important problems which do not fall into this category, but much of what I have to say is also relevant for a broader class of environmental problems.

Pollution of the type described above is a classical textbook example of a negative externality. A negative externality implies that the social cost of production is higher than the private cost. The classical economic policy to internalize such an externality is to introduce an emission tax which covers the difference between the social and private costs of production. Emission taxes are thus an obvious response to an environmental problem of this type.

In addition to emission taxes, there are, of course, other policies which may be used to reduce the amount of harmful emissions. However, emission taxes have the virtue of giving a cost-effective outcome: it is in each producer's own interest to equate his marginal abatement cost with the emission tax. As long as all producers face the same emission tax, marginal

---

* I am grateful to an anonymous referee for helpful comments and to Colin Forthun for useful assistance. I gratefully acknowledge financial support from the Nordic Council of Ministers under the Nordic Environmental Research Program 1993–1997, and from the Research Council of Norway under the SAMRAM Research Program.

abatement costs are therefore equalized across sources. This is a necessary and sufficient condition for cost effectiveness for homogeneous emissions, meaning that the environmental goal is achieved at as low costs as possible. Tietenberg (1990) has argued that the cost saving from using emission taxes instead of "command and control" instruments is in many cases substantial.

An emission tax is not the only policy instrument that gives a cost-effective outcome. Tradeable emission permits will also equalize marginal abatement costs across sources, provided markets are perfectly competitive. The argument of cost effectiveness is thus an argument for emission taxes or tradeable emission permits on one hand and non-tradeable quotas and other forms of direct regulation on the other.

More recently, several economists have focused on another advantage of emission taxes as compared to many other types of instruments. This advantage arises from the fact that lump-sum taxation is not a feasible tax form in practice. Therefore, existing taxes are generally distortionary. The revenue from an emission tax makes it possible to reduce other taxes, thus reducing distortions in the economy. Some economists and politicians have argued that there might be a "double dividend" associated with the introduction of an emission tax: not only does the environment improve, but the reduced distortions in the economy due to the reduction of other taxes may be welfare improving even without counting the environmental gain; see Goulder (1995) for an overview of some of the literature on "double dividends", and Bohm (1997) for a critical discussion of some of the issues in this literature.

Independently of whether or not a potential double dividend exists, the possibility of using the revenue from an emission tax to reduce other taxes is a desirable feature of an emission tax in comparison with other non-revenue-raising environmental policies. Goulder *et al.* (1996) have argued that the difference between revenue-raising and non-revenue-raising environmental policies might be quite substantial.

While an emission tax is the most obvious example of a revenue-raising environmental policy, it is not the only example. Another obvious example is tradeable emission permits, provided they are sold to the producers at their market price, e.g. through an auction. Tradeable emission permits of this type thus share both of the desirable properties of emission taxes: they give a cost-effective outcome, and they create revenue which may be used to reduce distortionary taxes.

Given the desirable properties of emission taxes as compared with many other environmental policy instruments, one might think that emission taxes (or tradeable emission permits sold by the regulator at their market price) would be the main instrument used in environmental policy. This is far from the case, however. Although environmental taxes are used a great deal in the OECD countries, see e.g. OECD (1995), various forms of quotas and direct regulation play a more important role than environmental taxes in most countries. There are many reasons why this is so, several of which have more to do with the process of policymaking than with economics in a narrower sense. Instead of a comprehensive discussion of these issues,[1] this paper focuses on four arguments which are often given against the use of emission taxes.

The first two arguments against emissions taxes (Sections II and III) are related to the possibility of achieving a particular environmental target. It is argued that policymakers give high priority to reaching a quantitative target with a high degree of accuracy, even in cases where the exact achievement of a quantitative target is not important from an economic point of view.

In Section IV, I consider the case in which it is costly/difficult/impossible to monitor emissions. Here, it may also be possible to use some type of environmental tax, but it is not obvious that environmental taxes in such cases are superior to appropriate forms of direct regulation.

Finally, Section V deals with emission taxes and other types of policy instruments in a situation with unemployment. Politicians often argue that emission taxes impose higher costs on producers than various forms of direct regulation, and may therefore be harmful to employment. The analysis in Section V does not give much support to this type of argument. On the contrary, it is shown that non-revenue-raising policy instruments may result in a lower level of employment than an emission tax.

II. Emission Taxes with Uncertain Abatement Costs

A concern among policymakers is that environmental taxes lack precision regarding emission quantities. When the regulator does not have complete knowledge of the properties of the abatement cost function, the effect of any given tax on emissions will be uncertain. To illustrate this, assume that we have the following type of asymmetric information. The firms know their abatement cost function and, if they are faced with an emission tax, they set their emission levels so that their marginal abatement costs are equal to the emission tax rate. The regulator, on the other hand, does not know the exact properties of the true aggregate abatement cost function at the time it sets the emission tax.

The tax is set based on the regulator's probability function over possible aggregate abatement cost functions. In the subsequent discussion, I use the

---

[1] General discussions of environmental taxes versus other policy instruments include Baumol and Oates (1971), Kneese and Schultze (1975), Yohe (1977) and Bohm and Russell (1985).

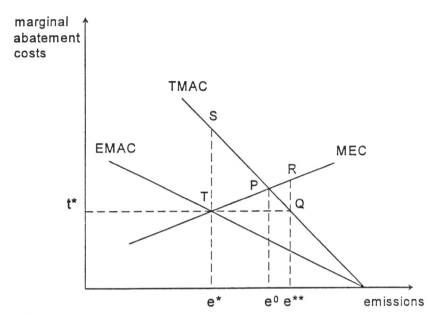

Fig. 1.

term "estimated abatement cost function" as a certainty equivalence to this distribution. In Figure 1, EMAC is the estimated marginal abatement cost function.

If the regulator has a target level of emissions equal to e^*, this can be achieved with the emission tax t^*. Assume, however, that the true marginal abatement cost function turns out to be TMAC instead of EMAC. Then the emission level resulting from the tax t^* will be e^{**} instead of the target level e^*. If quotas or other types of direct regulation specifying e^* directly had been used instead, the regulator would succeed in reaching his emission target. However, given that the true abatement function turns out to be TMAC, the cost associated with the target e^* will be higher than that following from the estimated cost function (EMAC). The "price" of reaching one's emission target precisely is thus a possibly large difference between estimated and true costs of achieving the target.

Weitzman (1974) was the first to make a rigorous analysis of whether a tax or a quota would be the best policy in this situation of asymmetric information. The main result is illustrated by Figure 1. Here, MEC is the marginal environmental cost. The target e^* is thus the emission level which would be optimal if the abatement cost were given by EMAC. For the true abatement cost function (TMAC), the optimal emission level is e^0. It is clear from Figure 1 that if an emission tax is used (at the rate t^*), the loss compared with the *ex post* optimal emission level e^0 is given by the triangle PQR. If, instead, emissions were fixed at e^* through direct regulation, the loss would be given by PST. It is also clear that PQR is smaller than PST. More generally, Weitzman showed that under specific assumptions (linear marginal costs, uncertainty only about the position of the marginal cost curves, and not their slopes, and no correlation between the uncertainty regarding the abatement cost and the environmental cost), the relative slopes of the marginal abatement cost function and the marginal environmental cost function are all that matters for determining whether an emission tax performs better or worse than direct regulation. Weitzman showed that an emission tax performs better than direct regulation if and only if the marginal abatement cost curve is steeper than the marginal environmental cost curve.

Since Weitzman's 1974 paper, several additional contributions on this topic fall into two categories: (i) by modifying the assumptions in Weitzman's analysis,[2] and (ii) by considering a richer class of policy tools than only an emission tax and a direct specification of the emission level.[3] It has been shown that the potential loss in social welfare associated with asymmetric information about abatement costs can be reduced by choosing more complex policies. In practice, however, these more sophisticated methods of environmental regulation have not been used by policymakers.

What can we say about the steepness of the marginal environmental cost curve compared to the steepness of the marginal abatement cost curve? In general, of course, not much. However, it is well known that numerical estimates of environmental costs are usually very uncertain. Numerical estimations usually limit themselves to estimating the costs at a very few levels of emissions. At each of these levels there is often a broad confidence interval of the estimated environmental costs. With estimates for two emission levels, the picture might look something like Figure 2, where the vertical lines cover, e.g., 90 percent confidence intervals. Based on such observations, it is difficult to have a strong opinion about the exact curvature of the underlying cost function (i.e., the steepness of the marginal cost function). It could in fact be argued that in many cases, a linear environment cost function, as illustrated by the line OA, in Figure 2, is perfectly consistent with the available estimates.

A linear cost function means that the marginal cost curve is horizontal. Thus, if one accepts the approximation of an environmental cost function OA, an emission tax will always be superior to direct regulation. Moreover,

---

[2] See e.g. Watson and Ridger (1984) and Stavins (1996).
[3] See e.g. Dasgupta *et al.* (1980), Kwerel (1977), McKitrick (1997) and Roberts and Spence (1976).

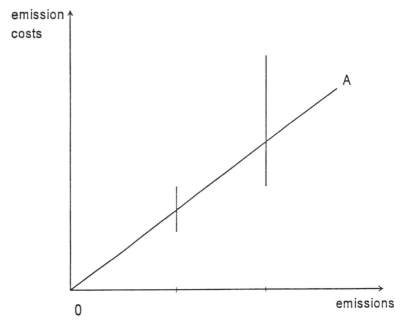

Fig. 2.

in this case, there is no need to search for more sophisticated environmental policies: when environmental costs are proportional to the emission level, there is no social welfare loss due to asymmetric information. The first-best optimum is achieved through an emission tax rate equal to the constant marginal environmental cost.

From the discussion so far, I would argue that in the presence of asymmetric information about abatement costs, there is a strong case to be made for emission taxes rather than direct regulation. However, the argument is based on an explicit function giving environmental costs for different levels of emissions. In many cases, policymakers will not have any clear conception of an environmental cost function. Implicitly, some cost function must, of course, exist, as there would otherwise be no need for environmental regulation. Nevertheless, an environmental target is often set without explicitly considering the underlying environmental cost function. And once the target is set, policymakers frequently give high priority to reaching the target with a high degree of accuracy. Under this procedure, policymakers regard direct regulation as more appealing than emission taxes. Economists' way of reasoning, as briefly sketched above, would attach much less weight to having a quantitative target in the first place. On the contrary, if environmental costs are proportional to emissions, an economist would argue in favor of a target value of the marginal cost of reducing emissions, leaving emissions to be determined endogenously without any specific quantitative target. The tendency for policymakers to prefer direct regulation in situations where economists would argue for an emission tax thus appears to be based on a fundamental difference between two ways of thinking about how policymaking should take place.

III. Non-Convex Abatement Costs

In simple textbook analyses of environmental economics, it is usually assumed that abatement costs and environmental costs are convex. However, this need not always be the case. For the purpose of this discussion, non-convexity of the environmental cost function is of limited interest and will, therefore, be ignored. On the other hand, non-convexity of the abatement cost function may be important for the choice between emission taxes and other environmental policies.

A simple example of a non-convexity is as follows. Consider first only one firm (I later extend the analysis to several firms). This firm has the choice between a conventional technology and a pollution-free technology. If the conventional technology is used, emissions can be reduced by conventional means (reducing production, factor substitution, etc.), giving abatement costs $c(e)$ (where $c'(e) < 0$, $c''(e) > 0$). Alternatively, the firm can pay a fixed cost f allowing it to switch to a pollution-free technology.

The marginal abatement cost for the firm is illustrated in Figure 3. The curve $-c'(e)$ is the marginal abatement cost when the conventional technology is used. However, if emissions are to be reduced below OB, the firm is best off by paying the fixed cost f and switching to the pollution-free technology. The emission level OB is given by $c(OB) = f$, i.e., the area ABC is equal to the fixed cost f. Reducing emissions to levels below OB is costless, once the fixed cost f has been paid. To the left of B, marginal abatement costs are therefore zero. The marginal cost curve is thus given by ACBO in Figure 3.

Whether or not this non-convexity of the abatement cost function is of practical importance depends on the position of the marginal environmental cost. If this latter curve intersects $-c'(e)$ to the left of C, it is clear that the social optimum will be to use the pollution-free technology. This is also the case if the marginal environmental costs curve intersects $-c'(e)$ to the right of, but sufficiently close to, C. In both of these cases the firm may be induced to use the pollution-free technology by introducing a sufficiently high emission tax.

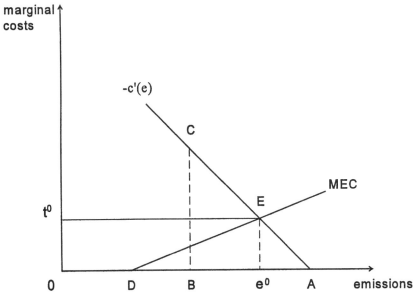

Fig. 3.

Consider next the case where the marginal environmental cost curve is given by MEC in Figure 3, with the area DEA smaller than f. In this case, the conventional technology should be used in the social optimum, with the emission level e^0. If an emission tax is to be used to achieve the emission level e^0 with the conventional technology, the tax rate must be given by t^0. In this case, the sum of abatement costs and emission taxes paid by the firm is given by $OAEt^0$. If this sum is lower than f, there is no problem. But if this sum exceeds f, the firm will be better off by switching to the pollution-free technology. Therefore, in this latter case, the socially optimal emission level cannot be achieved by using an emission tax.

Thus far, I have assumed that there is only one firm. Figure 4 illustrates the aggregate marginal abatement cost curve in the more realistic multi-firm case. For emission levels between OB and OA, abatement takes the form of all firms reducing their emissions from the no-regulation level, but continuing to use the conventional technology. For aggregate emission levels below OB, the cost-effective allocation is for some firms to switch to the pollution-free technology, while the remaining firms face an emission level e^0 given by $-c'(e^0) = (f - c(e^0))/e^0$; see Appendix 1 for details. This gives the aggregate abatement cost curve ACD.[4]

---

[4]Strictly speaking, the curve describes the limiting case in which the size of each firm (measured by e^0) is infinitesimally small.

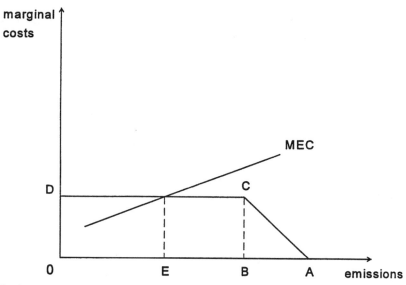

Fig. 4.

If the marginal environmental cost curve intersects the marginal abatement cost curve along the segment AC, the socially optimal emission level should be determined by this intersection. In this case, all firms should use the conventional technology in the social optimum, and each of them should have emissions at the level e^* determined by the intersection of the marginal abatement cost curve and the marginal environmental cost curve. It is shown in Appendix 1 that unlike the case with only one firm, firms will not have an incentive to switch to the pollution-free technology when the emission tax is given by $-c'(e^*)$.

If the marginal environmental cost curve is given by MEC as in Figure 4, the socially optimal emission level is given by OE, with some firms using the conventional technology and some firms using the pollution-free technology. The only tax rate which might give this social optimum is OD in Figure 4 (i.e., $t = (f-c(e^0))/e^0$). At this tax rate, firms are indifferent between using the pollution-free technology and the conventional technology (emitting e^0 per firm, where e^0 is given by $-c'(e^0) = (f-c(e^0))/e^0$). Although the optimal split of firms between the two groups (conventional and pollution-free technology) is supported by this emission tax, the equilibrium at this tax rate is not unique. Any distribution of firms in the two groups is an optimal response to the emission tax OD. The actual outcome will therefore (except by chance) differ from the social optimum.

It could be argued that, in practice, firms differ. In particular, the cost of switching to the pollution-free technology may differ among firms. If this is the case, the segment DC of the aggregate marginal abatement cost curve will be downward sloping instead of horizontal. A tax rate determined by the intersection of this curve and the MEC curve will in this case give a unique equilibrium which is the social optimum.

If the differences among firms are small, the segment DC will be almost flat. Unless the MEC curve is horizontal, it is therefore likely to be steeper than the marginal abatement cost curve. If there is asymmetric information about the position of the marginal abatement cost curve, it therefore follows from Section II that direct regulation of emission levels may be a better policy than emission taxes.

From the discussion above it is clear that non-convex abatement cost functions, in particular in combination with asymmetric information about these costs, may be an argument against using emission taxes. The obvious alternative which might perform better would be a system of tradeable emission permits. Other alternative policies might be worse than emission taxes. One such policy would be a form of direct regulation which specifies the technology firms must use. If all firms are to be treated equally, it is clear from our discussion that the social optimum cannot be achieved with this form of regulation if the environmental costs are given by MEC in Figure 4.

IV. Measuring Emissions

In order to have an emission tax, the regulator must be able to measure emissions from each source with a reasonable degree of accuracy. This is certainly not always the case. There is often some degree of asymmetric information regarding the level of emissions from a source. The decision maker(s) at the source (producers, consumers) will often know their emission levels with a higher degree of accuracy than the environmental regulator does, or can obtain information about the true emission level at lower costs than the regulator can.

In some cases it is almost impossible — or at least extremely costly — to obtain accurate information about emission levels, both for the decision-maker at the source of the emissions and for the environmental regulator. An example of this is NO_x emissions from road transportation. These emissions depend on vehicle type, equipment, fuel type, driving patterns, etc. Accurate measurement would require monitoring equipment on each vehicle, which would be so costly that it would far exceed the environmental cost of the emissions.

In many cases the problems of measuring emissions make it impossible not only to use traditional emission taxes, but also to set quotas on emissions, since violations of these quotas cannot be detected. There are cases in which quotas may be used, but not traditional emission taxes. Such cases are characterized by the regulator's possibility of obtaining — at reasonable costs — a rough, but not accurate measurement of emissions. Clearly, the accuracy needed to be able to prove "beyond reasonable doubt" that the quotas have been violated (at least for serious violations) is less than the accuracy needed to let taxes depend on the exact emission levels. Although traditional emission taxes are infeasible in such cases, taxes can be used in similar way as emission taxes: there can be a tax on reported emissions. Checking whether true emissions are higher than reported emissions is no more difficult than checking whether quotas have been violated. And the punishment for reporting less emissions than their true level could be of the same type as that used for violations of quotas. Harford (1978) has shown that given some assumptions on how the probability of detection depends on the violation, a tax on reported emissions with a rate equal to the marginal environmental costs gives the socially optimal level of emissions.[5]

A system very similar to the one above has been suggested by the "green tax commission" in Norway; cf. NOU (1996). For some types of pollutants, environmental regulation has consisted of firm-specific quotas. These quotas are given to firms by application, and the regulator decides how much each firm gets. The way the system works now, firms have no incentive to provide truthful reports on available pollution-reducing technologies, or to develop new low-pollution technologies (unless these technologies also reduce costs). The green tax commission has therefore suggested that the procedure for determining the size of quotas to each firm remain unchanged, but that firms must pay taxes proportional to their quotas. This gives firms an incentive to apply for low quotas, and to develop new low-pollution technologies. In addition, the tax revenue collected by the government in this way may have a beneficial effect on the economy (see Section V).

If neither the decision-maker at the emission source nor the environmental regulator can measure emissions at the source, one cannot use any type of environmental policy that relates directly to emission levels. Thus, traditional emission taxes, emission quotas and taxes on quotas or reported emissions are all ruled out. An alternative in this case is to regulate an input of production or a dimension of technology which is correlated with emissions. One possibility is direct regulation of some type. Alternatively, taxes and/or subsidies could be used to influence the input and/or tech-

---

[5] Schmutzler and Goulder (1997) have shown that when the monitoring costs of the regulator are taken into account, the social optimum may require the use of other policy instruments (an output tax in their model) instead of or in addition to a tax on reported emissions.

nology choice of producers. However, unlike a traditional emission tax, taxes/subsidies on inputs or technologies are no longer obviously at least as cost effective as direct regulation. To see this, consider the following simple example. Pollution comes from a particular sector of the economy, in which there are many producers, and output and input prices are given. Output from firm I is $\Phi(z_i, \boldsymbol{v}_i)$, where $(z_i, \boldsymbol{v}_i)$ is the input vector and z_j the particular input which is considered as a candidate for regulation or taxation. Alternatively, we may interpret z_i as a parameter describing the technology used by the firm. The price of the input vector is $(q, \boldsymbol{p})$.

The profit of firm i (before any taxes on z_i emissions) is (when the output price is set equal to 1)

$$\pi_i = \pi_i(z_i) = \max_{\boldsymbol{v}_i} [\Phi(z_i, \boldsymbol{v}_i) - \boldsymbol{p}\boldsymbol{v}_i]. \tag{1}$$

The input vector $(z_i, \boldsymbol{v}_i)$ also determines emissions from firm i, so that these are given by

$$e_i = h_i(z_i) = m_i(z_i, \boldsymbol{v}_i(z_i)) \tag{2}$$

where $\boldsymbol{v}_i(z_i)$ is given by the maximization problem in (1).

Assume that $\pi_i' > 0$ and $h_i' > 0$. Moreover, assume that the environmental regulator has a target level of emissions equal to E. Since output and input prices are given, the social optimum is the vector $(z_1, z_2, \dots)$ that maximizes $\sum_i \pi_i$ subject to $\sum_i e_i \leq E$. This gives

$$\frac{\pi_{i'}(z_i)}{h_{i'}(z_i)} \quad \text{same for all } i. \tag{3}$$

If the regulator knew all π_i- and all h_i-functions, the first-best optimum could be achieved by giving each firm the z_i- or $h_i(z_i)$-value following from (3) and $\sum_i e_i = E$. If the π_i- and h_i-functions are known at the firm level, but not by the regulator, an emission tax could be used instead of direct regulation. With an emission tax t, maximization of $\pi_i(z_i) - th_i(z_i)$ will give $\pi_i'/h_i' = t$. When all firms face the same emission tax, the condition (3) is thus satisfied. The target level of emissions will not be met, however, if the regulator's estimate of the aggregate abatement costs differs from the true costs; cf. Section II. Note, however, that in many instances the regulator has far more knowledge about the aggregate abatement cost function than about the individual $\pi_i(h_i^{-1}(e_i))$-functions. The error of target achievement may therefore be rather small. Moreover, as argued above, it is not obvious that the regulator should worry too much about not achieving a quantitative emission target with accuracy.

If the h_i-functions are unknown/highly uncertain also at the firm level, and the individual e_i's are unobservable, emissions cannot be regulated through regulating or taxing them directly. In this case, the x_i's can either be regulated or taxed. Considerations of fairness, predictability, etc., will usually require regulation to be the same for all firms. If the z_i's are taxed, this would mean that all firms should face the same tax. In this case, $\pi_i'(z_i)$ will be equalized across firms, which only implies (3) if the h_i-functions do not differ across firms.

Instead of a tax on the z_i's, the z_i's could be specified through direct regulation. Depending somewhat on the exact interpretation of z_i, equal treatment of firms will imply a particular restriction on how the z_i's may differ across firms. Even without any such restriction, the regulator will in general not be able to satisfy the optimality condition (3) when it does not know the h_i-functions. But it is not obvious whether the best feasible direct regulation of the z_i's performs worse or better than an equal tax on the z_i's.

We have just seen that if the h_i-functions happen to be equal across firms, direct regulation cannot be better than a tax. An example of the opposite case is if

$$\pi_i = \alpha_i \Pi(z_i) \tag{4}$$

and

$$h_i = \alpha_i H(z_i) \tag{5}$$

where the α_i's differ across firms. In this case, direct regulation in the form of equal z_i's for all firms will satisfy (3), while an equal tax on z_i for all firms will not.

It follows from the discussion above that when emissions cannot be taxed directly, it is no longer necessarily true that environmental taxes (in this case a tax on output or an input which is correlated with emissions) are more cost effective than various forms of direct regulation. In other words, one of the two main arguments given in the Introduction in favor of emission taxes is not necessarily valid in the present case. Another argument in the Introduction was the advantage of revenue-raising policy instruments over non-revenue-raising instruments. This argument in favor of some form of environmental tax is valid also when it is impossible to monitor emissions at the micro level.

V. Emission Taxes and Employment

Policymakers often argue that emission taxes imposed on producers give rise to an unnecessary cost increase. This argument is based on reasoning illustrated by Figure 5. Assume that the regulator wants emissions from a

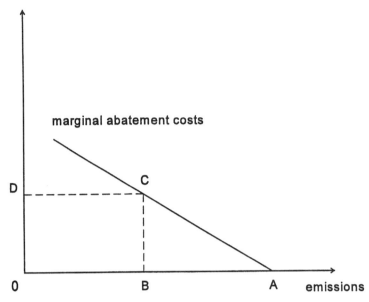

Fig. 5.

firm to be reduced from OA to OB. This gives the firm an abatement cost equal to ABC. If the emission reduction is achieved through an emission tax *t* at level OD, the firm has to pay an additional cost of OBCD. This 'unnecessary' component of the total cost - policymakers would typically argue - may be harmful to economic performance in general and to employment in particular.

Economists' response to this critique of emission taxes would typically be three (partly overlapping) arguments: (i) it is not particularly meaningful to consider the consequences of using an emission tax without simultaneously considering the consequences of using the emission tax revenue; (ii) the reasoning in Figure 5 is too partial; and (iii) the cost component OBCD is a type of lump-sum transfer (once the emission level is given at OB) which is not necessarily harmful to the performance of the economy.

To study this argument against an emission tax, and economists' typical response to such an argument, I present an extremely simple general equilibrium model with unemployment.

Consider a one-sector economy, where each firm's net output is given by

$$c = f(l, k, e) \tag{6}$$

where l and k denote input of labor and capital, and e is the level of emissions. I assume that f is increasing in its arguments (in particular, $f_e > 0$ implies that output is lower, the lower are emissions).

For reasons which will soon become obvious, I assume that the technology has increasing returns to scale for 'low' output levels, but constant or decreasing returns for 'high' output levels; see Appendix 2 for a description of the technology.

The emission level of each firm is specified by the environmental regulator, so that each firm regards e as given. Firms are price takers on the labor and capital markets, so profit maximization gives

$$f_l(l, k, e) = w \tag{7}$$

$$f_k(l, k, e) = r \tag{8}$$

where w is the wage rate and r is the interest rate. Firms also pay an emission tax $q \geq 0$. As long as $q \leq f_e$ this tax will not affect the firms' emission levels; for $q \geq f_e$ firms would never wish to reduce their emission levels below the upper limit given by the regulator. The cost component qe is thus zero for the limiting case of $q = 0$, and equal to the area OBCD in Figure 5 for the other limiting case of $q = f_e$.

In a long-run equilibrium, pure profits must be zero, i.e.,

$$f - wl - rk - qe = 0 \tag{9}$$

or, using (7) and (8)

$$f - (f_l l + f_k k + f_e e) = (q - f_e)e. \tag{10}$$

Using the equation

$$\varepsilon f = f_l l + f_k k + f_e e \tag{11}$$

where ε is the scale elasticity of the function f (note that $\varepsilon = \varepsilon(l, k, e)$), eq. (10) may be rewritten as

$$(1 - \varepsilon)f = (q - f_e)e. \tag{12}$$

From (12) it is clear that if $q < f_e$, we must have $\varepsilon > 1$, i.e., increasing returns to scale. If $q < f_e$, a competitive equilibrium can therefore only exist if the firms' production functions have increasing returns to scale for low output levels.

Denote the equilibrium number of firms by m. Aggregate employment, capital and emissions are then

$$L = ml \tag{13}$$

$$K = mk \tag{14}$$

$$E = me. \tag{15}$$

I assume that the economy is small and that it operates in a perfectly mobile international capital market. The rate of interest is therefore exogenous. Let K^0 be the stock of capital owned by domestic residents. Aggregate consumption in this economy is then given by

$$C = mf\left(\frac{L}{m}, \frac{K}{m}, \frac{E}{m}\right) - r(K - K^0) \tag{16}$$

Throughout, I assume that the policymakers have a given environmental goal, so that aggregate emissions E are exogenous. Consider first the full employment case, and assume that labor is inelastically supplied. L is therefore given in this case. When L, E, and K^0 are given, the only variables affecting aggregate consumption are K and m; see (16). Clearly, the value of K maximizing C must satisfy $f_k = r$. This optimum condition holds in a competitive economy; cf. (8). The optimal number of firms must be such that each firm operates at a scale minimizing its average costs, i.e., at a scale where $\varepsilon = 1$. This is satisfied if the regulator sets the emission tax so high that $q = f_e$ (implying that firms would not wish to increase their emission levels beyond the regulated level even if they were allowed to). If the regulator instead sets $q < f_e$ (where $q = 0$ is obviously an important special case), it follows from (12) that $\varepsilon > 1$. In this case there are therefore too many and too small firms, making aggregate consumption lower than its potential level. Thus, in a full employment economy, there is no loss associated with charging the firms the 'unnecessary' cost OBCD in Figure 5. On the contrary, by not making firms pay this cost component, entry is encouraged, making the equilibrium size of firms inefficintly small.

As argued in the beginning of this section, policymakers often argue that when firms have to pay the "unnecessary" cost component OBCD in Figure 5, this may be harmful to employment. To address this, we clearly cannot argue within the context of a full employment economy. Therefore, let us now assume that there is unemployment caused by the wage rate being exogenous. A detailed analysis of this case is given in Appendix 2 under the additional assumption that the production function f is homothetic.

Assume first that w is exogenous. It is shown in Appendix 2 that a reduction in q from $q = f_e$ to some lower level (e.g., $q = 0$) increases employment. If one accepts the assumption that w is exogenous, the argument that employment is hurt when firms have to pay the 'unnecessary' cost OBCD in Figure 5 is indeed correct. However, the case where the pre-tax wage w is exogenous is not particularly interesting. In this case unemployment could be eliminated by a direct subsidy to the use of labor, and the subsidy could be financed through a tax on labor income. Under the (unrealistic) assumption that w is exogenous, such a tax increase on labor income would not translate into higher wage costs. Therefore, let us instead assume that it is the after-tax wage, denoted by v, which is exogenous.

When the after-tax wage v is exogenous, we have

$$w = v + \frac{T-qE}{L} \tag{17}$$

where T is an exogenous tax revenue, so that $(T-qE)/L$ is the tax which each worker has to pay out of the gross wage w. As just mentioned, the direct effect of a reduction in q on employment is positive. However, from (17) w is no longer given. When q is reduced and v is given, w must increase. The isolated effect of this wage increase is to reduce employment. To find the net effect of reducing q we need to combine these two opposing effects. It is shown in Appendix 2 that the net effect of reducing q is a reduction in employment. This means that as q is reduced from the level $q = f_e$ to some level below f_e (e.g. to 0) total consumption C is reduced both for the reason given above (i.e., for a given value of employment) and because employment declines.

So far, I have assumed that the alternative to an emission tax is direct regulation in the form of non-tradeable quotas. An alternative form of direct regulation could be some kind of specification of which technologies firms may use. With regulation of the latter type, firms do not face an absolute limit on how much they can emit, but only a restriction on their choice of inputs and how these are used. In Appendix 3 it is shown that given some not too restrictive assumptions, this type of regulation may be written as

$$e \leq sh(l, k) \tag{18}$$

where h is homogeneous of degree 1 in l and k and increasing in these two variables. The parameter s in (18) is a measure of how strict the regulation is. For given values of l and k, permitted emissions are higher the higher s is (which has been assumed). These properties imply that if a firm facing a binding constraint on its emissions doubles its inputs, it will be permitted to double its emissions.

When (18) is binding, the profit per firm may be written as

$$\pi = f(l, k, sh(l, k)) - wl - rk - qsh(l, k). \tag{19}$$

Profit maximization gives

$$f_l + (f_e - q)sh_l = w \tag{20}$$

and

$$f_k + (f_e - q)sh_k = r. \tag{21}$$

Multiplying by l and k, respectively, adding, and using the homogeneity property $h = h_l l + h_k k$ gives

$$f_l l + f_k k + f_e e = wl + rk + qe. \tag{22}$$

Together with (18), (19) and the zero profit condition $\pi = 0$, this implies

$$f_l l + f_k k + f_e e = f. \tag{23}$$

But from (11) this implies that the scale elasticity must be equal to 1. With this type of direct regulation, the size of the firms is thus given by the size minimizing the average costs per firm. Or, from (16), m is given by the solution to

$$F(L, K, E) = \max_m mf\left(\frac{L}{m}, \frac{K}{m}, \frac{E}{m}\right). \tag{24}$$

Since h is homogeneous of degree 1, it is clear that when (18) is binding, s is given by

$$s = \frac{h(L, K)}{E} \tag{25}$$

where E is the exogenous target level of emissions.

Inserting (25) into the optimum conditions (20)–(21) and using $f_l = F_L$, $f_k = f_K$ and $F_e = F_E$ from (24) we get

$$F_L + (F_E - q)\frac{E}{F(L, K)} h_L = w \tag{26}$$

$$F_K + (F_E - q)\frac{E}{F(L, K)} h_K = r. \tag{27}$$

For the full employment case (L given), these two equations determine w and K for any value of $q \in [0, F_E]$. The value of K maximizing aggregate consumption is as before given by $F_K = r$ (see (16) and (24)), i.e., from (27), by $q = F_E$. Reducing the emission tax to a level below that which gives the target level of emissions withouot any further regulation thus harms the economy in the full employment case.

From (26) and (27) it is clear that reducing q below F_E works in the same way as a subsidy to labor and capital. If there is unemployment and w is exogenous, this individual subsidy to labor and capital will increase employment. (This will always be true if $F_{KL} \geq 0$. If $F_{KL} < 0$ and h_L is sufficiently small, a reduction in q may reduce employment.) For the more realistic case where the after-tax wage v is exogenous, we also have to take into consideration the increase in w which follows from the reduction in q. In Appendix 3 it is shown (for the case of a homothetic production function) that employment (and therefore also aggregate consumption) is lower for $q < F_E$ than it is for $q = F_E$.

The results in this section strongly suggest that emission taxes (or other revenue-raising policy instruments) are preferred to various types of non-revenue-raising instruments. This conclusion is not reversed in the presence of unemployment. On the contrary, the presence of unemployment as modelled here strengthens the case for using emission taxes: unemployment is higher with non-revenue-raising instruments than it is with an emission tax. The argument often made by politicians that emission taxes cause firms to incur an unnecessary cost (area OBCD in Figure 5), and therefore lead to higher unemployment than various forms of direct regulation, is therefore not supported by economic theory. Of course, we should not to be too categorical. It cannot be ruled out that other ways of modelling the economy and, in particular, other assumptions about wage determination under unemployment (instead of simply assuming that the after-tax wage is exogenous), could give different results. Nevertheless, the mechanisms of our simple model, whereby an emission tax is preferable to non-revenue-raising instruments, will remain valid under a much broader class of assumptions than those used here. To be taken seriously, arguments against emission taxes with reference to the effects on unemployment should therefore be based on much more sophisticated aspects than the reasoning related to Figure 5.

VI. Concluding Remarks

I have considered four arguments against the use of environmental taxes as a key instrument of environmental policy. At least the first three — all related to information asymmetries and non-convexities — are valid in the sense that they point to complications which make the use of environmental taxes less straightforward than suggested by elementary textbooks. Nevertheless, even in the presence of these arguments, environmental taxes may be better than most feasible alternatives. Moreover, two of the arguments (Sections II and III) suggest that if environmental taxes are not imposed, tradeable emission permits, and not direct regulation of the command and control type, should be used. The latter type of instrument may be justified if the regulator has high costs of monitoring emissions. However, even with high monitoring costs, some form of environmental taxes may be preferable to various forms of direct regulation, although we certainly cannot make general claims to this effect.

The fourth argument against the use of environmental taxes was related to the employment effects of different types of environmental policies in economies with unemployment. This is perhaps the argument most often used by politicians against environmental taxes. However, our analysis provided no justification for this type of argument. On the contrary: the analysis in Section V demonstrated that at least for the case of an exogenous after-tax wage, employment was higher with environmental taxes than with non-revenue-raising environmental policies.

Appendix

1. The Cost-Effective Allocation

Assume there are N firms, of which n use the pollution-free technology. Each of the $N-n$ firms using the conventional technology has the emission level e. The optimal values of n and e are given by the minimization problem

$$G(E) = \min_{n,e} \{nf + (N-n)c(e) | (N-n)e \leq E, n \geq 0\} \tag{A1}$$

where E is the aggregate level of emissions and $G(E)$ is the aggregate abatement cost function.

The Lagrangian associated with (A1) is

$$L = nf + (N-n)c(e) - \lambda[E - (N-n)e] \tag{A2}$$

and the first-order conditions are

$$f - c(e) - \lambda e \geq 0, \text{ with equality if } n > 0 \tag{A3}$$

$$-c'(e) = \lambda. \tag{A4}$$

If $n > 0$, the optimal emission level e^0 per firm using the conventional technology is therefore given by

$$f - c(e^0) + c'(e^0)e^0 = 0$$

or

$$-c'(e^0) = \frac{f - c(e^0)}{e^0}$$

If $n = 0$, the optimal emission level is determined by $e = E/N$, and in this case it follows from (A3) and (A4) that

$$-c'(e)e + c(e) \leq f. \tag{A5}$$

With an emission tax equal to $-c'(e)$, the l.h.s. of (A5) is the tax plus abatement cost of each firm. Since this total cost is no higher than the cost f of switching to the pollution-free technology, this emission level is achievable using an emission tax.

2. Description of the Technology

Consider a one-sector economy, where each firm's technology is given by

$$\varphi(l, k, \boldsymbol{v}, y, e) \geq 0 \tag{A6}$$

where l and k denote input of labor and capital, and v is a vector of other inputs. The "output" of the firm is (y, e), where y is regular output and e is the level of emissions. It is assumed that $\varphi'_y < 0$, while the other partial derivatives of φ are positive.

The net output from each firm is given by

$$c = y - pv. \tag{A7}$$

Maximization of c given (A7), and given (l, k, e), gives the net output function f in (6).

Consider an initial vector $(l^0, k^0, v^0, y^0, e^0)$ satisfying the production function (A6). I define the scale elasticity σ of this production function by considering two scalars α and β satisfying

$$\varphi(\alpha l^0, \alpha k^0, \alpha v^0, \beta y^0, \alpha e^0) = 0 \tag{A8}$$

The scale elasticity σ at the initial vector $(l^0, k^0, v^0, y^0, e^0)$ is defined as

$$\sigma = \left(\frac{d\beta}{d\alpha} \frac{\alpha}{\beta} \right)_{\alpha = \beta = 1}. \tag{A9}$$

It is straightforward to verify that

$$\sigma = \sigma(l, k, v, y, e) = \frac{\varphi_l l + \varphi_k k + \varphi_v v + \varphi_e e}{-\varphi_y y}. \tag{A10}$$

The function f is given by (6) is formally defined by

$$c = f(l, k, e) = \max_{y, v} \{ y - pv \mid \varphi(l, k, v, y, e) = 0 \}. \tag{A11}$$

The first-order conditions of this maximization problem are

$$1 + \lambda \varphi_y = 0, \qquad -p + \lambda \varphi_v = 0 \tag{A12}$$

where λ is a non-negative Lagrangian. Eliminating λ from (A12) gives

$$\frac{\varphi_{vi}}{p_i} = -\varphi_y, \qquad i = 1, \ldots, n. \tag{A13}$$

Moreover, applying the envelope theorem to (A11) and using (A12) gives

$$f_l = \frac{\varphi_l}{-\varphi_y}, \qquad f_k = \frac{\varphi_k}{-\varphi_y}, \qquad f_e = \frac{\varphi_e}{-\varphi_y}. \tag{A14}$$

If f is treated as a standard production function, the scale elasticity ε of this function is defined correspondingly to σ, i.e., with c as the only output. This gives

$$\varepsilon = \frac{f_l l + f_k k + f_e e}{f}. \tag{A15}$$

Inserting from (A14) and (A10) yields

$$\varepsilon = \frac{-\varphi_v v - \sigma \varphi_y y}{-\varphi_y f}. \tag{A16}$$

Since $f = y - pv$ (cf. (A11)) it follows from (A12) that $f\varphi_y = y\varphi_y + \varphi_v v$. Inserting this into (A16) and rearranging terms gives

$$\varepsilon - 1 = (\sigma - 1)\frac{y}{f}.$$ (A17)

Since f and y are both positive, it follows from (A17) that $\varepsilon - 1$ must have the same sign as $\sigma - 1$.

3. Restrictions on Technologies

Assume that the production function f is homothetic, i.e.,

$$f(l, k, e) = g(F(l, k, e))$$ (A18)

where F is homogeneous of degree 1, and that

$$g(x_0) = 0$$
$$g'(x) > 0 \quad \text{for} \quad x > x_0$$ (A19)
$$g''(x) < 0 \quad \text{for} \quad x > x_0$$
$$g(1) = g'(1) = 1.$$

These properties are illustrated in Figure A1. The variable x is a measure of the size of the firm, and with the normalizations given by (A19), the optimal firm size

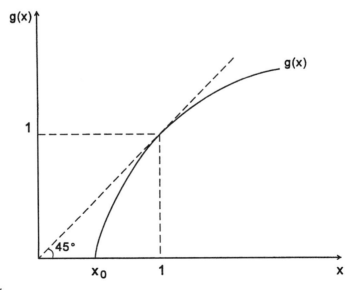

Fig. A1.

is given by $x = 1$.[6] The minimum firm size is x_0. Note that our results would not be changed if, instead of (A19), we assumed that $g'' > 0$ for sufficiently low x-values, in which case we could have $g(x) > 0$ for all positive x. For a homothetic production function of the type (A18), the scale elasticity is

$$\varepsilon = g'(x)\frac{x}{g(x)} \begin{cases} >1 & \text{for } x_0 < x < 1 \\ =1 & \text{for } x = 1 \\ <1 & \text{for } x > 1 \end{cases} \tag{A20}$$

It thus follows from (12) that $x < 1$ for $q < f_e$.

Since F is homogeneous of degree 1, it follows from (13)–(15) that $f(l, k, e) = g(F(L, K, E)/m)$. It therefore follows that (7) and (8) may be rewritten as

$$f_l = g'(x)F_L(L, K, E) = w \tag{A21}$$

$$f_k = g'(x)F_K(L, K, E) = r \tag{A22}$$

To find the effect of reducing q when w is given by (17) we proceed as follows. Since there are no pure profits in this economy, the value of total output must equal the sum of after-tax wages, return to capital, and taxes. Since $x = F(l, k, e) = F(L, K, E)/m$, total output is $mg(x) = F(L, K, E)g(x)/x$. We therefore have

$$\frac{g(x)}{x}F(L, K, E) - vL - rK - T = 0. \tag{A23}$$

The two equations (A22) and (A23) determine L and K for any given x. To see how L is affected by reducing x from $x = 1$ to a lower value, we differentiate these two equations, giving

$$\begin{pmatrix} \frac{g}{x}F_L - v & \frac{g}{x}F_K - r \\ g'F_{KL} & g'F_{KK} \end{pmatrix} \begin{pmatrix} \dfrac{\partial L}{\partial x} \\ \dfrac{\partial K}{\partial x} \end{pmatrix} = \begin{pmatrix} \dfrac{F}{x}\left(\dfrac{g}{x} - g'\right) \\ -F_K g'' \end{pmatrix}. \tag{A24}$$

Solving for $\partial L/\partial x$, we find

$$\frac{\partial L}{\partial x} = \frac{1}{D}\left[\frac{F}{x}\left(\frac{g}{x} - g'\right)g'F_{KK} + F_K g''\left(\frac{g}{x}F_K - r\right)\right] \tag{A25}$$

where

$$D = \left(\frac{g}{x}F_L - v\right)g'F_{KK} - g'F_{KL}\left(\frac{g}{x}F_K - r\right). \tag{A26}$$

Since $g/x \le g'$ for $x \le 1$, D will be positive if $F_{KL} \ge 0$ and T is sufficiently small. I assume that $D > 0$, as our economy would otherwise have the strange property

---

[6] It is straightforward to verify that the F-function defined in (24) is identical to the F-function in (A18) when f is given by (A18).

that an increase in the after-tax wage would increase employment. Since $F_{KK} < 0$, $g'' < 0$, and $g/x < g'$ for $x < 1$ (which from (A22) implies $gF_K/x < r$), the term in brackets in (A25) is positive. Together with $D > 0$ this means that as x is reduced from $x = 1$ to a value of $x < 1$ (implied by $q < f_e$), employment declines.

Consider next a form of direct regulation that gives some kind of specification of which technologies firms may use. With regulation of the latter type, firms do not face an absolute limit on how much they can emit, but only a restriction on their choice of inputs and how these are used. If the production function (A6) is smooth and there is no emission tax, this type of direct regulation will be inefficient in the sense that net output (c in (A7)) will not be maximized subject to a given vector (l, k, e). The reason for this is that whatever restriction is put on (l, k, e), a profit-maximizing firm will set $\varphi_e = 0$ (in the absence of an emission tax), which violates the conditions defining the function f in (A11)). To show that there is an *additional* inefficiency associated with this type of regulation, I ignore the inefficiency just mentioned. This is done by assuming there is no substitution between the two "outputs" y and e in (A6). The technology constraint may in this case be written as

$$y = \Phi(l, k, \boldsymbol{v}), \qquad e = m(l, k, \boldsymbol{v}). \tag{A27}$$

Assume that the firm faces a regulation of its inputs given by

$$z(l, k, \boldsymbol{v}) \geq 0 \tag{A28}$$

where z is assumed to be homogenous of degree 1.

When the technology is given by (A27) instead of (A6), maximization of $y - \boldsymbol{p}\boldsymbol{v}$ (given e) gives (instead of (A12))

$$\frac{\Phi_{vi} - p_i}{m_{vi}} \qquad \text{independent of } i. \tag{A29}$$

Assume that $m(l, k, \boldsymbol{v})$ is homogenous of degree 1. Profit maximization subject to a tax q in emissions and the constraints (A27) and (A28) gives

$$\Phi_l - w - qm_l + \lambda z_l = 0, \qquad \Phi_k - r - qm_k + \lambda z_k = 0, \qquad \Phi_v - \boldsymbol{p} - qm_v + \lambda z_v = 0. \tag{A30}$$

From (A29) and (A30), it is clear that the efficiency condition (A29) will hold only if z_{vi}/m_{vi} is the same for all inputs of the $\boldsymbol{v}$-vector. Only if this condition holds will consumption will be given by the efficient net output production function $f(l, k, e)$.

If the regulator knows the m-function, it can obtain the efficiency condition (A29), e.g. by choosing the following z-function:

$$z(l, k, v) = s - \frac{m(l, k, v)}{h(l, k)} \tag{A31}$$

where s is a positive parameter and h is any function which is homogenous of degree 1 and increasing in l and k. With the function (A31), the constraint (A28) may be rewritten as

$$e \leq sh(l, k) \tag{A32}$$

which is the constraint introduced in (18) in Section V.

Consider the effect of reducing emissions for the case where the after-tax wage v is exogenous. Equation (A23) remains valid (but now with $x = 1$). When $q = F_E$ we have $F_K = r$ (see (27)) which is the K-value which maximizes the l.h.s. of (A23). Reducing q below F_E will change K, and thus reduce the l.h.s. of (A23). To restore equality, L must change (since E, v, and T are given). For $D > 0$ to be valid also for F_K, r, it is clear that we must have $F_L - v < 0$ when $x = 1$ (see (A26)). But this means that the l.h.s. of (A23) is declining in L. To increase the left-hand side back to zero, L must therefore decline. This proves that employment (and therefore also aggregate consumption) is lower for $q < F_E$ than it is for $q = F_E$.

References

Baumol, W. J. and Oates, W. E.: The use of standards and prices for protection of the environment. *Swedish Journal of Economics 73* (1), 42–54, 1971; reprinted in P. Bohm and A. Kneese (eds.), *The Economics of the Environment: Papers from Four Nations*, Macmillan, London and Basingstoke, 1971.

Bohm, P.: Environmental taxation and the double dividend: Fact or fallacy? In T. O'Riordan (ed.), *Ecotaxation*, Earthscan, 1997.

Bohm, P. and Russell, C.: Comparative analysis of alternative policy instruments. In A. V. Kneese and J. L. Sweeney (eds.), *Handbook of Natural Resource and Energy Economics*, North-Holland, Amsterdam, 1985.

Dasgupta, P., Hammond, P. and Maskin, E.: On imperfect information and optimal pollution control. *Review of Economic Studies 47*, 857–860, 1980.

Goulder, L. H.: Environmental taxation and the "double dividend": A reader's guide. *International Tax and Public Finance 2*, 157–184, 1995.

Goulder, L. H., Parry, I. W. H. and Burtraw, D.: Revenue-raising vs. other approaches to environmental protection: The critical significance of pre-existing tax distortions. NBER WP 5641, Cambridge, MA, 1996.

Harford, J. D.: Firm behaviour under imperfectly enforceable pollution standards and taxes. *Journal of Environmental Economics and Management 5*, 26–43, 1975.

Kneese, A. V. and Schultze, C. L.: *Pollution, Prices and Public Policy*. Brookings Institution, Washington, DC, 1975.

Kwerel, E.: to tell the truth: Imperfect information and optimal pollution control. *Review of Economic Studies 44*, 595–601, 1977.

McKitrick, R.: Optimal pollution taxes under asymmetric information. Mimeo, University of Guelph, 1997.

NOU: Policies for a better environment and high employment. Norwegian Official Commission 1996: 9, Oslo, 1996.

OECD: *Environmental Taxes in OECD Countries*, OECD, Paris, 1995.

Roberts, M. and Spence, A. M.: Effluent charges and licences under uncertainty. *Journal of Public Economics 5*, 193–208, 1976.

Schmutzler, A. and Goulder, L. H.: The choice between emission taxes and output taxes under imperfect monitoring. *Journal of Environmental Economics and Management 32*, 51–64, 1997.

Stavins, R. N.: Correlated uncertainty and policy instrument choice. *Journal of Environmental Economics and Management 30*, 218–232, 1996.

Tietenberg, T.: Economic instruments for environmental regulation. *Oxford Review of Economic Policy 6* (1), 17–33, 1990.

Watson, W. D. and Ridker, R. G.: Losses from effluent taxes and quotas under uncertainty. *Journal of Environmental Economics and Management 11*, 310–326, 1984.

Weitzman, M.: Prices versus quantities. *Review of Economic Studies 41*, 477–491, 1974.

Yohe, G. W.: Comparisons of price and quantity controls: A survey". *Journal of Comparative Economics 1*, 213–233, 1977.

Scand. J. Economics 100(1), 105–108, 1998

Comment on M. Hoel, "Emission Taxes versus Other Environmental Policies"

Kerstin Schneider

University of Dortmund, D-44221 Dortmund, Germany

The choice of the appropriate instrument in environmental policy is not only a question of theoretical importance. It is also of considerable political relevance. While environmental taxes are sometimes used to control pollution, quotas and direct controls dominate in practice. If this observed bias is only due to the nature of policymaking and not supported by economic reasoning, politicians are not well advised to use quotas and direct controls instead of environmental taxes. Hoel discusses popular arguments that are often used by politicians in favour of direct controls and concludes that the results are typically not clear-cut. In this comment I would like to focus on the employment effects of revenue raising and non-revenue raising instruments.

Politicians as well as special interest groups often claim that emission taxes increase the cost of production, thereby harming employment. Clearly, in the face of high rates of unemployment in many industrialized countries, potentially negative employment effects of environmental regulation raise political resistance to green policy. The ongoing debate has put economists in the position of referees to assess the compatibility of environmental regulation and high rates of employment.

Inspired by the work of Bovenberg and de Mooij (1994), politicians and economists have argued about the existence of a "double dividend" resulting from the introduction of environmental taxes. The basic idea of the double dividend hypothesis is that using environmental tax revenue to reduce existing distortionary taxes might be welfare improving regardless of the environmental gain.

While politicians are inclined to adapt this idea — the European Commission (1997) recommends taxing the use of energy and recycling the revenue to reduce labor costs — economists remain more critical. Despite these differences, what is generally agreed upon is that environmental tax revenue should be used to reduce other distortionary taxes rather than to rebate the revenue lump sum. By the same line of reasoning, price instruments are recommended instead of direct controls, if the environmental rent can be extracted without inducing distortions. This became known as the weak form of the double dividend hypothesis; cf. Goulder (1995).

Hoel enriches the discussion by raising another question. Given the level of emissions, a byproduct of production, in an open economy with firm and factor mobility and imperfect labor markets, is it preferable to implement the target by means of revenue or non-revenue raising instruments of environmental policy? In other words, should environmental policy be used to raise revenue, or should the emission rent be left with the firms? In particular, if the economy is suffering from unemployment, the employment effects of taxes versus direct controls have to be controlled for.

It is well known that in a perfectly competitive economy with full employment and no factor or firm mobility, taxes and direct controls of emissions are equivalent instruments. This holds true, even with factor mobility, as long as the emission rent is appropriated within the country. This result is not surprising, because if the amount of emissions is predetermined, the return to emissions is pure rent income. Optimal taxation theory gives a definite answer to the question of the appropriate policy instrument. If the government has to finance a budget, pure rent income should be taxed, and can be taxed up to 100 percent, without inducing distortions.

When internationally traded factors of production or mobile firms that earn (part) of the emission rent are introduced, taxes and direct controls become distinct instruments. In a full-employment model with mobile firms, Wellisch (1995) shows that direct controls lead to inefficiently low levels of emissions, while taxes continue to produce an efficient outcome. Hoel's analysis of a full-employment economy is related to this. In a similar framework and with a fixed level of emissions, he argues that taxes are the efficient instrument, and the use of quotas leads to inefficiencies.

To gain a better understanding of the result, note that the return to emissions is no longer pure rent income, once it accrues to owners of not perfectly inelastically supplied factors of production. Assuming that the use of emissions is simply tied to the use of capital, raising the level of environmental taxes affects the use of capital. In fact, taxing emissions induces a capital outflow. However, this does not imply that emissions should not be taxed. On the contrary, if emissions are not taxed, too much capital will flow into the country and payments to foreigners will exceed the gains in the productivity of labor. Thus, in a world with factor mobility, where at least part of the environmental rent accrues to the mobile factor, emission taxes are the preferable instrument. The intuition behind this result is straightforward. If the emission rent is taxed, the rent income stays in the country, whereas part of it flows out of the country in a regime of direct controls.

In the literature, however, this issue is typically discussed in models of full employment. Thus, to understand the employment effects of taxes and quotas, labor market imperfections should be introduced. Hoel analyzes a model in which firms and capital are mobile, firms can differ in size, and labor is unemployed because the wage rate is exogenously given. In the most realistic scenario, the net wage is fixed, and the government chooses the optimal policy instrument. While the wage-setting process is not explicitly modelled, one can think of a Cournot game between the government and a union, in which the wage is set by a monopoly union and the government takes the net wage rate as given. Employment is no longer an exogenous variable, but depends on the cost of labor. Given that the return to emissions accrues to the owners of capital, and capital is immobile, the environmental rent is pure rent income that can be taxed at no cost. The tax revenue can be used to reduce the cost of labor, which in turn increases employment.

Thus we conclude that, contrary to politicians' intuition, factor and firm mobility as well as labor market imperfections of the simple type studied here provide strong arguments in favour of revenue-raising instruments. In fact, if allowing for pollution in production creates quasi rents that do not fully accrue to residents and taxes on labor raise the cost of not perfectly elastically supplied labor, taxes should be used instead of non-revenue raising instruments. Clearly, as Hoel indicates, it cannot be ruled out that allowing for other types of imperfections might change the results. My conjecture is that the result is fairly robust with respect to various types of labor market imperfections. The reason is the following. Assume that the rent on emissions accrues to owners of internationally mobile factors. Under these circumstances and without labor market imperfections, it is optimal to (fully) tax the emission rent income. For this result to change, one has to identify labor market distortions that render it optimal to subsidize mobile factors of production. Moreover, the second effect has to outweigh the first effect, for direct controls to be the preferable instrument.

The political and theoretical discussion of environmental tax reforms is an interesting attempt to satisfy three policy objectives simultaneously: pollution control, the reduction of unemployment, and to raise tax revenue. The initial enthusiasm about the potential of green tax reforms has been dampened by economic research. However, despite the still undecided theoretical and political debate on the welfare and employment effects of environmental tax reforms, two recommended policy strategies emerge from the discussion: first, use tax revenue to reduce existing distortionary taxes, and second, as Hoel has shown in his paper, quasi rents from emissions that accrue to owners of polluting mobile firms or mobile factors should be taxed. Imperfect labor markets strengthen the case for taxes instead of direct controls.

In closing I would like to add that Hoel has identified a form of the double dividend hypothesis that — similar to the weak form of the double dividend — is easy to reap and — until proven otherwise — is a safe policy strategy.

References

Bovenberg, A.L. and de Mooij, R.A.: Environmental levies and distortionary taxation. *American Economic Review 84*, 1085–1089, 1994.

European Commission: Proposal for Council Directors for restructuring the Community framework for the taxation of energy products. COM(97)30, Brussels, 1997.

Goulder, L.H.: Environmental taxation and the "double dividend": A reader's guide. *International Tax and Public Finance 2*, 157–183, 1995.

Wellisch, D.: Locational choices of firms and decentralized environmental policy with various instruments. *Journal of Urban Economics 37*, 290–310, 1995.

Scand. J. Economics 100(1), 109–112, 1998

Comment on M. Hoel, "Emission Taxes versus Other Environmental Taxes"

Peter Bohm

Stockholm University, S-106 91 Stockholm, Sweden

Michael Hoel highlights a set of factors that tend to blunt the traditional efficiency arguments in favor of using taxes instead of command and control (CAC) in environmental policy.[1] This is a valuable addition to other attempts, e.g., Weitzman (1974), to avoid oversimplification of economists' policy recommendations in this field, often questioned for good or bad reasons by non-economists.

I essentially agree with the way Hoel deals with the specific issues he has chosen for scrutiny. However, as a consequence of the general fashion in which he compares efficiency implications of environmental taxes and CAC, he leaves unobserved the fact that, in most real-world cases, emissions have time and/or location specific effects. Normally, such specificities tend to imply that "first-best" tax rates would vary from one emitter to the next.[2] However, (1) since transaction costs are likely to prohibit the use of such a "first-best" tax system, it is more doubtful to argue that optimal-feasible tax systems in general would be superior to specific CAC solutions. Moreover, in certain such cases, it may well be that an equi-proportionate cutback of emissions or an outright prohibition of emissions turns out to be more efficient than any optimal-feasible version of emission taxes.

Furthermore, with a target in terms of a maximum acceptable volume of pollution, emission taxes may still be a contending policy instrument. However, (2) if emission taxes are used, they would, in principle if not in fact, have to be adjusted to changes in exogenous variables. This adds, of course, to the transaction costs of this instrument and makes the CAC option look relatively better. This aspect is not made explicit in the paper.

---

[1] It may be noted that an early occasion, at which these traditional efficiency arguments were advanced, can be found in an article in the March 1971 issue of the Journal whose 100th anniversary is celebrated here; see Baumol and Oates (1971).

[2] This is "first best" in the quite usual, but somewhat strange, sense of defining optimality while abstracting from unavoidable facts of life such as transaction costs. Whenever such costs are non-trivial, this kind of "first best" could never exist or be implemented, in contrast to the technically achievable first best which can be attained by the removal of policy constraints creating the second best; see Bohm (1985).

As follows from point (1), the analysis in the paper is strictly speaking limited to the case where all emissions of a given type produce uniform environmental effects. This seems to be the case for emissions influencing the global environment, i.e., emissions of greenhouse gases (GHGs) and substances that deplete the ozone layer, but hardly for other types. International policy in the ozone-layer case has been, and in the GHG case is likely to be, determined by targets set by scientists' estimates and/or as politicians prefer to formulate their policy objectives, that is to say as a limit on emissions. This would tend to make point (2) — comparing taxes and CAC to attain a (here:) internationally agreed national emission quota — come into force.

Control of greenhouse gases and, in particular, CO_2 emissions from the combustion of fossil fuel, may emerge as a case of special importance in the years to come. Carbon taxes or their next of kin, auctioned tradable permits, as domestic instruments to support an international tradable quota system, may eventually dominate the scene and give rise to truly significant amounts of revenue from environmental policy; see IPCC, 1996, Ch. 11). This highlights a significant difference between the two policy options at issue, namely that in contrast to CAC, revenue-generating instruments offer the possibility of tax recycling, sometimes said to give rise to a double dividend; see Pearce (1990). This aspect is central in Hoel's paper, particularly in his discussion of his last two points. Still, he states somewhat enigmatically that "independently of whether or not a potential double dividend exists, the possibility of using the revenue from an emission tax to reduce other taxes is a desirable feature of an emission tax in comparison with other non-revenue-raising environmental polices". The remainder of my comments is an attempt to clarify this issue.

First, it turns out that Hoel uses the term "double dividend" of an environmental tax in the special sense introduced by Larry Goulder, and specified by him as a "strong double dividend", which means that the "environmental" tax, according to Hoel, is "welfare improving even without counting the environmental gain". If there is such a tax, it means, of course, that the pre-existing tax system is inefficient and that, to begin with, a fiscal tax reform is called for. Then, it follows that an *improved* tax system, but less likely, perhaps, an *efficient* tax system, could involve using a tax on certain emissions. It is only when (additional) taxes on emissions are no longer, if ever, needed for a fiscal tax reform, that the issue of an "*environmental* tax on emissions" arises. Since the emission tax as an environmental tax (!) cannot give rise to a "strong double dividend", it means that this particular concept is redundant. The possibly relevant concept is the original "double dividend", defined as the benefits from tax recycling (second benefit) in addition to the environmental (first) dividend, the latter of which is shared with the CAC option. Given the "pollution" of the double dividend concept that has occurred, it is no longer possible to use this concept without a definition, as the quotation in the preceding paragraph well illustrates.[3]

In the Introduction, Hoel refers to papers by Goulder (e.g. 1995) without explicitly mentioning Goulder's principal point that, within the framework of general equilibrium analysis, an environmental tax such as a carbon tax will increase consumer prices, reduce real wages and most likely employment and hence, revenue from labor taxes. If so, the resulting net revenue made available for tax recycling falls short of the revenue from the carbon tax. The net revenue may even be negative, although, as we shall see, this has no particular implication for the size of tax recycling relevant to the issue at hand.

Before elaborating on that argument, it should be noted that discussing aspects of the *choice* between taxes and CAC, as Hoel does, implies not explicitly observing that "both", *i.e.*, taxes *and* CAC, also constitute a feasible and quite meaningful option in many cases. Again, the climate change policy case can serve as an illustration. One particular reason why the combination of a tax (or tax-like instrument) and a quota/permit system may be more meaningful than using only one of them emerges when, in an international agreement, carbon emission quotas have been specified for individual countries. A cost-effective manner of implementing such a system would most likely be to let these quotas be internationally tradable and domestically attain compliance by a carbon tax to an *ex post* quota-trade quota or by auctioning domestic (tradable) permits in the amount of the initial quota; see IPCC(1996). In both cases, using the additional revenue incurred to reduce distortionary taxes would produce a double dividend, regardless of what happens to the labor tax revenue; see Bohm (1997a). The reason is as follows.

The introduction of an environmental tax (environmentally motivated auctioned permit system) presupposes an environmental policy target. In the present case, this is the agreed national emission quota. If the revenue-generating policy were not used, the targeted quota would have to be attained by a non-revenue-generating CAC — or grandfathered tradable-permit — system. (a) If a grandfathered permit system were used, the resulting permit price would equal, at least approximately, the permit price in the auctioned permit case, which in turn, at least approximately, equals the required tax rate. Thus, the change in the consumer price index and therefore, the indirect effects on labor taxes would also be the same. Hence, the only difference is the following: in the revenue-generating case

---

[3] This quotation could be paraphrased as saying that "independently of whether or not the possibility of a "strong double dividend" exists, the possibility of an "ordinary double dividend" is a desirable feature of an emission tax."

there is more government revenue than in the grandfathered-permit case, by an amount equal to that incurred from the new source of government revenue, now available for tax recycling. (b) If, in the non-revenue-generating case, a CAC solution were used that led to inefficiency somewhere — say, fossil fuel were allocated in a subefficient manner — the (shadow) consumer price index would increase even more and the reduction in labor taxes would be larger, given the assumptions made, than in the tax/auctioned-permit (tax, for short) case. Hence, we conclude that the indirect (negative) effects on pre-existing labor tax bases are at most as large in the tax case as in its baseline case. The tax-recycling benefit (the double dividend) therefore corresponds to at least the size of the revenue from the environmental tax, and not to anything less than that; see Bohm (1997b).

During 1993–95, the treatment of the double dividend in the literature was confused by a "school" of economists discussing a phantom "strong double dividend" and comparing the introduction of an environmental tax, given a presumed environmental policy target, with not introducing that tax *or any other environmental policy measure* — hence, with a situation in which there was no longer any environmental policy target; see e.g. Goulder (1995). To be sure, this mistake is not made in Hoel's paper. But the reader might be confused — in an otherwise clear presentation — by the quoted passage, in which Hoel talks about a "double dividend". A "strong double dividend" is what he purports to refer to here, but a "strong double dividend" of an environmental tax cannot exist unless the benefits from a fiscal tax reform are included among the dividends of environmental policy.

References

Baumol, W. J. and Oates, W. E.: The use of standards and prices for protection of the Environment. *Swedish Journal of Economics 73* (1), 42–54, Mar. 1971.
Bohm, P., Environmental taxation and the double dividend: Fact or fallacy? In T. O'Riordan (ed.), *Ecotaxation,* Earthscan, 1997a.
Bohm, P.: Public investment issues and efficient climate change policy. Keynote speech delivered at the 53rd Congress of the International Institute of Public Finance, Kyoto, August, 1997b; forthcoming in H. Shibata (ed.), *Public Investment and Public Finance,* Springer-Verlag, Tokyo..
Bohm, P.: Second best. *The New Palgrave,* Macmillan, Basingstoke, 1985.
Goulder, L.: Environmental taxation and the "double dividend": A reader's guide. *International Tax and Public Finance 2,* 157–184, 1995.
Intergovernmental Panel on Climate Change: *Climate Change 1995: The Economic and Social Dimensions of Climate Change.* Cambridge University Press, Cambridge, 1996.
Pearce, D.: The role of carbon taxes in adjusting to global warming. *Economic Journal 101,* 938–948, 1991.
Weitzman, M.: Prices versus quantities. *Review of Economic Studies 41,* 477–91, 1974.

Scand. J. of Economics 100(1), 113–141, 1998

Unemployment Insurance in Theory and Practice

Bertil Holmlund*

Uppsala University, Box 513, S-751 20 Uppsala, Sweden

Abstract

A hallmark of modern labor economics is the close interplay between the development of theory, data sources and econometric testing. The evolution of the economic analysis of unemployment insurance provides a good illustration. New theoretical approaches, in particular job-search theory, have inspired a large amount of empirical research, some of it methodologically innovative and most of it highly relevant for economic policy. The paper presents a broad survey and an assessment of the economic analysis of unemployment insurance as it has evolved since the 1970s.

I. Introduction

Public unemployment insurance (UI) is a social institution that emerged in a number of European countries during the first couple of decades of this century. Before public policies became established in this area, UI had often been provided by trade unions. The first union scheme was established in 1832 by the foundrymen's union in Britain. In Sweden, the first UI fund was created by the typographers' union in 1892, and by the turn of the century there were ten (out of 32) unions that ran some kind of UI scheme for their unemployed members.

The emergence of *public* UI seems to have originated in the Belgian town of Gent, where public support to union-administered insurance funds was introduced in 1901. An institution under which the government offers subsidies to union-affiliated UI funds with voluntary membership has become known as a "Gent system". Several European countries adopted Gent systems during the period prior to World War I, including France, Germany, Britain and the Nordic countries except Sweden. The Gent system turned out to be a short-lived institution in most countries, however. Compulsory UI was introduced in Britain in 1911, and a number of countries adopted compulsory UI schemes during or soon after World War I.

---

* I have received useful comments from Anders Björklund, Per-Anders Edin, Peter Fredriksson, Nils Gottfries, Ann-Sofie Kolm, Alan Manning, John Martin, Andrew Oswald, Steinar Strøm and Johnny Zetterberg.

The political trends in subsequent decades were largely in favor of compulsory systems. The Gent system survived in the Nordic countries except Norway, where compulsory UI was introduced in 1938. By the 1990s, the Gent system has only remained in effect in the other four Nordic countries, namely Denmark, Finland, Sweden and Iceland. Belgium has an intermediate system, with compulsory membership but union involvement in administration of the scheme. The remaining voluntary systems are subsidized by the governments to such an extent that they in many respects are indistinguishable from the compulsory systems prevailing in most of the advanced countries.

Traditional Keynesian macroeconomics, as it was taught and practiced in the postwar period, had little to say about UI, except perhaps that it may have desirable properties as an automatic stabilizer when the economy slides into a recession. However, a number of pre-Keynesian economists in the inter-war period had a great deal to say about UI that rings remarkably familiar to a reader in the 1990s. The British economists A. C. Pigou, John Hicks, Edwin Cannan and Henry Clay, as well as the Swedes Eli Hecksher and Gustav Cassel, emphasized the kind of incentive effects of UI that are still the focus of contemporary discussions of UI policies. They suggested that UI may strengthen the unions' bargaining position and thereby raise wage pressure; moreover, they argued that UI benefits are likely to affect job-search behavior and unemployment duration; they also noticed that UI can affect the nature of contracts between firms and workers; finally, they argued that UI may have effects on the allocation of labor across industries if the system entails net subsidies to some industries and net taxes on others.[1]

From the early 1970s and onwards, the analysis of UI has attracted considerable attention in the economics profession. There are several plausible explanations of this development. One is related to innovations in economics as a social science, in particular the emergence of job-search theory as a major framework for labor market analysis. This theoretical development has inspired a large amount of empirical research, some of it methodologically innovative and most of it relevant for economic policy. Indeed, a hallmark of modern labor economics is the close interplay between the development of theory, data sources and econometric testing.

The design of UI has implications for the macroeconomics of unemployment. The research devoted to UI in the past couple of decades is closely intertwined with the retreat of traditional Keynesian macroeconomics and the development of theories of the natural (or equilibrium) rate of unem-

---

[1] See Hicks (1932), Pigou (1933), Cassel (1902), Heckscher (1928), and the review in Casson (1983).

ployment. The natural rate framework was well suited to incorporate unemployment compensation as a policy instrument. In almost all natural rate models, there is a positive relationship between the (equilibrium) unemployment rate and the "generosity" of the UI system. In fact, in many simple models, the wage replacement rate provided by UI is often the only explicit exogenous variable that determines unemployment; see, for example, the survey of natural rate models by Johnson and Layard (1986) in the *Handbook of Labor Economics*.

The stubbornly high European unemployment since the 1980s has given some prominence to the idea that the equilibrium unemployment rate has increased along with the actual rate, possibly as a result of a more generous benefit system. Many governments have taken this possibility seriously and have attempted reforms to make UI less generous. Such policies have also been motivated by the need to offset the rise in budget deficits that has been associated with the rise in unemployment. Whatever the causes of high and persistent unemployment might be, the rise itself has brought UI to the fore in policy discussions about unemployment.

The present paper offers an exposition on the development of economic analysis of UI. The intention is not to provide an exhaustive survey, however; by and large, I take a bird's-eye view of the subject and focus on the common features of models and empirical investigations. Some issues, in particular concerning equilibrium unemployment, welfare economics and political economy, are dealt with in somewhat more detail. I take the existence of a *public* UI system as given and do not scrutinize the rationale for state intervention in this area. The paper is concerned with what economic theory and empirical work have to say about UI. What are the key mechanisms whereby UI affects the labor market? Are the theoretical results robust across alternative models? Are the theoretical results supported by the empirical studies? What normative conclusions, if any, can be deduced from the economic analysis of UI? I also briefly discuss some political-economy aspects of UI.

II. Job Search and Unemployment Insurance

The evolution of job-search theory has had a profound impact on labor market analysis. The theory provided economists with an analytical tool for exploring rational individual behavior during unemployment. The only pre-existing alternative was the standard model of labor-leisure choice, a model not well suited to deal with job search under imperfect information. The theoretical contributions have greatly influenced empirical work on unemployment in general, and microeconometric work on unemployment duration in particular.

Job-Search Theory

The first rigorous and detailed analysis of the impact of UI benefits on individual job-search behavior was provided by Mortensen (1977); see also Mortensen (1990) and van den Berg (1990). Mortensen derived several strong results using a model of sequential search where he incorporated some institutional features of labor markets, such as a fixed duration of benefit payments and an eligibility requirement that a certain amount of work must precede insured unemployment. Mortensen also allowed for (exogenous) layoff risks associated with accepted jobs as well as endogenous choice of search effort by the unemployed worker, in addition to the usual choice of reservation wage. The wage-offer distribution was taken as stationary and known by the unemployed searcher.

The most important implications derived were the following. First, the worker's reservation wage declines as he approaches the date at which benefits expire; hence the exit rate increases over the spell of (insured) unemployment. Second, an increase in the benefit level makes it more attractive for currently non-eligible workers to accept jobs and thereby become qualified for benefits in the future; the result is thus that the exit rate from unemployment to employment *increases* for workers who do not qualify for benefits, a response known as the "entitlement effect". Third, a rise in the benefit level will cause a newly unemployed worker to *increase* his reservation wage, but induce an insured worker close to benefit exhaustion to *reduce* his reservation wage. The exit rate thus decreases for newly unemployed workers but increases for workers who have come close to benefit exhaustion. The last property follows from the fact that a higher benefit level increases both the value of continued search as unemployed and the value of accepting an offer. The immediate value of higher benefits is small for workers close to benefit exhaustion, as they are almost in the same situation as workers not qualified for UI.

Mortensen's analysis brought out some of the complexities of predicting behavioral responses to changes in UI. The rather obvious adverse-incentive effects on job acceptance decisions among those who have just become unemployed are not valid for *all* unemployed; for some workers, in particular those who do not qualify (or have ceased to qualify), higher benefits will make work *more* attractive relative to unemployment. The effect of higher benefits on the duration of unemployment is therefore, in general, ambiguous.

Mortensen's work illustrates how the addition of institutional realism to the search model can generate important new results, some not immediately obvious. But search models offend advocates of realism in other respects. One critical factor is the assumption that unemployment benefits are essentially a subsidy to leisure, possibly subject to the restriction that the maximum duration of benefit payments is fixed. Workers who reject job offers continue to live on the dole; there is thus no work test whereby benefits can be withdrawn if workers reject job offers. It is clear that incentive effects will be unimportant if the work test is effective; however, complete enforcement would be prohibitively costly. The mere fact that the work test is ignored in the formal analysis does not make the theory irrelevant.

Job-search theory has been developed in several directions in order to shed light on other effects of UI. For example, there has been some work on the linkages between job search and labor supply. The fact that UI benefits are typically tied to previous earnings implies that the employed worker can influence his future benefit level by his choice of work hours. Higher UI benefits may therefore increase labor supply among employed workers; see Yaniv (1982). A rise in UI benefits will probably also encourage labor force participation since it increases the relative rewards from participation compared to non-participation; see Hamermesh (1980). It is conceivable that this participation effect may increase the number of effective job searchers in the labor market and hence in part offset the usual disincentive effects of UI.

Empirical Work

The development of job-search theory bred an empirical literature that by the mid-1990s had become voluminous. This research has exploited new types of data with information on the length of individual workers' unemployment spells. Search theory has provided a very useful theoretical framework for these empirical studies. Although most of these studies have been of the reduced-form rather than the structural variety, it is clear that the theory has been helpful, although perhaps not crucial, as a guide for selecting variables to be included and how the results should be interpreted. The evolution of job-search theory and its subsequent empirical applications is a good example of the close interaction between theory and empirical work that has characterized most of modern labor economics.[2]

To what extent, then, have the key predictions of the theory been supported by the empirical studies? Lancaster and Nickell (1980) reviewed some of the early empirical work and concluded that the theory was well supported: "We would regard the size of the effect of benefits (on unemployment duration) as being now a rather firmly established parameter". The review in Layard *et al.* (1991, p. 255) concluded that the "basic result is that the elasticity of expected duration with respect to benefits is gener-

---

[2] The book by Devine and Kiefer (1991) contains a detailed survey of the empirical work of the 1970s and the 1980s. See also Atkinson and Micklewright (1991).

ally in the range 0.2–0.9 depending on the state of the labour market and the country concerned".

The conclusion drawn by Lancaster and Nickell (1980) was surely premature. The effect of benefits on unemployment duration is far from a firmly established parameter that is comparable in robustness to, say, estimates of the returns to schooling. And not all economists would subscribe to the characterization in Layard *et al.* Some of the most careful (and most well-known) studies do find significant effects on unemployment duration from higher benefits; see e.g. Narendranathan *et al.* (1985). But there are also a number of studies which have been unable to detect significant effects; see Pedersen and Westergård Nielsen (1993) for a survey. In fact, as we have seen, there is no strong theoretical reason to expect unambiguous results if the entitlement effect is non-trivial.

The impact of fixed potential duration of benefits has been investigated much less than the effects of benefit levels. The evidence here is largely in favor of the theoretical prediction: exit rates from unemployment seem to increase as unemployed insured workers approach the time when benefits are due to expire. Evidence from the United States is reported by Moffitt (1985), Meyer (1990) and Katz and Meyer (1990), evidence for Canada by Ham and Rea (1987), and Swedish evidence by Carling *et al.* (1996). Although these results are good news for search theory, there is scope for alternative (implicit-contract) interpretations according to which employers recall laid-off workers just before their benefits run out. We will return to the implications of UI in contracting models.

One intriguing result in Mortensen's theory is that workers close to benefit exhaustion will respond by *lowering* their reservation wage when benefits are increased. This prediction has typically been ignored in empirical research. It has been common to include measures of benefits or replacement rates without allowing for a different effect between those who have just entered the unemployment pool and those who are close to benefit exhaustion. If the theory is correct, the estimates of benefit effects are likely to be sensitive to the duration composition of the samples at hand. Katz and Meyer (1990) report unsuccessful attempts to test for this effect on escape rates.

The effect of UI on transitions to employment is most often thought of as working through the unemployed worker's reservation wage, possibly also through search effort. There is not much direct evidence on the importance of these potential mechanisms, however. Feldstein and Poterba (1984) provided some direct evidence on the responsiveness of the reservation wage to benefits by using information on reported reservation wages along with information on benefits and found a significantly positive effect. Qualitatively similar results are reported by Harkman *et al.* (1997) in a study on Swedish data. The few available results concerning the impact of benefits on search effort do not give conclusive results. For example, Jones (1989) reports that higher benefits increase search effort among benefit recipients, whereas Harkman *et al.* (1997) are unable to find any effect from benefits.

A fundamental problem in many of the microeconometric studies in this field is the lack of truly *exogenous* benefit variation across unemployed individuals. Benefits are typically tied to previous earnings, which makes it difficult to disentangle the impact of benefits from the factors that affect earnings. In the United States, researchers have been able to exploit exogenous *state-level* variation in benefits, a procedure that has not been available in other applications. In Sweden — which has a voluntary UI system — most studies on micro data have compared UI recipients with non-recipients, an approach that may be hazardous because of self-selection into UI coverage (although it is not obvious which direction the bias will take).

Studies that make use of information on policy *changes* as natural experiments are rare in this field. Björklund (1978) used time series on outflow rates from unemployment to examine the effects of extensions of the Swedish UI system and found only very weak effects. A recent study by Jones (1996) investigates the effect of changes in the Canadian UI system that took effect in 1993. This study finds, surprisingly, that the cut in wage replacement rates (from 60 to 57 percent) was associated with *longer* spells of unemployment. Harkman *et al.* (1997) report results from a similar research strategy applied to Swedish data. The study offers modest, albeit imprecisely estimated, support for the hypothesis that the cut in replacement rates from 90 to 80 percent in 1993 increased transition rates from unemployment.

In the United States, a number of true social experiments of relevance for UI policies took place in the 1980s; see Meyer (1995) for a summary and an evaluation. Individuals were randomly assigned to treatment groups and control groups. The treatment groups were subject to certain programs and incentives, such as cash bonus payments for finding jobs quickly and keeping them for a given period of time. A consistent finding from these experiments was that the bonus treatments reduced the time spent on UI rolls. Meyer (1997) concludes that "the bonus experiments should convince any hardened skeptics that monetary incentives have a substantial effect on job finding."

In sum, there is little doubt that the microeconomic analysis of unemployment has been substantially enriched by the insights of job-search theory. It is hard to imagine that the same amount of empirical work would have been produced if the theory had not been developed. It would be wrong, however, to characterize the empirical application of search theory as an overwhelming success story. There is a fair amount of support for the theory, but the "benefit effect' is hardly a firmly established parameter. Some implications of the theory have rarely been tested, such as the role of the entitlement effect among workers close to benefit exhaustion. And there are potentially important real-world features of job search that have been largely ignored in theory and empirical work. The role of borrowing and savings is a case in point in this regard ; the standard model portrays job search in a setting where workers are either risk neutral or unable to use the credit market to smooth consumption.

From a policy perspective, however, the most severe limitation of the microeconometric studies on unemployment duration is their partial-equilibrium nature. This is, of course, not a criticism of the theory as such, since microeconomics naturally precedes macroeconomics. But we need to consider whether the partial-equilibrium results necessarily carry over to the general equilibrium. This is an issue to which we will return.

III. Contracts, Unions and Unemployment Insurance

There is evidence, initially pertaining to the US labor market, that a substantial fraction of unemployed workers are *rehired* by their most recent employer. Feldstein (1976) was one of the first to point out this feature of the labor market, estimating that as much as 75 percent of all layoffs in US manufacturing were "temporary" in the sense that the workers were rehired. For this case, job-search theory is not the most useful approach. UI still matters, but through other routes than job search.

Feldstein (1976) developed the basic implicit-contract model to examine the implications of UI with respect to the level and financing of benefits. The model features a firm with a pool of "attached" workers facing uncertain product demand. The firm and workers have to agree on a contract that specifies employment, wages and perhaps work hours for every possible realization of demand. For example, the contract specifies wages and employment in booms as well as slumps. The number of laid-off workers in each state of demand is simply given by the difference between the number of attached and employed workers. The model is particularly useful for investigating the role of *experience* rating in UI. In broad conformity with the system practiced in the United States, Feldstein assumed that firms that lay off workers have to finance part of the UI benefits for which their workers are eligible. The model implies that a rise in the UI subsidy — a decline in experience rating — causes a reduction in employment.

The general validity of Feldstein's result concerning experience rating has been questioned. For example, Burdett and Wright (1989) relaxed the assumption of a fixed pool of workers attached to the firm and allowed the firm to choose the number of workers. This modification has important implications. It turns out that higher experience rating does reduce layoff rates but also the number of attached workers. The intuitive explanation is that higher experience rating increases labor costs, which is bound to reduce the number of workers that the firm is willing to hire. The effect on average employment is ambiguous in general, and may plausibly be negative. It may also be noted that simulations undertaken by Mortensen (1994), using the Mortensen and Pissarides (1994) equilibrium model of job creation and job destruction, suggest that full experience rating would produce a small *increase* in unemployment, a result driven by the fact that experience rating effectively discourages *hirings* by making layoffs more costly to firms. The initial claim that experience rating reduces unemployment has thus not survived later elaborations of the theory.

Early empirical work on temporary layoffs seemed to suggest a strong case for the idea that benefits were an important explanation for the prevalence of temporary layoffs in the United States. Feldstein (1978) used micro data and explained the probability of being temporarily laid-off by, *inter alia*, the UI replacement rate. His results indicated strong effects: UI benefits were estimated to explain 50 percent of all temporary layoffs in the US. These results were questioned by Topel (1983), who argued that one has to distinguish between whether benefits are subject to experience rating or not; it is *subsidized* UI payments that matter for layoff decisions. Topel measured the extent of UI subsidization across different states in the US and found that subsidized UI, i.e., incomplete experience rating, accounted for around 30 percent of all spells of temporary-layoff unemployment. Nonsubsidized benefits were found to have a negligible impact on firms' layoff behavior.

The implicit-contract models considered by Feldstein and others have much in common with standard models of utility-maximizing trade unions; see Oswald (1985) and Pencavel (1991) for surveys. A popular model considers a trade union as attempting to maximize its members' expected utility, typically subject to the restriction that profit-maximizing firms determine employment. One of the implications is that the union's preferred wage is increasing in the benefit level, as a higher benefit level reduces the cost of unemployment to the members. This result for the monopoly-union case carries over to models with bargaining over wages.

Again, it is important to consider whether the implications from a partial-equilibrium analysis remain at least qualitatively intact when we turn to the general equilibrium. Some minor and plausible extensions of Feldstein's contract model have reversed a key policy conclusion concerning the financing of UI benefits. Are the implications from union models concerning benefits also fragile to minor changes in underlying assumptions? We discuss this issue using two standard models of equilibrium unemployment, namely a union-bargaining model and a search-matching model.

IV. Equilibrium Unemployment and Unemployment Insurance

Union-Bargaining Models

A popular model of unemployment features an economy with decentralized wage negotiations between symmetric firms and unions, subject to the "right-to-manage" constraint that employment is determined by firms; see e.g. Nickell (1990) for details. The negotiated wage in the single union-firm bargain will be set as a markup on a measure of "outside" labor market opportunities, captured by the general wage, the unemployment rate (a proxy for labor market tightness) and the benefit level. A higher benefit level thus increases the negotiated wage at the firm (or sectoral) level. When all union-firm pairs raise their negotiated wages, unemployment is bound to increase. Suppose that the benefit level is adjusted to the general wage through a fixed replacement rate (ρ) and that the worker's utility function takes the form $U = (1/\sigma)w^\sigma$, with $\sigma \leq 1$. We can then derive an expression for the symmetric-equilibrium unemployment rate (u) that takes the form

$$u = \frac{\kappa\sigma}{1-\rho^\sigma} \tag{1}$$

where κ is a measure of workers' bargaining power, in a broad sense. With fixed capital, perfect competition in the product market and a constant labor share, κ is constant and given as $\kappa = \beta(1-\gamma)/[(1-\beta)\gamma+\beta]$, where γ is the labor share and β is the measure of the union's power in the (Nash) bargain ($0 < \beta \leq 1$).

The unemployment rate is very sensitive to changes in the replacement rate in this model. Moreover, each percentage point increase in the replacement rate has a greater effect on unemployment the higher the initial unemployment rate is. When workers are risk neutral ($\sigma = 1$) we have $d \ln u/d \ln (1-\rho) = -1$. If one takes this model seriously enough to simulate it, it generates very large unemployment responses to changes in replacement rates. Suppose that workers have a degree of relative risk aversion of 2 ($\sigma = -1$) and choose a value of κ so as to generate an unemployment rate of 8 percent when the replacement rate is 50 percent. A rise in the replacement rate from 50 to 60 percent generates an increase in the unemployment rate by almost 4 percentage points with these assumptions. A rise from 50 to 80 percent implies a rise in unemployment from 8 to 32 percent. The magnitudes of these effects seem implausibly large considering the fact that actual replacement rates do vary substantially among countries without huge differences in unemployment rates.

Equilibrium Search Models

A search-matching model of the type developed in Pissarides (1990) is usually cast in terms of risk-neutral workers, but it is straightforward to reformulate the model with risk-averse workers (so long as there is no credit market that facilitates consumption smoothing). In this model there is a constant-returns-to-scale matching function that summarizes the interactions between unemployed job searchers and vacancies. Workers are either employed or unemployed and care about the expected present value of lifetime utility. Vacancies are opened as long as they yield positive expected profits. Firms' recruitment behavior gives a relationship between the real wage cost and labor market tightness, defined as the ratio between the number of vacancies and the number of unemployed. Wages are set in decentralized bargains between workers and firms, where higher labor market tightness increases the negotiated wage. By using the zero-profit condition for firms along with the wage equation, we can obtain an equation that determines the equilibrium value of labor market tightness (θ). This equation takes the form

$$\frac{\sigma\beta}{1-\beta}\left[r+\phi+\alpha(\theta)\right]\frac{a}{q(\theta)}+\rho^{\sigma}-1=0, \qquad \sigma \leq 1. \tag{2}$$

It is assumed that UI benefits are financed by a payroll tax and that hiring costs are proportional to after-tax wage costs, with a being the factor of proportionality. ρ is the replacement rate. The two assumptions that hiring costs are indexed to wage costs and that benefits are indexed to (consumer) wages are sufficient to make equilibrium tightness independent of the payroll-tax rate. The concavity of the utility function is measured by σ, β is the measure of the worker's bargaining power, r is the discount rate (taken as identical for workers and firms), ϕ the exogenous separation rate, $\alpha(\cdot)$ the job-finding rate, and $q(\cdot)$ the rate at which vacancies are filled. The rates at which workers find jobs and vacancies are filled are related to labor market tightness through the matching function, which implies $(\theta) > 0$ and $q'(\theta) < 0$.

The steady-state unemployment rate consistent with flow equilibrium is given as $u = \phi/(\phi + \alpha(\theta))$, which together with (2) determine labor market tightness and unemployment for alternative values of the replacement rate. The required tax rate is obtained from the government's budget restriction once unemployment is determined. Table 1 sets out some simulation results from this model. The model has been calibrated so as to

Table 1. *Equilibrium unemployment (%) and replacement rates (%) in the search-matching model*

Replacement rate	$\sigma = 1$	$\sigma = 0.1$	$\sigma = -1$
20	6.1	3.8	2.3
30	6.6	4.6	3.2
40	7.2	5.5	4.2
50	8.0	6.5	5.3
60	9.1	7.8	6.8
70	10.8	9.7	8.8
80	13.6	12.7	12.0
90	20.2	19.6	19.1

Notes: The model is calibrated so as to generate an unemployment rate of 8 percent when the annual separation rate is 20 percent, $\sigma = 1$ and $\rho = 0.5$. The matching function is specified as $H = 0.01295V^{0.6}U^{0.4}$, where V is the number of vacancies and U is the number of unemployed. The annual discount rate is set to 5 percent and the measure of workers' bargaining power (β) is set to 0.5. The hiring cost function is $k = aw(1+t)$, with $a = 1.5$.

generate 8 percent unemployment with risk-neutral workers and a replacement rate of 50 percent. The effects of varying the replacement rate are given in the first column for the risk-neutral case; the remaining columns show simulated unemployment rates when workers are risk-averse. All parameters except σ are kept constant across the columns.

The results from this exercise suggest a marked non-linear relationship between unemployment and the replacement rate, albeit less strong than in the bargaining model previously discussed. A rise in the replacement rate from 50 to 60 percent would, according to these examples, increase unemployment by a little more than 1 percentage point. A rise from 80 to 90 percent would increase unemployment by 7–8 percentage points.

Mortensen (1996) reports simulation results of UI policies in a parameterized version of the Mortensen and Pissarides (1994) model, which is an extended version of the Pissarides (1990) matching model to allow for endogenous job creation and job destruction. The effects of higher UI benefits are very large in this model. A rise in the replacement rate from 30 to 40 percent would increase unemployment by at least 4 percentage points, and possibly by more than 10 percentage points, according to these simulations. The most likely reason why benefit hikes apparently have a much stronger impact in Mortensen's experiments than in those reported in Table 1 is because Mortensen imputes a non-trivial value to leisure. This means that the "total" replacement rate, including the value of leisure, is much higher than the rate provided by UI. If the value of leisure is set to 40 percent of labor productivity (roughly Mortensen's assumption) in our simulations, we get results very similar to his.

Unfortunately, economists know virtually nothing about a reasonable estimate of the leisure value of unemployment. A liberal interpretation of some empirical evidence on unemployment and psychological well-being suggests that the value may well be *negative*; see e.g. Blanchflower and Oswald (1997). Policy simulations that hinge crucially on assumptions concerning unobservables should therefore be used with more than the usual caution as predictions of what is likely to happen if a particular policy is implemented.

Partial and General Equilibrium

Do the estimates from micro data give reliable answers to general-equilibrium questions about the effects of UI on unemployment? In general, the answer is no. There are a number of potential general-equilibrium effects that are ignored in the microeconometric studies of unemployed individuals' behavior. There can therefore be no presumption that the general-equilibrium effect is stronger — or weaker — than the estimated partial-equilibrium effect. The direction of the general-equilibrium effect is sensitive to the precise details of the general-equilibrium model.

Consider a search-matching model of the type sketched above. In some versions of this model there are non-trivial job search and job acceptance decisions taken by individual unemployed workers. A higher benefit level would then reduce the outflow from unemployment at a given level of labor market tightness. This is the effect captured by the partial-equilibrium studies of unemployment duration. There will also be an effect working through wage setting, however, which in general will reinforce the search effect by reducing labor market tightness. Using this model, then, the presumption is that the general-equilibrium effect of higher benefits is stronger than the partial-equilibrium effect.

These conclusions may be reversed when wages are set by firms, a theme that has been developed by Albrecht and Axell (1984) and Axell and Lang (1990). The driving force behind these results is that the equilibrium wage distribution is affected by benefit hikes in a way that encourages rather than discourages job acceptance among the unemployed. Low-wage firms may find it more difficult to recruit workers and therefore increase their wage offers. When the frequency of low-wage firms declines, it takes a shorter time for job-seekers to find acceptable offers. If this effect is sufficiently strong, the final outcome may conceivably be that unemployment actually *falls* when benefits are increased. The general insight offered by these models is that the effects on the wage-offer distribution need to be taken into account in general-equilibrium evaluations of UI reforms.

We may also note that surprising results can appear even in perfectly standard union-bargaining models once the possibility of multiple equilibria is entertained. Manning (1992) considers a model with increasing returns to scale in production. Increasing returns yield an aggregate price-setting schedule that is *positively* sloped in the real wage and employment space. There will in general be two equilibria in this model (at least with a Cobb-Douglas technology), one with low employment and one with high employment. A benefit increase will produce the usual result, i.e., higher unemployment, if the economy is located in the high-employment equilibrium. If the low-employment equilibrium obtains, however, the outcome of a rise in benefits (or other changes that increase wage pressure) would be *lower* unemployment. Manning's empirical work on British data finds some, albeit not overwhelming, support for this possibility.

It may be asked, then, whether the bottom line of this discussion is that we are bound to be lost in conflicting theoretical predictions. My own judgment is that the case for the conventional wisdom is reasonably strong: unemployment will probably increase if the benefit system is made more generous. Wage bargaining seems pervasive in most European labor markets. Firms are not typically free to set wages at their own discretion, so models of the bargaining variety seem more relevant for most of these countries than models of wage-setting firms. There is considerable uncertainty, however, regarding the *magnitude* of the effects.

Many equilibrium models of unemployment portray the UI system in an extremely simple way. For example, unemployment compensation is typically assumed to be available to all unemployed; benefits are paid for an infinite duration; there is no work test, i.e., no penalty for the refusal of job offers; there is no waiting period before benefits are paid, etc. These and other features of existing models are at variance with the institutional details of real-world UI systems, a point that has been forcefully made by Atkinson and Micklewright (1991). For example, most existing systems have time-limited UI benefits, a work test that involves some penalty for job rejections, and a waiting period before benefits are received. Unemployment compensation in the real world is clearly more than just a pure subsidy to leisure.

Does this apparent mismatch between models and reality mean that the stylized models are useless? This conclusion would be like throwing out the baby with the bathwater. All models are by necessity simplifications. Existing UI systems have a rich and complicated structure which it would be impossible to capture in detail in a manageable analytical model. The problem, as usual, is to strike the right balance between descriptive realism and analytical tractability. Although more detailed studies of existing UI features are needed, it seems difficult to argue that existing models have made incredible assumptions concerning UI. For example, a work test is built into most UI systems, but few would argue that it is effective enough to leave no room for individual search and acceptance decisions. UI benefits are often paid for a limited time period, but the assumption of infinite benefit duration may be innocuous for some purposes. The proof of the pudding lies in the eating, i.e., in the empirical performance of the models. The fact that some models seem to generate implausibly large unemployment responses to benefit changes may reflect weaknesses of the models that are unrelated to the treatment of unemployment compensation.

Empirical Work

How do the numbers from simulations of equilibrium models compare with available empirical results? The microeconometric studies of unemployment duration are of only limited use here, as they do not capture general-equilibrium effects. More relevant are studies that compare economies with different benefit regimes, and possibly also studies that exploit time series in order to examine how unemployment in a single economy responds to changes in UI policies.

The generosity of UI benefits seems to have increased gradually since the 1960s in most OECD countries. The OECD has calculated a summary measure of benefit generosity that takes into account benefit levels as well as the length of benefit periods.[3] According to these calculations, benefit generosity has doubled between the mid-1960s and the mid-1990s (see Table 2). The summary measure is a somewhat crude indicator, but the basic message is clear: unemployment benefits have become substantially more generous in most OECD countries over the past three decades. The rising trend in benefits relative to earnings must be considered as a prime suspect in any serious attempt to explain the trend rise in unemployment in most OECD countries.

There have been a few attempts to use cross-country data to explain unemployment differences by unemployment benefits and other variables;

Table 2. *The evolution of the summary measure of gross replacement rates (%) in the OECD*

	1961	1967	1973	1979	1985	1991	1995
OECD Europe	14	16	19	25	30	32	34
Total OECD	16	16	19	24	28	29	31

Source: Martin (1996).

---

[3] OECD has computed replacement rates for three different duration categories (one year, two or three years, and four or five years of unemployment). These calculations are applied to three family situations and two different levels of previous earnings. The summary measure is an unweighted mean of 18 computed replacement rates. The net (after-tax) replacement rates are higher than the gross rates, sometimes substantially. See Martin (1996).

the work by Layard *et al.* (1991) is the best known. In a simple cross-country regression, explaining average unemployment for the period 1983–88 in 20 OECD countries, they find that the replacement rate enters with a significant coefficient of 0.17. Layard *et al.* also find a significant positive effect from the maximum duration of benefit payments. Scarpetta (1996) reports results from a more ambitious study using panel data for the period 1983–93. A robust result in this study is that higher replacement rates increase unemployment; the estimated coefficient is 0.13, implying that an increase by 10 percentage points would increase unemployment by 1.3 percentage points. These results are broadly in line with the magnitudes implied by the simulation results in Table 1 for replacement rates in the range 50 to 70 percent.[4]

The empirical results from studies that use time series for single countries have produced diverse results concerning the effects of UI policies, although typically in the expected direction. Manning (1993) estimated unemployment equations for Britain and found significantly positive replacement rate effects. Forslund (1995) found similar results for Sweden. Other studies, e.g. Layard and Nickell (1985) and Minford (1983), have derived positive benefit effects on unemployment via estimated real wage equations.

When evaluating these and similar studies, the possibility of reverse causality cannot easily be ignored. Is the rise in unemployment driven by more generous UI systems? Or has the rise in unemployment increased the political pressure to make UI more generous? Benefit variables are often treated as endogenous in the empirical studies, but it is an open question whether the identification problems have really been solved.

UI and Unemployment Persistence

Most theoretical investigations of how UI affects unemployment have focused on steady states rather than the dynamic adjustment. Some recent work in the search and matching framework has suggested that UI may have important implications for how unemployment adjusts to shocks. The papers by Ljungqvist and Sargent (1996) and Millard (1996) are two examples; the recent paper by Marimon and Zilibotti (1997) is another.

Ljungqvist and Sargent (1996) develop a model where workers experience stochastic accumulation and depreciation of skills. Unemployed workers face a risk of skill loss and their UI benefits are based on the wage

---

[4] Most equilibrium models of unemployment ignore the fact that benefits are typically paid for a limited time period rather than forever. This makes it difficult to relate the OECD summary measure to the replacement rates used in parameterized models.

in the most recent job. The model is used to simulate the dynamic behavior of two economies, referred to as "laissez faire" and "welfare state". The welfare state features a benefit replacement rate of 70 percent of previous earnings, whereas there are no benefits in the laissez-faire economy. It turns out that the steady states of the two economies are very similar, but their dynamic responses to shocks differ substantially. A transient economic shock causes a prolonged period of long-term unemployment in the welfare state, while adjustment is fast in the laissez faire-economy. The reason for this difference appears to be that the unemployed in the welfare state adjust their reservation wages more slowly, and search less intensively, than the unemployed in the corresponding laissez-faire economy without benefits. The two economies also differ markedly with respect to their responses to an increase in a measure of "economic turbulence". Unemployment in the laissez-faire economy stays roughly constant whereas unemployment in the welfare state increases sharply as more workers experience large skill losses while being entitled to 70 percent of their previous earnings.

Millard (1996) applies a calibrated version of the Mortensen and Pissarides (1994) model of job creation and job destruction to study the dynamics of unemployment. A basic finding is that the average unemployment rate as well as the degree of unemployment persistence are increasing in the replacement rate. An adverse but transient productivity shock leads to prolonged unemployment when replacement rates are high, a result very similar to what Ljungqvist and Sargent (1996) report.

The above-mentioned papers identified effects of UI that had been largely ignored in the previous literature. The possibility that generous benefits can cause severe unemployment persistence has not been modeled carefully in earlier research.[5] And the observation that technological shocks may interact with generous UI to produce high unemployment is novel. In general, the simulations of parameterized search and matching models are very useful as exercises to identify effects that are not easily derived from simpler analytical models, but there is much more to be done before they can be used to confidently predict how an economy will respond to UI policies. For example, it is disturbing that some results depend heavily on assumptions concerning unobservables, such as the value of leisure. Many of these models are also seriously incomplete as guides to how policies *should* be undertaken, the reason being that they feature risk-neutral agents and thereby ignore the benefits from income insurance as a means to smooth consumption.

---

[5] There is some empirical evidence that long-term benefits magnify the increase in unemployment following disinflationary policies; see Ball (1996).

V. The Welfare Economics of Unemployment Insurance

The economics of UI has first and foremost been concerned with positive analysis of the effects of various UI policies. Much less attention has been devoted to the normative issue: what is the *optimal* level of UI benefits in an economy with risk-averse workers? Despite the moral-hazard problems related to wage setting and job search incentives, the optimal UI policy may well involve quite high replacement rates if workers are risk averse and do not have access to credit markets. To illustrate this claim we can again make use of a parameterized version of the search-matching model.

Optimal Unemployment Insurance in a Search-Matching Model

In this model the expected lifetime utility of being employed (W^e) and unemployed (W^u) can be derived as a function of the replacement rate, the real wage, the transition rates and the discount rate. The corresponding flow values of being employed and unemployed take the form:

$$rW^e = \left[\frac{r+\phi\,\rho^\sigma+\alpha(\theta)}{r+\phi+\alpha(\theta)}\right]\frac{w^\sigma}{\sigma} \tag{3}$$

$$rW^u = \left[\frac{(r+\phi)\,\rho^\sigma+\alpha(\theta)}{r+\phi+\alpha(\theta)}\right]\frac{w^\sigma}{\sigma}. \tag{4}$$

With positive discounting ($r>0$), we have $rW^e>rW^u$. As the discount rates approaches zero, rW^e approaches rW^u and the limiting value is simply given by the worker's expected steady-state utility:

$$rW = (1-u)\frac{w^\sigma}{\sigma}+u\,\frac{(\rho w)^\sigma}{\sigma}. \tag{5}$$

The budget restriction, absent administration costs, is given as $t(1-u) = \rho u$, where t is the payroll-tax rate. Equation (2) determines labor market tightness for any given replacement rate, unemployment is obtained from the flow-equilibrium equation, and the tax rate follows from the budget restriction. To determine the optimal replacement rate we need to consider the effect on the consumer wage. Let y denote labor productivity. Labor cost, $w_c \equiv w(1+t)$, is related to labor market tightness through the free-entry condition. This takes the form

$$w_c(\theta) = \frac{yq(\theta)}{q(\theta)+\phi a} \tag{6}$$

when the discount rate approaches zero. Labor productivity must exceed wage costs so as to cover expected vacancy costs; the per-period cost of holding a vacancy is aw_c, with $a > 0$. The expression for steady-state utility can then be written as

$$rW = \frac{1}{\sigma}\left(\frac{w_c(\theta)}{1+t(\cdot)}\right)^{\sigma}[1-u(\theta)+u(\theta)\rho^{\sigma}].\tag{7}$$

The tax rate is a function of labor market tightness as well as the replacement rate, $t = t(\theta, \rho)$. Tightness is determined by (2) as a function of the replacement rate, i.e., $\theta = \theta(\rho)$.

Holding tightness constant, an increase in the replacement rate has a direct positive welfare effect associated with higher consumption when unemployed and a direct negative welfare effect due to the higher tax rate that has to be paid. In addition there are indirect effects operating through the reduction in tightness (increase in unemployment). If the indirect effects are ignored, the optimum with risk-averse workers involves full insurance ($\rho = 1$), as is easily established by differentiating (7) while holding tightness (and hence labor cost) constant. Full insurance is not optimal under moral hazard, however.

From inspection of eqs. (6) and (7) it is clear that the level of productivity does not influence the optimal replacement rate. Table 3 shows optimal replacement rates implied by a parameterized version of the model. The optimal rates are calculated for three separation rates and two utility functions. By varying the separation rate we get variations in the equilibrium unemployment rate for any given replacement rate. The exercises illustrate that the optimal replacement rate can be quite high, around 50 percent, despite the adverse effects on unemployment. Of course, these numbers will be sensitive to the assumptions concerning the leisure value of unemployment (which is ignored here). Another critical assumption is the lack of capital markets. If workers could engage in precautionary savings the case for generous UI would probably be weaker. Some recent papers, e.g. Costain (1997) and Valdivia (1996), have addressed this issue using calibrated search-equilibrium models with precautionary savings.

Table 3. *Optimal replacement rates (%) in the search-matching model*

	Annual separation rate (%)		
	10	20	30
$\sigma = -0.1$	47	46	46
	(3.1)	(5.9)	(8.9)
$\sigma = -1.0$	57	56	56
	(3.1)	(5.8)	(9.0)

Notes: See notes to Table 1. The discount rate is set to zero. Unemployment rates at the optimum solutions are shown in parentheses.

Costain reports that optimal replacement rates in the range of 30 to 40 percent seem to arise very easily, and Valdivia's results are similar. Gruber (1997) applies the model of Baily (1978) along with new empirical esti- mates of the consumption smoothing effect of UI in the United States; he finds that the optimal replacement rate is below 0.5 even at very high levels of risk aversion.

The Optimal Time Profile of Benefits

Early contributions to the welfare economics of UI include papers by Baily (1978), Flemming (1978), and Shavell and Weiss (1979). One issue concerned the optimal time profile of UI benefits. Should UI compensa- tion be paid indefinitely at a fixed rate or should it decrease (or increase) over the worker's spell of unemployment? One formulation of the problem portrays a government with a given amount of resources to spend on UI payments. The unemployed worker chooses search effort and a reservation wage to maximize expected utility. The problem is to find the optimal time profile of unemployment compensation, defined as the profile that maxi- mizes the unemployed worker's expected utility.

The design of optimal UI policy in this framework involves a tradeoff between, on the one hand, the desirability of smoothing consumption and, on the other hand, the positive incentive effect arising from a scheme where benefits decline over the spell of unemployment. One (unsurpris- ing) result from this analysis is that a constant time profile of benefits is optimal if job search is effectively monitored by the UI administration so that the moral-hazard problems are eliminated. The more the job searcher can affect the job-finding probability, and the more sensitive the job- finding probability is with respect to the benefit level, the stronger the case for a declining time profile (possibly including a lump-sum severance payment). Allowing for private savings may overturn some results from models without credit markets. Shavell and Weiss (1979) show that the optimal solution may include an introductory period with a rising benefit level, followed by a declining time profile.

Some recent papers have reexamined the question of the optimal sequencing of benefits by using equilibrium models of unemployment. Davidson and Woodbury (1997) ask whether benefits should be paid indef- initely or for a fixed number of weeks. The analysis exploits a search- matching framework with endogenous search effort among the unemployed, although wages and the number of jobs are taken as exoge- nous. Davidson and Woodbury argue that the optimal UI program should entail *indefinite* potential duration of UI payments for risk-averse workers. Their result is driven by a comparison between two extremes, i.e., a program with indefinite potential duration of a fixed level of compensation and a program where benefits drop to zero after a certain number of weeks. Cahuc and Lehmann (1997) also investigate the effects of the time sequence of UI benefits. Their model ignores job search but allows for endogenous wage determination through union-firm bargaining. They find that a constant time sequence yields lower unemployment than a program with a declining time profile. The reason is that a declining benefit schedule increases the welfare of the short-term unemployed at the expense of the long-term unemployed, which raises wage pressure. In a third paper on the same theme, Fredriksson and Holmlund (1998) develop an equilibrium search-matching model with endogenous wage determination as well as endogenous search effort. Their key result is that a socially optimal UI policy implies a declining sequence of unemployment compensation over the spell of unemployment. This result is driven by a version of the "entitlement effect", i.e., the fact that an increase in benefits will raise search effort among those not currently qualified for benefits. A declining time sequence provides incentives for active search among workers who have lost their initially high benefit level.

VI. The Political Economy of Unemployment Insurance

There are a number of reasons why preferences over UI policies may differ in the population. Heterogeneity in unemployment risks is an obvious possibility, which has been explored in detail by Wright (1986) in a model without moral hazard. UI preferences may also differ among intrinsically identical individuals because their current labor market status will differ; some will be employed and others unemployed at each point in time. The *timing* of spells of employment and unemployment matters for the preferred UI compensation so long as the discount rate is positive.

In the context of the search-matching model that we have used here, a positive discount factor generates a difference between the value of employment and the value of unemployment, as given by (3) and (4); with positive discounting we have $rW^e > rW^u$. The unemployed have more to gain immediately from a rise in benefits than the employed; they receive the higher benefits now whereas the employed get the increase if they become unemployed in the future.

We computed replacement rates preferred by employed and unemployed workers for a parameterized version of the search-matching model, setting the annual discount rate to 5 percent. These calculations maximize the steady-state present values of being employed and unemployed, respectively. As one might expect, the unemployed worker prefers a higher replacement rate than the employed according to these simulations. The differences in preferred compensation are relatively small, however, ranging from 2 to 6 percentage points depending on the specific assumptions regarding the separation rate and the degree of risk aversion. The political outcome is plausibly determined by the employed voter, so the political equilibrium would in these examples generate lower replacement rates than a procedure where individuals voted on the UI policy *before* they knew their current labor force status.

It is easily verified that the politically chosen replacement rate is independent of labor productivity in this model, a property that seems to be in accordance with the facts. Benefit levels are typically adjusted upwards as real wages increase.

Benefit Generosity and Bargaining Structure

The model that we have considered presupposes decentralized wage bargaining, the outcome of which is taken into account by the median (employed) voter. However, if the employed workers were able to choose wages as well as replacement rates, the optimum solution would be different. Suppose that the worker has access to an encompassing monopoly union. The worker's wage choice would then effectively determine labor market tightness in the economy. By making use of a "labor demand" relationship analogous to eq. (6) as well as the government's budget restriction, we can write the worker's objective as a function of the replacement rate and labor market tightness, i.e.,

$$rW^e = \Psi(\rho, \theta, w(\theta, t(\theta, \rho))) = \Psi(\rho, \theta, w(\theta, \rho))) \tag{8}$$

where $\theta = \theta(\rho)$. The choice of replacement rate could then be made without considering the impact on labor market tightness, by the envelope theorem.[6] The solution to this problem would then seem to imply full insurance ($\rho = 1$), exactly as in the case where incentive considerations are ignored altogether.

There are at least two caveats to this conclusion, however. A minor one is that the employed worker will not prefer full insurance in a model with positive discounting, as can be verified by differentiating (3) while holding labor market tightness constant, subject to the budget-balance condition and the relationship between the consumer wage and the producer wage, i.e., $w = w_c/(1 + t)$. Full insurance is the outcome only with zero discounting. The higher the discount rate, the lower the preferred replacement

---

[6] The first-order condition for optimal tightness is $\Psi_\theta + \Psi_w w_\theta = 0$. The first-order condition for the optimal replacement rate is then given as $\Psi_\rho + \Psi_w w_\rho = 0$, where the envelope theorem is invoked.

rate, taking labor market conditions as given.[7] The other caveat is that centralized wage setting may easily lead to full employment. A requirement for an interior solution is that it must be possible to increase the consumer wage through a reduction in aggregate employment. In fact, a condition for an interior maximum with full insurance is that the labor demand elasticity (ε) is smaller than unity, which is a quite restrictive condition.[8] However, interior solutions with $\rho < 1$ and $\varepsilon > 1$ are possible.

The "envelope argument" suggesting that very high replacement rates should be observed in labor markets where the median voter can exercise unilateral wage setting power is thus somewhat fragile, since it only works for relatively low labor demand elasticities. Of course, it is also questionable because it presupposes that employers have no influence over wages, an implausible assumption. We nevertheless take a brief look at the data to see if there is anything that can confirm the idea. Are replacement rates higher in countries where unions are strong and wage bargaining centralized?

A frequently used measure of union power is the "coverage rate", i.e., the number of employees covered by collective agreements as a percentage of the total number of employees. There is a positive and relatively strong correlation between benefit generosity and coverage rates in cross-country data for the early 1990s ($R = 0.70$). Figure 1 shows a scatter plot between benefit generosity and coverage rates for 17 countries. The benefit variable is the summary measure calculated by the OECD, expressed as an average replacement rate; see Martin (1996). The slope of the estimated relationship is 0.29 with a t-value of 3.78. The correlation between benefit generosity and union density is much weaker ($R = 0.40$). Table 4 presents several regressions which all confirm the positive and significant association between replacement rates (*RRATE*) and coverage rates (*COV*).[9]

Is there then any evidence suggesting that benefits are more generous where bargaining is more centralized, as the envelope argument would suggest? Table 4 reports the results of including a dummy (*CEN*) for countries with relatively centralized wage bargaining; the variable is a somewhat arbitrary dichotomization of the rankings in Calmfors and

---

[7] Similar results appear in Wright (1986), Saint-Paul (1996) and Hassler and Rodriguez Mora (1996).

[8] Differentiation of the consumer wage with respect to the producer wage and recognizing the labor demand relationship as well as the government's budget restriction verifies the claim.

[9] Saint-Paul (1996) finds a positive correlation between union density and another measure of benefit generosity, namely the share of GDP devoted to unemployment compensation divided by the unemployment rate. This measure is equal to the average benefit payment relative to average labor productivity.

Driffill (1988). The centralization dummy never has a significant effect on the replacement rate.

If the political-economy perspective is taken seriously, it will have consequences for empirical work on unemployment and unemployment compensation. Unemployment and benefit generosity would both be endogenous variables, and the identification issues would have to be addressed. Many studies include measures of benefit generosity in unemployment equations. Other authors have included unemployment among the variables explaining benefit generosity; see Di Tella and MacCulloch (1995), and Saint-Paul (1996). It is difficult, however, to think of theoretically satisfactory exclusion restrictions that would achieve identification in this case; all variables affecting unemployment would in general influence the policy decision.

VII. Concluding Remarks

The economics of unemployment insurance has been a very active research area in labor economics over the past 25 years or so. What have we learned? A lot, surely, at least at the conceptual and theoretical level. The

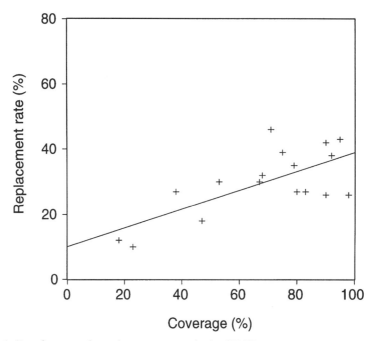

Fig. 1. Benefit generosity and coverage rates in the OECD

Table 4. *Benefit generosity and bargaining structure*

	Dependent variable			
	RRATE	RRATE	ln RRATE	ln RRATE
Constant	10.09	10.90	0.424	0.420
	(1.82)	(1.79)	(0.82)	(0.69)
COV	0.288	0.266		
	(3.78)	(2.70)		
ln COV			0.701	0.703
			(5.65)	(4.60)
CEN		1.837		−0.002
		(0.38)		(0.01)
$\bar{R}^2$	0.454	0.421	0.659	0.634

Notes: RRATE is a summary measure of benefit generosity (%) in the mid-1990s; see Martin (1996). *COV* is the coverage rate (%) in 1990; see OECD (1994). *CEN* is a dummy for centralized wage bargaining based on the rankings in Calmfors and Driffill (1988). *CEN* = 1 for Austria, Belgium, Finland, Germany, Netherlands, Norway and Sweden; *CEN* = 0 for the other countries. The 17 countries included in the regressions are: Australia, Austria, Belgium, Canada, Finland, France, Germany, Japan, Netherlands, New Zealand, Norway, Portugal, Spain, Sweden, Switzerland, United Kingdom and the United States. Absolute *t*-values in parentheses.

numerous theoretical studies have identified many routes whereby the design of UI may affect the operation of labor markets. As compared to where we were around 1970, this is a major achievement. In the late 1990s economists have access to many more tools for systematically examining UI policies than they had around 1970.

A notable feature of the economic analysis of UI is the close interplay between theory and empirical testing. Search theory, in particular, has had a major impact on how we think about labor market statistics and how we undertake econometric investigations. It would be tempting, therefore, to characterize past research on UI as an overwhelming success story. But I hesitate to make such an unqualified claim. If a success story is character-ized by repeated empirical confirmation of theoretical predictions, with reasonably robust parameter estimates, the economics of UI do not quite measure up to the requirements. The weight of the evidence suggests that increased benefit generosity causes longer spells of unemployment and probably higher overall unemployment as well. But there remains a considerable degree of uncertainty regarding the magnitudes of these effects.

There are also various fine details of UI policies, such as the choice between a change in benefit levels and a change in benefit duration, where we have little empirical grounds for making predictions as guides to policy-makers. What would happen to unemployment (duration) if, say, benefit levels were increased while benefit durations were shortened by a prescribed amount? Although there have been attempts to answer such questions in some empirical studies, e.g. Katz and Meyer (1990), we are a long way from a situation where economists can with any confidence provide policymakers with reliable menus for choice among key UI parameters.

A recurrent theme of the paper has been that policy prescriptions require an equilibrium framework; partial-equilibrium results rarely carry over unaltered to the general equilibrium. Policy prescriptions should also recognize the ultimate rationale for UI, namely its provision of income insurance to risk-averse individuals. It is only recently, however, that equilibrium approaches to unemployment have taken the insurance motive for UI seriously. Simply looking at changes in unemployment is not sufficient to gauge the welfare effects of UI policies.

The nature of capital market imperfections plays a crucial role in the appropriate design of UI policies. If workers can self-insure through saving and borrowing, the case for (generous) public UI is weakened. Other forms of self-insurance are conceivable in a family context: a reduction in household income due to one family member's job loss can to some extent be offset through increased labor supply of another family member. These are areas where little research has been undertaken so far. Much more needs to be done, theoretically and empirically, in order to deepen our understanding of the interactions between private self-insurance and public unemployment insurance.

References

Albrecht, J. and Axell, B.: An equilibrium model of search unemployment. *Journal of Political Economy 92*, 824–840, 1984.

Atkinson, A. and Micklewright, J.: Unemployment compensation and labor market transitions: A critical review. *Journal of Economic Literature 29*, 1679–1727, 1991.

Axell, B. and Lang, H.: The effects of unemployment compensation in general equilibrium with search unemployment. *Scandinavian Journal of Economics 92*, 531–540, 1990.

Baily, M. N.: Some aspects of optimal unemployment insurance. *Journal of Public Economics 10*, 379–402, 1978.

Ball, L. : Disinflation and the NAIRU. NBER WP 5520, 1996.

Berg, G. van den: Nonstationarity in job search theory. *Review of Economic Studies 57*, 255–277,1990.

Björklund, A.: On the duration of unemployment in Sweden, 1965–1976. *Scandinavian Journal of Economics 80*, 422–439, 1978.

Blanchflower, D. and Oswald, A.: The rising well-being of the young. NBER WP 6102, 1997.

Burdett, K. and Wright, R.: Optimal firm size, taxes, and unemployment. *Journal of Public Economics 39*, 275–287, 1989.

Cahuc, P. and Lehmann, E.: Equilibrium unemployment and the time sequence of unemployment benefits. WP 97.49, Université de Paris I, Panthéon-Sorbonne, 1997.

Calmfors, L. and Driffill, J.: Bargaining structure, corporatism and macroeconomic performance. *Economic Policy*, No. 6, 13–61, 1988.

Carling, K., Edin, P.-A., Harkman, A. and Holmlund, B.: Unemployment duration, unemployment benefits, and labor market programs in Sweden, *Journal of Public Economics 59*, 313–334, 1996.

Cassel, G.: *Socialpolitik* (Social Policy). Hugo Gebers Förlag, Stockholm, 1902.

Casson, M.: *Economics of Unemployment: An Historical Perspective*. MIT Press, Cambridge, MA, 1983.

Costain, J.: Unemployment insurance in a general equilibrium model of job search and precautionary savings. Manuscript, Department of Economics, University of Chicago, 1997.

Davidson, C. and Woodbury, S.: Optimal unemployment insurance. *Journal of Public Economics 64*, 359–387, 1997.

Devine, T. and Kiefer, N.: *Empirical Labor Economics: The Search Approach*. Oxford University Press, Oxford, 1991.

Di Tella, R. and MacCulloch, R.: The determination of unemployment benefits. Applied Economics DP 180, Institute of Economics and Statistics, University of Oxford, 1995.

Feldstein, M.: Temporary layoffs in the theory of unemployment. *Journal of Political Economy 84*, 937–957, 1976.

Feldstein, M.: The effect of unemployment insurance on temporary layoff unemployment. *American Economic Review 68*, 834–846, 1978.

Feldstein, M. and Poterba, J.: Unemployment insurance and reservation wages. *Journal of Public Economics 23*, 141–167, 1984.

Flemming, J. S.: Aspects of optimal unemployment insurance: search, leisure, savings and capital market imperfections. *Journal of Public Economics 10*, 403–425, 1978.

Forslund, A.: Unemployment: is Sweden still different? *Swedish Economic Policy Review 2*, 15–58, 1995.

Fredriksson, P. and Holmlund, B.: Optimal unemployment insurance in search equilibrium. WP, Department of Economics, Uppsala University, 1998.

Gruber, J.: The consumption smoothing benefits of unemployment insurance. *American Economic Review 87*, 192–205, 1997.

Ham, J. and Rea, S.: Unemployment insurance and male unemployment duration in Canada. *Journal of Labor Economics 5*, 325–353, 1987.

Hamermesh, D.S.: Unemployment insurance and labor supply. *International Economic Review 21*, 517–527, 1980.

Harkman, A., Jansson, F., Källberg, K. and Öhrn, L.: *Arbetslöshetsersättningen och arbetsmarknadens funktionssätt* (Unemployment Insurance and the Functioning of the Labor Market). The Swedish National Labor Market Board, 1997.

Hassler, J. and Rodriguez Mora, J. V.: Employment turnover and unemployment insurance. CEPR DP 1609, 1996.

Heckscher, E.: Den ekonomiska innebörden av offentliga åtgärder mot arbetslöshetens verkningar (Economic aspects of public unemployment policies). Bilaga 1 till SOU 1928:9. *Betänkande och förslag angående arbetslöshetsförsäkring, arbetsförmedling och reservarbeten*, Norstedts, Stockholm, 1928.

Hicks, J.: *The Theory of Wages*. Macmillan, London, 1932.

Johnson, G. and Layard, R.: The natural rate of unemployment: Explanation and policy. In O. Ashenfelter and R. Layard (eds.), *Handbook of Labor Economics*, North-Holland, Amsterdam, 1986.

Jones, S.: Job search methods, intensity and effects. *Oxford Bulletin of Economics and Statistics 51*, 277–296, 1989.

Jones, S.: Effects of benefit rate reduction and changes in entitlement (Bill C-113) on unemployment, job search behaviour and new job quality. Human Resource Development Canada, Ottawa, 1996.

Katz, L. and Meyer, B.: The impact of the potential duration of unemployment benefits on the duration of unemployment. *Journal of Public Economics 41*, 45–72, 1990.

Lancaster, T. and Nickell, S.: The analysis of re-employment probabilities for the unemployed. *Journal of the Royal Statistical Society A 143*, 141–165, 1980.

Layard, R. and Nickell, S.: Unemployment in Britain. *Economica* (Supplement) S121–S169,1986.

Layard, R., Nickell, S. and Jackman, R.: *Unemployment: Macroeconomic Performance and the Labour Market*. Oxford University Press, Oxford, 1991.

Ljungqvist, L. and Sargent, T.: The European unemployment dilemma. Manuscript, Department of Economics, University of Chicago, 1996.

Manning, A.: Multiple equilibria in the British labour market: Some empirical evidence. *European Economic Review 36*, 1333–1365, 1992.

Manning, A.: Wage bargaining and the Phillips curve: The identification and specification of aggregate wage equations. *Economic Journal 103*, 98–118, 1993.

Marimon, R. and Zilibotti, F.: Unemployment vs. mismatch of talents: Reconsidering unemployment benefits. NBER WP 6038, 1997.

Martin J.: Measures of replacement rates for the purpose of international comparisons: A note. *OECD Economic Studies*, No. 26, 99–115, 1996.

Meyer, B.: Unemployment insurance and unemployment spells. *Econometrica 58*, 757–782, 1990.

Meyer, B.: Lessons from the U.S. unemployment insurance experiments. *Journal of Economic Literature 33*, 91–131, 1995.

Millard, S.: The cyclical effects of labour market policy. Paper presented at the Applied Econometrics Association Conference on the Econometrics of Unemployment, Gothenburg, 1996.

Minford, P.: Labour market equilibrium in an open economy. *Oxford Economic Papers* (Supplement) *35*, 207–244, 1983.

Moffitt, R.: Unemployment insurance and the distribution of unemployment spells. *Journal of Econometrics 28*, 85–101, 1985.

Mortensen, D.: Unemployment insurance and job search decisions. *Industrial and Labor Relations Review 30*, 505–517, 1977.

Mortensen, D.: A structural model of unemployment insurance benefit effects on the incidence and duration of unemployment. In Y. Weiss and G. Fishelson (eds.) *Advances in the Theory and Measurement of Unemployment*, Macmillan, London, 1990.

Mortensen, D.: Reducing supply-side disincentives to job creation. In *Reducing Unemployment: Current Issues and Policy Issues*, Reserve Bank of Kansas City, 1994.

Mortensen, D.: Search equilibrium approaches to labor market policy analysis. Paper presented at the meeting of the European Association of Labour Economists, Chania, 1996.

Mortensen, D. and Pissarides, C.: Job creation and job destruction in the theory of unemployment. *Review of Economic Studies 61,* 397–415, 1994.

Narendranathan, W., Nickell, S. and Stern, J.: Unemployment benefits revisited. *Economic Journal 95*, 307–329, 1985.

Nickell, S.: Unemployment: A survey. *Economic Journal 100*, 391–439, 1990.

OECD: *Employment Outlook*. OECD, Paris, 1994.

Oswald, A.: The economic theory of trade unions: An introductory survey. *Scandinavian Journal of Economics 87*, 160–193, 1985.

Pedersen, P. and Westergård Nielsen, N.: Unemployment: A review of the evidence from panel data. *OECD Economic Studies,* No. 20, 65–114, 1993.

Pencavel, J.: *Labor Markets under Trade Unionism.* Basil Blackwell, Oxford, 1991.

Pigou, A. C.: *The Theory of Unemployment.* Macmillan, London, 1933.

Pissarides, C.: *Equilibrium Unemployment Theory.* Basil Blackwell, Oxford, 1990.

Saint-Paul, G.: Exploring the political economy of labour market institutions. *Economic Policy* No. 23, 265–300, 1996.

Scarpetta, S.: Assessing the role of labour market policies and institutional settings on unemployment: A cross-country study. *OECD Economic Studies*, No. 26, 43–98, 1996.

Shavell, S. and Weiss, L.: The optimal payment of unemployment insurance benefits over time. *Journal of Political Economy 87*, 1347–1362, 1979.

Topel, R.: On layoffs and unemployment insurance. *American Economic Review 73*, 541–559, 1983.

Topel, R.: Unemployment and unemployment insurance. In R. Ehrenberg (ed.) *Research in Labor Economics*, vol. 7, JAI Press, London, 1985.

Valdivia, V.: Evaluating the welfare benefits of unemployment insurance. Manuscript, Department of Economics, Northwestern University, 1996.

Wright, R.: The redistributive roles of unemployment insurance and the dynamics of voting. *Journal of Public Economics 31*, 377–399, 1986.

Yaniv, G.: Unemployment insurance benefits and the supply of labor of an employed worker. *Journal of Public Economics 17*, 71–87, 1982.

Scand. J. Economics 100(1), 143–145, 1998

Comment on B. Holmlund, "Unemployment Insurance in Theory and Practice"

Alan Manning

London School of Economics, London WC2A 2AE, England

This paper is an admirably clear and concise overview of the impact of unemployment insurance on labour markets. I have no quarrels with it on questions of substance: I would just differ in emphasis. In my comments I would like to make three main points:

   i) theoretical models (and policy discussion based on these models) may overestimate the role of benefits in determining the reservation wages of unemployed workers;
   ii) the strength of the evidence linking the generosity of the benefit system and unemployment is not as strong as we would like and our belief in such a link derives more from the theory than from the evidence;
   iii) it is often not just the level of benefits that matters: the structure of them may be as or more important.

In many models of the labour market (for example, the union and matching models mentioned in this paper), the reservation wage of workers without jobs is crucial in determining wage pressure and, hence, the equilibrium rate of unemployment. In most of these models (and many others) the reservation wage is assumed to be given by the level of benefits plus possibly the value of leisure. In the notation of the paper we have that:

$$R = B^\sigma = \rho^\sigma W^\sigma$$

where we have assumed that benefits are indexed to the average wage. This specification implicitly assumes that all the unemployed receive welfare benefits. But, in reality, many of those without jobs receive little or no benefits. For example Table 1 shows the proportions of those classed as unemployed (in the EU Labour Force Surveys) who are receiving any welfare benefits or assistance. In some countries, particularly those in Southern Europe, these proportions are surprisingly low, yet these are often countries where unemployment is very high. In the absence of benefits from the state, these people are generally supported by their family, friends or accumulated savings. On its own, this will tend to make estimates of the income available to the unemployed higher than simply looking at benefits would suggest. But, on the other hand, it will also make

Table 1. *Percentage of unemployed receiving any welfare benefit or assistance, 1995*

Austria	66	Belgium	81
Denmark	66	Finland	73
France	45	Germany	70
Greece	9	Ireland	67
Italy	7	Netherlands	50
Portugal	27	Spain	24
Sweden	70		

Source: Eurostat Labour Force Survey, 1995.

the reservation wage less sensitive to changes in benefits so that equations like (1) are likely to overstate the extent to which changes in benefits change the reservation wage. To see this, suppose that a fraction α of the unemployed live on benefits getting benefit B and the other live on income from the family which it is reasonable to assume is also proportional to the wage. We then might have something like the following:

$$R = (B^{\alpha}(\beta W)^{1-\alpha})^{\sigma} = \beta^{\sigma(1-\alpha)}\rho^{\alpha\sigma}W^{\sigma}.$$

The point to note is that the elasticity of the reservation wage with respect to benefits is lower in (2) than (1).

The second point I want to make is that the strength of the empirical evidence linking benefit generosity and unemployment is weaker than often claimed. For example consider the following quotation from the OECD Jobs Study (1994, p. 78):

"In Canada, entitlements rose in 1972 and unemployment unusually in 1978 and more strongly around 1983. In Finland, entitlements rose in 1972 and unemployment rose sharply ... through to 1978; in Ireland, changes increasing entitlements occurred over 1971 to 1985 and its rise in unemployment was particularly large ... from 1980 to 1985. In Norway, major increases in entitlement occurred in 1975 and 1984 (although also before and after this date) and unemployment rose exceptionally around 1989. Entitlements rose in Sweden in 1974 and in Switzerland in 1977 with major rises in unemployment in 1991 in both cases."

Taken on its own, I think that we would all agree that this is absurd. In fact, one could write a very similar paragraph relating performance in the Eurovision Song Contest to unemployment. Sweden won in 1991 (as well as 1974) and Switzerland in 1988, so this alternative hypothesis would seem better able to explain the rise in unemployment in 1991 in both countries. The clincher would seem to be that Norway notoriously got 'null points' on more than one occasion and has a particularly low level of unemployment.

The point I want to make is not that there is no good evidence of a link between unemployment and benefits (the paper does an excellent job in summarizing the respectable studies which do show evidence of such a link), but that we have very strong *a priori* beliefs from theory that there should be such a link, beliefs that are so strong that we can read paragraphs like the one above and not think anything is amiss. We need to be honest about the fact that theory plays a disturbingly large part in informing discussion about the impact of unemployment insurance on the labour market.

The third point I want to make is that it is not just the level of benefits that matters for its impact on the labour market: that the structure of benefits may be just as important. For example, in the UK, the level of unemployment insurance is not generous relative to pay in a full-time job. But most of the jobs on offer to the unemployed are part-time and not attractive to someone on benefits so there is a serious incentive problem. The policy of reducing benefits so that there is an incentive for workers to take part-time jobs would make benefits unacceptably low. A better option would seem to be to provide the unemployed with better incentives to take one (or two) part-time jobs while not losing all benefits. In this case, improving incentives is more than a simple question of raising or lowering benefits as many of the theoretical models imply.

But all of these points should not distract us from the point that this paper performs a valuable service in providing an accessible overview of the voluminous literature on the subject.

Scand. J. Economics 100(1), 146–152, 1998

Comment on B. Holmlund, "Unemployment Insurance in Theory and Practice"

Steinar Strøm

University of Oslo, N-0317 Oslo, Norway

Introduction

Holmlund's exposition on the development of the economic analysis of unemployment insurance is well balanced. It covers theoretical contributions — micro and macro — as well as analyses of the welfare and political economy aspects of unemployment insurance.

Empirical evidence is also reported. As mentioned by Holmlund, this evidence is rather mixed and does not give any unambiguous support to the conclusions derived in theory say, between unemployment insurance and unemployment duration. My comments go a little further than Holmlund's exposition in emphasizing the mixed character of the empirical evidence.

Predictions from Job-Search Theory and Empirical Evidence

Prediction no. 1. A worker's reservation wage declines as he approaches the date at which benefits expire and hence the exit rate (out of unemployment and into jobs) increases over the spell of unemployment. The empirical and testable implication is that there should be a positive duration dependence among insured unemployed individuals.

Hernæs and Strøm (1996) have estimated duration models on observations of all those who registered as unemployed in Norway in October 1990 (28,090 individuals). After correcting for unobserved (gamma-distributed) heterogeneity and applying joblessness as a criteria for unemployment, they found: i) a positive duration dependence among those entitled to unemployment benefits (63% of the sample), and ii) a negative duration dependence among those not entitled to unemployment benefits.

Thus, these results indicate that the probability of exiting unemployment as unemployment is prolonged is increasing among insured individuals, while the contrary is the case among the non-insured. These results are in accordance with the prediction from job-search theory. However, although the estimated coefficients are as predicted, the difference in magnitude is rather small.

Prediction no. 2. The higher the replacement rate is, the longer unemployment will last. Pencavel (1994) claims that the differences in the level and extent of unemployment benefits are of major significance in explaining why Britain has a higher unemployment rate and longer average duration than the US.

This view is in line with the results reported in Layard *et al.* (1991). They found that the elasticity of the probability of leaving unemployment with respect to unemployment benefits is numerically on the order of 0.4–0.5 or even higher (0.9).

Arulampalam and Stewart (1995) point out, however, that this evidence is based on data for the 1970s and earlier. They argue that the benefit elasticity may be numerically lower when aggregate unemployment is higher. Accordingly, they found that for those who entered unemployment in 1978, the (numerical value of the) elasticity is estimated to 0.4, but for those who entered unemployment in 1987 it is estimated to 0.1.

Hernæs and Strøm (1996) find that, for those who entered unemployment in October 1990, with entitlement to unemployment benefits and without any unemployment periods prior to October 1990, the numerical value of the elasticity is 0.17. For those with unemployment periods prior to October 1990, the elasticity is not significantly different from zero.

Thus the impact of unemployment benefits on unemployment duration may be rather weak and it will depend on the business cycle and on unemployment history that may vary substantially across workers.

Prediction no. 3. The effect of benefits on the probability of leaving unemployment increases when unemployed workers come close to benefits exhaustion. Arulampalam and Stewart (1995) found some empirical support for this hypothesis.

Prediction no. 4. An increase in the benefit level makes it more attractive — among those not entitled to unemployment benefits — to accept jobs and thus become entitled to unemployment benefits in the future ("the entitlement effect"). To my knowledge, this hypothesis has not yet been tested in empirical work. The possible reason may be that it is hard to find suitable data.

Predictions from General Equilibrium Models

The problem in macroeconomic theory is that no consensus has been reached with respect to what is the best modelling framework. Holmlund presents a variety of approaches, including a union bargaining model. The most important assumptions in this model are: i) wage levels are determined in Nash-bargains between unions and firms; ii) firms determine employment; iii) workers' utility depends on consumption only, where consumption is derived from labor income (Holmlund allows for risk-averse workers and proportional taxation of labor income); iv) the alternatives to work in a firm are either work in other firms or unemployment.

Holmlund derives the following relationship for the (long-run) equilibrium unemployment rate

$$u = \frac{k\sigma}{1-\rho^\sigma} \tag{1}$$

where u is the unemployment rate, $\sigma \leq 1$ reflects risk aversion, ρ is the replacement ratio and k is a constant. With risk-neutral workers ($\sigma = 1$), (1) becomes

$$u = \frac{k}{1-\rho} \tag{2}$$

and

$$\frac{\partial \ln u}{\partial \ln \rho} = \frac{\rho}{1-\rho} = 1 \quad \text{(when } \rho = 0.5\text{).} \tag{3}$$

Thus, (3) implies that if the replacement rate is raised from, say, 0.5 to 0.6 when the unemployment rate is 0.10, the unemployment rate increases to 0.12. This long-run impact of a higher replacement ratio on aggregate unemployment is rather strong, and much stronger than what microeconometric results suggest. As pointed out by Holmlund, the microeconometric models are partial equilibrium models. These partial equilibrium results do not necessarily carry over to the general equilibrium, in particular since wage formation is endogenous in general equilibrium models and may be strongly affected by the generosity of unemployment insurance.

However, some of the assumptions introduced by Holmlund are rather restrictive and we need to consider the consequenses when these restrictions are relaxed. Thus, we extend the model to account for progressivity in taxation, and utility derived from both consumption and leisure. We also introduce labor market programs.

Progressivity in taxation. If consumption is equal to disposable income, we can specify consumption as

$$C = \delta(wh)^d, \qquad 0 \leq d \leq 1 \tag{4}$$

where C is consumption, w is the wage rate, h is hours of work, and d is the degree of progressivity in taxation. If $d = 1$, then we have a proportional tax system. δ is a positive constant.

Utility derived from consumption and leisure. If T is total time, the utility function can be specified as

$$v = C^\sigma e^{\beta_0(T-h)^{\beta_1}} \tag{5}$$

where $(T-h)$ is leisure and the parameters β_0 and β_1 are both assumed to be positive. The risk-aversion parameter, σ, is the same as above.

Labor market programs. Labor market programs are available at an exogenously given rate q. Thus, open unemployment will be equal to $(u-q)$ where total unemployment is given by u. Both u and q are positive and less than, or equal to, 1. The alternatives to working in a specific firm at the wage rate w are: i) working in another firm at the general wage-level $\bar{w}$, with probability $(1-u)$; ii) being unemployed and receiving a benefit per hour of $\rho\bar{w}$, with probability $(u-q)$; and iii) being selected for a labor market program and receiving a compensation per hour of $a\bar{w}$, with probability q.

The expected utility thus is

$$v_E = (1-u)\bar{v} + (u-q)v_b + qv_a \tag{6}$$

where (when $\sigma = 1$)

$$\bar{v} = \delta(\bar{w}h)^d\, e^{\beta_0(T-h)^{\beta_1}}$$

$$v_b = \delta(\rho\bar{w}h)^d\, e^{\beta_0 T^{\beta_1}}$$

$$v_a = \delta(a\bar{w}h)^d\, e^{\beta_0(T-h)^{\beta_1}}.$$

It is assumed that hours of work are equal across all jobs and labor market programs and that they are exogenously set by firms and/or the government. Inserting and rearranging give us

$$v_E = \delta(\bar{w}h)^d\, e^{\beta_0(T-h)^{\beta_1}} f(u) \tag{7}$$

where

$$f(u) = (1-u) + (u-q)\rho^d g(h) + qa^d \tag{8}$$

and where

$$g(h) = e^{\beta_0[T^{\beta_1} - (T-h)^{\beta_1}]} \geq 1.$$

The firms are assumed to face a given demand curve in the product market. The unions' preferences are represented by

$$V = N(v - v_E) \tag{9}$$

where N is the number of employed workers, and v_E is the expected utility derived from being in other labor market states than in the firm considered.

The firm maximizes its profit

$$\Pi = R - whN \tag{10}$$

subject to the production function

$$x = ehN \tag{11}$$

and the revenue function

$$R = x^{1/m}, \qquad m \geq 1 \tag{12}$$

For expository reasons the productivity level, e, is set equal to 1. The parameter m is the common mark-up on marginal cost across sectors in long-run equilibrium, where $m = 1$ in the case of perfect competition. m depends on the demand elasticity. The Nash solution of a bargain between union and firm is the outcome of maximizing the Nash product

$$\mathcal{L} = V \cdot \Pi$$

and can be shown to yield the following solution for the wage rate w:

$$w = \frac{(1+m)}{2} f(u)\bar{w}. \tag{13}$$

In the long-run equilibrium the wage rate in the representative firm will equal the wage rate in all other firms. We then get (when $\sigma = 1$), using (8):

$$u = \frac{q[a^d - \rho^d g(h)] + [1 - 2/(1+m)]}{1 - \rho^d g(h)} \tag{14}$$

which is the unemployment rate in long-run equilibrium.

In order to secure voluntary participation in labor market programs, the compensation rate when on a labor market program must be higher than the compensation received as unemployed:

$$a > bg(h).$$

Being unemployed gives a gain in utility in addition to the unemployment benefit ratio since it involves more leisure. Accordingly, we must have that

$$1 > \rho^d g(h)$$

if jobs are to be preferred to unemployment.

Holmlund's model is just a special case of the extended version above. To see this, assume that $q = 0$, and $d = g(h) = 1$. We then get

$$u = \frac{k}{1-\rho} \tag{15}$$

where

$$k = 1 - \frac{2}{1+m}$$

see (2) above.

In the Swedish case of today, the parameters in the model are approximately $q = 0.05$, $a = 0.9$, $\rho = 0.5$, $d = 0.9$, $m = 1.1$. $g(h)$ can be calibrated to yield the Swedish rate of unemployment (0.12). $g(h)$ then becomes 1.1.

From (14) we then get

$$\frac{\partial \ln u}{\partial \ln \rho} = 0.75,$$

which should be compared to the results based on Holmlund's specification, (3). What happens if one of the parameters is assigned another value? Let, for example, $g(h) = 1$, which will be the case if there is no utility derived from leisure when being unemployed. This yields

$$\frac{\partial \ln u}{\partial \ln \rho} = 0.55.$$

In this case, which is obtained by slightly modifying the model discussed by Holmlund, the replacement ratio elasticity is nearly halved, compared to Holmlund's case (3). If we allow for heterogeneity with respect to unemployment history and entitlement to unemployment benefits, and assume less than full union coverage, the replacement rate elasticity will most likely be further reduced.

Macroeconometric evidence. In macroeconometric analyses it has been common to estimate the linkage between unemployment and unemployment benefits on cross-country time series; see e.g. Layard *et al.* (1991). A critical aspect in this vein of research is that possible policy rules are ignored. In addition to the possibility that unemployment is affected by unemployment benefits, there may be a policy rule at work which relates unemployment benefits to previous unemployment rates. If so, this raises an identification problem: has the generosity of the unemployment benefit system been enlarged by politicians to ease the burdens of the unemployed, or has unemployment risen because of higher unemployment benefits? Thus, the autonomy of the estimated macroeconometric equations can be questioned. Such autonomy is a topic with a lengthy history in the econometric literature; see e.g. Haavelmo (1944), Frisch (1948) and Lucas (1976). It is surprising that this problem has not been considered in macroeconometric analyses of unemployment insurance.

Conclusion

Neither microeconometric nor macroeconometric results give strong and/or convincing support to the predictions of a strong positive relationship between unemployment and unemployment benefits as indicated in microeconomic and macroeconomic theory. Moreover, there is no support for the strong beliefs, held by many economists and others, of a strong positive relationship between unemployment benefits and duration of unemployment.

References

Arulampalam, W. and Stewart, M. B.: The determinants of individual unemployment durations in an era of high unemployment, *Economic Journal 105*, 321–332, 1995.

Frisch, R.: Repercussion studies at Oslo, *American Economic Review 38* (3), 367–372, 1948.

Haavelmo, T.: The probability approach in econometrics, *Econometrica 12* (Suppl.), i–viii, 1–118, 1944.

Hernæs, E. and Strøm S.: Heterogenity and unemployment duration, *Labour 10* (2), 269–296, 1996.

Layard, R., Nickell, S. and Jackman, R.: *Unemployment*, Oxford University Press, Oxford, 1991.

Lucas, Jr., R. E.: Econometric policy evaluation: A critique. In K. Brunner and A. H. Meltzer (eds.): *The Phillips Curve and Labour Markets*, Carnegie-Rochester Conference Series on Public Policy, Vol. 1, *Journal of Monetary Economics* (Suppl.), 19–46, 1976.

Pencavel, J.: British unemployment: Letter from America, *The Economic Journal 104*, 621–632, 1994.

Scand. J. of Economics 100(1), 153–179, 1998

Modelling Policy Issues in a World of Imperfect Competition*

Egbert Dierker

University of Vienna, A-1010 Vienna, Austria

Birgit Grodal

University of Copenhagen, DK-1455 Copenhagen, Denmark

Abstract

General equilibrium theory constitutes a sound basis for the discussion of policy issues if firms do not have market power. However, if firms influence prices strategically, the concept of profits loses its meaning due to the price normalization problem. Hence, it is unclear how to model the behavior of oligopolistic firms. In order to provide a conceptual foundation for the analysis of policy issues in the case of imperfect competition, we discuss ways to formulate the objective of a strategic firm. In particular, we investigate the concept of real wealth maximization that is based on profits as well as on shareholders' aggregate demand.

I. Introduction

In many models of imperfect competition in micro- as well as macro-economics, firms are assumed to maximize profits. However, it is well known from the literature that this objective is ill-defined since firms strategically influence prices; see e.g. Gabszewicz and Vial (1972), H. Dierker and Grodal (1986), Böhm (1994) and Grodal (1996). In these models the (absolute) price level remains undetermined. As a consequence, profits are normalized by using one of the commodities as numéraire or, more generally, by applying some price normalization rule. But different price normalizations entail profit functions which are in general not related to each other by monotone transformations. Hence, maximization of profits in different normalizations amounts to firms pursuing different objectives. In particular, firms have different "optimal" actions. Of course, different response functions give rise to different Nash equilibria. Clearly, if price normalization rules and hence firms' objectives fail to

---

* We are grateful to Hildegard Dierker for valuable discussions. We would also like to thank Nina Maderner for helpful comments on an earlier version of this paper. E. Dierker and B. Grodal wish to thank the Department of Economics, University of Copenhagen, and the Department of Economics, University of Vienna, respectively, for their hospitality.

be based on economic considerations, only ill-founded, arbitrary conclusions can be drawn from such models.[1]

Since imperfectly competitive markets abound in the real world, policy questions are often analyzed in models with strategically acting firms. However, the lack of a sound economic foundation for firms' payoffs described above often leads to confusion if such models are used as a basis for policy recommendations. To illustrate this point, Ginsburgh (1994) constructs an example in which a simple change of the numéraire, and hence the firms' objectives, entails a larger welfare gain than the abolition of all taxes. Similarly, Kletzer and Srinivasan (1994) propose a model representative of those used in the trade literature with oligopoly, e.g. Eaton and Grossman (1986), and show that the effects of policy changes on welfare and resource allocation are sensitive to the choice of a numéraire in these models. Ginsburgh's example and the analysis by Kletzer and Srinivasan clearly demonstrate that in models of imperfect competition, there is a need for a concept of profit maximization that rests on firm grounds. Without such a concept, policy conclusions can lead us astray.

The price normalization problem does not arise, of course, if perfect competition prevails and, moreover, markets are complete, since one system of relative prices is then taken as given and suffices to compare the values of all different production plans. Furthermore, in this case profit maximization serves the needs of the shareholders, since it maximizes their wealth at the given price system. Note that a similar link between the objective of a firm and the desires of its shareholders is missing in the above-mentioned literature on imperfect competition.

Moreover, consider the following standard model of imperfect competition. There is precisely one composite good which is used as numéraire. Firms maximize profits measured in terms of this numéraire. This particu-

---

[1] It is often argued that money should be used to express profits. However, if money is interpreted as a good or service playing the role of a numéraire, the difficulties associated with the price normalization problem are bound to appear. Thus, some kind of fiat money is needed. However, in an economy with fiat money, there remains the problem that shareholders' real wealth is not only affected by the amount of money available, but also by its purchasing power. Clearly, the purchasing power of money depends, in general, on the prices resulting from the strategic interaction of firms. Hence, it must be assumed that shareholders' income is separated from their expenditures, as is common in partial equilibrium models of Industrial Organization, see below; also, see the island model of Hart (1985). Of course, such an assumption can be introduced as well in the absence of fiat money! Thus, there is no reason to introduce fiat money and to face the resulting difficulties. More importantly, the assumption that shareholders do not spend any income on the market on which their firm operates should be avoided, since it imposes limitations on the validity of policy conclusions. In this paper we show that the assumption becomes superfluous, if an appropriate conceptual framework is adopted.

lar objective is justified only if shareholders are not allowed to consume or own any good other than the numéraire.

The situation is summarized in Kreps' (1990, p. 727) textbook on microeconomic theory: "The notion that shareholders necessarily want managers of their firms to maximize profits is a long-standing component of the folklore of capitalism. But it is incorrect folklore, if the firm has market power and if its shareholders participate, even indirectly, in the markets that are affected by the operations of the firm."

A similar remark applies to the issue of shareholder value maximization that has recently provoked a heated political debate. Kreps also points out (p. 729): "The usual pat answer to all these questions is: The firm should maximize the value of current shareholder's equity. There is a large literature concerning why this might be so (and what it means), which comes down to: This makes sense (once again) only if the firm is a price-taker, where being a price taker in this context involves many more conditions."

Both quotations emphasize the need for a general, clear formulation of the objectives of firms with market power. Obviously, if the characteristics of the shareholders could be aggregated into a social preference ordering, that ordering could be used to define the objective of the firm. However, such an aggregation of shareholders' characteristics cannot be achieved unless extremely restrictive conditions are imposed, which should, in general, be avoided. Therefore, the notion of profit maximization has to be given a meaning of its own, which should not depend on some artifacts of the underlying model such as the way in which prices are normalized. Such a foundation is necessary, since policy conclusions should only rely on the underlying economic circumstances.

To resolve the price normalization problem arising in models of imperfect competition, we address the following questions:

(i)   Assume that the objective function of a firm is to maximize profits using a specific normalization rule. For instance, suppose that prices are normalized such that the value of a certain commodity bundle x always equals 1. Can a profit maximum then be characterized in terms of *relative* prices only, without recourse to the specific normalization rule?

(ii) How can an objective of a firm that is based on profits and shareholders' desires be defined?

To answer the first question, we consider a specific example in Section II. As we shall see, it is indeed possible to characterize a maximum of the objective function given in this example such that it becomes invariant with respect to price normalizations. In particular, the first-order condition for a maximum of the objective function depends on relative prices only. However, to obtain the invariance, it is essential to take shareholders' expenditures explicitly into account. In other words, to overcome the price normalization problem, both aspects have to be considered simultaneously, the way profits are earned by the firm and the way they are spent by the shareholders on the market.

We present another example in Section II, where the notion of consumer surplus is unambiguously defined. In this case it is natural to consider strategies maximizing shareholders' social surplus, i.e., the sum of the producer surplus (profits) and shareholders' consumer surplus. Again, this problem turns out to be well-defined independently of any price normalization due to the following fact. The concept of social surplus combines the generation of profits (producer surplus) with their final use for consumption (shareholders' consumer surplus). In this way, a clear link is established between the objective of a firm and the desires of its shareholders. Such a link is missing if the firm only takes its producer surplus into account.

Maximization of shareholders' social surplus amounts to the selection of a particular (shareholder constrained) Pareto optimum. Since the shareholders of a firm differ with respect to their characteristics, i.e., preferences and initial endowments of commodities and shares, there will, in general, be many different strategies that are Pareto efficient for them. However, surplus maximization abstracts from these distributional aspects by definition and is thus linked to the more powerful concept of potential Pareto efficiency.

We argue that potential Pareto efficiency leads to severe existence problems due to an intrinsic nonconvexity of the aggregate budget set of the shareholders. The use of potential Pareto improvements entails the same difficulty that was pointed out by Guesnerie (1975) in his seminal article on the nonoptimality of marginal cost pricing equilibria in the case of a nonconvex technology. Hence, we are led to use a definition that requires less than potential Pareto efficiency.

We say that shareholders' real wealth at σ_1 can be increased by σ_2, i.e., $\sigma_1 \prec_{rw} \sigma_2$, iff the shareholders can afford to buy more units of their aggregate demand at σ_1 if the firm chooses σ_2 rather than σ_1. A real wealth maximizing strategy is a strategy such that shareholders' real wealth cannot be increased. Observe that real wealth maximization does not take the aggregate preferred set of the shareholders into account and requires only knowledge of the composition of shareholders' aggregate demand.

Real wealth maximization generalizes the concept of profit maximization in the case of perfect competition. The same holds true in the special case of imperfect competition, where there is a numéraire commodity that is the only good consumed and owned by the shareholders and that is used to measure profits. In general, however, the composition of shareholders' demand varies with the relative price system in the economy and, therefore, with the firm's strategy. In the case of real wealth maximization, the firm uses the aggregate demand of its shareholders as a reference bundle when it evaluates another strategy, and it seeks to maximize the number of units of this bundle.

In Section II we also explore different ways to overcome the price normalization problem in the theory of imperfect competition. This leads us to define real wealth increases, i.e., the relation $\prec_{rw}$, in Section III.[2] Imposing a certain monotonicity assumption on shareholders' aggregate demand, we show that the relation $\prec_{rw}$ is acyclic. As a consequence, real wealth maxima exist. Moreover, we analyze the first-order condition for a real wealth maximum and show the existence of a real wealth maximizing strategy provided the profit function is concave. We also show how our approach can be applied if shareholders decide on the strategy of their firm by majority voting.

II. How Can the Price Normalization Problem be Overcome?

Example 1: Invariant Formulation of Profit Maximization

To investigate the price normalization problem in a particularly simple setting, consider an economy with two commodities and one firm. Good 0, which is referred to as the numéraire, is used by the monopolistic firm to produce good 1 with constant returns to scale. In order to produce one unit of good 1, the monopolist uses c units of the numéraire. Consumers are denoted by $i = 1, \ldots, m$. Consumer i has the initial endowment $e^i = (e_0^i, e_1^i)$ and owns the share $\vartheta^i \geq 0$, where $\sum_{i=1}^{m} \vartheta^i = 1$. The group of shareholders is denoted $\mathscr{A} = \{i | \vartheta^i > 0\}$. The strategy P of the firm is the decision to offer one unit of the product in exchange for P units of the numéraire.

We assume that all consumers are initially endowed with the numéraire commodity only, i.e. $e_1^i = 0$, and that the shareholders of the firm do not consume its product. Then the natural objective of the firm is the maximization of profits in terms of the numéraire. Thus, if the firm chooses the strategy P and prices take the form $(1, P)$, the firm maximizes profits[3]

$$\Pi_N(P) = (P - c) \sum_{i \notin \mathscr{A}} d_1^i((1, P), e_0^i), \tag{1}$$

where d_1^i stands for consumer i's demand for good 1.

Now let prices be $\alpha(P)(1, P)$, $\alpha > 0$, instead of $(1, P)$. Since individual demand functions d^i are homogeneous of degree 0, nominal profits with

---

[2] The resulting concept of a real wealth maximum is identical to the one introduced in E. Dierker and Grodal (1996).

[3] We use the subscript N when good 0 is used as numéraire, whereas we use the subscript Δ when prices are normalized such that they lie on the unit simplex.

respect to prices $\alpha(P)(1, P)$ are $\alpha(P)\Pi_N(P)$. Observe that the amount of the numéraire that can be bought out of these profits is, as before, $\Pi_N(P)$. As we shall see, the objective of the firm can also be expressed in terms of the prices $\alpha(P)(1, P)$. However, maximizing $\Pi_N(P)$ and maximizing $\alpha(P)\Pi_N(P)$ are obviously two different goals and accordingly yield different first-order conditions. Let us, for example, normalize prices such that they add up to 1. Then $\alpha(P) = 1/(1+P)$ and the price system corresponding to P is $(1/(1+P), P/(1+P))$. Profits in this normalization are

$$\Pi_\Delta(P) = (P/(1+P) - c/(1+P)) \sum_{i \notin \mathcal{A}} d_1^i((1/(1+P), P/(1+P)), 1/(1+P)e_0^i),$$

i.e.,

$$\Pi_\Delta(P) = (1/(1+P)) \Pi_N(P).$$

The first-order condition for maximizing $\Pi_\Delta(P)$ is $(d/dP)\Pi_\Delta(P) = 0$ or, equivalently, $(d/dP)\Pi_N(P) = (1/(1+P))\Pi_N(P)$.

We now show how the profit function corresponding to prices $(1/(1+P), P/(1+P))$ rather than to $(1, P)$ can be used to maximize the original objective $\Pi_N(P)$ of the firm. Let $\hat{\Pi}_N = \Pi_N(\hat{P})$ be the maximal profit if the N-normalization is used, and let $\hat{Z}_0$ denote the amount of good 0 share-holders buy out of profits at $\hat{P}$, i.e. $\hat{Z}_0 = \hat{\Pi}_N$. As noted above, if prices are normalized such that they add up to 1, then the strategy $\hat{P}$ still allows shareholders to buy exactly $\hat{Z}_0$ units of good 0.

Since profits $\Pi_N(P)$ at any strategy P do not exceed $\hat{\Pi}_N$, we have

$$\Pi_N(P) - (1, P)\hat{Z} = \Pi_N(P) - \hat{Z}_0 \leq 0 \tag{2}$$

with equality for $P = \hat{P}$. Hence $\Pi_N(P) - \hat{\Pi}_N$ reaches its maximum at $\hat{P}$. Obviously, maximizing $\Pi_N(P) - \hat{\Pi}_N$ amounts to maximizing $\Pi_N(P)$. Observe, however, that (2) becomes independent of any normalization due to the seemingly superfluous constant $\hat{\Pi}_N = (1, P)(\hat{Z}_0, 0)$. Indeed, if the Δ-normalization is used, the value of shareholders' net trade $(\hat{Z}_0, 0)$ turns into $[1/(1+P)]Z_0$ and (2) becomes

$$\Pi_\Delta(P) - \frac{1}{1+P}\hat{Z}_0 = \frac{1}{1+P}(\Pi_N(P) - \hat{Z}_0) \leq 0, \tag{3}$$

which is obviously equivalent to the original version (2).

Note that the optimal value $\hat{\Pi}_N$ must be explicitly taken into account for the following reason. Consider any differentiable function $f(P)$ such that $(d/dP)f(\hat{P}) = 0$ and let τ be a transformation with nonvanishing derivative. In our interpretation $f(P)$ and $\tau(P)f(P)$ stand for the same objective of the firm. Hence both functions should satisfy the first-order condition for optimization at identical points, i.e., at $\hat{P}$ in our example. Obviously $(d/dP)(\tau(P)f(P)) = f(P)(d/dP)\tau(P) + \tau(P)(d/dP)f(P)$ vanishes at $\hat{P}$ if and only if f does. Hence the objective function has to be adjusted such that its optimal value becomes zero. This is achieved in (2) by putting $f(P) = \Pi_N(P) - \hat{\Pi}_N$.

Of course, the first-order condition $(d/dP)\Pi_N(\hat{P}) = 0$ for (2) and that for (3), i.e.,

$$\frac{d}{dP} \Pi_\Delta(\hat{P}) = -\frac{1}{(1+\hat{P})^2} \hat{Z}_0,$$

must be equivalent. This fact also results from an elementary calculation, but needs to be explained in economic terms. Recall that $\hat{Z}_0 = \hat{\Pi}_N$ is the amount of good 0 shareholders can buy out of profits at the optimal strategy $\hat{P}$. The expenditure which shareholders incur when buying $\hat{Z}_0$ at prices $(1/(1+P), P/(1+P))$ is $[1/(1+P)]\hat{Z}_0$. The first-order condition

$$\frac{d}{dP} \Pi_\Delta(\hat{P}) = -\frac{1}{(1+\hat{P})^2} \hat{Z}_0$$

corresponding to (3) states that the increase $(d/dP)\Pi_\Delta(\hat{P})$ in profits has to equal the change in expenditures $(d/dP)(1/(1+P)\hat{Z}_0)$ on the optimal net trade. If this condition were violated, the firm could choose a strategy P enabling its shareholders to buy more than $\hat{Z}_0$. Note that there is, by definition, no change in expenditures if we use the N-normalization, since the value $1 \cdot \hat{Z}_0$ of $\hat{Z}_0$ is independent of the strategy P. However, in the Δ-normalization, the value $[1/(1+P)]\hat{Z}_0$ of $\hat{Z}_0$ is affected by the choice of P. To summarize, the traditional statement that marginal profits have to vanish at the optimum is quite misleading. An economically meaningful (as well as mathematically invariant) way to express the first-order condition for an optimal decision of the firm is the following: *marginal profits must equal total marginal expenditures of all shareholders on their optimal net trades.*

It is important to distinguish between objective functions and normalized profit functions. If a firm has a well-defined goal such as to enable its shareholders to buy as many units of a given consumption bundle $x \geq 0$, $x_0 \neq 0$, as possible out of profits, then we can proceed as in the above example, where x equals $(1, 0)$. If $\hat{\lambda}x$ is optimal in the sense that $\hat{\lambda}x$ is feasible and shareholders' net trade can never exceed $\hat{Z} = \hat{\lambda}x$, then the firm's objective function can be written in the N-normalization as $\Pi_N(P) - (1, P)(\hat{\lambda}x)$. In the α-normalization, i.e., for prices of the form $\alpha(P)(1, P)$, the objective of the firm is to maximize the function

$$\Pi_\alpha(P) - \alpha(P)(1, P)(\hat{\lambda}x) = \alpha(P)[\Pi_N(P) - (1, P)(\hat{\lambda}x)] \leq 0. \tag{4}$$

Thus, the goal of the firm can be expressed using an arbitrary normalization rule α.

Although (2), (3), or (4) describe profit maximization in a way that is obviously independent of any price normalization, these formulas suffer from the drawback that the value of shareholders' optimal aggregate net trade enters explicitly. Thus we may ask whether the firm has to anticipate shareholders' optimal net trade. The answer turns out to be *no* due to the following fact. Consider (4) and recall that it is based on the assumption that the firm measures profits in terms a given consumption bundle x. We claim that nothing more than the bundle x needs to be known to the firm. Indeed, consider the first-order condition for profit maximization. It can obviously be rephrased in elasticity terms. But the elasticity of the value $\alpha(P)(1, P)(\hat{\lambda}x)$ of $\hat{\lambda}x$ equals the elasticity of the value of x so that the maximal number $\hat{\lambda}$ of units of x drops out. Thus, the first-order condition for an optimal strategy of the firm obtains as: *the elasticity of the profit function must equal the elasticity of the value of the bundle x.*

Observe that shareholders are no longer explicitly mentioned here, but it is implicitly assumed, of course, that the underlying bundle x reflects their interests appropriately. The method just used to reformulate the first-order condition can also be used to reformulate (4) itself. The value of profits in terms of the bundle x is $\Pi_N(P)/((1, P)x)$ and the firm's goal is to maximize this expression. Of course, if the α-normalization is used, the numerator and the denominator of $\Pi_N(P)/((1, P)x)$ are both multiplied with $\alpha(P)$.

Our answer to the question of whether the firm needs to anticipate shareholders' optimal net trade $\hat{Z}$ hinges on the existence of some bundle x used to measure profits. For instance, if we would have taken $\alpha(P) = 1/\sqrt{1 + P^2}$ and the firm would have been assumed, for some unknown reason, to maximize $\alpha(P)\Pi_N(P)$, then $\hat{Z}$ could not have been eliminated in that way.[4] Thus, rational expectations about shareholders' optimal aggregate net trade will, in general, be needed if firms are supposed to maximize profits computed with respect to price normalization rules such as the Euclidean norm, which is unrelated to shareholders' demand or taste.[5] However, as explained above, this issue does not arise if profits have an economic interpretation based on consumption bundles.

---

[4] Even in this case it is not true that the information needed to write down profits invariantly is qualitatively different from the informational requirements in the theory of perfect competition. If competition is perfect, consumers have to anticipate their wealth correctly in order to specify their consumption plans. Since wealth depends on profits, Walras' law is based on the assumption that shareholders have rational expectations about profits. If we assume that a firm maximizes an arbitrary function $\alpha(P)\Pi_N(P)$, then we need expectations to be reciprocal: A firm must form expectations about the aggregate net trade of its shareholders and shareholders must form expectations about the profits they will receive.

[5] Except perhaps for their preference for Euclidean geometry.

There are, of course, several ways in which attempts can be made to incorporate shareholders' wishes. If the firm were omniscient, then it could base its decision on the individual characteristics of every shareholder. But economic theory provides no tool to exploit such detailed knowledge, since preferences cannot, in general, be aggregated. The rest of this section is devoted to a discussion of concepts related to utility theory and Hicksian demand. We argue that even if informational constraints could be ignored, utility theory would not provide a generally satisfactory solution.

Before taking utility considerations into account, we would like to point out that the choice of a strategy P does, in general, affect shareholders in two ways. If the firm's decision has an influence on the relative prices of the goods initially owned by its shareholders, then their wealth changes not only because profits do, but also because their initial wealth depends on P. Thus, in the above discussion of the maximization of Π_N, we have assumed that shareholders do not have initial endowments of commodity 1. In this case profit maximization and wealth maximization coincide, provided prices are of the form $(1, P)$. In general, shareholders are, of course, interested in the purchasing power of their total wealth and not only in that part stemming from profits.

Example 2: Surplus Maximization

Now we give up the assumption that shareholders consume the numéraire only. Also, we no longer assume that all shareholders have identical utility functions. However, we retain the assumption that they initially only own good 0. We consider the following situation. Each shareholder $i \in \mathcal{A}$ has a quasilinear utility function $u^i(x_0^i, x_1^i) = x_0^i + f^i(x_1^i)$. Thus, every value u^i gives rise to a Hicksian demand function $h_1^i(\cdot, \cdot, u^i)$ for the product that is independent of the particular utility level chosen (as long as the corresponding indifference curve does not hit the vertical axis $x_0 = 0$). Moreover, the Walrasian demand $d_1^i(\cdot, \cdot, W^i)$ for the product is independent of the wealth W^i (as long as W^i is not too small) and coincides with the Hicksian demand. Due to quasilinearity we are thus in a setting in which the Marshallian notion of demand $x_1^i(p)$ for the product is unambiguously defined. Let $x_0^i(p)$ denote the demand for the numéraire after the profits have been distributed to the shareholders according to their shares (cf. the next subsection). In Figure 1 we have drawn the Scitovsky indifference curves, which indicate the boundaries of shareholders aggregate preferred sets or, equivalently, the sum of their Hicksian demands, for three different utility profiles corresponding to three different strategies of the firm. The important property here is that Scitovsky indifference curves do not intersect each other because of quasilinearity.

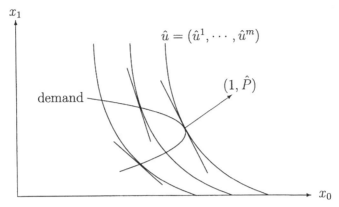

Fig. 1. Nonintersecting Scitovsky curves and feasible budget lines

The surplus of consumer i at price system $(1, P)$ is given by $\int_P^\infty x_1^i(p)\mathrm{d}p$ and the consumers' surplus aggregated over all shareholders equals $\sum_{i \in \mathscr{A}} \int_P^\infty x_1^i(p)\,\mathrm{d}p$.[6] Assume now that the monopolist's objective is to maximize the *social surplus of all shareholders*, that is to say the sum of profits and the aggregate consumers' surplus of its shareholders. More precisely, the firm's goal is to

$$\text{maximize } \Pi_N(P) + \sum_{i \in \mathscr{A}} \int_P^\infty x_1^i(p)\,\mathrm{d}p. \tag{5}$$

Observe that the firm is not supposed to maximize profits $\Pi_N(P)$! Since shareholders also consume the product, the firm has to take the consumers' surplus of its shareholders into account. We now show that the surplus maximization problem *(5)* is indeed independent of how prices are normalized. Recall that strategies are relative prices and let $\hat{P}$ be the surplus maximizing strategy of the firm and $\hat{u}^i$ the corresponding utility level of shareholder i. Denoting i's expenditure function by E^i the budget identity of i obtains as $e_0 + \vartheta^i \Pi_N(\hat{P}) = E^i((1, \hat{P}), \hat{u}^i)$. Since $\hat{P}$ maximizes shareholders' social surplus, we have $\Pi_N(P) + \sum_{i \in \mathscr{A}} \int_P^\infty x_1^i(p)\,\mathrm{d}p \le \Pi_N(\hat{P}) + \sum_{i \in \mathscr{A}} \int_{\hat{P}}^\infty x_1^i(p)\,\mathrm{d}p$ for any other strategy P. This inequality together with the budget identities yields

$$\Pi_N(P) + \sum_{i \in \mathscr{A}} e_0^i \le \sum_{i \in \mathscr{A}} \left(E^i((1, \hat{P}), \hat{u}^i) + \int_{\hat{P}}^P x_1^i(p)\,\mathrm{d}p \right) = \sum_{i \in \mathscr{A}} E^i((1, P), \hat{u}^i),$$

since $E^i((1, \hat{P}), \hat{u}^i) - E^i((1, P), \hat{u}^i) = -\int_{\hat{P}}^P x_1^i(p)\,\mathrm{d}p$. Obviously, using the function $\alpha(P)$ to normalize prices (cf. example 1), the last inequality is

---

[6] In Figure 1 the preferences are such that $x_1^i(p) = 0$ for large enough p. Hence the integral $\int_{\hat{P}}^\infty x_1^i(p)\,\mathrm{d}p$ exists.

equivalent to $\Pi_\alpha(P) + \alpha(P)\sum_{i \in \mathscr{A}} e_0^i \leq \alpha(P)\sum_{i \in \mathscr{A}} E^i((1, P), \hat{u}^i)$. Hence $\hat{P}$ solves the surplus maximization problem (5) if and only if

$$\Pi_\alpha(P) + \alpha(P)\sum_{i \in \mathscr{A}} e_0^i \leq \sum_{i \in I} E^i(\alpha(P)(1, P), \hat{u}^i)$$

with equality for $P = \hat{P}$. This shows that, as in the previous subsection, the objective of the firm is independent of any price normalization, if shareholders' expenditures are taken into account. Of course, in the particular case where the demand $x_1^i(p)$ for the product is identically equal to 0, there is no consumers' surplus and surplus maximization reduces to the maximization of profits $\Pi_N(P)$. Note that, in this particular case, the argument just given reduces to the one presented in the context of (2), (3) and (4) in example 1.

The first-order condition for shareholders' social surplus maximization is

$$\frac{d}{dP} W_N(P) = \frac{d}{dP} \Pi_N(P) = \sum_{i \in \mathscr{A}} x_1^i(P), \tag{6}$$

where $W_N(P)$ equals shareholders' aggregate wealth. Since the $(x_1^i)_{i \in \mathscr{A}}$ are Hicksian demand functions by assumption, the absolute value $\sum_{i \in \mathscr{A}} x_1^i(P)$ of marginal consumers' surplus aggregated over the group of shareholders must equal the derivative of the shareholders' aggregate expenditure function by Shephard's lemma. The first-order condition requires this expression to be equal to marginal profits. If profits and expenditures are computed with respect to the same price normalization rule, then it is irrelevant which rule has been selected. Thus, the first-order condition, which is stated above in terms of the numéraire, depends on relative prices only and can be expressed as saying that marginal profits must equal the total marginal expenditures of all shareholders on their net trades at the surplus maximum.

Expressed in terms of surplus maximization, *the confusion caused by the price normalization problem in imperfect competition can be attributed to the lack of distinction between shareholders' social surplus and producer's surplus (profits)*. On the other hand, we have made the extremely strong assumption that utility is quasilinear. Below we discuss the question of whether one can successfully generalize the notion of shareholders' social surplus beyond the case of quasilinear utility functions or a representative owner (cf. the subsection on potential Pareto improvements).

The computation involving the expenditure function (following formula (5) above) can be summarized as saying that shareholders' aggregate wealth, i.e., the value of their aggregate initial endowment together with profits, never exceeds the expenditures needed to guarantee each shareholder i his utility level $\hat{u}^i$ reached at strategy $\hat{P}$. That is to say, for no strategy P does the corresponding aggregate budget set of all shareholders intersect the interior of the aggregate preferred set corresponding to the utility profile $(\hat{u}^i)_{i \in \mathscr{A}}$. By contrast, the considerations in the preceding subsection amount to the following statement: for no strategy P does shareholders' aggregate demand $\sum_{i \in \mathscr{A}} e^i + \hat{Z}$ lie in the interior of the corresponding aggregate budget set of all shareholders. It is obvious that both statements depend on relative prices only since budget sets do. Clearly, the first property of the strategy $\hat{P}$ is strictly stronger than the second one (assuming local nonsatiation). However, the first statement also requires more information, since Scitovsky indifference curves must be known. If quasilinearity of all utility functions is assumed, then, of course, all aggregate preferred sets are known if one is. Although we hesitate to make such a demanding assumption, we want to explore its consequences below in the context of potential Pareto improvements.

Basic Model and Notation

We maintain the simple setting consisting of an economy with two commodities and one monopolist producing good 1 using good 0, the numéraire, as input. The analysis is essentially the same as that of a price setting firm in an oligopolistic market, if the prices of its competitors are thought of as fixed. For simplicity, we also retain the assumption that the firm has fixed unit costs c. The strategy P of the firm is the decision to offer one unit of the product in exchange for P units of the numéraire. Profits obtained at prices $(1, P)$ are denoted $\Pi_N(P)$. As before, the firm has a large set $\mathscr{A}$ of shareholders taking their budget sets as given. Assume for simplicity that the consumption set of every consumer equals $\mathbb{R}^2_+$ and that no consumer has initial endowments of the product, i.e., consumer i has the initial endowment $e^i = (e^i_0, 0)$ where $e^i_0 > 0$. All consumers have demand functions $d^i, i \in \{1, \ldots, m\}$, which are continuous, homogeneous of degree 0, and satisfy the budget identity $(1, P)d^i((1, P), W^i) = W^i$. The wealth of consumer i at prices $(1, P)$ is described by the continuous function $W^i_N(P) = (1, P)e^i + \vartheta^i \Pi_N(P)$. We assume throughout that profit expectations are correct, i.e., the demand based on consumers' wealth expectations generates precisely the expected profits, if the monopolist satisfies the demand for its product. That is to say, profits fulfill the equation $\Pi_N(P) = Pd_1(P) - cd_1(P)$, where $d_1(P) = \sum_{i=1}^m d^i_1((1, P), \vartheta^i \Pi_N(P) + (1, P)e^i)$ is the total demand of all consumers for good 1 if prices are $(1, P)$ and profits are $\Pi_N(P)$. Let $D^i(P) = d^i((1, P), \vartheta^i \Pi_N(P) + (1, P)e^i)$ denote shareholder i's demand corresponding to strategy P. Shareholders' aggregate demand is $D(P) = \sum_{i \in \mathscr{A}} D^i(P)$. We assume that $\Pi_N(P)$ attains its maximum in the interior of the set of strategies $\mathscr{P} = [c, \bar{c}]$ and that $W_N(P) \geq 0$ for all $P \in \mathscr{P}$.

In order to define the objective of the firm we look at the aggregate budget set of all shareholders and their aggregate demand. Each strategy P defines a budget line

$$BL(P) = \{(x_0, x_1) \in \mathbb{R}^2 | x_0 + Px_1 = W_N(P)\} \tag{7}$$

and a corresponding budget set

$$AB(P) = \{(x_0, x_1) \in \mathbb{R}^2_+ | (1, P)(x_0, x_1) \leq W_N(P)\} \tag{8}$$

for the group of shareholders. Their aggregate budget set becomes $AB = \bigcup_{P \in \mathscr{P}} AB(P)$. Note that AB is compact, since $\mathscr{P}$ is compact and W_N is continuous. Since $\mathbb{R}^2_+ \backslash AB(P)$ is convex for every P and $AB = \mathbb{R}^2_+ \backslash \bigcap_{P \in \mathscr{P}} (\mathbb{R}^2_+ \backslash AB(P))$, the aggregate budget set is the complement of a convex set. The northeast boundary of AB is called the *aggregate budget curve ABC*. More precisely,

$$ABC = \{x \in AB | \nexists z \gg 0 \text{ such that } x + z \in AB\}. \tag{9}$$

Potential Pareto Improvements

In the surplus maximization problem (5) the firm abstracts from all distributional aspects related to profits $\Pi_N(P)$. Furthermore, the firm also ignores the distribution of consumer surplus among its shareholders, i.e., it ignores differences between shareholders' willingnesses to pay for the firm's product. It is instructive to consider the (degenerate) special case in which total surplus reaches its maximum in the whole interval $[P_1, P_2]$. Let $P_1 < P < P_2$. Then the consumer surplus of shareholder i decreases by the amount $x_1^i(P)$ if P is marginally raised. On the other hand, i obtains the share ϑ^i of marginal profits $\Pi_N'(P)$. Since we have not made any assumption on the relationship between the size of individual shares and the size of individual demand, shareholder i will in general not be indifferent with respect to the marginal change in the firm's strategy P. Some shareholders gain and others lose, but for the firm itself each strategy $P \in [P_1, P_2]$ is equally optimal. Surplus maximizing strategies can be characterized in terms of potential Pareto improvements.

Definition. *Strategy P' is potentially Pareto dominated by strategy P, in symbols $P' \prec_{pp} P$, iff shareholders' aggregate demand $D(P)$ can be redistributed among them such that the resulting allocation Pareto dominates $(D^i(P'))_{i \in \mathscr{A}}$.*[7]

---

[7] Of course, potential Pareto domination can be expressed in a weak or strict way. The difference is of minor importance for our purposes and will mostly be ignored. Whenever arguments become formal, we use strong Pareto dominance.

Note that we are in a second-best framework here, since shareholders must use the market to obtain the product. The fact that all $P \in [P_1, P_2]$ considered above are equally optimal from the viewpoint of the firm can be restated as saying that these strategies are "potentially Pareto equivalent". Indeed, the shareholders' aggregate preferred set $\hat{U}$ is the same for all $P \in [P_1, P_2]$. For each such P, the set $\hat{U}$ is supported by the budget line $BL(P)$ at $\sum_{i \in \mathscr{A}} x^i(P)$. Consider any $\hat{P} \in [P_1, P_2]$ and the corresponding utility profile $(\hat{u}^i)_{i \in \mathscr{A}}$. Then, at any other strategy $P \in [P_1, P_2]$, profits $\Pi_N(P)$ are just sufficient to allow each $i \in \mathscr{A}$ to reach the utility level $\hat{u}^i$ after a suitable redistribution of wealth. Expressed in physical terms, the aggregate demand $x(P)$ can be redistributed in such a way that every $i \in \mathscr{A}$ receives the same utility as at strategy $\hat{P}$. In this sense shareholders' total real wealth is constant on $[P_1, P_2]$.

Observe that, by the argument above, some shareholder i with a demand $x_1^i(P)$ for the product that is large (small) in comparison to i's share in profits $\Pi_N(P)$ will object to a price increase (decrease) even if $P < P_1$ ($P_2 < P$). Thus there are many strategies outside $[P_1, P_2]$ which are Pareto optimal for the shareholders. The strength of the notion of potential Pareto improvements is the following: by disregarding distributional aspects, the firm is able to select among the possibly very large set of strategies which are Pareto optimal for its shareholders. In the setting of example 2 the surplus maximizing strategies are precisely those among the Pareto optimal ones at which no potential Pareto improvement is possible.

We would like to remark that the following stronger property holds at a surplus maximizing strategy $\hat{P}$. Even if the firm could, given some arbitrary strategy P, simply take any bundle x on the budget line $BL(P) = \{x \mid (1, P)x = W_N(P)\}$ and distribute x freely among its shareholders, it would be impossible for the firm to Pareto improve on the allocation $(x^i(P))_{i \in \mathscr{A}}$.

More formally, let P be an arbitrary strategy and $(x^i(P))_{i \in \mathscr{A}}$ be the optimal consumption plans of the shareholders corresponding to P. Put $U^i(P) = \{x^i \mid x^i \succ_i x^i(P)\}$ and $U(P) = \sum_{i \in \mathscr{A}} U^i(P)$. Due to the quasilinearity of the utility functions we have $U(P') \subseteq U(P'')$ or $U(P'') \subseteq U(P')$ for any pair (P', P''). For any surplus maximizing strategy $\hat{P}$ and for any arbitrary strategy P, the budget line $BL(P)$ never intersects $U(\hat{P})$.[8] In particular,

---

[8] In the preceding paragraph we gave an interpretation of the fact that $BL(P) \cap U(\hat{P}) = \emptyset$. This explanation should not be taken too verbally. If shareholders' demand $D(P)$ would be replaced by x, then shareholders' contribution to total profits $\Pi_N(P)$ would change. This would lead to an inconsistency, because the budget equation underlying $BL(P)$ would then be violated.

shareholders' aggregate demand $x(P)$ does not lie in $U(\hat{P})$ for any P, i.e., $\hat{P}$ is a $\prec_{pp}$-maximal strategy.

In the quasilinear case the firm has a representative owner and surplus maximization coincides with the maximization of the representative owner's utility.[9] Clearly, individual shareholders differ in their opinion from each other and also from their representative, who, by definition, abstracts from distributional issues. If the representative owner's utility is maximized at strategy $\hat{P}$, profits could, in principle, be redistributed so as to induce all shareholders to agree to $\hat{P}$, since $U(\hat{P}) \subseteq U(P)$ for all P.

Thus, we are led to examine the question of whether the notion of potential Pareto improvements can be used to extend the definition of a surplus maximum beyond the case treated in example 2.[10] In general multi-owner models, the aggregate (strictly) preferred sets $U(P)$ corresponding to the profile of shareholders' demand at P are often incomparable. However, maximal elements can still be described as follows. The goal of the firm is to find a strategy $\hat{P}$ such that no point in $U(\hat{P})$ can be reached by choice of another strategy P. This statement can have the following two interpretations:

i) there is no strategy P such that $D(\hat{P}) \prec_{pp} D(P)$;
ii) no budget line $BL(P)$ intersects $U(\hat{P})$.

We argue below that both versions lead to the same serious nonexistence problem.

As noted above models of imperfect competition contain an intrinsic nonconvexity that is absent in the case of perfect competition. That is to say, the aggregate budget set AB is the complement of a convex set and hence nonconvex. This fact leads to problems similar to those discussed in Guesnerie (1975).

We now analyze the intimately related questions of the existence and multiplicity of potential Pareto optima. An illustration is given in Figure 2, where several budget lines corresponding to different strategies of the firm under consideration and one indifference curve $\hat{I}$ are drawn. Assume for the moment that the firm is owned by a representative consumer, whose optimal utility level is obtained on $\hat{I}$. Observe that the indifference curve I is simultaneously tangent to the aggregate budget set at two different points, denoted A and B. There is a third point C on the boundary of the

---

[9] Notice that the owner as a consumer is supposed to take prices and wealth as given. In this respect the representative owner behaves differently from an individual owner, who ought to be aware of the fact that the amount he pays in excess of unit costs is fully returned to him as part of the firm's profits.

[10] We abstain from using one of the popular surplus concepts, such as the compensating or the equivalent variation, because of the confusion they have created for many years. The main point stated below can be understood more clearly without mentioning any of them.

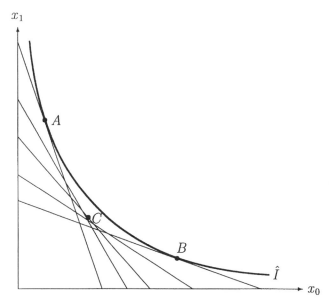

Fig. 2. A and *B* are both optimal

aggregate budget set which is tangent to some indifference curve. However, the utility of the representative owner at C is lower than at A or B and we have only drawn the highest indifference curve $\hat{I}$ the representative owner can reach.

Obviously Figure 2 presents a special, degenerate case. However, as long as we assume that the firm has a representative owner, the simultaneous tangency at two different points is irrelevant for the existence of potential Pareto optima. Therefore, let us now give up the assumption that a representative owner exists and let us slightly perturb the preferences of the shareholders as depicted in Figure 3.[11] As in the case of Figure 2 it is assumed that shareholders' aggregate demand is in the interior of their aggregate budget set for all strategies P except for those leading to A, B and C. In both Figures 2 and 3, the point C is potentially Pareto dominated by A as well as by B. Thus, the only candidates for a potential Pareto optimum in Figure 3 are A or B. Note, however, that the perturbation of the preferences yields a situation in which A and B cease to be potential Pareto optima. This is due to the fact that the Scitovsky indifference curve touching the boundary of the aggregate budget set at A cuts into the aggregate budget set near B and vice versa. Therefore, we have $A \prec_{\mathrm{pp}} B$ and

---

[11] In Figure 3 we focus on the essentials by leaving out all but the three budget lines corresponding to the points A, B and C.

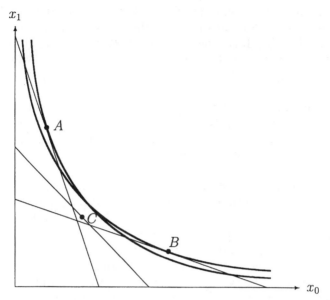

Fig. 3. $A \prec_{pp} B$ and $B \prec_{pp} A$

$B \prec_{pp} A$. Moreover, the situation is robust with respect to small perturbations. Thus, it is too demanding to ask for potential Pareto optimality. There need not be any $\hat{P}$ satisfying condition i) above. Clearly, ii) is even harder to fulfill. This non-existence result shows that it does not help to make the heroic assumption that the firm knows the characteristics of its shareholders. The situation illustrated in Figure 3, in which the optimality of both A and B has been destroyed, is, of course, reminiscent of the one pointed out in Guesnerie's seminal paper (1975) in the context of marginal cost pricing in the case of a nonconvex technology.

Observe that potential Pareto improvements can still be used locally even if the firm has no knowledge of shareholders' preferences. Assume that shareholders' marginal wealth at P exceeds shareholders' marginal expenditures. In this case the first-order condition (6) is violated at P. Then the shareholders' aggregate demand curve $(D(P))_{P \in \mathscr{P}}$ intersects their budget line $BL(P)$ and hence the Scitovsky indifference curve corresponding to strategy P transversely at $D(P)$. Therefore, there is $\Delta P > 0$ such that $D(P) \prec_{pp} D(P + \Delta P)$. This fact has been illustrated in Figure 1.[12]

This fact will be exploited as follows. In Section III we define a binary relation $\prec_{rw}$ on strategies that captures increases of shareholders' real

---

[12] Look at the intermediate Scitovsky curve, change the price vector in the direction of $(1, \hat{P})$ so that shareholders' demand $D(P)$ moves towards the optimum.

wealth and does not require the firm to know shareholders' preferences. The relation $\prec_{rw}$ allows us to replace the last sentence of the preceding paragraph by the following statement: there is $\Delta P > 0$ such that $P \prec_{rw} P + \Delta P$. Moreover, the relation $\prec_{rw}$ is consistent with potential Pareto efficiency in the sense that $\prec_{rw}$ never rejects a potential Pareto optimum.

The objective of the firm is to choose a strategy $\hat{P}$ that maximizes shareholders' real wealth, i.e., a $\hat{P}$ that is $\prec_{rw}$-maximal. The advantage of this definition is that it does not require the firm to know more than the composition of shareholders' aggregate demand $D(P)$. Moreover, we shall show the existence of real wealth maximizing strategies.

The crucial difference between the maximization of shareholders' real wealth and potential Pareto optimality discussed above lies in the fact that the former is not expressed in terms of utility theory. Therefore, it is much closer in spirit to the concept of profit maximization as used in both the theory of perfect competition and the partial equilibrium literature on imperfect competition. Moreover, the informational requirements are much weaker than they would be, if the concept were grounded on potential Pareto improvements. Of course, there is a cost associated with this advantage, since dispensing with utility entails the following consequences. Suppose that the firm has a representative owner and consider the situation depicted in Figure 2. Then all three points, A, B and C, do satisfy the definition proposed in Section III. In other words, a utility maximum does necessarily maximize shareholders' real wealth. However, a point such as C does as well, since a comparison between, say, A and C is impossible without taking indifference curves into account. Observe, though, that this does not mean that real wealth maximization focuses on first-order conditions. Rather, it is a global concept as is reflected by the fact that no budget line passes above any of the three points A, B and C.

III. Real Wealth Maximization

Definition of a Real Wealth Maximum

We now define the objective of the monopolist without making *a priori* assumptions on the demand behavior of the shareholders. Consider two different strategies P_1, P_2 and the corresponding aggregate budget sets $AB(P_1)$ and $AB(P_2)$. First, we look at the extreme case in which $AB(P_1)$ is contained in the interior (relative to $\mathbb{R}^2_+$) of $AB(P_2)$. Let $x \geq 0$, $x \neq 0$, be any commodity bundle. Clearly, the number of units of the bundle x which the shareholders can afford, if the firm chooses the strategy P_2, is strictly larger than the number of units they can buy if the firm chooses the strategy P_1. Whatever bundle the firm uses to evaluate the real wealth of the shareholders, their aggregate wealth is larger at P_2 than at P_1. We assume that a real wealth maximizing firm choosing between P_1 and P_2 will select P_2, although it may very well be that some shareholders, due to distributional effects, prefer the strategy P_1 to P_2.

In general, the budget sets corresponding to different strategies of the firm will not be ordered by inclusion. Hence the ordering of the budget sets according to number of units of the bundle x which can be bought out of shareholders' aggregate wealth depends on the choice of reference bundle x. However, when the firm considers a strategy P, it is assumed to know the composition $x(P) = D(P)/\|D(P)\|$ of shareholders' aggregate demand at P. In our opinion it is natural for the firm to use $x(P)$ as the reference bundle. Thus we are led to introduce the following definition.

Definition. *Shareholders' real wealth at $P_1 \in \mathscr{P}$ can be increased by the strategy $P_2 \in \mathscr{P}$, in symbols $P_1 \prec_{rw} P_2$, if for some $\lambda > 1$, $\lambda D(P_1) \in BL(P_2)$. That is to say, $P_1 \prec_{rw} P_2$ iff $(1, P_2)D(P_1) < W_N(P_2)$.*

Without assumptions on shareholders' aggregate demand function D, the relation $\prec_{rw}$ need not be asymmetric, i.e., it can be that $P_1 \prec_{rw} P_2$ and $P_2 \prec_{rw} P_1$. Therefore, we impose a monotonicity property on D. It states that the aggregate demand for the numéraire commodity increases, if the relative price P of the product increases and profits after the price change suffice to allow shareholders to buy the original bundle $D(P)$.

Definition. *Shareholders' aggregate demand D_0 for the numéraire is monotone in the interval $[P_a, P_b] \subset \mathscr{P}$, if $D_0(P_1) < D_0(P_2)$ holds for all $P_1, P_2 \in [P_a, P_b]$ such that $P_1 < P_2$ and $(1, P_2)D(P_1) < W_N(P_2)$.*

Remark 1. *If shareholders' aggregate demand D_0 for the numéraire is monotone on $[P_a, P_b] \in \mathscr{P}$, then the relation $\prec_{rw}$ is asymmetric on $[P_a, P_b]$.*

The objective of the firm is to choose a strategy $\hat{P}$ such that there is no other strategy P which allows the group of shareholders to buy more units of the bundle $D(\hat{P})$. Formally:

Definition. *The strategy $\hat{P} \in \mathscr{P}$ maximizes shareholders' real wealth if there does not exist a strategy $P \in \mathscr{P}$ and $\lambda > 1$ such that $\lambda D(\hat{P}) \in AB(P)$, that is $D(\hat{P}) \in ABC$.*

Clearly, the set of real wealth maximizing strategies is identical to the set of maximal elements for the relation $\prec_{rw}$.

Existence of Real Wealth Maximizing Strategies

The proof of the existence of a real wealth maximizing strategy is based on the fact that the relation $\prec_{rw}$ is acyclic if the above monotonicity assumption applies and D satisfies the budget identity. To show acyclicity we first prove the following lemma.

Lemma. *Assume that D_0 is monotone on $[P_a, P_b] \subset \mathcal{P}$. Let $P_1, P_2, P_3 \in [P_a, P_b]$ satisfy $P_1 \prec_{rw} P_2$, $P_2 \prec_{rw} P_3$, $P_1 \not\prec_{rw} P_3$, and $P_1 < P_2$. Then $P_2 < P_3$.*

Proof: Let P_1, P_2, P_3 fulfill the assumptions of the lemma. First, notice that $P_2 \prec_{rw} P_3$ and $P_1 \not\prec_{rw} P_3$ amount to $(1, P_3)D(P_2) < W_N(P_3) \leq (1, P_3)D(P_1)$. Hence

$$(1, P_3)D(P_2) < (1, P_3)D(P_1). \tag{10}$$

Also, $P_1 \prec_{rw} P_2$, i.e.,

$$-(1, P_2)D(P_2) < -(1, P_2)D(P_1). \tag{11}$$

Adding the two inequalities (10) and (11) we obtain

$$(P_3 - P_2)D_1(P_2) < (P_3 - P_2)D_1(P_1). \tag{12}$$

Clearly, the conclusion $P_2 < P_3$ follows if we know that $D_1(P_2) < D_1(P_1)$. In order to see this, observe that $P_1 < P_2$ and $P_1 \prec_{rw} P_2$ imply that $D_0(P_1) < D_0(P_2)$, since D_0 is monotone. Therefore, the inequality $D_1(P_2) < D_1(P_1)$ follows from (10).   □

Theorem 1. *Assume D_0 is monotone on $[P_a, P_b] \subset \mathcal{P}$. Then $\prec_{rw}$ is acyclic on $[P_a, P_b]$.*

Proof: Assume by way of contradiction that $\prec_{rw}$ has a cycle in $[P_a, P_b]$. Then there exists a cycle $(P_i)_{i=1}^n$ of minimal length, where P_1 is chosen such that $P_1 \leq P_k$ for all $k \in \{1, \ldots, n\}$. Clearly, $P_i \neq P_k$ for all $i \neq k$. For ease of notation put $P_{n+1} = P_1$. Thus,

$$P_1 \prec_{rw} P_2 \prec_{rw} \cdots \prec_{rw} P_n \prec_{rw} P_{n+1} = P_1 \quad \text{and} \quad P_1 < P_2. \tag{13}$$

We claim that, for all $k \in \{1, \ldots, n-1\}$,

$$P_k < P_{k+1} \text{ implies } P_{k+1} < P_{k+2}. \tag{14}$$

Assume $P_k < P_{k+1}$. We have $P_k \prec_{rw} P_{k+1} \prec_{rw} P_{k+2}$. Since $(P_i)_{i=1}^n$ has minimal length, we know that $P_k \not\prec_{rw} P_{k+2}$. Hence the above lemma applies and we obtain $P_{k+1} < P_{k+2}$.

Since $P_1 < P_2$, we have $P_2 < P_3$ by (14). Successively applying (14) we get

$$P_1 < P_2 < \ldots < P_n < P_{n+1} = P_1, \tag{15}$$

a contradiction. Thus, $\prec_{rw}$ is acyclic on $[P_a, P_b]$.   □

Proposition 1. *Assume D_0 is monotone on $[P_a, P_b] \in \mathcal{P}$. Then there exists a maximal element $\tilde{P}$ for the restriction of $\prec_{rw}$ to $[P_a, P_b]$.*

Proof: Recall that D, and hence, by the budget identity, W_N are continuous. Let $P \in [P_a, P_b]$ and let $\mathcal{O}(P) = \{P' \in [P_a, P_b] | P' \prec_{rw} P\} = \{P' \in [P_a, P_b] | (1,$

$P)D(P') < W_N(P)\}$. Note that $\mathcal{O}(P)$ is open relative to $[P_a, P_b]$. Assume that the restriction of $\prec_{rw}$ to $[P_a, P_b]$ does not have a maximal element. Then we obtain $\bigcup_{\{P \in [P_a, P_b]\}} \mathcal{O}(P) = [P_a, P_b]$. As the interval $[P_a, P_b]$ is compact, there exists a finite set $\{P_1, .., P_n\}$ such that $\bigcup_{j=1}^n \mathcal{O}(P_j) = [P_a, P_b]$. Hence, there exists, for each $k \in \{1, .., n\}$, some $k_j \in \{1, .., n\}$ such that $P_k \prec_{rw} P_{k_j}$. Therefore, $(P_i)_{i=1}^n$ contains a cycle for $\prec_{rw}$ in $[P_a, P_b]$, but this contradicts Theorem 1. Thus, there exists a maximal element $\hat{P}$ for the restriction of $\prec_{rw}$ to $[P_a, P_b]$. □

Recall that a strategy $\hat{P}$ maximizes shareholders' real wealth iff $\hat{P}$ is a maximal element for $\prec_{rw}$ on $\mathcal{P}$. Thus, putting $[P_a, P_b] = [c, \bar{c}] = \mathcal{P}$ in Proposition 1 we obtain:

Theorem 2. *Assume that D_0 is monotone on $\mathcal{P}$. Then there exists a strategy $\hat{P}$ maximizing shareholders' real wealth.*

First-Order Condition for Real Wealth Maximization and Concave Profit Functions

In the preceding subsection we have proven the existence of a real wealth maximizing strategy using the acyclicity of $\prec_{rw}$, which was derived from the monotonicity of shareholders' demand D_0 for the numéraire. The purpose of this subsection is to show that the monotonicity assumption can be dispensed with provided that the profit function Π_N is concave. This result is due to the fact that a real wealth maximum is fully characterized by its first-order condition if Π_N is concave.

For convenience, we assume that the strategy $P = c$, at which the firm sets the price of the product equal to unit costs, does not maximize shareholders' real wealth.

Remark 2. *Suppose that, at $P = c$, the aggregate demand $D_1^{ns}(c)$ of the non-shareholders for the product is positive. Then $P = c$ does not maximize shareholders' real wealth.*

Proof: Consider any $\delta > 0$ and $\varepsilon > 0$ such that $D_1^{ns}(P) > \varepsilon$ for all $P < c + \delta$. At any strategy $P < c + \delta$ the firm gets profits $\Pi_N(P) \geq (P - c)\varepsilon + (P - c)D_1(P)$. Now choose $\delta' < \delta$ such that $D_1(P) > D_1(c) - \varepsilon/2$ for all $P < c + \delta'$. Then $\Pi_N(P) \geq (P - c)\varepsilon + (P - c)(D_1(c) - \varepsilon/2) > (P - c)D_1(c)$ for all $P \in]c, c + \delta'[$. Hence we obtain $W_N(P) = \sum_{i \in \mathcal{A}} e_0^i + \Pi_N(P) > (1, c)D(c) + (P - c)D_1(c) = (1, P)D(c)$. Thus $c \prec_{rw} P$ for all $P \in]c, c + \delta'[$. □

Let $\bar{P} \in \mathcal{P}$ be the highest price at which Π_N takes its maximal value. Recall that we have assumed that the upper bound $\bar{c}$ on the strategy space $\mathcal{P}$ is so high that all strategies which maximize Π_N are in the interior of $[c, \bar{c}]$, (see the subsection on the basic model and notation). Thus $\bar{P} < \bar{c}$. It follows that no $P > \bar{P}$ maximizes shareholders' real wealth. Indeed, if $P > \bar{P}$ and

$W_N(P) < W_N(\bar{P})$, the budget set $AB(P)$ is strictly contained in $AB(\bar{P})$. Hence $P \prec_{rw} \bar{P}$. Thus, a strategy $\hat{P}$ maximizing shareholders' real wealth must satisfy $\hat{P} \leq \bar{P} < \bar{c}$.

To summarize, under the above assumptions, $\hat{P}$ must lie in the interior of the strategy space $\mathscr{P} = [c, \bar{c}]$. We now state and interpret the first-order condition for a real wealth maximum.

Proposition 2. *Assume that there exists $P \in \mathscr{P}$ such that $c \prec_{rw} P$. If Π_N is C^1 and $\hat{P} \in \mathscr{P}$ maximizes shareholders' real wealth, then*

$$\Pi_N'(\hat{P}) = \left[\frac{d}{dP}((1, P)(D(\hat{P}) - \sum_{i \in \mathscr{A}} e^i)) \right]_{P = \hat{P}}. \tag{16}$$

Proof: Assume that $\hat{P} \in \mathscr{P}$ maximizes shareholders' real wealth. Then $W_N(P) \leq (1, P)D(\hat{P})$ for all $P \in \mathscr{P}$ with equality for $P = \hat{P}$. We know from above that $\hat{P} \in \text{int}\,\mathscr{P}$. Consequently,

$$W_N'(\hat{P}) = \left[\frac{d}{dP}((1, P)D(\hat{P})) \right]_{P = \hat{P}}.$$

Since $W_N(P) = (1, P) \sum_{i \in \mathscr{A}} e^i + \Pi_N(P)$, the result holds. □

The first-order condition (16) generalizes the ones derived in examples 1 and 2 in Section II. Denote shareholders' aggregate net trade at $\hat{P}$ by $\hat{Z} = D(\hat{P}) - \sum_{i \in \mathscr{A}} e^i$. An infinitesimal price change ΔP has two effects. First, it entails a profit change $\Delta \Pi_N$. Second, ΔP also has a "price effect", which captures the change in the value of shareholders' transactions if the firm infinitesimally varies its strategy. Since shareholders' consumption is optimally adjusted to the price system, the envelope theorem implies that shareholders' change ΔD in consumption does not enter the first-order condition. Thus, the change in shareholders' expenditures is given by

$$\left[\frac{d}{dP}((1, P)\hat{Z}) \right]_{P = \hat{P}} = \hat{Z}_1.$$

If $\hat{\Pi}$ maximizes shareholders' real wealth, then the profit effect and the price effect must be equal, i.e., marginal profits must equal marginal expenditures on shareholders' net trade $\hat{Z}$.

If the price effect vanishes, i.e., if

$$\left[\frac{d}{dP}((1, P)\hat{Z}) \right]_{P = \hat{P}} = 0,$$

the first-order condition reduces to the familiar equation $\Pi_N'(P) = 0$. The polar case with vanishing price effect underlies most of the partial equilibrium literature in industrial organization, where it is (implicitly) assumed that shareholders neither own nor demand the firm's product, that is to say $D_1 - \Sigma_{i \in \mathscr{A}} e_1^i$ is identically equal to 0. In this polar case, real wealth maximization coincides with the maximization of profits expressed in terms of the numéraire (cf. example 1).

In more general settings the price effect does not disappear and must be taken into account. Assume that $\tilde{P}$ is a price at which Π_N takes its maximal value, hence $\Pi_N'(\tilde{P}) = 0$. Furthermore, suppose that

$$\left[\frac{d}{dP}((1, P)(D(\tilde{P}) - \Sigma_{i \in \mathscr{A}} e^i))\right]_{P=\tilde{P}} = D_1(\tilde{P}) - \Sigma_{i \in \mathscr{A}} e_1^i > 0.$$

Thus, the first-order change in profits induced by an infinitesimal change ΔP of $\tilde{P}$ is zero, but the induced first-order change in shareholders' expenditures is $\Delta P(D_1(\tilde{P}) - \Sigma_{i \in \mathscr{A}} e_1^i) \neq 0$. Since profits $\Pi_N(P)$ are maximized at $P = \tilde{P}$, we obtain $W_N(P') = \Pi_N(P') + (1, P') \Sigma_{i \in \mathscr{A}} e^i > (1, P') D(\tilde{P})$ for small $\Delta P < 0$ and $P' = \tilde{P} + \Delta P$. That is to say $\tilde{P} \prec_{\text{rw}} P'$. Thus $\tilde{P}$ does not maximize shareholders' real wealth. The argument shows that if shareholders' aggregate net trade in the firm's product is positive, a real wealth maximizing price must always be below $\tilde{P}$.

We have expressed the first-order condition for real wealth maximization in terms of the N-normalization. This condition can, of course, also be stated in any other normalization. Let prices corresponding to the strategy P be $(\alpha(P), \alpha(P)P)$ where α is a C^1 function (see Section II). Using the definition of profits in the basic model above, we obtain that profits $\Pi_\alpha(P)$ at strategy P are given by $\Pi_\alpha(P) = \alpha(P)\Pi_N(P)$.

Hence, in terms of the α-normalization, the first-order condition reads as

$$\Pi_\alpha'(\hat{P}) = \left[\frac{d}{dP}((\alpha(P), \alpha(P)P)(D(\hat{P}) - \sum_{i \in \mathscr{A}} e^i))\right]_{P=\hat{P}}, \qquad (17)$$

which again states that marginal profits equal marginal expenditures on the aggregate net trade $D(\hat{P}) - \Sigma_{i \in \mathscr{A}} e^i$.

In the model of this paper the strategy space $\mathscr{P}$ is 1-dimensional, since the firm produces one good only. In the multiproduct case the right- and left-hand sides of (16) or (17) must be read as total derivatives. In other models of imperfect competition, for instance in models of Cournot competition, a strategy σ_j of firm j influences the price system that j's shareholders face as consumers indirectly. It is assumed that each strategy profile (σ_j, σ_{-j}) gives rise to a relative price system, e.g. through a market clearing condition. In such a setting, prices as well as profits and wealth become, for any strategy combination σ_{-j} of the competitors of firm j, functions of the strategy σ_j. The concept of real wealth maximization then is: the strategy $\hat{\sigma}_j$ maximizes shareholders' real wealth given σ_{-j}, if there is no other strategy σ_j such that $W(\sigma_j, \sigma_{-j})$ exceeds the value

$p(\sigma_j, \sigma_{-j})D(p(\hat{\sigma}_j, \sigma_{-j}))$ of shareholders' aggregate demand. The first-order condition for a real wealth maximum then states that the profit change induced by an infinitesimal change $\Delta\sigma$ of the strategy $\hat{\sigma}$ equals the change in shareholders' expenditures entailed by $\Delta\sigma$.

Theorem 3. *Assume Π_N is concave and C^1. Then:*

a) *If $\hat{P}$ satisfies the first-order condition for shareholders' real wealth maximization, then $\hat{P}$ maximizes shareholders' real wealth.*
b) *Let $[P_a, P_b] \subset \mathscr{P}$ be such that $W'_N(P_a) > D_1(P_a)$ and $W'_N(P_b) < D_1(P_b)$. Then there exists a strategy $\hat{P} \in]P_a, P_b[$ maximizing shareholders' real wealth.*
c) *There exists a strategy $\hat{P} \in \mathscr{P}$ that maximizes shareholders' real wealth.*

Proof: To show *a*), define the linear function $h: \mathscr{P} \to \mathbb{R}$ by $h(P) = (1, P)D(\hat{P})$. By the budget identity $h(\hat{P}) = W_N(\hat{P})$. The first-order condition states that $h'(\hat{P}) = D_1(\hat{P}) = W'_N(\hat{P})$. As W_N is concave, $W_N(P) \le W_N(\hat{P}) + (P - \hat{P})W'_N(\hat{P})$ for all $P \in \mathscr{P}$. Hence $W_N(P) \le h(\hat{P}) + (P - \hat{P})h'(\hat{P}) = (1, P)D(\hat{P})$ for all P, that is to say $\hat{P}$ maximizes shareholders' real wealth.

Let P_a and P_b satisfy the assumptions of part *b*). Since W'_N is continuous, there exists $\hat{P} \in]P_a, P_b[$ such that $W'_N(\hat{P}) = D_1(\hat{P})$. Hence, by part *a*), $\hat{P}$ maximizes shareholders' real wealth.

To prove *c*), notice first that the argument given in the proof of *a*) shows that the strategy $\hat{P} = c$ is a real wealth maximizing strategy if $W'_N(c) \le D_1(c)$. Therefore, assume that $W'_N(c) > D_1(c)$. Observe that the definition of $\bar{c}$ together with the concavity of W_N imply that $W'_N(\bar{c}) < 0$ and hence $W'_N(\bar{c}) < D_1(\bar{c})$. Consequently the existence of a real wealth maximizing strategy $\hat{P} \in]c, \bar{c}[$ follows from statement *b*).   □

Theorem 2 relies on the monotonicity of shareholders' demand D_0 for the numéraire. If Π_N is concave on $\mathscr{P}$, then, according to Theorem 3, the existence of a strategy which maximizes shareholders' real wealth obtains without imposing any monotonicity assumptions on shareholders' demand. A geometric explanation of the fact that monotonicity is irrelevant in the setting of Theorem 3 is given in E. Dierker and Grodal (1996).

The concavity assumption underlying Theorem 3 is formulated with respect to the numéraire normalization and it may be asked to what extent the concavity of the profit function is invariant with respect to price normalizations. Indeed, it can be shown that Π_N is concave if and only if Π_x is concave for any commodity bundle $x \in \mathbb{R}_2 \backslash \{0\}$, where Π_x denotes profits measured in terms of units of x as a function of the output price (also taken in the x-normalization); see E. Dierker and Grodal (1996, Proposition 2). Thus the concavity of profits as a function of the output price is invariant as long as one does not leave the framework of economically meaningful normalizations.

Median Voter

In this paper the objective of the firm has been based on shareholders' aggregate budget sets and their aggregate demand. Hence we have disregarded distributional effects (cf. Section II). However, we could, in principle, also have taken the view that shareholders decide about the strategy of their firm by majority voting. In this case the median shareholder would play a central role.

To illustrate this point, consider the following simple modification of example 1 in Section II. We retain the assumption that shareholders consume the numéraire commodity only, but assume now that shareholders have initial endowments of the firm's product, i.e., $e_1^i > 0$ for $i \in \mathscr{A}$.[13] In this way we can easily model the distributional conflict between different shareholders. Since the shareholders sell their initial endowments e_1^i of good 1, the firm faces the residual demand. If the firm sets the price P, shareholder i obtains the consumption bundle $(\vartheta^i \Pi_N(P) + P e_1^i + e_0^i, 0)$. Consequently, shareholder i's preference relation $\succcurlyeq_i$ on the strategies of the firm is given by the indirect utility function $\vartheta^i \Pi_N(P) + P e_1^i + e_0^i = W_N^i(P)$. Notice that, for any pair $P' < P$, we have $P \succcurlyeq_i P'$ if and only if

$$\frac{\Pi_N(P') - \Pi_N(P)}{P - P'} \leq \frac{e_1^i}{\vartheta^i}.$$

Now assume that $\# \mathscr{A}$ is odd and that no two shareholders have the same composition of wealth e_1^i / ϑ^i. In this case there exists a median shareholder I in the sense that $\# \{ j | e_1^j / \vartheta^j < e_1^I / \vartheta^I \} = \# \{ j | e_1^j / \vartheta^j > e_1^I / \vartheta^I \}$. Clearly, the strategy $\hat{P}$ is not defeated by majority voting if and only if $\hat{P}$ is a $\succ_I$-maximal strategy, i.e., iff $\vartheta^I \Pi_N(P) + P e_1^I + e_0^I \leq \vartheta^I \Pi_N(\hat{P}) + \hat{P} e_1^I + e_0^I$ for all strategies P.

This last statement can be interpreted as saying that the firm maximizes the real wealth of the median shareholder I in the following sense. There does not exist a strategy P such that $(1, P) D^I(\hat{P}) < W_N^I(P)$. In a more general setting in which the shareholders of the firm consume all commodities, the median shareholder would still play a central role. In general, a strategy is not defeated by majority voting if and only if the strategy maximizes his indirect utility function. However, the existence of a median shareholder requries strong assumptions on the shareholders' character-istics. In an oligopoly model the assumptions are even stronger, since the preferences of the shareholders over strategies of their own firm will in general depend on the strategies of its competitors. These problems are

---

[13] Note that this constitutes a trivial extension of the basic model which does not affect our results in any essential manner.

avoided if the objective is based on shareholders' aggregate demand and wealth.

IV. Conclusion

Many policy issues are most naturally analyzed without making the assumption of perfect competition. Consider, for instance, a model of international trade with two countries and one domestic firm in each country. Important facts about trade flows can only be explained if competition is imperfect. Clearly, a meaningful comparison of different trade policies is impossible if firms' objectives are modelled as profit maximization in some arbitrary price normalization. Economic policy, and hence the objective of each firm, has to be linked to the characteristics of the consumers in its country.

As mentioned in the introduction, extremely restrictive assumptions are required to aggregate the characteristics of the consumers on whose behalf a firm is supposed to act (owners, inhabitants of a country) into a social preference ordering. In this paper we have shown that policy issues can be analyzed without making any such assumption. For that purpose we have extended the notion of profit maximization to the case of imperfect competition in such a way that a firm's objective becomes independent of any price normalization. As a consequence, there is no need for policy conclusions to depend on unrealistic assumptions made only in order to describe the behavior of firms.

To overcome the price normalization problem in models of imperfect competition, we have given an interpretation of profits in real terms using some appropriate, endogeneously determined commodity bundle. Clearly, if a firm acts in the interests of its shareholders, then the bundle used to measure this firm's profits should be linked to its shareholders' demand. In this way both sides of the coin are taken into account, viz. the profits and the expenditures that shareholders incur as consumers. For that reason, we have introduced the real wealth comparison in terms of the relation $\prec_{rw}$ and the maximization of shareholders' real wealth.

We have suggested that a firm maximizes the real wealth of its shareholders, but it should be apparent that it is of minor importance whether one uses the aggregate demand (net trade) of the shareholders as in this paper, a weighted average with shares as weights, the demand of a median shareholder, or some other bundle suggested by the economic context of the particular model at hand. It is imperative, however, that firms' objectives are modelled by purely economic considerations to ensure that policy conclusions drawn from models with strategically acting firms do not lead us astray.

References

Böhm, V.: The foundation of the theory of monopolistic competition revisited. *Journal of Economic Theory 63*, 208–218, 1994.

Dierker, E. and Grodal, B.: The price normalization problem in imperfect competition and the objective of the firm. WP 9616, Department of Economics, University of Vienna, 1996.

Dierker, H. and Grodal, B.: Non existence of Cournot-Walras equilibrium in a general equilibrium model with two oligopolists. In W. Hildenbrand and A. Mas-Colell (eds.), *Contributions to Mathematical Economics*. North-Holland, Amsterdam, 1986.

Eaton, J. and Grossman, G.: Optimal trade and industrial policy under oligopoly. *Quarterly Journal of Economics 101*, 383–406, 1986.

Gabszewicz, J. and Vial, J. P.: Oligopoly "à la Cournot" in a general equilibrium analysis. *Journal of Economic Theory 4*, 381–400, 1972.

Ginsburgh, V. A.: In the Cournot–Walras general equilibrium model, there may be "more to gain" by changing the numéraire than by eliminating imperfections: A two good example. In J. Mercenier and T. N. Srinivasan (eds.), *Applied General Equilibrium and Economic Developments: Present Achievements and Future Trends*. University of Michigan Press, Ann Arbor, 1994.

Grodal, B.: Profit maximization and imperfect competition. In B. Allen (ed.), *Economics in a Changing World 2*. Macmillan, London, 1996.

Guesnerie, R.: Pareto optimality in non-convex economies. *Econometrica 43*, 1–31, 1975.

Hart, O.: Imperfect competition in general equilibrium: An overview of recent work. In K. Arrow and S. Honkapohja (eds.), *Frontiers of Economics*, Basil Blackwell, New York, 1985.

Kletzer, K. and Srinivasan, T. N.: Price normalization and equilibria in general equilibrium models of international trade under imperfect competition. Yale Economic Growth Center DP 710, 1994.

Kreps, D.: *A Course in Microeconomic Theory*. Harvester Wheatsheaf, Hemel Hempstead, 1990.

Scand. J. Economics 100(1), 181–183, 1998

Comment on E. Dierker and B. Grodal, "Modelling Policy Issues in a World of Imperfect Competition"

Heracles M. Polemarchakis*

CORE, Université Catholique de Louvain, B-1348 Louvain-la-Neuve, Belgium

Imperfect Competition in General Equilibrium

Preferences and beliefs are characteristics of individuals; equilibrium is a consistent profile of optimal actions; this is the case in the theory of general competitive equilibrium and, also, in non-cooperative game theory.

Firms are not optimizing agents with the required preferences and beliefs; they act on behalf of individuals — in particular, shareholders; this is also the case for other aggregate bodies, such as governments or labor unions.

The actions of firms are unambiguous when the interests of shareholders coincide; in a competitive economy with a complete system of markets they do: shareholders, who may differ in their preferences, even their beliefs, but who optimize under one, overall budget constraint, agree that the firm should maximize profit. The information necessary for the firm to implement the unanimous choice of the shareholders is available in the market; it consists of the prices of commodites and only that; no information on the characteristics of shareholders is necessary; prices aggregate the diverse preferences and beliefs of shareholders.

The fundamental role played by prices at a competitive equilibrium is not matched by an appropriate specification of the formation of prices; the specification of the model of general competitive equilibrium is agnostic on this issue.

Models of imperfect competition assign the role of setting prices to the optimizing agents in the model, who, thus, perceive their market power: competition is imperfect.

Non-cooperative market games assign price setting to individuals. The specification of markets as non-cooperative games offers the advantage of a complete description of economic activity at or out of equilibrium, which

---

* This text presents results of the Belgian Program on Interuniversity Poles of Attraction initiated by the Belgian State, Prime Minister's Office, Science Policy Programming. The scientific responsibility is assumed by its authors. The Commission of the European Communities provided additional support through the Human Capital and Mobility grant ERBCHRXCT940458.

may be a disadvantage for the modelling of complex and partly understood situations.

Market oriented models of imperfect competition assign the role of setting prices to firms; since firms are not optimizing agents, the criterion that guides their production and pricing decisions must be derived from the preferences and beliefs of individuals. After firms, j, have made their production decisions, y^j, competitive equilibrium prices, p, are formed and individuals, i, exchange commodities and consume, x^i

$$(\ldots, y^j, \ldots) \rightarrow p, (\ldots, x^i, \ldots).$$

Firms decide on their production plans; they know the production decisions of other firms and, to some extent, the dependence of equilibrium prices and allocations of consumption plans on the allocation of production plans — in particular, their production plan.

The specification of a decision criterion for firms encounters three problems:

  i) shareholders may not agree on their preferences over allocations of consumption plans;
  ii) there may be multiple equlibrium allocations of consumption plans associated with an allocation of production plans;
  iii) full knowledge of the equilibrium correspondence, which maps allocations of production plans to competitive equilibrium prices and allocations of consumption plans, is rather demanding.

In order to economize on the informational requirements of the decision criterion, one is led to consider criteria that employ the equilibrium prices of commodities, but not the equilibrium allocations of consumption plans that are associated with an allocation of production plans. The profits or market values of firms, py^j, are a natural candidate; but this leads to a conundrum: competitive equlibrium does not determines the level of prices; if $p(\ldots, y^j, \ldots)$ are competitive equilibrium prices associated with the allocation of production plans $(\ldots, y^j, \ldots)$, so are $k(\ldots, y^j, \ldots) p(\ldots, y^j, \ldots)$, for any $k(\ldots, y^j, \ldots) > 0$. For the profit criterion to be well defined, a normalization rule is necessary.

Arbitrary normalization rules may prevent the existence of equilibria; or, they may implement arbitrary allocations at equilibrium. Alternatively, the normalization rule which uses as price index the index derived from the aggregate consumption of the shareholders of a firm guarantees that no deviation by the firm would allow an increase in the aggregate consumption of its shareholders; see Dierker and Grodal (1996).

Monetary policy determines, possibly, the level of prices; it can be seen as a normalization rule. In perfectly competitive markets, the normalization rule and, hence, monetary policy, do not affect the allocation of resources at equilibrium; when competition is imperfect and firms naxi-mize profits, this is not the case. This raises the question of effective and optimal monetary policy under imperfect competition.

As with imperfectly competitive markets, the decision criteria of firms are not evident when the asset market is incomplete. The difficulties encountered in specifying a decision criterion for firms when the asset market is incomplete parallel the difficulties encountered with imperfect competition. In both cases, normalizations matter. A comparison is of interest and may lead to interesting conclusions on the effectiveness and optimality of monetary policy.

Reference

Dierker, E. and Grodal, B.: The price normalizatin problem in imperfect competition and the objective of the firm. WP 9616, Department of Economics, University of Vienna, 1996.

Scand. J. Economics 100(1), 184–186, 1998

Comment on E. Dierker and B. Grodal, "Modelling Policy Issues in a World of Imperfect Competition"

Seppo Honkapohja
University of Helsinki, FIN-00014 Helsinki, Finland

The paper by Egbert Dierker and Birgit Grodal is a challenging one. As a piece of economic theory it is a nice example of the fine "Copenhagen tradition" in mathematical economics. This tradition has always excelled in detailed and rigorous analysis; this paper makes no exception to these standards.

The twofold goal of the paper is to offer a systematic perspective and propose a resolution to an old challenge in general equilibrium theory. The issue concerns the proper objective of the firm under imperfect competition. As is well known, general equilibrium models with imperfect competition can face fundamental problems, when one moves to more general frameworks than the simple models that have been used in much of the applied and partial equilibrium literature.

In earlier work it has been found that the notion of profit maximization is not well founded for many such models. Only in special cases can it be justified. At a general level the problem concerns both existence and number of equilibria. This issue can have serious consequences, as the set of equilibria can change dramatically in conjunction with the choice of the normalization or, using standard jargon, the choice of the unit of account.

We are accustomed to thinking that the choice of measuring rod is not of great economic significance, but this paper and the related literature suggest that this is not so. Taken literally, it would say, for example, that by itself creation of the Euro could dramatically alter the economic outcome in Europe because of different prices indices and so on.[1] Another example is the choice of invoicing currencies in international trade deals. If the problem in the paper is a real one, then these invoicing choices could have dramatic consequences.

The paper and the associated technical literature do not stop at illustrations of the problem. This is indeed as it should be. Many of us probably

---

[1] I am taking some liberties in this illustration, since the models in the paper are not monetary economies.

venture as a first guess that the choice of the unit of measurement does not, in itself, create major economic changes. In other words, we do not believe in the "unit of account" illusion in steady state or static settings. (Here I am leaving out the more sophisticated dynamic stories based on imperfect information, etc.)

The paper cites some instances where the choice of the numéraire has been shown to have major consequences for the equilibria in some international trade models. Luckily enough, some other models in the applied literature seem to have a consumption and ownership structure fitting the special cases, where profit maximization is justified. For example, in a trade model, consumers in a country may consume only (varieties of) products from other countries and have initially only labor. While the developers and users of these models may be relieved, the progress of applied economics is such that more general applied models will probably be developed in the future. Then the constructive results in the paper may be helpful.

The paper suggests as the resolution that shareholders' wealth maximization is a well-justified objective function for firms operating under imperfect competition. The analysis provides a precise formulation of this and considers its relationship to profit and surplus concepts arguing that e.g. the surplus maximization works as an alternative, but only under very special assumptions.

I have no comments on the technical aspects of the paper. I have two further remarks on the relationship of the resolution to other literature.

First, in the field of corporate taxation, there is a fairly sizeable literature in which, for tax reasons, the interests of the shareholders and the objective of the firm cannot be separated even under perfect competition. If I recall correctly, in this literature shareholders' wealth maximization is commonly used as the objective function for decision-making by firms. This appears to accord with the suggestion put forward by Dierker and Grodal. The potential relationship between this paper and the tax literature should perhaps be explored further in the future.

Second, the paper takes up only briefly the connection of the approach to positive models of corporate decision-making. It is shown how the median voter approach can be consistent with the approach in the paper, provided the median voter exists. There is, to my knowledge, further literature on decision-making procedures in public corporations, for example the one-share-one-vote models. Some of these lead to the median voter approach, but I believe that other models could also be contemplated. Again the relationship to that literature might be explored.

In this paper there is complete information, no uncertainty and no stock market, but generalizing the approach to incomplete markets would be of interest for future work. How much of this approach will survive when there is uncertainty and markets are incomplete? If stock markets open, should firms maximize the wealth of those who are owners before or after stock-trading? These are usually different agents with active stock markets. What about asymmetric information? These extensions may eventually place the approach closer to some much debated topics, such as corporate governance and the market for corporate control.

To conclude, this is a fine but abstract paper. I hope that my discussion shows how this technical piece does, in fact, have some relationships to more applied areas and therefore even to policy.

Scand. J. of Economics 100(1), 187–206, 1998

Pitfalls in the Theory of International Trade Policy: Concertina Reforms of Tariffs, and Subsidies to High-Technology Industries

J. Peter Neary*

University College Dublin, Dublin 4, Ireland

Abstract

This paper explores the links between international trade theory and the practice of trade and industrial policy in open economies, with special attention to three areas where theoretical lessons have been misunderstood in policy debates. I argue that the "concertina rule" for tariff reform justifies reductions in high tariffs but not moves towards uniformity and particularly not *increases* in low tariffs. I show that the basic principles of tariff reform are the same in unilateral, multilateral and customs union contexts. Finally, I suggest that the theory of strategic trade policy does not justify subsidies to high-technology industries.

I. Introduction

Among the many difficulties of economic policy-making is the need to understand the relevant economic theory. In this paper, I want to illustrate the delicate and subtle steps from theory to policy advice by means of some examples from recent work in international trade.

To set the scene, let me start with three policy questions:

1. What kinds of tariff change will raise welfare in a small open economy?
2. Should countries liberalize trade unilaterally or only multilaterally?
3. Should export-oriented high-technology firms be subsidized?

I think it is self-evident that these questions are important and interesting. They arise in many real-world contexts and non-economists care about the answers. By contrast, consider the following three theoretical questions:

* This paper was begun during a stimulating visit to the Chinese University of Hong Kong. For helpful comments I am grateful to participants at seminars in Florence (EUI), Hong Kong and Mainz and especially to Harry Flam and Alasdair Smith, who presented the paper on my behalf at the *SJE*'s symposium on "Public Policy and Economic Theory". Section IV draws heavily on my joint work with Dermot Leahy. This paper forms part of the International Economic Performance Programme of the Centre for Economic Performance at the London School of Economics. An earlier version was circulated as Discussion Paper No. 1740 of the Centre for Economic Policy Research, London.

1. Should models of tariff reform contain a numéraire good?
2. How many *distinct* theorems of tariff reform are there?
3. Do governments have greater commitment power than firms?

Clearly, these are not questions which would ever occur to a non-economist. I suspect that even many economists would find them dry and uninteresting. Their focus on the literature rather than on the real world suggests that only specialists, and pedantic ones at that, are likely to care about the answers.

Yet, as I hope to show, the answers to the three theoretical questions above are intimately bound up with the answers which our current knowledge allows us to offer to the three policy questions. Moreover, I believe that misunderstandings of the theoretical subtleties involved have led to some misleading if not downright wrong policy recommendations. I say "misunderstandings" rather than "errors" because as a profession we are well trained in rooting out analytic mistakes and there are none such in the literature I review below. However, we may be less sensitised to appreciating the qualifications which need to be made in applying theoretical results. I illustrate this in the three sections which follow. Each deals with one of the three policy questions posed above, drawing attention to statements in the literature which are at best redundant and at worst highly questionable.

II. Tariff Reform in a Small Open Economy

The first topic I consider is that of tariff reform in a perfectly competitive economy which cannot influence its external prices. The main results in this area are well-known since the work of Hatta (1977) and others. In the absence of externalities or "non-economic" motives for protection, such a small open economy should not impose tariffs. If it does so, then the first-best policy is to abolish them. If this is not feasible, then there are two types of "piecemeal" change which are guaranteed to raise welfare. One is a uniform radial reduction of tariffs; the other is a "concertina" reform, i.e., a reform which compresses the tariff structure. The concertina reform rule (subject to a well-known qualification about substitutability which I discuss below) is widely advocated in practice and is often used, by the World Bank and others, to justify tariff reforms which reduce the variance of the tariff structure, lowering exceptionally high and raising exceptionally low tariffs.

Exactly how well-founded in theory are these policy recommendations? To examine this I need to review the theory of tariff reform. Before doing so, I want to note three results which have been derived in the literature in models without a numéraire good. These results are correct as stated but

I will argue later that they are not very helpful in policy contexts. So, I label them "POMPs" for "*Po*tentially *M*isleading *P*ropositions"! They are:

POMP 1: [Diewert, Turunen-Red and Woodland (1989)] A tariff change of the form $d\tau = \delta\pi^* - \varepsilon\tau$, $\delta + \varepsilon > 0$, must raise welfare.

Here τ and π^* are vectors of specific tariffs and world prices of *all* goods respectively, while δ and ε are arbitrary scalars. Hence POMP 1 states that welfare will rise if tariffs are increased in proportion to world prices or decreased in proportion to their initial levels.

POMP 2: [Diewert et al. (1989)] There always exists some increase in tariffs which will raise welfare.

This is just a corollary of POMP 1, with ε set equal to zero, so the tariff change takes the form $d\tau = \delta\pi^* > 0$.

POMP 3: [Hatta (1977), Fukushima and Hatta (1989)] An increase in the lowest tariff rate will raise welfare, provided the good in question is a net substitute for all others.

This completes my list of POMPs. In order to substantiate my criticisms of them, I need first to present the basic theory of tariff reform.[1]

Tariff Reform in a Small Open Economy with a Numéraire Good

I consider a small open economy which consumes and produces $n + 1$ goods which it trades at fixed world prices. For the present, I choose one good, indexed by zero, as numéraire and I denote by p and p^* the $n \times 1$ vectors of domestic and world prices of non-numéraire goods respectively. It turns out to be very convenient to summarise the behaviour of consumers and firms in terms of a single function. Following Neary and Schweinberger (1986) I call this the trade expenditure function, defined as the difference between consumer spending and GNP. These in turn are equal to standard expenditure and GNP functions respectively:

$$E(p, u) \equiv e(p, u) - g(p). \tag{1}$$

This function embodies a number of assumptions: consumer spending is the outcome of a single utility-maximising individual's decisions; and all goods and factor markets are perfectly competitive with no barriers to efficient intersectoral factor movements. These assumptions are standard but still heroic. They can be justified as allowing a clear focus on the contribution of trade policy to efficiency. The great convenience of the

---

[1] The exposition which follows is based on Neary (1995). For extensions to economies with quotas and non-traded goods as well as tariffs, see Falvey (1988), Anderson and Neary (1992) and Neary (1995).

trade expenditure function is that its price derivatives (denoted by a subscript "p") equal the economy's compensated net import demand functions:

$$E_p(p,u) = e_p(p,u) - g_p(p) = m(p,u). \tag{2}$$

(This follows because, by Shephard's and Hotelling's Lemmas, e_p and g_p equal the economy's consumption and net output vectors, respectively.) Moreover, these import demand functions are well-behaved: the substitution matrix $S \equiv -E_{pp} = -m_p$ may be assumed to be positive definite.[2] Finally, the utility derivatives of the trade expenditure function equal those of the household expenditure function. Thus, $E_u = e_u$, the marginal cost of utility, which it is convenient to normalise to equal one initially; and $E_{pu}/E_u = x_1$, the vector of Marshallian income derivatives.

We are now ready to summarise the equilibrium of a tariff-distorted small open economy. First, domestic prices equal world prices plus tariffs (by definition there is no tariff on the numéraire good "0", so $p_0 = p_0^* = 1$):

$$p = p^* + t. \tag{3}$$

Second, tariff revenue is redistributed costlessly and so equals net spending by the private sector:

$$E(p,u) = t'm, \tag{4}$$

where a prime denotes the transpose of a vector. Totally differentiating equations (2) to (4) gives the basic expression for the welfare effects of tariff changes in a small open economy:[3]

$$(1 - t'x_1)\, du = -t'S\, dt. \tag{5}$$

The coefficient of welfare change on the left-hand side may reasonably be assumed to be positive: if it was not, then the government could raise welfare by imposing a lump-sum *tax* on the private sector and destroying the proceeds.[4] Hence our concern is with the right-hand side of (5).

---

[2] The full $(n+1) \times (n+1)$ matrix of substitution effects (including those between the numéraire and other goods) is singular and so only positive semi-definite. Provided there is some substitutability between the numéraire good and at least one other good, the $n \times n$ matrix S will be positive definite and it is convenient to assume this henceforward.

[3] To obtain this equation, totally differentiate (4), setting $dp = dt$ from (3) and using (2) to eliminate dm.

[4] The inverse of this coefficient, $(1 - t'x_1)^{-1}$, is known as the "shadow price of foreign exchange", since it measures the welfare effect of a unit transfer of the numéraire good to this country. If the economy were so distorted that this term were negative, it would be unnecessary to seek small tariff changes which would raise welfare. See Smith (1982, 1987) and Neary (1995) for details and references.

The uniform reduction result follows immediately. Since S is positive definite, a tariff change of the form $dt = -\varepsilon t$, $\varepsilon > 0$, must raise welfare. However, the more difficult question is what can be said when tariff changes are not equi-proportionate. This is where the concertina rule comes in.

To derive the concertina reform result, disaggregate the tariff vector into t_1 (a scalar) and t_2; and assume that t_2 is fixed. Partitioning the S matrix conformably into its sub-matrices allows (5) to be written as:

$$(1 - t'x_1)\,du = -(t_1 S_{11} + t'_2 S_{21})\,dt_1 \tag{6}$$

$$= -[t_1 + t'_2 S_{21} S_{11}^{-1}] S_{11}\,dt_1. \tag{7}$$

Now, if we switch from specific tariffs t_i to *ad valorem* tariffs, $r_i = t_i/p_i$, and make use of the linear homogeneity of E in *all* prices (p_0, p), this equation can be written as:[5]

$$(1 - t'x_1)\,du = -\left(r_1 - \sum_{i \neq 1} \omega_{i1} r_i\right) p_1 S_{11}\,dt_1. \tag{8}$$

Recalling that S_{11} is positive, this equation states that a cut in the tariff on good 1 ($dt_1 < 0$) will raise welfare provided the tariff rate on good 1 exceeds a weighted average of the tariff rates on all other goods (including the zero "tariff" on the numéraire). This is where substitutability comes in. The expression in (8) is not a true weighted average unless all the weights ω_{i1} are positive. This in turn requires that good 1 be a general equilibrium net substitute for every other good: $\omega_{i1} > 0$ if and only if $S_{i1} < 0$. Hence we finally reach our statement of the concertina rule:

Proposition 1. *If good 1 has the highest tariff rate, a sufficient condition for a reduction in r_1 to raise welfare is that good 1 is a net substitute for all other goods.*

Note that the requirement that good 1 be a net substitute for all other goods is an over-strong sufficient condition. All that is required is that $r_1 > \sum \omega_{i1} r_i$. For example, complementarities *per se* (some $\omega_{i1} < 0$) are not a problem. Lowering the highest tariff can only reduce welfare if the good in question is a sufficiently strong complement for some goods that it is also strongly *substitutable* for some other goods which are subject to high tariffs.

---

[5] Linear homogeneity of E in all prices implies that $p_0 S_{01} + p_1 S_{11} + p'_2 S_{21} = 0$. Rearranging and recalling that S_{11} and p_1 are scalars gives $p_1 S_{11} = -\sum_{i \neq 1} p_i S_{i1} > 0$, where the summation is over *all* goods *except* good 1 but *including* the numéraire. Dividing by $p_1 S_{11}$ leads to the weights $\omega_{i1} = -p_i S_{i1}/p_1 S_{11}$, $i = 0, 2, 3, \ldots, n$, which must sum to unity: $\sum_{i \neq 1} \omega_{i1} = 1$.

Tariff Reform in a Small Open Economy without *a Numéraire Good*

Having reviewed the theory of tariff reform when one good is explicitly selected as numéraire, let me now follow the same route in the same model but using a notation which treats all $n+1$ goods symmetrically. This cannot change the substantive results, of course. However, it can open the way to misunderstandings.

Since the model is unchanged, its specification is as before, except that I use Greek letters to denote $(n+1) \times 1$ vectors which include the numéraire good. Thus, paralleling equations (2) to (4), excess demand equals net imports:

$$E_\pi(\pi, u) = \mu; \tag{9}$$

domestic prices equal world prices plus tariffs:

$$\pi = \pi^* + \tau, \qquad \pi = \{p_0, p\}, \qquad \pi^* = \{p_0^*, p^*\}, \qquad \tau = \{t_0, t\}; \tag{10}$$

and net spending at world prices is zero:

$$\pi^{*\prime}\mu = 0, \qquad \mu = \{m_0, m\}. \tag{11}$$

Totally differentiating yields a slightly different version of equation (5):

$$\pi^{*\prime}X_1\, du = \pi^{*\prime}S_{\pi\pi}d\tau, \tag{12}$$

where X_1 is the $(n+1) \times 1$ vector of income derivatives of demand for all goods and $S_{\pi\pi}$ is the full $(n+1) \times (n+1)$ matrix of price responses and is positive semi-definite. As before, we assume that the coefficient of du, $\pi^* . X_1$, is positive,[6] so the efficacy of tariff reform hinges on the sign of the right-hand side term.

Why "POMPs" are POM

We are now ready to see why the theorems I presented at the outset may be described as "potentially misleading". Consider first POMP 1, which states that a tariff change of the form $d\tau = \delta\pi^* - \varepsilon\tau$ must raise welfare. Using this expression to eliminate $d\tau$ from (12), it is easy to prove the result.[7] But what exactly does this prove? From (10), a tariff reform of the kind specified in the proposition, $d\tau = \delta\pi^* - \varepsilon\tau$, is the same as

---

[6] This is sometimes called the "Hatta normality term" and is easily seen to equal the left-hand side coefficient in (5): $\pi^{*\prime}X_1 = (\pi - \tau)'x_1 = 1 - t'x_1$, using homogeneity and setting $t_0 = 0$.

[7] The proof makes use of the linear homogeneity of the trade expenditure function in the vector of *all* prices π. This implies that $S_{\pi\pi}\pi = 0$, which, since $\pi = \pi^* + \tau$, implies in turn that $S_{\pi\pi}\tau = -S_{\pi\pi}\pi^*$. It follows immediately from (12) that the change in welfare is proportional to $(\delta + \varepsilon)\pi^{*\prime}S_{\pi\pi}\pi^*$. Assuming that $\delta + \varepsilon$ is positive, this is proportional to a quadratic form in the positive semi-definite matrix $S_{\pi\pi}$ and so is always non-negative and is strictly positive provided $S_{\pi\pi}$ is of rank n and π^* is not proportional to π.

$d\tau = \delta\pi - (\delta + \varepsilon)\tau$; in words it is the same as raising all tariffs, by a factor δ, in proportion to *domestic* prices and then lowering them, by a factor $\delta + \varepsilon$, in proportion to their initial values. The only difficulty with this is that, since raising all tariffs in proportion to domestic prices does not change relative prices, it cannot affect any real magnitudes. In particular, it has no effect on welfare! All it amounts to is a rescaling of domestic prices; or put differently, to a change in the numéraire. Hence, the tariff change $d\tau = \delta\pi^* - \varepsilon\tau$ is equivalent to a proportional reduction of tariffs of $(\delta + \varepsilon)\%$, no more and no less: POMP 1 is just a restatement of the uniform radial reduction rule.

The same argument applies to POMP 2. It is technically true that welfare will increase if all tariffs are increased in proportion to world prices. But such a tariff change (of the same form as before with $\delta > 0$ and $\varepsilon = 0$) is really a uniform tariff *reduction* of $\delta\%$.

Finally, what about POMP 3? There is no need to prove the concertina rule a second time, since the proof already given makes explicit the role of all $n+1$ goods. Equation (8) as it stands shows that welfare will definitely increase when the tariff rate on good 1 is *increased*, provided it is *lower* than that on all other goods and good 1 is a net substitute for all of them. But in the absence of a numéraire, what does it mean to "raise the lowest tariff"? Either the lowest tariff is negative or it is not. If it is negative, then it is in effect an import *subsidy* and "raising" it really means *reducing* a distortion, since the subsidy rate is moved closer to zero. Alternatively, if the lowest tariff rate is not negative, then we can, without changing any real magnitudes, rescale all domestic prices in the manner already described until one tariff rate becomes zero. Now, raising this tariff rate is equivalent from homogeneity to an equiproportionate reduction in the tariffs on all other goods. In this case, POMP 3 (like POMPs 1 and 2) is just another restatement of the uniform reduction rule.

In conclusion, I should stress that the papers where these propositions originate make many important contributions other than the ones which I have criticised.[8] However, I believe that propositions of this sort have done potential harm in appearing to provide a case for tariff increases in distorted small open economies.[9] For example, the World Bank appears to have implemented this advice in some of its structural assistance packages in sub-Saharan Africa. There may of course be other justifications for

---

[8] Their authors also join a distinguished group whose conclusions have been criticised for failing to recognise the implications of excluding a numéraire good; see, for example, the criticisms of Hotelling (1938) by Frisch (1939); of Dixit (1970) by Sandmo (1974); and of Deaton (1979) by Stern (1986).

[9] Michaely, Papageorgiou and Choksi (1991) review the experience of trade liberalisation in developing countries.

raising some tariffs: the desire to avoid a loss of tariff revenue is one possibility.[10] However, to the extent that the models I have surveyed here are relevant they do *not* justify raising tariffs. In the real world, the conditions for the concertina theorem to apply are unlikely to hold in the case where low (but positive) tariffs are raised, since there are typically many goods (such as exports) with zero or even negative trade distortions.

III. Unilateral versus Multilateral Reform of Trade Policy

The second topic I review is that of multilateral tariff changes. Here I do not want to suggest that there are misleading results in the literature but rather that the fundamental similarity between apparently different results has not been appreciated. These results I therefore label "ARTs" for "*A*rguably *R*edundant *T*heorems". Consider the following:

ART 1: Proportional reductions in tariffs raise welfare in a small open economy.
ART 2: Given substitutability, concertina reforms of tariffs raise welfare in a small open economy.
ART 3: Proportional reductions in tariffs by all countries are Pareto-improving.
ART 4: Given substitutability, concertina reforms of tariffs by all countries are Pareto-improving.
ART 5: [Ohyama (1972), Kemp and Wan (1976)] If a group of countries keeps its net external trade fixed, then a Pareto-improving tariff reduction exists.

ARTs 1 and 2 repeat the two small-open-economy results considered in Section II. I have already noted (as is well known) that they are both special cases of the general expression for welfare-improving tariff changes, (5). ARTs 3 and 4, by contrast, relate to a very different substantive question, pioneered by Vanek (1964): when will coordinated tariff changes by all countries in the world lead to a welfare improvement for all of them? Finally, ART 5 deals with yet another problem, that of characterising the tariff changes which will ensure a welfare improvement for a customs union. The Ohyama–Kemp–Wan theorem is one of the few clear-cut results in the whole of customs union theory.

As in the last section, I first begin by sketching an analytic framework. Fortunately, much of the necessary work has already been done. Consider

---

[10]Though, if this is the case, they should be modelled explicitly. Attempts to do this to date do not provide clear support for increases in low tariffs; see, for example, Falvey (1994) and Anderson (1997).

a world with many countries, indexed by $j = 1,...m$, each of which can be characterised in just the same way as the small open economy of Section II. Thus in each country (indexed by a superscript j) net imports equal the derivatives of the trade expenditure function:

$$E_p^j(p^j, u^j) = m^j, \qquad j = 1,\ldots, m; \tag{13}$$

domestic prices equal world prices plus tariffs:

$$p^j = p^* + t^j, \qquad j = 1,\ldots, m; \tag{14}$$

and net domestic spending equals tariff revenue:

$$E^j(p^j, u^j) = t^{j\prime} m^j, \qquad j = 1,\ldots, m. \tag{15}$$

This gives *3m* equations for the *3m* country-specific endogenous variables, $\{u^j\}$, $\{p^j\}$ and $\{m^j\}$. The specification of world equilibrium is completed by adding the requirement that world markets must clear:

$$\sum_k m^k = 0. \tag{16}$$

This last equation determines the remaining unknown, p^*.

Solving the model in full is complicated. Fortunately, we do not need to do this, since all we seek are conditions for Pareto-improving tariff changes. First, differentiate (13) to (15) as in the small open economy case, and then sum over all countries:[11]

$$\sum_j (1 - t^{j\prime} x_1^j)\, du^j = -\sum_j t^{j\prime} S^j dp^j, \tag{17}$$

where the notation of Section II is extended to the multi-country case in an obvious way. (For example, country j's substitution matrix is: $S^j \equiv -E_{pp}^j$.) To simplify further, we need an expression for the change in world prices, which comes from differentiating (16):

$$dp^* = S^{-1} \sum_k (x_1^k\, du^k - S^k\, dt^k), \tag{18}$$

where $S \equiv \Sigma S^k$ is the world substitution matrix. Finally, substitute in (17) and collect terms:

$$\sum_j (1 - T^{j\prime} x_1^j)\, du^j = -\sum_j T^{j\prime} S^j\, dt^j. \tag{19}$$

where:

$$T^{j\prime} = t^{j\prime} - \sum_k t^{k\prime} S^k S^{-1}. \tag{20}$$

Equation (19) is the key equation in this section. I have deliberately written it in a notation which brings out its similarities with equation (5) in the

---

[11] The term $-\Sigma m^{j\prime} dp^*$ vanishes because of (16).

small open economy case, but it clearly differs from it in two respects. First, the left-hand side is not the change in utility in one country but a weighted sum of utility changes in all countries. This is because we seek only tariff changes which are *potentially* Pareto-improving; or, put differently, which ensure efficiency gains for the world as a whole. Translating these gains into *actual* Pareto improvements requires that international lump-sum transfers be available.[12] The assumption that lump-sum transfers are available also allows us to sign the coefficients of du^j. They must all be positive since otherwise a Pareto improvement could be achieved by transferring the numéraire good from countries with negative towards those with positive coefficients.

The second difference between equation (19) and the small open economy equation (5) is that in the latter the substitution and income effects are multiplied by actual tariffs t whereas in the former they are multiplied by T^j, the deviations of each country's tariffs from their world-wide weighted average, $\Sigma t^{k\prime} S^k S^{-1}$. (The weights are positive definite matrices and sum to the identity matrix: $\Sigma S^k S^{-1} = I$.) Thus in the multi-country context it is relative rather than absolute tariff levels which are crucial for welfare reform. I will refer to the T^j terms as "shadow premia" since it is easy to show that they equal the differences between domestic prices in each country and world shadow prices.[13]

We can now state a single general result which follows immediately by inspection of (19) and which encompasses all five ARTs:[14]

Proposition 2: *A necessary and sufficient condition for a potential Pareto-improving tariff change is that the right-hand side of (19) is positive.*

Proposition 2 is a powerful result. It shows that, as far as efficiency is concerned, international tariff harmonisation is always desirable. Moreover, the number of countries which choose to harmonise their tariffs does not matter. It can be only a single country harmonising its tariffs with the world average (as envisaged in ARTs 1 and 2) or all countries in the world (as envisaged in ARTs 3 and 4) or any intermediate group of countries.

---

[12] Making such transfers explicit requires adding a term b^j, with $\Sigma b^k = 0$, to the right-hand side of (13). Conditions for actual Pareto improvements in the absence of lump-sum transfers are much more stringent; see Turunen-Red and Woodland (1993).

[13] From (20), $T^{j\prime} = p^{j\prime} - (p^{*\prime} + \Sigma t^{k\prime} S^k S^{-1})$. The term in parentheses (which is independent of country j) measures the increase in potential world welfare (measured by the left-hand side of (19)) as a result of lump-sum increases in world endowments of goods. Note that these shadow prices are *not* equal to world prices, unlike in the well-known Little–Mirrlees (1968) result which applies to the small open economy of Section II.

[14] Essentially the same result is obtained by Turunen-Red and Woodland (1991) using Motzkin's theorem of the alternative. However, they do not interpret the shadow premia as deviations from a weighted average and they do not note the general applicability of the result as I do here.

Note that, if all countries have identical tariff structures, then no further Pareto gains are possible. This is because if the same relative prices prevail in all countries, the remaining common tariffs are equivalent to lump-sum taxes and have no welfare cost.

It is straightforward to show that all five ARTs are corollaries of Proposition 2. ARTs 1 and 2 follow trivially. In this context, a small open economy is one whose substitution effects are negligible relative to the world matrix S: $S^k S^{-1}$ is zero. Ignoring tariffs in other countries, the usual uniform reduction and concertina reform results follow as in Section II. ARTs 3 and 4 also follow straightforwardly. The only qualification is that, to ensure a Pareto improvement with many countries, the theorems must be stated in terms of the shadow premia (20). Thus, the uniform reduction result requires that all tariffs in a given country are reduced in proportion to their shadow premia; and the concertina reform result requires that (given substitutability) the tariff on the good with the highest shadow premium rate (not the highest tariff rate) should be reduced.

Finally, what about ART 5, the Ohyama–Kemp–Wan result? Formally, this is just another corollary of Proposition 2: Pareto-improving reforms of tariffs by all members of a customs union exist, provided their external trade is kept fixed. The interpretation is different because the countries considered comprise only a subset of the world. In deriving ARTs 1 to 4, we could invoke the differential of (16), $\Sigma\, dm^k = 0$, because there were no other countries in the world; now it holds (even though $\Sigma m^k = 0$ does not) because the union's common external tariff is adjusted as necessary to ensure that its external trade does not change. Note finally, that this version of the Ohyama–Kemp–Wan result is constructive in that it characterises a sequence of internal tariff changes which ensure successive Pareto improvements rather than merely showing that the abolition of all internal tariffs (given a fixed volume of external trade) is Pareto-improving. Proposition 2 thus extends the existing theory of tariff reform in significant ways as well as encompassing all the earlier theorems.

IV. Subsidies to High-Technology Firms

The third substantive issue I wish to review is whether governments should support export-oriented high-technology firms. Since such firms typically compete in oligopolistic industries, traditional trade theory, with its focus on perfectly competitive general equilibrium models, has relatively little to say on this topic. However, in the past fifteen years an explosion has taken place in the field of strategic trade policy, applying the insights of modern industrial organisation theory to open economies. The result in my view has been a rich crop of novel theoretical insights but as yet no robust recommendations for policy. The latter point has been made by a number of writers, such as Krugman (1987), yet the impression persists that new and important guidelines for policy have been developed. Among the strong and non-so-strong claims which have been made, let me single out three, which I label "QUARTs" for "*Q*uestionable *A*ssertions *R*esembling a *T*heorem":

QUART 1: [*The Economist* (1996)] Export subsidies should be targeted towards firms in high-technology sectors.

QUART 2: [Brander (1995)] Subsidies to pre-competition variables (such as investment or R&D) are a more robust recommendation than subsidies to market-period variables (output or price) because the former are more likely to be strategic substitutes.

QUART 3: [*The Economist* (1996)] The strategic case for subsidies is strengthened by R&D spillovers.

Once again, to put my claims in context I need to devote a little time to an exposition of the theory. I will concentrate on a canonical model, due to Brander and Spencer (1985) which considers the case for subsidising a single domestic firm which exports all its output (so domestic consumption can be ignored) in competition with a single foreign rival.

The Optimal Export Subsidy in a One-Period Duopoly

QUART 1 resembles the basic result of Brander and Spencer (1985). They showed that if the home and foreign firm engage in a one-shot Cournot game, then an export subsidy is optimal. This result has subsequently been shown to be sensitive to a relaxation of many of the model's assumptions (a fact of which *The Economist* is clearly aware). For example, if firms play a Bertrand price-setting game rather than a Cournot quantity-setting game, then the result is reversed. To see this, consider a general setting where the firms choose an unspecified "action", which could be either output or price, a for the home firm and b for the foreign firm. (This specification follows Brander (1995).) The home firm's profits equal its net revenue from production and sales, $R(a, b)$, plus the revenue it receives from a subsidy to its action at a rate s:

$$\pi(a, b, s) = R(a, b) + sa. \tag{21}$$

This specification encompasses both the Cournot case, where a and b are home and foreign output respectively and output is subsidised; and the Bertrand case, where a and b are home and foreign prices respectively and price is subsidised. (In Bertrand competition, a subsidy to price has the same allocative effect as, and so is equivalent to, a *tax* on the (differentiated) domestic good.) Finally, the home government is assumed to maximise domestic welfare which equals profits less subsidy income:

$$W(a, b) = \pi(a, b, s) - sa = R(a, b). \tag{22}$$

The basic result is now easily obtained. The home firm's first-order condition is:

$$\pi_a = R_a + s = 0. \tag{23}$$

A symmetric problem faced by the foreign firm leads to a similar condition, though with no subsidy term, since I assume for simplicity that the foreign government is passive: $R_b^*(b, a) = 0$. The latter condition implicitly defines the foreign firm's reaction function, which relates its action to that of the home firm:

$$b = B(a). \tag{24}$$

This reaction function is downward-sloping (so its derivative B_a is negative) if and only if the foreign firm's action is a *strategic substitute* for the home firm's.[15] This is usually considered the normal case in Cournot competition, for example.

Now, totally differentiate the welfare function (22):

$$dW = R_a \, da + R_b \, db. \tag{25}$$

Setting this equal to zero and substituting from (23) and the total differential of (24) gives the solution for the optimal subsidy:

$$s = R_b B_a. \tag{26}$$

The Brander–Spencer result follows immediately. In Cournot competition when goods are substitutes in demand, R_b is negative; and B_a is negative in the normal case where outputs are strategic substitutes. Hence the right-hand side is positive and the optimal policy is an export subsidy. The counter-result of Eaton and Grossman (1986) also drops out. In Bertrand competition, a and b are prices; R_b is positive assuming the goods are substitutes in demand; and B_a is positive (the foreign reaction function is upward-sloping) in the normal case where prices are strategic complements. Once again the right-hand side is positive, but now this means that *price* should be subsidised, which is equivalent to an export *tax*.

While the sign of the optimal subsidy differs between the Cournot and Bertrand cases, the rationale for government intervention is the same in

---

[15] To see this in more detail, totally differentiating the foreign firm's first-order condition gives: $B_a = -R_{ba}^*/R_{bb}^*$. The denominator R_{bb}^* must be negative from the foreign firm's second-order condition; while the numerator R_{ba}^* is negative if and only if the foreign firm's action is a strategic substitute for the home firm's, meaning that its marginal profitability is reduced by an increase in a.

both. The government is assumed to have the power to commit credibly to a subsidy or tax which affects the environment in which the two firms take their decisions. Optimal policy requires that the government exercise this power to do what the home firm cannot credibly do alone: move the equilibrium to the one which would prevail if the home firm had a first-mover Stackelberg advantage. This allows us to answer the third theoretical question posed in Section I: strategic trade policy is justified provided the home government has superior commitment power to the home firm.

What about the corresponding policy question from Section I: does equation (26) justify export subsidies to high-technology firms? Even if we stay with the Cournot case, I claim that it does not, for there is *nothing* in the specification of the model which identifies the industry as a high-technology one. The existence of a duopolistic market structure requires only that barriers to entry are high. While this may be true of the rivalry between Airbus and Boeing in aerospace it is just as true of that between *The Economist* and *Time* and *Newsweek* in news magazines; between Unilever and Proctor and Gamble in detergents; or between Bowater and Kimberly-Clark in paper tissues. Indeed, in the Brander–Spencer framework the only consideration determining which firms within a group of oligopolistic industries should be subsidised is which ones have the greatest potential for increasing their profits at the expense of their foreign competitors; see Neary (1994). So, to sum up, QUART 1 is not a reasonable restatement of the Brander–Spencer result.

Optimal Subsidies to R&D

How might the model be extended to focus more specifically on high-technology industries? An obvious feature of such industries is that production must be preceded by extensive investment in research and development. This suggests that a two-period framework, in which firms first make such investments and then compete in the product market, should be more relevant to the high-technology case. Following Spencer and Brander (1983) and Neary and Leahy (1996), the model just presented can be extended in this direction.

Suppose that in period 1 the home firm must incur fixed costs $F(k)$ which are increasing in the level of its spending on R&D, k. The payoff to such spending is that it lowers production costs in period 2. This is captured by including k as an argument in the period-2 revenue function, with $R_k > 0$.[16]

---

[16] For example, $R(k, a, b)$ might equal $pq - c(k)q$, where pq is sales revenue and $c(k)$ is marginal cost, independent of output q and decreasing in k.

Finally, R&D spending benefits from a subsidy σ. Under these assumptions the firm's profit function becomes, instead of (21):

$$\pi(k, a, b, \sigma, s) = -F(k) + R(k, a, b) + \sigma k + sa. \tag{27}$$

Now, assume that the home government and the two firms engage in a subgame-perfect three-stage game. In the first stage the government sets the two subsidy rates; in the second stage the firms choose their R&D levels; and in the third stage they choose their actions as before.[17] To solve the model, we work backwards through the stages. In the final stage the firms play a static game just as in the preceding subsection. The home firm's first-order condition is once again (23). In the second stage the firms choose their optimal levels of R&D, taking account of their effects on the third-stage game. Thus the home firm's choice of R&D spending takes account both of its direct or "non-strategic" effect on future profitability as captured by π_k; and also of its strategic effect in influencing the environment in which the period-2 game is played. The first-order condition for R&D is therefore:

$$\frac{d\pi}{dk} = \pi_k + \pi_b \left.\frac{db}{dk}\right|_{k^*} = 0, \tag{28}$$

where $\pi_k = -F' + R_k + \sigma$ and $\pi_b = R_b$. The term db/dk is the effect on the foreign firm's action in the second period which the home firm anticipates will result from an increase in its R&D. It is calculated by solving the two period-2 first-order conditions, which is why it is specified as conditional on the foreign firm's choice of R&D, k^*.

What is the government's optimal policy in this case? As before, with no domestic consumption, welfare equals profits less subsidy payments:

$$W(k, a, b) = \pi(k, a, b, \sigma, s) - \sigma k - sa = R(k, a, b) - F(k). \tag{29}$$

Totally differentiating this and substituting from the home firm's first-order conditions gives:

$$dW = \left[-\sigma - \pi_b \frac{db}{dk} \right] dk - s\, da + R_b\, db. \tag{30}$$

The government's problem is straightforward. With two instruments at its disposal (σ and s), it effectively controls the home firm's choice of k and a directly. As for the foreign firm's choice of b, it controls this indirectly by

---

[17] I assume that the government commits to its output subsidy before the firms choose their R&D levels. Reversing this sequencing leads to a four-stage game in which firms have an additional strategic incentive to choose their R&D levels with a view to influencing the output subsidy. The implications of this are considered in Leahy and Neary (1998) and Neary and Leahy (1996).

moving the foreign firm along its reaction function, just as in the one-period model of the preceding subsection. The only additional complication is that the relevant reaction function is now more complex, since it is the solution to *both* the foreign firm's first-order conditions, which are (corresponding to (23) and (28)):

$$\frac{\partial \pi^*}{\partial b} = R_b^* = 0 \quad \text{and} \quad \frac{d\pi^*}{dk^*} = R_{k^*}^* + R_a^* \frac{da}{dk^*}\bigg|_k = 0. \tag{31}$$

The government solves these conditions to obtain the foreign firm's action as a function of the home firm's two actions:

$$b = B(a, k). \tag{32}$$

Substituting the derivatives of this into (30) and equating to zero yields the optimal subsidies:

$$\sigma = -\pi_b \frac{db}{dk}\bigg|_{k^*} + R_b B_k \quad \text{and} \quad s = R_b B_a. \tag{33}$$

This can be simplified by setting the term B_k to zero: since the two firms do not compete directly in the first period, the effect of k on b is of second-order importance and may safely be ignored.[18] The optimal policies in (33) then exhibit a clear division of labour. The period-2 export subsidy s serves to commit the home firm to the Stackelberg choice of period-2 action, while the R&D subsidy σ exactly offsets the strategic effect. Moreover, the signs of these two instruments display exactly the same ambiguity as in the static game. The formula for the period-2 export subsidy is identical to that in the static case and so it too is positive or negative depending on whether period-2 actions are strategic substitutes or complements. As for the R&D subsidy, it has the opposite sign to that of s. When period-2 actions are strategic substitutes, the strategic effect is positive. In the terminology of Fudenberg and Tirole (1984), the home firm adopts a "top dog" strategy, "over-investing" (relative to the social-cost-minimising optimum where $R_k = F'$) to give itself an advantage in the period-2 game. The optimal policy is an R&D tax to "restrain" the firm. By contrast, when period-2 actions are strategic complements, the firm adopts a "puppy dog" strategy of "underinvestment". For example, in Bertrand competition, the firm has

---

[18] Foreign profits R^* are a function of (k^*, a, b) only and so the derivatives of R^* in (31) do not depend directly on k. Hence k can affect b directly (i.e., for given a) only to the extent that changes in k affect the slope of the home firm's period-2 reaction function and hence affect the term da/dk^* in (31). This effect vanishes, for example, in the case of Cournot competition where marginal costs are independent of output: see Spencer and Brander (1983) and Leahy and Neary (1996).

an incentive to reduce investment in order to raise its rival's price. In this case the optimal policy is an R&D subsidy: the puppy dog should be "encouraged".

The result for strategic substitutes was obtained by Spencer and Brander (1983); that for strategic complements does not appear to have been noted prior to Neary and Leahy (1996). Taken together, these results suggest that this branch of the theory of economic policy exhibits an aesthetically pleasing unity, but they provide little comfort to policy activism. Contrary to the conjecture of Brander (1996) which I have labelled QUART 2, the ambiguity which plagues the static theory of strategic trade policy is magnified rather than reduced when dynamic behaviour is incorporated.

R&D Spillovers and the Case for Industrial Policy

The final issue I want to address is the implications for strategic trade policy of allowing R&D to have non-appropriable spillover effects, so that it reduces the costs of firms other than those of the firm which engages in it. QUART 3 suggests that such spillovers strengthen the strategic trade policy case for supporting innovating firms. However, Leahy and Neary (1997b) show that this inference is not valid. Of course, the presence of positive externalities in itself justifies a subsidy (assuming that the private sector cannot internalise them in Coasian fashion). But this is an old argument, due to Pigou rather than to the theory of strategic trade policy. The relevant question is what *additional* basis for intervention, if any, is provided by strategic considerations.

The answer turns out to be surprising. When spillovers accrue to firms in the same industry, a Cournot oligopolist has a strategic incentive to reduce its R&D to reduce the technology transfer to its rivals.[19] This indeed provides a strategic motive for a government subsidy. But note that the subsidy should be provided even if the firms which benefit from the spillovers are foreign! The point of the subsidy is not to encourage diffusion of new technology but to avoid inefficient underinvestment for strategic reasons. Of course, if the other firms are domestic, it is well known that the strategic case for export subsidies is also weakened.

What if the firms that benefit from the spillovers are domestic but not in the same industry? Now there is a pure Pigovian basis for subsidising R&D. But, if competition is Cournot then, from the previous section, there is also a strategic motive for taxing R&D, to counteract the 'top dog'

---

[19] This incentive has been extensively studied in the closed economy context; see d'Aspremont and Jacquemin (1988) and Leahy and Neary (1997a).

overinvestment behaviour already noted. Thus, the exact type of intervention which is justified is ambiguous and at least in the Cournot case the strategic argument works against rather than in favour of R&D subsidies.

V. Summary and Conclusion

In this paper I have reviewed and extended some recent contributions to three areas in the theory of international trade policy. In each case, I have used a simple canonical model to derive the main results in a compact fashion and I have related this model to the principal results in the literature.

In the case of tariff reform in a small open economy, I have drawn attention to some results in the literature which are potentially misleading. In particular, I take issue with suggestions that tariff *increases* in a small open economy may be desirable. I argue that such recommendations are artifacts of models which do not include a numéraire good. When a numéraire good is included (which is equivalent to saying, when the implications of linear homogeneity in prices are recognised) the case for tariff increases ceases to hold.

Turning to the conditions for Pareto-improving tariff changes I have suggested that a number of results in the literature can be seen as equivalent. A consequence of this perspective is that the same basic principles of tariff reform apply in unilateral, multilateral and customs union contexts. Moreover, I have shown that the Ohyama–Kemp–Wan theorem can be extended beyond an existence result and have shown how the internal tariffs of a customs union can be adjusted to ensure Pareto gains for the members, provided the union's external trade is kept fixed.

Finally, I have reviewed the theory of strategic trade policy and shown that it does not provide a secure case for subsidies to high-technology firms. Indeed, the basic one-period result due to Brander and Spencer merely justifies subsidies to firms in industries with high barriers to entry. These are just as likely to be technologically unsophisticated incumbents in established markets as high-technology firms in growing sectors. The theory can be extended to allow for investments in R&D prior to the competitive stage, thus more closely approximating the conditions in high-technology industries. But here too the ambiguity which characterises the static theory persists: policies appropriate to firms which compete on quantity are the opposite to those which should be applied to price competitors. Of course, R&D spillovers provide a clearcut justification for subsidising, though in this case too the optimal subsidy may be reduced or even reversed when firms behave strategically. In the light of recent research, the case for subsidising firms in high-technology sectors is not particularly strong.

References

Anderson, J. E.: Trade reform with a government budget constraint. In J. Piggott and A. D. Woodland (eds.), *International Trade Policy and the Pacific Rim*. Macmillan, London, forthcoming, 1997.

Anderson, J. E. and Neary, J. P.: Trade reform with quotas, partial rent retention, and tariffs. *Econometrica 60*, 57–76, 1992.

Brander, J. A.: Strategic trade policy. In G. Grossman and K. Rogoff (eds.), *Handbook of International Economics, Volume III*. North-Holland, Amsterdam, 1395–1455, 1995.

Brander, J. A. and Spencer, B. J.: Export subsidies and international market share rivalry. *Journal of International Economics 18*, 83–100, 1985.

d'Aspremont, C. and Jacquemin, A.: Cooperative and noncooperative R&D in a duopoly with spillovers. *American Economic Review 78*, 1133–1137, 1988.

Deaton, A. S.: The distance function in consumer behaviour with applications to index numbers and optimal taxation. *Review of Economic Studies 46*, 391–405, 1979.

Diewert, W. E., Turunen-Red, A. H. and Woodland, A. D.: Productivity and Pareto-improving changes in taxes and tariffs. *Review of Economic Studies 56*, 199–215, 1989.

Dixit, A. K.: On the optimum structure of commodity taxes. *American Economic Review 60*, 295–301, 1970.

Eaton, J. and Grossman, G. M.: Optimal trade and industrial policy under oligopoly. *Quarterly Journal of Economics 101*, 383–406, 1986.

Economist, The: Economics focus: How to beggar your neighbour. 78, 3 February 1996.

Falvey, R. E.: Tariffs, quotas and piecemeal policy reform. *Journal of International Economics 25*, 177–183, 1988.

Falvey, R. E.: Revenue enhancing tariff reform. *Weltwirtschaftliches Archiv 130*, 175–190, 1994.

Frisch, R.: The Dupuit taxation theorem. *Econometrica 7*, 145–150, 1939.

Fudenberg, D. and Tirole, J.: The fat-cat effect, the puppy-dog ploy, and the lean and hungry look. *American Economic Review (Papers and Proceedings) 74*, 361–366, 1984.

Fukushima, T. and Hatta, T.: Why not tax uniformly rather than optimally? *Economic Studies Quarterly 40*, 220–238, 1989.

Hatta, T.: A theory of piecemeal policy recommendations. *Review of Economic Studies 44*, 1–21, 1977.

Hotelling, H.: The general welfare in relation to problems of taxation and of railway and utility rates. *Econometrica 6*, 242–269, 1938.

Kemp, M. C. and Wan, Jr., H. Y.: An elementary proposition concerning the formation of customs unions. *Journal of International Economics 6*, 95–97, 1976.

Krugman, P. R.: Is free trade passé? *Journal of Economic Perspectives 1*, 131–144, 1987.

Leahy, D. and Neary, J. P.: International R&D rivalry and industrial strategy without government commitment. *Review of International Economics 4*, 322–338, 1996.

Leahy, D. and Neary, J. P.: Public policy towards R&D in oligopolistic industries. *American Economic Review 87* (4), 642–662, 1997a.

Leahy, D. and Neary, J. P.: R&D spillovers and the case for industrial policy in an open economy. WP No. 1671, Centre For Economic Policy Research, London, 1997b.

Leahy, D. and Neary, J. P.: Learning by doing, precommitment and infant-industry promotion. *Review of Economic Studies* (forthcoming), 1998.

Little, I. M. D. and Mirrlees, J. A.: *Manual of Industrial Project Analysis in Developing Countries, Vol. 2*. OECD, Paris, 1968.

Michaely, M., Papageorgiou, D. and Choksi, A.: *Liberalizing Foreign Trade: Lessons of Experience in the Developing World*. Basil Blackwell, Oxford, 1991.

Neary, J. P.: Cost asymmetries in international subsidy games: Should governments help winners or losers? *Journal of International Economics 37*, 197–218, 1994.

Neary, J. P.: Trade liberalisation and shadow prices in the presence of tariffs and quotas. *International Economic Review 36*, 531–554, 1995.

Neary, J. P. and Leahy, D.: Strategic trade and industrial policy towards dynamic oligopolies. Mimeo., University College Dublin, 1996.

Neary, J. P. and Schweinberger, A. G.: Factor content functions and the theory of international trade. *Review of Economic Studies 53*, 421–432, 1986.

Ohyama, M.: Trade and welfare in general equilibrium. *Keio Economic Studies 9*, 37–73, 1972; reprinted in J. P. Neary (ed.), *International Trade, Volume I (International Library of Critical Writings in Economics)*. Edward Elgar, Cheltenham, 1995.

Sandmo, A.: A note on the structure of optimal taxation. *American Economic Review 64*, 701–706, 1974.

Smith, A.: Some simple results on the gains from trade, from growth and from public production. *Journal of International Economics 13*, 215–230, 1982.

Smith, A.: Shadow price calculations in distorted economies. *Scandinavian Journal of Economics 89*, 287–302, 1987.

Spencer, B. J. and Brander, J. A.: International R&D rivalry and industrial strategy. *Review of Economic Studies 50*, 707–722, 1983.

Stern, N. H.: A note on commodity taxation: The choice of variable and the Slutsky, Hessian and Antonelli matrices (SHAM). *Review of Economic Studies 53*, 293–299, 1986.

Turunen-Red, A. H. and Woodland, A. D.: Strict Pareto-improving multilateral reforms of tariffs. *Econometrica 59*, 1127–1152, 1991.

Turunen-Red, A. H. and Woodland, A. D.: Multilateral reforms of tariffs without transfer compensation. In H. Herberg and N. van Long (eds.), *Trade, Welfare, and Economic Policies: Essays in Honor of Murray C. Kemp*. University of Michigan Press, Ann Arbor, 145–166, 1993.

Vanek, J.: Unilateral trade liberalization and global world income. *Quarterly Journal of Economics 78*, 139–147, 1964.

Scand. J. Economics 100(1), 207–209, 1998

Comment on J. P. Neary, "Pitfalls in the Theory of International Trade Policy: Concertina Reforms of Tariffs, and Subsidies to High-Technology Industries"

Alasdair Smith*

University of Sussex, Brighton BN1 9QN, UK

This is a characteristically thoughtful and thought-provoking paper from Peter Neary. It makes deceptively simple points using elegant techniques, forcing us to think quite carefully about the interpretation of some central results in open economy welfare economics. I will focus on the part of the paper that draws on the literature which, from the mid-1970s onwards, developed an elegant formal synthesis of the economics of second-best welfare analysis in the open economy.

Neary's message in Section II is that we need to be particularly careful in interpreting results in models in which the numeraire of the price system is not explicitly specified. The welfare effects of two kinds of distortion changes, radial and "concertina" reductions, are discussed.

The version of the model without an explicit numeraire gives the clearest results on radial reductions in distortions. It follows from equation (12) that changes in tariff rates proportional to world prices or, using homogeneity, proportional to the negative of the tariff rates, are guaranteed to be welfare improving. The possible confusions to which Neary draws our attention are best avoided by focusing on the most fundamental version of the proposition: moving the domestic price vector radially closer to the world price vector is an unambiguous reduction in distortions and is therefore welfare improving.

The "concertina" theorem states that in a small open economy in which a particular condition is satisfied by the substitution matrix, it is desirable to reduce the largest distortion and increase the smallest. Neary is concerned about the way the "concertina" result is used in practice to justify the raising of low tariff rates. If we suppose that prices are defined in such a way that there is an untaxed numeraire among the goods whose prices are being analysed, then the lowest trade distortion is either in the numeraire good itself, an increase in whose tax rate is equivalent to a radial

---

* A longer version of this comment, including some technical detail, is available by e-mail from Alasdair.Smith@sussex.ac.uk.

reduction in all the other, positive, tax rates, or a subsidy for which an "increase" in the tax rate is actually a reduction in the subsidy. In neither case is there a justification for raising the lowest tariff rate. The essential point is that correct application of any result about the effects of changing the highest or the lowest distortion requires one to make sure that *all* relevant prices are taken into consideration.

The full power and elegance of the approach which is followed in this paper can only be appreciated in a more general setting with non-traded goods as well as traded goods, quotas as well as tariffs, and endogenous world prices, as presented in Neary (1995).

In such a more general model, Motzkin's dual inequality theorem, cf. Diewert *et al.* (1989), can be used to establish the existence of shadow prices that for traded goods are world prices, cf. Little and Mirrlees (1974), and for non-traded goods are the cost at shadow prices of changes in the net supply of traded goods required to keep the markets for non-traded goods in equilibrium when supplies of non-traded goods change. Duality also formally establishes the requirement that the cost at shadow prices of a lump-sum transfer to consumers, the "Hatta normality term", should be positive (as discussed in footnotes 4 and 6 of the paper). With endogenous world prices, the shadow prices of traded goods are the marginal foreign exchange cost of the goods themselves, *plus* the value at shadow prices of the change in domestic net demands generated by the terms-of-trade change. The equations provide a precise statement of the claim, by e.g. Little and Mirrlees (1974), that with world prices endogenous, the shadow price of a traded good is the marginal foreign exchange cost of imports. We also obtain the notable result of Falvey (1988) and Neary (1995) that if quotas are held constant, welfare analysis of tariff reduction can be conducted as if the distortions arising from the quotas did not exist.

Thus such a more general and more formal approach demonstrates the central role that shadow prices play in the development of a unified treatment of second-best welfare economics.

Presenting the radial reduction result in a model with non-traded goods gives an untroublesome way of dealing with the numeraire: it can be safely tucked in among the non-traded goods, and ignored for the purpose of this argument. Now the general version of the radial reduction result is that a change in tariff rates proportional to shadow prices moves the domestic price vector of traded goods radially closer to the shadow price vector, is therefore an unambiguous reduction in distortions, and is welfare improving.

Two versions of the concertina result are now available: one referring only to traded goods, one to all goods: a rise in a trade tax rate will be welfare improving if that good has a smaller proportional distortion between its market price and its shadow price than any other *traded* good;

and a rise in a trade tax rate will be welfare improving if that good has a smaller proportional distortion between its market price and its shadow price than *any* other good, *traded or non-traded*; subject to slightly different substitution conditions in the two cases.

In the practical application of this theory to tariff reform it is surely essential to take account both of the existence of non-traded goods and of endogenous world prices of traded goods. Because there is a version of the concertina result that applies only to traded goods, we do not need to take explicit account of non-traded goods in the expression of the rule, but we do need, as Neary's analysis emphasises, to make sure that all traded goods are included in the calculation. We also need to take account of endogeneity in world prices in defining the shadow prices of traded goods, and therefore to take account of *all* distortions in the calculation of shadow prices. Given the wide range of distortions between market prices and true opportunity costs that exist in many economies and the pervasiveness of imperfect competition, there are many reasons why the selection of the lowest import tariff rates in the published tariff schedules is unlikely to identify the good for which the concertina rule justifies an increase in the domestic price, and the informational requirements of correct application of the rule are formidable. Practical policymakers should use the theory as a guide to the principles of good policymaking, not as a source of simple recipes.

References

Diewert, W. E., Turunen-Red, A. H. and Woodland, A. D.: Productivity and Pareto-improving changes in taxes and tariffs. *Review of Economic Studies 56*, 199-215, 1989.

Falvey, R. E.: Tariffs, quotas and piecemeal policy reform. *Journal of International Economics 25*, 177-183, 1988.

Little, I. M. D. and Mirrlees, J. A.: *Project Appraisal and Planning for Developing Countries.* Heinemann, London, 1974.

Neary, J. P.: Trade liberalisation and shadow prices in the presence of tariffs and quotas. *International Economic Review 36*, 531-554, 1995.

Scand. J. Economics 100(1), 210–212, 1998

Comment on J. P. Neary, "Pitfalls in the Theory of International Trade Policy: Concertina Reforms of Tariffs, and Subsidies to High-Technology Industries"

Harry Flam

IIES, Stockholm University, S-106 91 Stockholm, Sweden

Peter Neary makes three points in his discussion of subsidies to high-technology industries. First, the standard Brander–Spencer one-period duopoly model does not provide an argument for subsidies to high-technology industries. There is nothing in the model that identifies the firms as high-tech. If anything, the fixed and small number of firms is a description of any industry with high barriers to entry, low-tech as well as high-tech. Second, the Brander–Spencer three-period duopoly model does capture an important feature of high-technology industries, namely substantial initial investment in R&D. In the model, the government decides first about taxes or subsidies to the domestic firm's R&D and output (or price). The firm invests in R&D in the first (actually second) period, which has a strategic effect on its rival both in the first and second period, when production takes place. But it turns out that the three-period model is plagued by the same kind of ambiguity as the one-period model, only doubly so. When second-period actions are strategic substitutes, the firm overinvests in the first period to give it a strategic advantage in the second period. The welfare-maximizing policy is to subsidize output in the second period and tax R&D in the first. When second-period actions are strategic complements, policies should be the opposite. Third, when R&D has positive spillovers to other firms, domestic and foreign, a subsidy is called for to prevent underinvestment by the domestic firms. Thus, there may be reasons to tax and to subsidize R&D at the same time, which makes for even more ambiguity.

I would like to add to the ambiguity concerning subsidies to high-technology industries by investigating the effects of subsidies under other assumptions about market structure and conduct. Nothing in what I have to say is new, but a serious consideration of the potential for public policy must be broader in scope than the market structure of two firms, no domestic consumption and strategic interaction.

Consider first the case of perfect competition. A subsidy to exports is certain to decrease welfare, by creating distortions in consumption and production, and by deteriorating the terms of trade, if the exports are sufficiently large to have an influence on the world market price. A *tax*, on the other hand, may be welfare-improving, as long as the improvement in the terms of trade is greater than the distortions created by the tax. The case for an export tax is, of course, not particular to high-technology industries. My guess is that it would be hard in practice to convince policymakers to tax high-tech exports, since that would be completely against their common (non)sense.

Consider next the case of monopolistic competition. A small export subsidy or tax will affect welfare by changing the terms-of-trade (even for a small country) but also the degree of competition (the price-cost margin) and product variety. The net effect of a subsidy or tax is ambiguous, and depends among other things on the competition between sectors over resources; see Flam and Helpman (1987). Monopolistic competition is characterized by a large number of firms with some market power and no strategic interaction, as surely some high-technology industries also are.

We do not have to venture outside the framework of oligopoly with strategic interaction to find other sources of ambiguity surrounding policies that aim to support high-technology industries and enhance national welfare. Take the case of a domestic oligopoly, Cournot or Bertrand, and perfect competition abroad. Here the optimal policy is to tax exports regardless of market conduct. A small tax on exports improves the terms of trade and has relatively small distortionary effects. Or take the case where there are more than one domestic and one foreign firm. If the strategic variable is output, a subsidy to exports will serve to shift profits from the foreign to the domestic firms, the Brander–Spencer effect. However, it will also serve to shift profits among domestic firms. To avoid the latter effect, exports should be taxed. Hence, whether exports should be taxed or subsidized depends on the number of domestic relative to the number of foreign firms. Yet another possibility is that entry prevents the existence of pure profits in the oligopolistic industry. In this case there are no foreign profits to capture. The optimal policy is again to tax exports in order to improve the terms of trade.

Most of the strategic trade policy analysis is done within the framework of partial equilibrium. A general equilibrium framework introduces general equilibrium effects that can overturn policies that are welfare improving in partial equilibrium. One example is when there are more than one oligopolistic industry with pure profits. Subsidies to one of the industries will draw resources to it from other industries, possibly from other oligopolistic industries with greater profits. If so, the policy acts as a tax on the other industries, and the net effect will be a shifting of profits from domestic to foreign firms and lower welfare; see Dixit and Grossman (1986).

Finally, it is usually assumed that the country that exploits other countries can do so without fear of retaliation. This, of course, is not likely. Retaliation may make matters worse than in the equilibrium without any government intervention. That is the case when actions are strategic substitutes. All countries are worse off in the equilibrium where they use subsidies. They would be better off by cooperating and setting a tax that achieves the monopoly equilibrium. The case of strategic complements, on the other hand, calls for cooperation to set a higher tax than what is individually optimal in the no-retaliation situation.

I hope that these examples make the point that any attempt by governments to favor their high-technology industries and firms can easily do harm instead of good. The information and knowledge about the workings of the real economy that are necessary to carry out a beneficial policy — if such a policy exists — are simply not available.

References

Dixit, Avinash and Grossman, Gene: Targeted export promotion with several oligopolistic industries. *Journal of International Economics 21*, 23–49, 1986.

Flam, Harry and Helpman, Elhanan: Industrial policy under monopolistic competition. *Journal of International Economics 22*, 79–102, 1987.

Scand. J. of Economics 100(1), 213–237, 1998

Business Cycles: Theory, Evidence and Policy Implications

*Russell W. Cooper**

Boston University, Boston, MA 02215, USA

Abstract

This paper looks at recent advances in the study of aggregate fluctuations. The emphasis is on three prominent areas of research: the stochastic growth model, economies which exhibit macroeconomic complementarities and models that emphasize heterogeneity. Each section of the paper outlines the theory, examines relevant empirical evidence and then discusses some policy implications of the analysis.

I. Introduction

The point of this paper is to bring together positive and normative aspects of ongoing research on the sources and consequences of aggregate fluctuations. First, from the positive perspective, does the consideration of government policy bring the predictions of the models closer to the data? As we shall see, this is particularly relevant for real business cycle models. Second, what do these models suggest as the appropriate form of intervention?

While there are numerous active areas of investigation into the sources and consequences of business cycles, here we focus on three: real business cycles, models built on macroeconomic complementarities and models with non-convexities and heterogeneity. I have chosen to highlight these models partly due to their prominence in the ongoing debate over the aggregate fluctuations and partly due to the unique perspective they bring to policy questions.

II. Stochastic Growth Models

Kydland and Prescott (1982) provide the intellectual starting point of this branch of macroeconomics. With its emphasis on complete contingent

*I am grateful to the organizers of the *SJE*'s symposium on "Public Policy and Economic Theory" for inviting this presentation, to Jean-Pierre Danthine, Nils Gottfries and the referee for comments and suggestions and to the conference audience for insightful questions and further commentary. Jon Willis provided outstanding reserarch assistance and the National Science Foundation provided much appreciated financial support.

markets and technology shocks (broadly defined) as the primary source of fluctuations, the Kydland–Prescott paper spawned a literature built around a framework commonly termed the "real business cycle" model, hereafter RBC model. For the purposes of this presentation, with its emphasis on policy, we start out discussion with a variant of the RBC model which emphasizes fiscal policy. We then turn to versions of the stochastic growth model with other policy shocks.

Basic RBC Model with Fiscal Policy

Consider an economy composed of a large number of infinitely lived individuals all solving for optimal consumption and capital accumulation paths. The production function for each agent has the usual arguments of capital and labor as well as an exogenous technological parameter which, at least initially, will be a source of fluctuations in the economy. Add to this model a government which produces a public good and finances its expenditures through a variety of taxes. Our presentation begins with the general specification of this problem in Braun (1994).

The optimization problem of a representative agent is given by:

$$\max \mathrm{E}\left\{\sum_{t=0}^{\infty} \beta^t u\left(c_t, l_t\right)\right\} \tag{1}$$

where c_t is total period t consumption and l_t is period t leisure, β lies between zero and one and the utility function is strictly increasing and concave. Consumption in period t comes from two sources: private consumption (c_t^p) and government consumption (g_t). Braun assumes that these components enter linearly to determine total consumption: $c_t = c_t^p + \gamma g_t$ where γ is a parameter of the preferences. The household faces a time constraint that leisure plus work time (n_t) sums to the time endowment, normalized at 1. The transition equation for household capital (wealth) is:

$$k_{t+1} + k_t + (1 - \tau_t) w_t n_t + (1 - \tau_t)(1 - \tau_t^k)(r_t - \delta) k_t + TR_t - c. \tag{2}$$

In this expression, τ_t is the period t tax on income (both labor and capital) and τ_t^k is the period t tax on capital income, net of depreciation.[1] In (2), TR_t are lump-sum transfers.

Braun utilizes a statistical framework to represent government policy. In particular, income taxes, capital taxes and spending, along with a

---

[1] This tax structure reflects the double taxation of capital income in the U.S.

technology shock (described below) follow a stationary autoregressive process. Thus the model allows some feedback from the state of the system to government policy. In addition, the government is required to balance its budget each period through the transfers.

Firms produce using a constant returns to scale stochastic technology in which output is produced from capital and labor. So, output is given by

$$Y_t = A_t F(K_t, N_t). \tag{3}$$

Households supply both inputs and all markets are competitive. The first-order conditions for the firm relate the rental rate on capital (r_t) and the wage rate (w_t) to the marginal products of capital and labor respectively. The equilibrium conditions then guarantee that these factor prices clear markets using the predetermined capital level and the household labor supply.

The equilibrium is characterized by the following two necessary conditions:

$$u_2(c_t, 1-n_t) = u_1(c_t, 1-n_t) A_t F_2(k_t, n_t)(1-\tau_t) \tag{4}$$

$$\beta E u_1(c_{t+1}, 1-n_{t+1})(1-\tau_{t+1})(1-\tau_{t+1}^k)$$
$$\times [A_{t+1} F_1(k_{t+1}, n_{t+1}) - \delta] + 1) = u_1(c_t, 1-n_t). \tag{5}$$

Intratemporal optimality is characterized by (4), taking into account the period t taxation of labor income. The Euler equation for intertemporal optimality is given in (5) where the expectation is taken with respect to both the future state of technology as well as the future taxes on labor and capital income. These conditions are then supplemented by the government budget constraint, the individual budget constraint and the resource constraint that output equals consumption (private plus government) plus investment to fully characterize an equilibrium.

It is quite well known that this model without fiscal policy does a good job of matching some observed movements in U.S. data.[2] In particular, the presence of technology shocks gives rise to procyclical productivity. The curvature of the utility function yields consumption smoothing so that the variance of consumption is less than the variance of output and the variance of investment exceeds that of output. Further, the labor input is procyclical.

---

[2] See Danthine and Donaldson (1993) and Fiorito and Kollintzas (1994) for a discussion of cross-country evidence. Interestingly, investment is more volatile than output for all of the countries in the Danthine–Donaldson study but consumption is smoother than output in only six of ten cases.

However, Christiano and Eichenbaum (1992a) argued that the RBC model fails to match the observed correlation in U.S. data between hours worked and average productivity. In U.S. data this correlation is about 0 while in most RBC models, the correlation is quite close to 1.[3] Also, the actual variability in hours is close to that of output, contrary to the model's prediction.

In order to match the low correlations between hours and productivity, the labor supply curve must shift along with labor demand. Thus a one-shock model is unable to match observations. Christiano and Eichenbaum (1992a) introduce stochastic fiscal policy into the analysis.

In particular, they consider a variant of model outlined above in which public and private consumption goods are imperfect substitutes ($\gamma \neq 1$). Government spending is financed by lump-sum taxes: τ_l and τ_l^k are both set to zero and TR_l is negative. So, government spending is just subtracted from gross output in the resource constraint.

For the extreme case in which government spending has no effect on individual's utility, fiscal policy has only pure wealth effects which do lead to variations in the labor supply curve of the representative agent. Periods of large government expenditures are matched with large wealth reducing taxes which increase the labor supply of the individual household. Intuitively, from (4), increases in lump-sum taxes, reduce consumption and thus increase the marginal utility of consumption, keeping savings fixed. This, in turn, increases the labor supply of the agent in order for the intratemporal condition to hold. Thus, it is through these labor supply effects that increases in government spending lead to increases in employment and output. Empirically, the model still substantially overstates the correlation between hours and average productivity.[4]

Braun (1994) takes this approach a step further. He admits differential taxation of capital and labor incomes and estimates the fiscal policy process using U.S. data where the tax rates are actually average marginal rates.[5] Braun finds that the labor income tax is quite persistent compared to the capital income tax.

The movement away from a specification in which the government relies solely on lump-sum taxation is important since increases in spending create substitution effects through the link between spending and distortionary taxes. In this regard, Braun finds that the correlation between government

---

[3] Though, as emphasized by Christiano and Eichenbaum (1992a), one must be very careful about the measurement of hours.
[4] Though Christiano–Eichenbaum do argue that their fiscal shock model combined with an elastic labor supply schedule cannot be rejected.
[5] In fact, many of the model's parameters are estimated using GMM though there is some structure imposed, such as log preferences over consumption and leisure.

spending and hours is quite close to zero in a model economy with distortionary taxes while it is about 0.5 in an economy with lump-sum taxes only. This correlation is about 0.09 in U.S. data.

Braun finds that allowing for the taxation of capital and labor income, in a manner consistent with the time series representation of these taxes, brings the standard deviation of hours relative to output much closer to U.S. data. Further, the presence of these tax shocks creates enough variability in labor supply that the resulting correlation between hours and average productivity is actually negative as in U.S. data.[6] These results certainly support the view that taxes represent important shiters of labor supply.

Thus, from a positive perspective of inquiring about the properties of the stochastic growth model with taxation and government spending, we find that introducing these elements does enhance the capability of the model to match observations. In particular, some of the labor market anomalies, for U.S. data, disappear upon the introduction of stochastic fiscal policy.

Given the results of Christiano–Eichenbaum and Braun, as well as McGrattan (1994), it is interesting to see if differences in fiscal policy processes can explain observed differences across countries. In a recent effort along these lines, Jonsson and Klein (1996) study the interaction between fiscal policy and the behaviour of aggregate variables in Sweden. They consider a model with stochastic government spending, payroll taxes and consumption taxes. The latter seems particularly important in that consumption is slightly more volatile than output in Sweden. The model seems to do a very good job of matching this relative volatility as well as the near zero correlation between productivity and employment.

Overall, these papers illustrate the capability of using the stochastic growth model to analyze fiscal policy. This framework can clearly be used to evaluate a wide variety of policies. Further, the model is based upon optimizing behavior and is internally consistent: there are no assumed decision rules or other restrictions on behaviour imposed from outside of the model.

Still, one can certainly be unconvinced about the impact of fiscal policy from these exercises. First, the models clearly lack a variety of elements, such as market frictions, heterogeneity and so forth that some macroeconomists consider essential to any macroeconomic model. Second, one could be critical from the perspective that the fiscal policy functions do not emerge from a well-specified optimization problem for the government. Put differently, one could inquire about the implications

---

[6] In fact, the point estimate of this correlation is even more negative than in U.S. data.

of optimal policy rather than focus on the consequences of a purely statistical representation of policy.

Not surprisingly, this approach is more difficult for a couple of reasons. Conceptually, one immediately faces the question of the basis for government intervention. Strictly speaking, there is no role for the government in the standard RBC model with complete markets, no externalities and so forth. Still, one could imagine the need for government spending (provision of public goods) comes into play though this is not really a stabilization role for the government. Thus any attempt to rationalize stabilization policy within this framework must be in terms of a model with frictions that creates a welfare gain for policy.[7]

A second difficulty emerges in the determination of optimal policy. If we actually model the government as a player in a dynamic economy, then it is natural to move away from a purely competitive framework in that the government is a large player. This immediately leads to considerations of commitment by this player.

The paper by Chari, Christiano and Kehoe (1994) is an important step forward in this research program. In particular, they characterize optimal fiscal policy in a version of the stochastic growth model assuming that the government is able to commit to its tax and spending policies. The policies they derive are quite different from those used in the fiscal policy exercises described above: labor taxes fluctuate very little and the *ex ante* tax on capital is close to zero. While the authors compare statistics from an economy with optimal policy to one more representative of actual U.S. policy, they do not present the labor market correlations. One would conjecture though that the model with optimal policy would not create enough labor supply variation to reduce the correlation between productivity and employment to zero.

The gap between this model and, for example, the analysis by Braun is troubling. If the underlying model of the economy and that of the policymaker is correct, then the positive and normative exercises ought to yield similar results. There are clearly two ways to go. First, the optimal policy problem studied by Chari *et al.* could be modified to reflect additional constraints, such as commitment, and political economy considerations. Second, the underlying economic model ought to be modified to give more of a role to the policymaker. That is, in an economy with frictions, the policymakers may have a larger stabilization role to play.[8]

---

[7] For example, see Hairault, Langot and Portier (1997) for a discussion of alternative means of financing unemployment compensation is a distorted environment.

[8] Hairault et al. (1995) study stabilization policy in an economy with frictions due to market power and liquidity constraints.

Monetary and Financial Shocks

A final line of work within these models concerns monetary interventions. As has been well understood for quite a long time, any study of monetary policy must deal with two hurdles: generating a demand for money and creating a source of non-neutrality.

One approach is to study the liquidity effects of a monetary shock, as in Christiano and Eichenbaum (1992b), Christiano, Eichenbaum and Evans (1996), Fuerst (1992) and Lucas (1990). The idea is that a representative household is involved in a number of distinct activities: buying goods, selling labor, borrowing/lending and so forth. These models create a demand for money through some form of cash-in-advance constraint and the non-neutrality of money arises from lump sum transfers of new money directly to financial intermediaries. These funds flow from banks to firms to finance labor costs. Within this framework, many injections may lead to lower interest rates and expansions of activity. According to the quantitative analysis in Christiano and Eichenbaum (1992b), the monetary shock also leads investment and consumption to move in opposite directions. Further, the basic models in this literature do not contain a mechanism to endogenously propagate these shocks.

One of the activities of the monetary authority, at least in the U.S., is to regulate banking activity. Cooper and Ejarque (1996) assume that the technology that converts savings into new capital is a stochastic and nonlinear process. In fact, one interpretation of this structure is that government regulations, such as reserve requirements, act as a tax on the intermediation process.[9]

The effects of variations in the productivity of the intermediation process are fairly intuitive.[10] In particular, in times of productive intermediation (such as a low reserve requirement), more resources will be invested and less consumed. Further, due to the higher return on investment, employment will increase as well. As a result, the impact of a shock to the intermediation process is to create negative comovement between consumption and employment and between consumption and investment. The transitional dynamics of the standard model reinforce this negative correlation.[11] Thus, Cooper–Ejarque find that one implication of these models in which fluctuations arise from variations in the productivity of the intermediation process is the negative comovement.[12] Further, Cooper–

---

[9] This point is also raised in Loungani and Rush (1995).

[10] Greenwood, Hercowitz and Huffman (1988) have a related model in which there are shocks to capital accumulation which they interpret as investment shocks. See their lengthy discussion of the negative correlations that can be generated in this class of models.

[11] This point is discussed in some length by King, Plosser and Rebelo (1988).

[12] Interestingly, Baxter and King (1993) find similar effects in some of their fiscal policy exercises. In fact, it is easy to see that variations in an investment tax credit would behave in

Ejarque find that these shocks cause capital to be more volatile than output.

From an empirical perspective, the issue is whether there is evidence of these negative correlations. For U.S. data, the unconditional correlations between consumption, investment and employment are all positive and capital is less volatile than output. Clearly, these shocks to the process of intermediation can not be the sole driving process for fluctuations. However, if one looks at particular periods in U.S. history (such as the 1966 credit crunch episode or the 1937 recession), there does appear to be some evidence of the predicted negative comovement between consumption and investment. Further, a VAR structure with dummy variables for credit crunches predicted some negative comovements in response to interme-diation shocks as did the empirical work of Loungani and Rush (1995) on the effects of varying reserve requirements.

Summary

Over the past 15 years, the stochastic growth model has become a main tool for business cycle analysis. The discussion here points to a number of policy exercises within the real business cycle structure that ought to be informative to policymakers considering the impact of a wide variety of fiscal and monetary interventions.

Still, considerable doubt remains over the value of the strict RBC model for understanding business cycles. The complete contingent markets model with fluctuations driven by technology shocks is far less accepted than the methodology itself. Further, some of the criticisms raised early on concerning the predominance of technology shocks have not been adequately addressed. Even taking the models as given, problems match-ing certain labor market observations and concern over measurement of the Solow residual, as in Burnside, Eichenbaum and Rebelo (1995) remain.

What are the key features of the basic model that, at least in principle, are most objectionable? First, there is the assumption of complete contin-gent markets. Second, the standard RBC model rests too much upon the representative household structure. Finally, potentially important issues associated with nonconvexities are assumed away. Hence, in the sections that follow, these modeling features are emphasized.

---

a similar fashion as "intermediation shocks" on new capital expenditures. How economies actually respond to investment tax credits is an issue worthy of more study.

Strategies of all others

Single		1	2
Players	1	800	800
Strategy	2	0	1000

Fig. 1. Coordination game.

III. Macroeconomic Complementarities and Multiple Equilibria

The representative agent model with complete contingent markets avoids a number of important issues. First, choices are obviously made by a multitude of agents and trade occurs in all economies. Second, perhaps it is better to think of real economic life as the interaction of heterogeneous units, each with the ability to influence the trading opportunities of others in environments where external effects are present.

Consider the following game played by a large number of agents. Each agent in the economy chooses one of two strategies. In general, payoffs for a single agent will depend on the profile of choices by all agents.[13] In Figure 1, let the row strategies represent the choices of a single agent and the columns the choice of all other agents. This construction uses a restriction to symmetric equilibria. The numbers displayed in the matrix are the payoffs to the single agent given the action of that player for each possible action of *all* other players.

For this game, there are two pure strategy equilibria: (1, 1) and (2, 2). From the figure, playing 1 (2) is a best response to that choice by all others. These pure strategy equilibria are Pareto ordered. Yet, a single player has no incentive for unilateral defection.

In terms of macroeconomics jargon, in the Pareto inferior Nash equilibrium there are $100 bills laying on the sidewalk. This statement was often used to criticize models in which some mutually advantageous trades were not executed. Here, in this coordination game there are sub-optimal equilibria because it takes the actions of many agents to pick up the $100 bills. Thus, it is the lack of coordination among agents that underlies the unexploited gains to trade.[14]

---

[13] In this sense, we are again back to the representative agent model though only in equilibrium.

[14] One issue, beyond the scope of this paper, concerns equilibrium selection. The experimental evidence on coordination games indicates that Pareto-optimal equilibria are not always selected; see e.g. Cooper, Dejhong, Forsythe and Ross (1994) and Van Huyck *et al.* (1990).

What are the critical features of this type of game? As discussed by Cooper and John (1988) for simple games and Milgrom and Roberts (1990) and Vives (1990) for complex environments, the key to this type of situation is a complementarity in the interactions of agents. Put simply, coordination games have a structure such that "... if others work more, a single agent will as well". With small numbers of agents, this positive interaction is often call strategic complementarity. In a model with a large number of small agents, this is a macroeconomic complementarity.

Sources of Complementarity

In macroeconomics, there are three main lines of research on coordination games. These avenues of investigation are distinguishable by their departure from the Arrow–Debreu model.

A. Production Complementarities. The first approach, associated with the contribution of Bryant (1983), models the complementarity as stemming from the interaction of agents through the production function. Thus, if other agents work or produced more, then the remaining agent is assumed to be more productive. This will, under the restriction that input supplies are increasing in their real return, induce the remaining agent to produce more.

For example, suppose that an agent chooses a level of work (or effort) $e \in [0, 1]$. The agent's prefernces are given by $u(c) - g(e)$, where $u(c)$ is an increasing, concave function of consumption (c) and $g(e)$ is increasing and strictly convex. Because of the production complementarity, assume that the production of consumption depends on both own work (e) and the level (or average) of work effort by others in the economy, (E). That is, let $c = f(e, E)$, where $f(\cdot)$ is thus a production function. If $f_{12} > 0$, then increases in the level of effort by all others in the economy will increase E and also increase the productivity of more effort by the single agent.

Bryant (1983) considers an example in which the production function is given by $f(e, E) = \min(e, E)$. While this is not a continuously differentiable function, it still has the important property of complementarity: if other agents work more, my effort is more productive too.[15] When $u(c)$ is strictly increasing and strictly concave and $g(e)$ is strictly increasing and strictly convex, then there will exist a unique effort level, call it e^{**}, which represents the social optimum. Bryant proves that the set of symmetric Nash equilibria includes any effort level between 0 and e^{**}. Thus in this extreme case, the set of Nash equilibria is a continuum and the equilibria are Pareto ranked.

---

[15] For the approach of Milgrom and Roberts (1990), the min function is a prime example.

B. Search. Starting with Diamond (1982), macroeconomists have explored the importance of increasing returns in the search process as a basis for complementarity.[16] Here we can think of search quite generally to encompass any form of trading frictions. The key aspect of this approach is that these costs of trading fall as the number (fraction) of traders increase. That is, there is a thick market effect operating through the magnitude of these frictions.

In Diamond's model, agents have a choice of undertaking an expensive project. There is heterogeneity in the economy; some projects are more expensive than others. If an agent chooses to produce, then that agent must trade output with another agent to consume. In contrast to the Arrow–Debreu complete contingent markets view, trade does not occur in well-organized markets. Instead, agents must search for each other which is represented by a matching function. Diamond assumes that this matching function exhibits increasing returns to scale: the larger the fraction of agents searching, the easier it is to find a trading partner.

Using this form of increasing returns, Diamond shows that this model may have multiple Pareto-ranked equilibria. In one equilibrium, very few agents participate in the production of goods so that trading opportunities are not very good. Hence only low cost projects are undertaken. In a second equilibrium, many agents will undertake production so that, through the increasing returns, trading probabilities are relatively high. That the equilibria are Pareto ordered arises from the fact that in the equilibrium with high activity, all agents that produce could have chosen not to produce, thus obtaining their payoffs from the other equilibrium.

C. Imperfect Competition. A final area of investigation for coordination games arises in models of imperfect competition. Here the departure from the Arrow–Debreu model comes from the introduction of market power, principally to the sellers of goods.

Consider an economy consisting of many sectors producing distinct goods. Each sector consists of a few firms producing the same product who interact in the market for their homogeneous product. The demand for their product reflects, among other things, the activity levels of firms in the other sectors. Firms take their sectoral demand curve as given, as they are small relative to the rest of the economy. This is essentially the structure of Hart (1982).

Suppose that firms play a Cournot–Nash game within a sector; they choose output given the output levels of others. This interaction is well-

---

[16]The most well-known case is the Kiyotaki and Wright (1993) model of money in a search theoretic setting. González (1996) provides an example in which increased market participation by some agents increases the informativeness of signals and thus induces participation by others.

defined and generally there is an equilibrium for a sector *given sectoral demand*. In fact, the interaction of firms within a sector is one of the strategic substitutability; as other firms expand, the remaining firm will contract output.

However, the interaction across sectors is generally one of strategic complementarity. As firms in other sectors expand their production levels, the demand curve facing a given sector will shift out, inducing firms in that sector to expand as well. Thus the complementarity arises quite naturally from the normality of goods.

In the presence of imperfect competition, this complementarity creates the basis for a coordination game. Heller (1986) and Cooper (1994) construct examples of multiple, Pareto-ranked equilibria in this type of economy, while Kiyotaki (1988) generates multiplicity in a related model of monopolistic competition.

Positive Implications

Perhaps not surprisingly, the specification of the complementarities model that has received most attention in the quantitative macroeconomics literature is the production externality model. This largely reflects its tractability and the ease of placing it in the context of a stochastic growth model.

The Baxter and King (1991) specification fits nearly into our discussion of stochastic growth models. Consider the household optimization problem specified in (1)–(2) assuming that all fiscal policy variables are set to 0. Further, suppose the production technology of an individual producer is given by

$$y_t = A_t F(k_t, n_t) Y_t^\varepsilon. \tag{6}$$

In the specification Y_t represents the economny wide average level of output while y_t represents output for a particular individual. Being small, the individual firm takes Y_t as given in optimizing. In (6), ε measures the magnitude of the effect of average activity on the productivity of a single agent. This specification is one simple representation of a production complementarity: high activity by others makes the remaining individual more productive.

With this production function in mind, solution of the individual's intertemporal optimization problem will yield decision rules for employment, consumption and investment given the state contingent process for aggregate output. The first-order conditions are:

$$\frac{u_2(c, 1-n)}{u_1(c, 1-n)} = AF_2(k, n) Y^\varepsilon \tag{7}$$

$$\beta E u_1(c', 1-n')[A'F_1(k', n')(Y')^\varepsilon + (1-\delta)] = u_1(c, 1-n) \tag{8}$$

and

$$k' = k(1-\delta) + AF(k, n)Y^\varepsilon - c. \tag{9}$$

Since there are no differences across agents, an equilibrium arises when the individual and aggregate processes coincide. So in (7)–(9), determining an equilibrium amounts to imposing the restriction that the choices of the single agent and the average agent coincide. This, combined with a Cobb–Douglas technology leads to a final set of equilibrium conditions.

A key step is parameterization of the model, particularly the size of the production externality. Baxter and King (1991) use an instrumental variables estimation routine on aggregate data to identify this parameter. The instruments chosen are arguably independent of any technology shock in the economy to enable identification. From this exercise, they set ε at 0.23.[17] However, these estimates have been widely disputed and remain a topic of continued research.

A model with production complementarity will tend to magnify an underlying technology shock. When technology improves for exogenous reasons, the increased activity by each agent will cause aggregate activity to increase which, acting through the complementarity, will magnify the initial shock. This interaction can be seen directly in (8) where the level of output by others acts like a shock to total factor productivity. The complementarity does not add persistence.[18]

Baxter–King also consider taste shocks in the model through exogenous variations in the marginal utility of consumption. Using the model with external returns to scale and taste shocks alone, Baxter–King report that the model produces: (i) positively correlated fluctuations in the key components of aggregate GNP, (ii) fluctuations which are persistent in terms of their deviations from trend and (iii) consumption which is less volatile than output which is, in turn, less volatile than investment. These are the same features that are prominently displayed by models which are driven by technology shocks though here they arise with demand shocks *if* there are external increasing returns to scale.

---

[17] Cooper and Haltiwanger (1993) describe the estimation issues in some detail and discuss an attempt by Braun and Evans (1991) to estimate this parameter using seasonal data. The use of seasonal data is a natural way to identify the social returns to scale since one would generally not argue that seasonal fluctuations are predominantly due to technology shocks. More recent evidence by Basu and Fernald (1995) questions conclusions based on the use of value added data in these exercises.

[18] Cooper and Johri (1996) estimate a model with dynamic complementarities which does produce considerable persistence.

Note that while the Baxter–King formulation contains a complementarity in production, this is not an economy with multiplicity. One form of multiplicity and sunspot equilibria arises in models with multiple steady state equilibria. Cooper and Ejarque (1995) look at a version of the stochastic growth model in which intermediaries play a critical role in the process of capital accumulation. In this formulation, there are increasing returns to scale in the intermediation process that leads to a multiplicity of steady states. In one steady state, agents are pessimistic about the returns to intermediated activity and thus do not invest. The low level of intermediated activity leads to an unproductive process and thus this equilibrium is self-fulfilling. Similarly, there is another equilibrium in which the intermediation process is quite productive and this is consistent with a high level of intermediated activity. Sunspot equilibria are then created by randomizing between the neighborhoods of these two steady states producing stochastic shifts between periods of optimism and pessimism. The model is consistent with some aspects of the U.S. Great Depression period, though, as in the linearized version of the model discussed earlier, the model still implies too much negative correlation across consumption, employment and investment relative to observations over the 1920–40 period.

Benhabib and Farmer (1994) and Farmer and Guo (1994) take the Baxter–King specification an additional step and investigate a second form of multiplicity in a dynamic model. In an economy with very elastic labor supply, a production complementarity considerably larger than that used by Baxter–King and a slightly larger labor share, Benhabib–Farmer and Farmer–Guo argue that the basic neoclassical growth model has sunspot equilibria. That is, the steady state is no longer a saddle. Instead, it becomes a sink and thus there are multiple paths leading to the steady state. It is feasible to randomize across paths and generate sunspot equilibria.

Farmer and Guo (1994) evaluate the quantitative implications of these sunspots. The introduction of the sunspots essentially adds a bit to the intertemporal Euler equation. This model possesses many properties of the basic RBC model: there is consumption smoothing and investment is more volatile than output. More interestingly though, the sunspot model generates serial correlation in output, consumption and investment with iid shocks. Due to the strong external returns, the model also generates procyclical productivity.

The model with production externalities has also been used to investigate price rigidity and monetary shocks by Beaudry and Devereux (1993). They use the multiplicity of equilibria to support an outcome where money is not neutral: among the set of equilibria, there is one in which prices are predetermined. In this way, the ex post price rigidity is generated as part of the equilibrium rather than through an outside assumption.[19] Further, the large returns to scale creates a basis for the propagation of the monetary shocks. Thus, Beaudry–Devereux are able to match the observed implications of positive monetary shocks: output, consumption, investment and employment rise, interest rates initially fall and average labor productivity rises.

Policy Implications

One of the interesting aspects of models based on macroeconomic complementarities are their policy implications. In contrast to the RBC model, there are real gains to coordination in these models. Put differently, the multiplicity of equilibria allows for a positive coordinating role for the government. In fact, this need not be an active role in the sense of spending and taxation. Instead, the government can provide confidence and thus influence the choice of an equilibrium in the event of multiplicity. At the same time, the presence of the government may itself provide an additional source of instability.

The role of the government as a stabilizer in coordination models is nicely brought out in the bank runs model of Diamond and Dybvig (1983). As is well known, there are multiple equilibria in this model due to the illiquidity of the banking system. In one equilibrium, agents have faith and leave their funds in the banks while in another, agents lose confidence and extract their funds. The government can provide confidence in the intermediation process through the introduction of deposit insurance. This effectively breaks the complementarity: even if all others withdraw their funds, the residual agent should not withdraw. Of course, in the unique equilibrium the government actually never takes any actions!

There are numerous examples though in which the presence of a government is, in fact, the source of multiplicity. Consider the static optimization problem of an agent choosing how much to work (n) to minimize $u(An(1-\tau), n)$ where A is a measure of productivity and τ is a tax rate. The agent takes the tax rate as given and the optimal choice of hours would be given by $n^*(A, \tau)$. Assume that substitution effects dominate so that $n_1 > 0$ and $n_2 < 0$. Further, suppose that the government faces a financing constraint that $\tau AN = G$, where N is the average level of employment in the economy. Hence there is an implicit relationship between taxes and activity given by $\tau(N)$ with $\tau'(N) < 0$. Inserting this into the optimal employment rule yields $n = n^*(A, \tau(N))$ with n^* *increasing* in N. That is, as

---

[19] Cooper (1990) argues that equilibria with predetermined wages and prices exist in a bilateral contracting model since these contracts jointly provide insurance to risk adverse workers.

the level of activity increases, the tax rate will fall and this will support the higher activity level. This upward sloping relationship between the action of one agent and all others is a complementarity that can lead to multiple equilibria.[20]

Schmitt-Grohe and Uribe (1996) analyze multiplicity in a dynamic model in which the government must balance the budget using distortionary labor taxes.[21] They show that the steady state is indeterminate if labor supply is sufficiently elastic. Suppose that forward-looking agents anticipate high labor taxes in the future. Thus, they anticipate a lower labor input in the future and hence lower productivity of capital. So, the current demand for investment is lower and thus output in the current period will be lower. Therefore, the government will have to raise taxes today to raise the necessary revenues to balance the budget. In a sense there is an intertemporal complementarity at work here: higher tax rates in the future lead to higher tax rates today.

IV. Heterogeneity and the Making of Economic Policy

The last class of models we consider has two key components: discrete choice at the microeconomic level and heterogeneity. From the perspective of these models, decisions at the micro level are not taken continuously but instead are taken infrequently, perhaps due to some non-convexities in the costs of adjustment. The heterogeneity arises because individuals will generally have different probabilities of acting, reflecting both the current values of relevant state variables and underlying heterogeneity across decision units.

These models are clearly more complicated than the standard stochastic growth model due to the heterogeneity and non-convexities. Advocates of these models argue that the complexity brings a benefit in terms of a deeper understanding of the economy's response to different shocks and a new source of propagation. Critics argue that aggregation adequately smooths over both the non-convexities and differences across agents so that these models provide relatively little new insights into aggregate behavior.

---

[20] An early example of this point appears in Persson and Tabellini (1990) and more recently in a growth context in Gloom and Ravikumar (1995). Eaton (1987) analyzes a model of capital flight in which tax policies creates a complementarity across investors and thus the prospect of multiple equilibria.

[21] In a related effort, Christiano and Harrison (1996) explore the large set of equilibria for an economy with both production complementarities and government expenditures financed by income taxes with lump sum transfers used for budget balance.

This section of the paper describes some examples from this class of models and provides some insights into this controversy. Then, we discuss the policy insights from models which rest on heterogeneity and discrete choices. As we shall see, one lesson for policymakers is that the impact of interventions may be quite sensitive to current distributions of state variables across agents. A second point is that the evolution of the cross sectional distribution created by the policy intervention can be substantial and thus ought to be considered in the policy analysis.

Basic Structure

A useful starting point is a generic model described by Caballero and Engel (1993). The economy is populated by a group of agents indexed by $i = 1, 2, ..., I$. At each point of time t, the agent is described by two variables. The first, denoted by x_{it}, represents the current state of the agent. The second, denoted by x_{it}^* is the desired state of the agent if adjustment was costless in the period. Thus, $z_{it} \equiv x_{it} - x_{it}^*$ measures the distance between the actual and desired state.

A stationary decision rule is then some function of the current state, say $\phi(z)$.[22] In the discrete choice setting, this decision rule has the interpretation of a hazard function: $\phi(z)$ is the probability that an agent in state z will act.[23] Note that by construction, the optimal action of an agent is to set $x_{it} = x_{it}^*$.

What are the properties of this decision rule? It is natural to conjecture that the likelihood of an agent acting is increasing in $|z_{it}|$. The exact nature of the hazard function is generally determined in two ways. Either, one takes the hazard as a primitive object and specifies a functional form which is then estimated. Alternatively, one can start with an underlying dynamic programming problem and then generate the hazard as the optimal decision rule. These alternatives are described in more detail below in the context of a particular example. For now, we take $\phi(z)$ as given to illustrate some of the properties of the model.

The nonlinearities and propagation in the model come from the cross sectional distribution. Let $f_t(z)$ denote the period t cross sectional distribution of z across the agents. Further, let Y_t denote the level of activity in

---

[22] Here we ignore the subscripts and just use z to denote the current state.

[23] An alternative model, described by Caballero and Engel (1993), would have agents adjusting partially toward their target so that $\phi(z)$ would be the magnitude of partial adjustment between the current state and the target. While these interpretations appear undistinguishable at the aggregate level, they are very different views of optimal descisions at the micro level.

period t. By activity, we mean the change in the variable x_{it} for all of the agents. So,

$$Y_t = \int z\phi(z)f_t(z)\,\mathrm{d}z. \tag{10}$$

To interpret this expression, recall that the adjustment of an active agent is z and the probability of action is $\phi(z)$. The dynamics stem from the evolution of the cross sectional distribution.

When the economy experiences a shock, the resulting change in the distribution of z will lead to an adjustment by some agents and not by others, dictated by the shape of $\phi(z)$. Further, the response of those who act is much larger than the average response across agents. There is also a nonlinear response to shocks in these models. The effects of a common shock that, say, reduces the values of z for all agents will depend on the distribution of z prior to the shock. For some distributions, the shock will cause a large fracton of agents to act and for other distributions the shock will have a much smaller influence.

As for propagation, the law of motion for the distribution summarizes the manner in which history influences current activity. From (10), even in the absence of aggregate disturbances, the level of activity will vary along with the cross sectional distribution. Of course, the magnitude and nature of the propagation will depend on the hazard function, $\phi(z)$. An important issue is how much propagation can actually be generated by this mechanism.

While compelling due to its generality, this structure is not quite convincing in a couple of respects. First, there is no guarantee that the actual state of the system can be so conveniently summarized through a single dimensional variable, z. Second, the hazard function is not derived directly from an optimization problem. This is problematic for certain policy analyses, particularly those that are not encompassed by historical precedence.[24]

A Durable Goods Example

To deal with some of these potential problems and to make the linkages to policy as well as the properties of nonlinearity and propagation explicit, we turn to a specific example from Adda and Cooper (1997).[25] The problem

---

[24] That is, a government may wish to implement certain policies that have no historical precedent making predictions of their effects impossible without knowing underlying decision rules.

[25] This same structure is used by Cooper and Haltiwanger (1993) and Cooper, Haltiwanger and Power (1996) to study lumpy investment. See Bar-Ilan and Blinder (1992) for further motivation on the appropriateness of discreteness.

concerns the optimal scrapping of cars and the policy exercise relates to recent attempts in some countries, such as France, to stabilize the automobile market by subsidizing the scrapping of cars.

Consider the problem of an individual household owning a car of age i. The household enjoys a service flow from this good given by s_i and so gains utility from other goods, denoted by c. Assume that households have either 0 or 1 cars. Each period, the household can keep the car, sell it or scrap it. In the event of a sale or a scrapping, a new car may be purchased. If we assume for now that all households are identical except for the age of their car, then in equilibrium there will be no trades of intermediately aged cars.

The household's discrete dynamic choice problem is then to choose between retaining the car and scrapping it. Letting c denote the cost of a new car, y the income of the household and π the scrap value of a car, the dynamic programming problem is given by:

$$V_i(c, y, \pi) = \max\left(u(s_i, y) + \beta EV_{i+1}(c', y', \pi'), (u(s_1, y + \pi - c)\right.$$
$$\left. + \beta EV_2(c', y', \pi')\right). \tag{11}$$

In this problem, V_i is the value of an agent of an age i car. The agent can hold that car and earn a utility flow of $u(s_i, y)$ within the period and then have a car of age $i+1$ in the next period. Alternatively, the agent can scrap the car and buy a new one at cost c and then have a car of age 2 in the following period. Note that this construction assumes that the utility from car ownership exceeds the cost of a new car, c. The state of the system is given by the age of a particular agent's car and the common variable (c, y, π), which we again denote as z.

The solution to (11) takes the form of a stochastic stopping problem: for each value of the state vector, there is a critical age, denoted $I(z)$ such that cars are scrapped iff $i > I(z)$. Let $\phi_i(z)$ be the probability of scrapping and buying a new car in state z if the current car age is i. Note that since z includes the entire set of variables influencing the individual's choice, $\phi_i(z) \in \{0, 1\}$. If there are unobservable components to the agent's problem not included in z, such as taste shocks, then $\phi_i(z) \in [0, 1]$. In this case, $\phi_i(z) < \phi_{i+1}(z)$ for all z; i.e. the hazard is increasing in car age.

As in (10), the level of new car sales is determined by the interaction between the hazard and the cross sectional distribution over the car ages, $f_i(i)$. So, given the realized aggregate shocks (c, y, π), the level of new car sales is given by:

$$Q_t = \sum_{i=1}^{I(z)} \phi_i(z) f_t(i) \tag{12}$$

where $I(z)$ is again the optimal scrapping age and $i = 1$ is a new car. The evolution of the cross sectional distribution is:

$$f_{t+1}(1) = Q_t, \qquad f_{t+1}(i+1) = (1 - \phi_i(z))f_t(i). \tag{13}$$

The factors that determine the sensitivity of durables purchases to variations in the aggregate variables are now easy to see. Consider the effects of shocks to aggregate income. In this model, variations in income will influence the hazard for cars of age i. From an analysis of (11) with a two-state process for y, Adda and Cooper (1997) find that $\phi_i(z)$ is increasing in income.

From (12), the impact of the income shocks on car sales will depend partly on the magnitude of the hazard shift and partly on the cross sectional distribution of the car vintages. This is precisely the source of nonlinearity. If there are many new cars in the population then a high income realization will lead to a relatively small increase in new car sales.

Following this income shock, the dynamics of the cross sectional distribution will take over. In general for these models, the transitional dynamics are dampened cycles.[26] To see why, suppose that the initial cross sectional distribution places considerable weight on young cars. Given that the hazard is increasing in car age, car sales will be low. Over time, the age distribution will adjust with more weight placed on older cars. This will increase car sales. Eventually, the population of cars will again be fairly young and car sales will be relatively low.

Adda–Cooper consider a more complicated version of this model to study the impact of policies in the automobile market undertaken recently in Europe. In particular, the French, Italian and Spanish governments have provided subsidies for the scrapping of old cars followed by the purchase of a new one. In the model, this is simply a variation in the scrap value, π.

Evaluating the impact of these types of policies is quite difficult. One approach would be to specify a hazard function which included a scrapping subsidy as an argument. However, for some policy exercises, such as the case of these subsidies in France, the novelty of these policies precludes this approach. Instead, Adda–Cooper estimate the parameters of preferences from the dynamic programming problem, (11), and then use these estimates to simulate the effects of the policy on sales and government revenues.

The points raised earlier on nonlinear responses and dynamics appear in the policy exercise. First, to forecast the impact of the policy on sales requires some knowledge of the cross sectional distribution of car vintages as well as the ability to predict the shifts in the hazard functions. Scrapping

---

[26] See Bar-Ilan and Blinder (1992) for an earlier argument of this point. Cooper, Haltiwenger and Power (1996) discuss this in some detail for an investment example. As pointed out by Jess Benhabib, the cyclical nature of these models dates to at least Marx's interest in replacement cycles.

subsidies when the population of cars is relatively young are not very effective since the policy will not induce considerable additional sales.

Second, the stimulative effects of these policies can be rather short lived. That is, a successful policy will lead quickly to a distribution with relatively young cars and thus relatively little new sales until the young stock ages. The resulting pattern of boom and bust is not quite what is meant by "stabilization policy"!

Price Rigidities Revisited

Another application of the dynamic stochastic discrete choice framework concerns price setting behavior by firms who face a lump sum cost of changing their prices. At the start of each period, a firm would choose to adjust its price or not, recognizing the influence of this choice on its future state. This choice of adjusting or not adjusting is very close to the replacement problem described above. In fact, one could directly embed this into a dynamic programming problem similar to (11), allowing a wide variety of aggregate and idiosyncratic shocks to influence the pricing decision of the firm.[27] That is, consider:

$$v(p, P, M, \theta) = \max[\pi(p, P, M, \theta) + \beta \mathrm{E}v(p, P', M', \theta'),$$

$$\max_x \pi(x, P, M, \theta) - F + \beta \mathrm{E}v(x, P', M', \theta')]. \tag{14}$$

Here p is the current price for a firm, P is a measure of aggregate prices, M is the shock of money and θ represents an idiosyncratic shock to the firm's current profits, represented by $\pi(p, P, M, \theta)$. The first line entails no price change by the firm so that its price in the next period is also p. The second line allows the firm to optimally choose a new price (x) but the firm pays an adjustment cost of F. To solve this dynamic programming problem requires the firm to know the distribution of exogenous random variables (M, θ) as well as the state contingent evolution of the aggregate price level, P. This is a big issue since it requires the solution of an equilibrium problem along with the optimization problem of an individual firm.

Dotsey, King and Wolman (1996) consider a model where firms solve an optimal price setting problem where the fixed cost of changing a price is random across firms. As in the car example, the state of a firm is partially determined by the time since its last price change. For their economy, Dotsey *et al.* argue that there is a maximal time between price changes which creates a finite state space for their analysis: they follow the distribution of firms in each of these states to characterize their equilibrium. With

---

[27] Caballero and Engel (1993c) make essentially the same point using the gap between actual and desired price as a proxy for the firm's current state and then investigating the implications of an (S, s) rule.

this structure, they can evaluate a number of monetary policy experiments and compare the properties of their economy to the more traditional, but less convincing, time dependent rules. Dotsey *et al.* find that less persistent money shocks have larger real impacts since most firms will not pay the cost of adjustment given the temporary nature of the shock. Further, their economy displays underlying cycles as part of the transitional dynamics, just as the car example given above. Finally, their economy also generates some persistence through the evolution of the cross sectional distribution.

Caplin and Leahy (1997) study the equilibrium of a stochastic monetary economy in which firms optimally adopt (S, s) policies. These authors stress the importance of strategic complementarity between the firms in a monopolistically competitive environment. In an equilibrium with staggering of pricing decisions, Caplin–Leahy find that as the degree of strategic complementarity is increased, the range of output fluctuations will increase as well though the size of price adjustments will be lower.

V. Concluding Thoughts

In the U.S., the IS/LM model is now rarely taught above the intermediate undergraduate level. Yet, in the corridors of our capital and the columns of our newspaper, the implicit (and often explicit) model that underlies economic conversation is, in fact, the basic IS/LM model with a Phillips curve. Is this ever present gulf a sign of the failure of researchers to communicate their discoveries to policymakers or is it simply evidence that, in terms of policy questions, macroeconomics has made little progress over the past years?

My reading of recent literature suggests that policy relevant contributions are being made. The basic RBC model has provided us with tools for evaluating the positive aspects of a variety of fiscal policies. Further, quantitative research has gone well beyond the complete contingent markets, representative agent paradigm and will eventually allow us, in principle, to understand the impact of policy in a very rich set of alternative environments.[28] This same methodology has been extended to study economies with price rigidities, providing additional policy insights.

Finally, the models with heterogeneity provide a novel perspective on policy. These models suggest that it is important to know the cross sectional distribution of relevant variables in assessing the impact of a

---

[28] One could, for example, consider fiscal policy experiments in a version of the Baxter–King model and undertake an analysis of optimal policy in that environment.

particular policy. Further, these models suggest that policymakers should be aware of both the immediate and more long-run implications of these actions through the dynamics induced by the cross sectional distribution.

References

Adda, J. and Cooper, R., Balladurette and Juppette: A discrete approach. NBER WP 6048, 1997.

Bar-Ilan, A. and Blinder, A.: Consumer durables: Evidence on the optimality of doing nothing. *Journal of Money, Credit and Banking 24*, 253–272, 1992.

Basu, S. and Fernald, J.: Are apparent productive spillovers a figment of specification error? *Journal of Monetary Economics 36*, 165–188, 1995.

Baxter, M. and King P.: Productive externalities and business cycles. DP 53, Institute for Empirical Macroeconomics, Federal Reserve Bank of Minneapolis, Nov. 1991.

Baxter, M. and King P.: Fiscal policy in general equilibrium. *American Economic Review 83*, 315–334, 1993.

Beaudry, P. and Devereux, M.: Monopolistic competition, price setting and the effects of real and monetary shocks. Mimeo, University of British Columbia, 1993.

Benhabib, J. and Farmer, R.: Indeterminacy and increasing returns. *Journal of Economic Theory 63*, 19–41, 1994.

Braun, T.: Tax disturbances and real economic activity in the postwar United States. *Journal of Monetary Economics 33*, 441–462, 1994.

Braun, T. and Evans, C.: Seasonal Solow residuals and Christmas: A case for labor hoarding and increasing returns. WP-91-20, Federal Reserve Bank of Chicago, Oct. 1991.

Bryant, J.: A simple rational expectation Keynes-type model. *Quarterly Journal of Economics 97*, 525–529, 1983.

Burnside, C., Eichenbaum, M. and Rebelo, S.: Capital utilization and returns to scale. In B. Bernanke and J. Rotemberg (eds.), *NBER Macroeconomics Annual*, MIT Press, Cambridge, MA, 67–123, 1995.

Caballero, R. and Engel, E.: Microeconomic adjustment hazards and aggregate dynamics. *Quarterly Journal of Economics 108*, 359–384, 1993a.

Caballero, R. and Engel, E.: Explaining investment dynamics in U.S. manufacturing: A generalized (S, s) approach. Mimeo, ?place, Dec. 1993b.

Caballero, R. and Engel, E.: Heterogeneity and output fluctuations in a dynamic menu-cost economy. *Review of Economic Studies 60*, 95–119, 1993.

Caplin, A. and Leahy, J.: Aggregation and optimization with state dependent pricing. *Econometrica 65*, 601–626, 1997.

Chari, V. V., Christiano, L. and Kehoe, P.: Optimal fiscal policy in a business cycle model. *Journal of Political Economy 102*, 617–652, 1994.

Christiano, L. and Eichenbaum, M.: Current real-business-cycle and aggregate labor market fluctuations. *American Economic Review 82*, 430–450, 1992.

Christiano, L. and Eichenbaum, M.: Liquidity effects and the monetary transmission mechanism. *American Economic Review 82*, 344–353, 1992.

Christiano, L. and Eichenbaum, M. and Evans, C.: The effect of monetary shocks: Evidence from the flow of funds. *Review of Economics and Statistics 78*, 78–93, 1996.

Christiano, L. and Harrison, S.: Chaos, sunspots and automatic stabilizers. Staff Report 214, Federal Reserve Bank of Minneapolis, Aug. 1996.

Cooper, R.: Predetermined wages and prices and the impact of expansionary gvernment policy. *Review of Economic Studies 57*, 205–214, 1990.

Cooper, R.: Equilibrium selection in imperfectly competitive economies with multiple equilibria. *Economic Journal 104*, 1106–1123, 1994.

Cooper, R., DeJong, D., Forsythe, R. and Ross, T.: Alternative institutions for resolving coordination problems: Experimental evidence on forward induction and preplay communication. In J. W. Friedman (ed.), *Problems of Coordination in Economic Activity*, Kluwer Academic Publishers, Boston, 1994.

Cooper, R. and Ejarque, J.: Financial intermediation and the Great Depression: A multiple equilibrium interpretation. *Carnegie-Rochester Conference Series on Public Policy 43*, 285–323, 1995.

Cooper, R. and Ejarque, J.: Financial intermediation and aggregate fluctuations: A quantitative analysis. Revised version of NBER WP 4819, July 1996.

Cooper, R. and Haltiwanger, J.: The aggregate implications of machine replacement: Theory and evidence. *American Economic Review 83*, 360–382, 1993.

Cooper, R., Haltiwanger, J. and Power, L.: Machine replacement and the business cycle: Lumps and bumps. NBER WP 5260, Sept. 1995.

Cooper, R. and John, A.: Coordinating coordination failures in Keynesian models. *Quarterly Journal of Economics 103*, 441–463, 1988.

Cooper, R. and Johri, A.: Dynamic complementarities: A quantitative analysis. NBER WP 5691, July 1996; forthcoming in *Journal of Monetary Economics*.

Danthine, J.-P. and Donaldson, J.: Methodological and empirical issues in real business cycle theory. *European Economic Review 37*, 1–35, 1993.

Diamond, D. and Dybvig, P.: Bank runs, deposit insurance and liquidity. *Journal of Political Economy 91*, 401–419, 1983.

Diamond, P.: Aggregate demand management in search equilibrium. *Journal of Political Economy 90*, 881–894, 1982.

Dotsey, M., King, R. and Wolman, A.: State dependent pricing and the general equilibrium dynamics of money and output. Mimeo, University of Virginia, Oct. 1996.

Eaton, J.: Public debt guarantees and private capital flight. *World Bank Economic Review 3*, 377–395, 1987.

Farmer, F. and Guo, J. T.: Real business cycles and the animal spirits hypothesis. *Journal of Economic Theory 63*, 42–72, 1994.

Fiorito, R. and Kollintzas, T.: Stylized facts of business cycles in the G7 from a real business cycles perspective. *European Economic Review 38*, 235–269, 2994.

Fuerst, T.: Liquidity, loanable funds and real activity. *Journal of Monetary Economics 29*, 3–24, 1992.

Gloom, G. and Ravikumar, B.: Endogenous public policy and multiple equilibria. *European Journal of Political Economy 11*, 653–662, 1995.

González, F.: Individual experimentation and aggregate fluctuations. Mimeo, Boston University, 1996.

Greenwood, J., Hercowitz, Z. and Huffman, G.: Investment, capacity utilization and the real business cycle. *American Economic Review 78*, 402–417, 1988.

Hairault, J.-O., Langot, F. and Portier, F.: On the effectiveness of automatic stabilizers. Mimeo, MAD, Université de Paris I, Sept. 1995.

Hairault, J.-O., Langot, F. and Portier, F.: Financing unemployment benefits in the business cycle: Stabilization, welfare and equity issues. Ch. 10 in J.-O. Haircault, P.-Y. Henen and F. Portier (eds.), *Business Cycles and Macroeconomic Stability: Should We Rebuild Built-in Stabilizers?* Kluwer Academic Publishers, Boston, 231–250, 1997.

Hall, R.: Market structure and macroeconomic fluctuations. *Brookings Papers on Economic Activity*, 285–322, 1986.

Hart, O.: A model of imperfect competition with Keynesian features. *Quarterly Journal of Economics 97*, 109–138, 1982.

Heller, W.: Coordination failure under complete markets with applications to effective demand. In W. Heller, R. Starr and D. Starrett (eds.), *Equilibrium Analysis, Essays in Honor of Kenneth J. Arrow*, Volume II, Cambridge University Press, Cambridge, 1986.

Howitt, P.: Transactions costs in the theory of unemployment. *American Economic Review* 75, 88–101, 1985.

Jonsson, G. and Klein, P.: Stochastic fiscal policy and the Swedish business cycle. *Journal of Monetary Economics 38*, 245–268, 1996.

King, R., Plosser C. and Rebelo, S.: Production growth and business cycles. *Journal of Monetary Economics 21*, 195–232, 1988.

Kiyotaki, N.: Multiple expectational equilibria under monopolistic competition. *Quarterly Journal of Economics 103*, 695–714, 1988.

Kiyotaki, N. and Wright, R.: A search theoretic approach to monetary economics. *American Economic Review 83*, 63–77, 1993.

Kydland, F. and Prescott, E.: Time to build and aggregate fluctuations. *Economedtrica 50*, 1345–1370, 1982.

Lee, B. S. and Ingram, B.: Simulation estimation of time-series models. *Journal of Econometrics 47*, 197–205, 1991.

Loungani, P. and Rush, M.: The effects of changes in reserve requirement on investment and GNP. *Journal of Monetary, Credit and Banking 27*, 511–526, 1995.

Lucas, R.: Liquidity and interest rates. *Journal of Economic Theory 50*, 237–264, 1990.

McGratten, E.: The macroeconomic effects of distortionary taxation. *JOurnal of Monetary Economics 33*, 573–601, 1994.

Milgrom, P. and Roberts, J.: Rationalizability, learning and equilibrium in games with strategic complementarities. *Econometrica 58*, 1255–1278, 1990.

Persson, T. and Tabellini, G.: *Macroeconomic Policy, Credibility and Politics*. Harwood Academic Press, New York, 1990.

Schmitt-Grohe, S. and Uribe, M.: Balanced budget rules, distortionary taxes and aggregate instability. Mimeo, Federal Reserve Board of Governors, 1996.

Vives, X.: Nash equilibrium with strategic complementarities. *Journal of Mathematical Economics 19*, 305–321, 1990.

Van Huyck, J. B., Battalio, R. and Beil, R.: Tacit coordination games, strategic uncertainty and coordination failure. *American Economic Review 80*, 2134–2148, 1990.

Weil, P.: Increasing returns and animal spirits. *American Economic Review 79*, 94, 1989.

Weitzman, M.: Increasing returns and the foundation of unemployment theory. *Economic Journal 92*, 787–804, 1982.

Scand. J. Economics 100(1), 239–242, 1998

Comment on R. W. Cooper, "Business Cycles: Theory, Evidence and Policy Implications"

Jean-Pierre Danthine*

Université de Lausanne, CH-1015 Lausanne, Switzerland

Russell Cooper's paper usefully and interestingly surveys three strands of literature which, until recently, would have been viewed as largely antagonistic: stochastic growth models on one hand, models building on macroeconomic complementarities and heterogeneity on the other. The reason for grouping them together in a selective survey of business cycle research can be read between the lines: in the author's view, the RBC methodology has become largely accepted, although this is not the case for the complete contingent markets/representative agent model. Accordingly, the stochastic growth model can be used as a platform or a generic analytical framework for business cycle research, but it should be extended - on *a priori* grounds or with the objective of improving its ability to replicate key stylized facts - and the author's preferences as to the directions of extension are revealed in his choice of topics in Sections III and IV. I fully agree with this view on the state of business cycle theory and the research program that results. And, although my own preferences differ somewhat, I find the proposed directions for extending the basic model particularly challenging.

Keeping with the occasion, the title of the paper includes the terms 'policy implications' and Cooper indeed concludes his contribution by asserting that "policy relevant contributions are being made". Making explicit the argument that begins there, this suggests that he views the gulf between researchers — who have stopped using or teaching the IS-LM model — and practitioners — who predominantly continue to rely on it — as a sign of "the failure of researchers to communicate their discoveries to policymakers". One may disagree on this score. I, for one, am not sure that even this well-crafted survey would convince policymakers that they should abandon their favorite tool for macroeconomic analysis. That is, I am not convinced that any of the models presented here provide, in their current state of development, adequate foundations for policy analysis.

Beyond this apparently pessimistic assessment, I am willing to argue, however, that the extension of the stochastic growth/real business cycle

---

*These comments draw on Danthine (1997).

model in the directions sketched in this paper — macroeconomic complementarities and, perhaps, heterogeneity — and along several other dimensions, is likely to give rise to the new synthesis the profession has been
awaiting for 20 years. This would be in line with the prediction of Campbell
(1994): "Ultimately, a stochastic growth model incorporating [real and
nominal macroeconomic] rigidities holds out the promise of a new synthesis in macroeconomics".

For this to be the case, a number of requirements have to be fulfilled,
however. First, a balance has to be struck between the legitimate ambitions
of researchers in terms of the rigor and generality of their model and the
relative simplicity that is required for a model to serve as an intuitive tool
for everyday policy analysis. Compared with the new breed of dynamic
general equilibrium models, IS-LM was extraordinarily simple. It will not
be possible to satisfy all the demands of academics aware of the main
lessons of recent research and still fulfill this simplicity requirement.
Models with meaningful heterogeneity, as reviewed in Section IV, pose
particularly difficult problems. In the end, the question of the existence of
a true successor to IS-LM may well reside in economists' ability to
summarize in a simple enough model the various lessons of the last 20
years of macroeconomics.

At another level, the successor to IS-LM will have to be better than
current models in reproducing the key stylized facts of macroeconomics.
While generally considered surprisingly good on this score, the benchmark
RBC model nevertheless fails to explain important macroeconomic or
financial regularities. Cooper focuses on the near-zero correlation
between hours worked and average productivity because the preferred
solution to this puzzle is the introduction of a richer policy set-up, namely
government expenditures and distortionary taxes. Several other puzzles
have drawn the attention of business cycle researchers: the employment
volatility puzzle, the consumption volatility puzzle, the equity premium
puzzle and a score of additional anomalies appearing once open economy
considerations are introduced. What I find interesting is that the solutions
to these puzzles almost always entail extending the model in directions that
are close in spirit to those advocated by Cooper: incomplete financial
markets are considered an essential element of the possible solutions for
the international and financial puzzles; labor market puzzles have led to
grafting the dynamic GE model with important pieces of the new Keynesian research program. Dynamic GE models with efficiency wages and
labor contracts have thus appeared, often with significant explanatory
success.

There is no dispute that these observations about reality, which are
puzzling because they are in conflict with the prediction of the standard
business cycle model, can be taken as falsification of the pure neo-classical

growth model. The uncovering of these puzzles has, however, been used profitably to modify and enrich the model context beyond what previously appeared to be formidable technical barriers. This systematic process of model enrichment following the confrontation with observations is precisely what makes it possible, in my view, to foresee the dynamic GE models developed around the neoclassical stochastic growth model — but possibly evolving towards friction-prone non-Walrasian models — growing into the successor to IS-LM.

Third, the future synthesis should not only be relatively simple and transparent as well as demonstrate a satisfactory ability to replicate the key macroeconomic and financial stylized facts. In addition, it should be expected to do so while relying on intuitively plausible economic mechanisms. A problem with most current models of the RBC class is that they look and sound implausible to a large fraction of the profession. Plausibility is likely to be a decisive criterion for success in the contest for the IS-LM successorship. Plausibility is, however, subject to change: what is considered implausible today may well become part of the consensus tomorrow. Indeed, how are we supposed to react, if not by modifying our priors, if, repeatedly and convincingly, the models best able to match the stylized facts are those based on what we view, *a priori*, as implausible mechanisms, while the more plausible models systematically fail to account for some major observations?

This said, one may indeed question the plausibility of solving the near-zero correlation puzzle alluded to earlier by relying on shifts of the labor supply occurring at quarterly frequencies as a result of changes in the tax burden of the representative agent. Similarly, Aiayagari (1996) has suggested that the multiple equilibria route followed by Benhabib and Farmer (1994) and Farmer and Guo (1994) and reviewed by Cooper does not pass the plausibility test, in that the ability of these models to reproduce the observations is predicated on the twin assumptions of an upward sloping labor demand curve and a downward sloping labor supply curve.

More constructively, it is possible today to make what many would view as an extra step in the direction of a plausible short-run macroeconomic model and build a true Keynesian dynamic GE model. By that I mean a dynamic model economy in which, because of price rigidities, a negative demand shock, originating in macro policies or the current account or possibly consumer confidence, is met with quantity adjustments across sectors rather than pure price adjustments as implicitly hypothesized in the standard business cycle model. In other words, a dynamic GE model where Keynesian spillovers reappear. Gali (1996) sketches such a model with imperfect competition, sticky prices and variable efforts, arguing that such a model stands a better chance than more traditional RBC models of explaining what he sees as a negative (conditional) correlation between shocks identified as technology shocks and employment. Most recently, Goodfriend and King (1997) have also proposed — and put to work for the analysis of monetary policy — a similar model, not hesitating to label it "the new neoclassical synthesis". These newest developments make it ever more likely that the gulf between policymakers and academic economists will soon be reduced to at most a communication gap, as diagnosed, only slightly prematurely, by the author.

References

Aiayagari, S. R.: Comments on Farmer and Guo's "The econometrics of indeterminacy: An applied study" (1994). Federal Reserve Bank of Minneapolis Staff Report 196, 1995.

Benhabib, J. and Farmer, R.: Indeterminacy and increasing returns. *Journal of Economic Theory 63*, 19–41, 1994.

Campbell, J.: Inspecting the mechanism - An analytical approach to the stochastic growth model. *Journal of Monetary Economics 33*, 463–506, 1994.

Danthine, J. P.: In search of a successor to IS-LM. *Oxford Review of Economic Policy 13*(3), 135–144, Fall 1997.

Gali, J.: Technology, employment and the business cycle: Do technology shocks explain aggregate fluctuations? CEPR DP 1499, London, 1996.

Goodfriend, M., and King, R. G.: The new neoclassical synthesis and the role of monetary policy. Mimeo, University of Virginia, 1997.

Scand. J. Economics 100(1), 243–245, 1998

Comment on R. W. Cooper, "Business Cycles: Theory, Evidence and Policy Implications"

Nils Gottfries

Uppsala University, S-751 20 Uppsala, Sweden

Cooper's paper reviews some current research directions in macroeconomics. The paper made me worried about the state of macroeconomic research and my comments below consist of some critical remarks on the methodological approach in the literature reviewed in the paper.

A Depressing Picture of Macroeconomic Research

In order to build a basic macroeconomic model we need to understand consumption, investment, labor demand, labor supply, wage setting, price setting and a few other things. If we combine these, we get a simple macroeconomic model. We want the model to be based on rational optimizing behavior - and personally I am sympathetic to representative agents models. Usually when we try to interpret macroeconomic data, we implicitly assume that the aggregation problems are not too serious; so in that sense most journalists who write about macroeconomic developments think in terms of representative agents. If we could get a reasonable representative agent model to explain 70 percent of the variation in key macroeconomic variables, such a model would be of great help in discussions of macroeconomics.

There are quite a few theories available and we need to learn from the data which of them are relevant. Here, econometric theory tells us almost everything we want to know about what we can and what we cannot learn from the data, using all the information in the data, taking account of complicated error structures, etc. With modern computers, extremely sophisticated estimation can be done quite easily. So with quite a few theories and powerful econometric estimation methods available we should, by now, know a great deal about how the macroeconomy works, shouldn't we?

Reading this paper, one gets the impression that we know close to nothing about how the macroeconomy works. Every paper starts more or less from scratch. Economists are fumbling with various theories which are very different from each other and which are tested in extremely crude ways by checking whether they are able to reproduce a few covariances between key macroeconomic variables. Judging from this review, there is no 'received wisdom' in macroeconomics today. Why is this?

The key problem is the *identification problem* in econometrics. We cannot make controlled experiments; whatever estimation we make, and whatever correlations we look at, there are typically several possible interpretations. Most of the econometric evidence that has accumulated over the years can be critisized on the grounds that the regressions may pick up spurious correlations: causation may go the other way or some third factor may create a correlation between two variables. Thus it is hard to produce decisive evidence for or against some particular hypothesis. Of course, the same applies to the rudimentary form of econometrics where one only tries to reproduce a small number of correlations between macroeconomic variables.

This does not mean that macroeconomic data are useless for testing theories. No, checking whether a model can reproduce key macroeconomic correlations is useful, and so is more sophisticated econometric estimation. But considering the severe problems with macroeconometrics we should not regard it as the only way to the truth - other sources of information should be regarded as equally important. We need to use all the information that we have: microeconomic data, observed behavior on the microeconomic level, accounts by journalists and businessmen, answers to questionaires, etc. All this information must be weighted together in an informal way and in the end we must ask ourselves whether the story is *plausible*.

Scientific Discipline?

But the methodology in much recent macroeconomic research seems to be to disregard much of what we know, to set up a very limited number of macroeconomic statistics and to ask *only* whether the model is able to reproduce these statistics. If a model is able to reproduce one or two correlations more than the previous one, it is regarded as a step forward. One systematically ignores the question of whether the model is plausible and consistent with other types of information, e. g. what we know about how firms and workers behave on the microeconomic level.

It is as if a doctor would base his diagnosis only on the results of a very limited set of "quantitative" medical test results, refusing to see the patient because what the patient says is not sufficiently "quantitative". What is, after all, "a stomach ache"? It is a subjective perception which cannot be measured! No, let's only use the hard facts! Most patients would hesitate to consult such a doctor, but in economics this is regarded as the highest form of scientific discipline.

More specifically, a theme that runs through the paper is the question: how can we get employment to vary with the business cycle? The traditional view of this problem is that there is a non-clearing labor market and nominal wages and prices adjust slowly; so both demand and supply shocks may cause variations in employment. To me there seems to be overwhelming evidence to support this traditional view — evidence of all the different kinds that I referred to above — suggesting that the features mentioned above should be important elements in any theory of the business cycle. Standard textbooks in intermediate macroeconomics, such as Mankiw (1997) and Blanchard (1997), refer to such evidence. They also illustrate the usefulness of the traditional approach for understanding the consequences of major policy experiments such as a shift to a more contractionary monetary policy or a devaluation. I do not see why we should disregard this evidence as well as the various theories which have been constructed in order to explain non-clearing labor markets and wage and price rigidity.

Ignoring the key combination of nominal wage rigidity and a non-clearing labor market, researchers turn to very implausible stories about the business cycle. Contrived stories are told about how money could be non-neutral although prices are flexible. Enormous externalities between firms are introduced to get large effects of shocks and multiple equilibria. Taxes are supposed to play an important role in creating cyclical variations in labor supply. A very elastic labor supply is assumed in order to generate multiple equilibria. But why should we ignore the observed fact that labor contracts typically fix nominal wages for periods of between one and three years? Are there any microeconomic examples of the massive externalities assumed in macroeconomic simulations? Does anyone believe that unemployment increases in recessions because the tax system makes people withdraw from the labor market? Why should we disregard microeconometric estimates which suggest that the elasticity of labor supply is small? Don't economists see that there are unemployed workers out there who become happy if they get a job?

Now, introducing wage and price rigidities does not solve all the problems in macroeconomics. But if we allow them to play a role, we may focus on the true mysteries of macroeconomics rather than on constructed ones. My main point, however, is that we need to take a broader view when we evaluate macroeconomic theories than is done in the survey and in the cited literature.

References

Blanchard, O.: *Macroeconomics.* Prentice Hall, Englewood Cliffs, NJ, 1997.
Mankiw, G.: *Macroeconomics.* Worth, New York, NY, 1997.

Scand. J. of Economics 100(1), 247–275, 1998

Open-Economy Macroeconomics: Developments in Theory and Policy

Maurice Obstfeld *

University of California, Berkeley, CA 94720, USA

Abstract

This paper views developments in open-economy macroeconomics through the lens of the debate over European monetary unification. The empirical tendency for nominal exchange rate regimes to affect the variability of nominal and real exchange rates alike can be rationalized by sticky-price theories or models of asset-market liquidity effects. But plausible liquidity models have difficulty generating enough persistence to match the data. Thus, the macroeconomic stabilization costs of forgoing the exchange-rate realignment option seem pertinent. It is argued that our theories of efficiencies due to a common currency remain unsatisfactory, despite recent advances. The paper concludes by reviewing theories of currency crisis

I. Introduction

The evolution of the international gold standard stands out as the central factor in European (indeed, world) macroeconomic history in the first half of the twentieth century. When future historians look back over Europe's macroeconomic performance in the early twenty-first century, a similarly dominant role will no doubt be attached to the evolution of economic and monetary union (EMU). The drive toward EMU has its roots in European reconstruction a half-century ago, and it is scheduled to reach fruition, at least for a first wave of participants, on January 1, 1999. It is now difficult to believe that some form of EMU will not be put in place on that date. This paper is focused on the question of international monetary

---

* My discussants at the *SJE*'s symposium on "Public Policy and Economic Theory", Patrick Kehoe and Asbjørn Rødseth, provided useful criticism, as did Andy Neumeyer, two anonymous referees, the editors, and seminar participants at MIT. I am grateful to Olivier Jeanne, Kenneth Rogoff, and Alan Taylor for ongoing discussions, to Matthew Jones and Reza Baqir for excellent research assistance, and to the National Science Foundation for support. All errors and opinions are mine. An earlier version of this paper was presented as the Mackintosh Lecture at Queen's University in October 1996.

unification, which provides a useful lens for examining much of the recent thinking and progress in open-economy macroeconomic analysis.

In its interwar incarnation, the international gold standard had staggering costs in terms of output and employment, as is now widely agreed; see Eichengreen (1992). EMU will aid countries with inflationary histories in achieving more stable price levels (while possibly delivering more inflation than Germany would like). But will EMU entail significant output and employment costs? The answer depends in part on the efficacy of macro-economic (especially monetary) policy for stabilization of output and employment. Motivated by the need to understand macroeconomic policy effects, I devote Sections II and III to understanding what nominal and real exchange rate movements can tell us about the flexibility of nominal prices. If nominal prices are sticky in the short run, there is a strong presumption that national authorities can deploy monetary and fiscal policy to offset unexpected shocks to output and employment. Under EMU, however, member countries may largely be constrained from responding to unpleasant macroeconomic surprises.

If EMU is costly in terms of macroeconomic stability, its membership could be unstable. But monetary union is thought to involve offsetting *microeconomic* benefits — wholly apart from the political dividends that have been a dominant factor propelling EMU from the idea's inception. These microeconomic benefits involve efficiency gains in exchange and production, such as transaction-cost savings and a more rational international division of labor. Balancing the economic costs and benefits, one arrives at the notion of an optimum currency area, which I discuss in Section IV. In that section I also explore some models and empirical results pertinent to the efficiency benefits of monetary unification, though these results are largely conjectural. As Krugman (1995) has observed, the theoretical foundation for our beliefs about the efficiency benefits of common currencies remains quite narrow.

A final question, addressed in Section V, has implications for the transition to EMU and its operation as it evolves. Prior to January 1, 1999 speculative attacks on European Monetary System (EMS) exchange parities remain a logical possibility. Uncertainty over the eventual conversion rates between member currencies could lead to volatile capital flows. Even after EMU is inaugurated, the "outs" who target the euro in the hope of ultimately entering EMU remain vulnerable to attack, and such attacks could trigger intervention by the "in" bloc. A new literature on currency crises suggests that even countries following conservative monetary and fiscal policies may become vulnerable to attack. In the final substantive section, I review the implications of these models, along with some new questions they raise.

II. Currency Movements in Light of Sticky-Price Theories

Are nominal prices sticky in the short run? This question, central to all of macroeconomic debate, also is critical for assessing the influence of the nominal exchange rate regime on the macroeconomy. The joint distribution of real and nominal exchange rates provides some of the most striking evidence that models with sticky prices can potentialy explain international macroeconomic data. This point was forcefully made by Mussa (1986). Developments since his seminal article was published only reaffirm its findings.

The basic empirical regularities are two under moderate inflation rates. First, changes in the nominal exchange rate regime appear systematically related to the variability of real as well as nominal exchange rates. Shifts from regimes of controlled nominal rates to floating rates apparently cause short-run real exchange rate volatility to rise, whereas opposite shifts reduce short-run real exchange rate volatility. High-frequency real and nominal volatility tend to be approximately the same under floating rates. Second, under floating exchange rates, though not necessarily under more controlled exchange rate regimes, real and nominal exchange rate movements are nearly perfectly correlated in the short run.[1]

The findings are easily explained if price levels are slow to adjust compared with nominal exchange rates, so that nominal exchange rate changes translate virtually one-for-one into international relative price level changes. Under conditions of very high inflation, however, matters are different: floating nominal rates are more volatile than the corresponding real rates when inflation is high, and the short-run correlation between changes in the two rates lies substantially below unity. These changes are consistent with flight from nominal contracting in conditions of monetary instability.

Evidence from Moderate-Inflation Economies

The case of the lira/deutschemark rate (see Table 1) illustrates how the preceding regularities operate in cases of moderate and low inflation.[2] Let

---

[1] The high short-run correlation between real and nominal exchange rates under floating has been ascribed by some to real or output-market shocks that alter nominal exchange rates without much affecting national price levels. The seeming dependence of real rate volatility on the nominal regime is, however, evidence against the "real shock" view. Further evidence that monetary shocks indeed have played a big role comes from long-run data on price levels and exchange rates. Over the period since 1973, industrial-country price levels have changed quite a bit; see e.g. Obstfeld 1995, p. 123, figure 1). The cumulative inflation furnishes a *prima facie* case that monetary shocks have been important.

[2] Real exchange rates in Tables 1 and 2 are based on consumer price indexes and monthly average nominal exchange rates. Wholesale price indexes, when available, imply very smilar behavior. Data, measured at monthly frequency, are taken from International Monetary

Table 1. *Italy/Germany*

Period	Std ($\hat{e}$)	Std ($\hat{r}$)	Corr ($\hat{e}, \hat{r}$)
February 1957–February 1973	0.008	0.010	0.89
March 1973–February 1979	0.027	0.027	0.97
March 1979–December 1989	0.009	0.009	0.85
January 1990–August 1992	0.004	0.006	0.78
September 1992–November 1996	0.029	0.029	0.99
December 1996–June 1997	0.009	0.009	0.98

e denote the nominal exchange rate (the domestic-currency price of foreign currency) and r the real exchange rate, ep^*/p (where p^* and p are foreign and home money CPIs). Table 1 (like the two tables that follow it) displays the standard deviations of the monthly log differences in e and r, denoted by hats, as well as the correlation coefficient between $\hat{e}$ and $\hat{r}$. Notice that on the above measure of volatility, a currency depreciating at a constant rate (as in a steady crawling peg) would display zero variability. The variables $\hat{e}$ and $\hat{r}$ are graphed in Figure 1 for Italy relative to Germany.

Nominal and real rate volatility are low under Bretton Woods, but with the advent of floating both increase roughly threefold and the real-nominal correlation coefficient rises. Italy's ± 6 percent ERM band (1979–89) reduces exchange rate volatility to Bretton Woods levels, realignments notwithstanding, and the shift to the ERM's ± 2.25 percent narrow band in January 1990 reduces volatility further. The real-nominal correlation drops in that period because most real rate variation comes from price-level movements. During Italy's absence from the ERM (September 1992–November 1996), volatility and correlation return to the same pattern as in the pre-EMS float, 1973–79. Italy's end-1996 return to the ERM in order to qualify for EMU brings a sharp drop in real as well as nominal volatility. In all episodes real and nominal variability are close or equal.

Evidence from High-Inflation Economies

Somewhat different empirical regularities apply in cases of high or hyper-inflation, as stressed by Leiderman and Bufman (1995). Table 2 and Figure 2 show data on Israel's exchange rate against the dollar, calculated consistently on the basis of the present Israeli currency. The year 1973 ushered in

Fund, *International Financial Statistics*. The relative-price data in Table 3 below, which are based on relative export price indexes rather than relative CPIs, come from the same source.

a period of sharply higher Israeli inflation. Thus, until the stabilization of July 1985, nominal volatility rises with almost *no corresponding average increase in real volatility*. Furthermore, the real-nominal correlation drops sharply (having been dominated by realignments before 1973). One theory

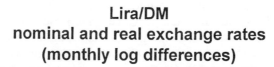

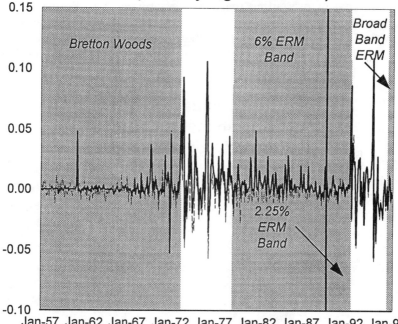

Fig. 1.

Table 2. *Israel/United States*

Period	Std ($\hat{e}$)	Std ($\hat{r}$)	Corr ($\hat{e}, \hat{r}$)
February 1957–February 1973	0.036	0.039	0.93
March 1973–June 1985	0.063	0.042	0.69
July 1985–August 1996	0.030	0.020	0.68

explaining this development is that nominal contracting simply becomes too costly when inflation is high and variable. In response, dollarization spreads through the economy. Similar patterns characterize recent data for other sometime high-inflation economies, such as Argentina, and for interwar inflationary episodes; see, for example, De Grauwe, Janssens, and Leliaert (1985).

The stabilization initiated under Michael Bruno's governorship of the Bank of Israel began with a pegged exchange rate, but has since followed more flexible forms of exchange rate targeting, most recently a crawling target zone. This flexibility has allowed some accommodation of inflation with the goal of preventing real currency appreciation. Both real and nominal volatility have dropped under nominal exchange rate targeting, as one would expect, but the correlation between real and nominal exchange rate movements has not risen relative to the period of high inflation. This

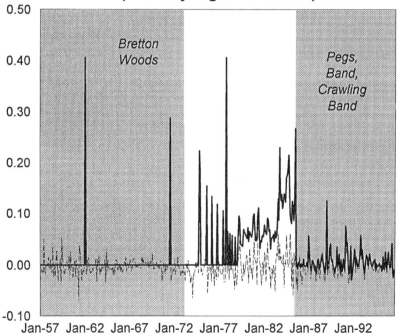

Fig. 2.

may be due to the accommodative exchange rate policy of the Israeli authorities, which resists incipient real currency appreciations through nominal exchange rate adjustments.

Exchange Rates and Terms of Trade

The above empirical regularities have been developed from the perspective of real exchange rates defined in terms of consumer prices. Similar regularities hold, albeit somewhat less strongly, for comovements between nominal exchange rates and terms of trade. Figure 3 shows changes in the France/Germany nominal exchange rate along with changes in French relative to German export prices.[3] The statistics in Table 3 suggest that in

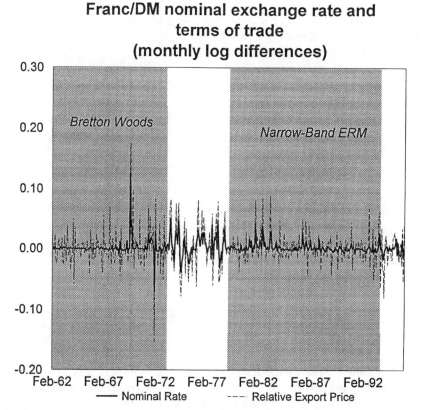

Fig. 3.

---

[3] For the analogous picture with CPIs, see Obstfeld (1995, p. 131).

Table 3. *France/Germany*

Period	Std ($\hat{e}$)	Std ($\hat{r}$)	Corr ($\hat{e}, \hat{r}$)
February 1962–February 1973	0.014	0.035	0.68
February 1962–July 1969	0.003	0.022	0.06
March 1973–February 1979	0.019	0.038	0.83
March 1979–July 1993	0.007	0.022	0.61
August 1993–December 1995	0.009	0.031	0.55

general both nominal exchange variability and variability in relative export prices rise when currencies float (or when there are large discrete realignments, as in 1969–73). The numbers also suggest that exchange rate changes are highly correlated with changes in relative export prices in a flexible-rate regime. Even in the short run, however, terms of trade display considerably more variability than the nominal exchange rate regardless of the monetary regime. This behavior could be due to different export composition and destination for the two countries, and differences in pricing-to-market.

Macromodels and the "Purchasing Power Parity Puzzle"

The acceptance of a sticky-price basis for the comovements between relative prices and nominal exchange rates has important implications for stabilization policy. Price stickiness provides a channel through which macropolicies can offset shocks that were not anticipated when prices were set, and that potentially have real effects pending the complete adjustment of prices. In an open economy with nominal price and wage stickiness, the government's option to adjust the exchange rate in response to unexpected shocks has a stabilization value that is forgone under an irrevocably fixed exchange rate or currency union.

The modified IS–LM model of Mundell, Fleming, and Dornbusch, which has been the workhorse analytical tool of policymakers for decades now, is consistent with the preceding conclusions. But the model does not come to grips with several important areas quite critical for the evaluation of stabilization policies. Among these are the dynamics of current accounts, the dynamics of fiscal imbalances, and the foundations of aggregate supply.

Recent intertemporal models of price setting by imperfectly competitive firms and/or unions provide a framework for exploring these issues; see e.g. Obstfeld and Rogoff (1996, Chapter 10). The best way to introduce nominal and real rigidities so as to capture the stylized facts of business cycles remains the subject of active research. Alternative calibration exercises by Chari, Kehoe, and McGrattan (1996) and by Kollmann (1996) consider models with monopolistic elements and sticky nominal prices and/or wages (*à la* Calvo). The first of these papers assumes complete asset markets, while the second, more realistically, assumes that monies and nominally risk-free bonds are the only assets available. Taken together, however, the papers show that nominal price and wage rigidities offer the potential to rationalize the exchange-rate behavior discussed above, along with other regularities, such as a persistent effect of nominal shocks on real exchange rates; see e.g. Clarida and Gali (1994) and Schlagenhauf and Wrase (1995).

The models developed to date still leave some important business-cycle phenomena unexplained, and no doubt will be extended. For example, the persistence of monetary effects on real exchange rates, while high in the models mentioned above, is not as extremely high as the real exchange rate persistence seen in the data. Generally it is found that the half-life of real exchange rate deviations from trend is on the order of four to five years, far longer than the typical business cycle. Stockman (1988) asked how that discrepancy could be consistent with a monetary-*cum*-sticky price account of real exchange rate movements. Rogoff (1996) calls the conundrum the "purchasing power parity puzzle".

There are (at least) two responses to the puzzle. The first observes that the rate of reversion of real exchange rates to a linear trend need not measure the pace of adjustment to a specifically monetary shock. For example, let u_t be a positive shock to national aggregate output demand. The shock follows a first-order autoregressive process with serial correlation $\rho \in (0, 1)$. Let r_t denote the real exchange rate, defined as the price of foreign in terms of domestic goods. In the log-linear Mussa (1982) model of exchange rates, it can be shown that the real exchange rate evolves according to the process

$$\Delta r_{t+1} = -\theta\delta r_t + (1 - \rho - \theta\delta)\frac{u_t}{\delta} + \varepsilon_{t+1},$$

where θ is the speed of nominal price response to excess output demand, δ is the real exchange rate elasticity of output demand, and ε_t is a random date t disturbance.

If u_t were constant, applying least squares to the preceding equation — the exercise prevalent in the PPP literature — would yield a consistent estimate of the adjustment speed to nominal shocks, $\theta\delta$. But in truth real shocks do occur, and r_t and u_t tend to be *negatively* correlated because a rise in aggregate demand causes real currency appreciation. If real shocks are at all persistent (ρ near 1), so that $1 - \rho - \theta\delta < 0$, then least squares regression of Δr_{t+1} on r_t alone gives an estimate of $\theta\delta$ that is biased toward zero. The estimate appears to imply slower elimination of monetary shocks' real effects than is the case in reality, because the data confound persistent real shocks with monetary shocks. Nonetheless, monetary shocks might still explain most exchange rate variability at relatively short horizons.

A second response to the PPP puzzle is based on the observation that real rigidities, when coupled with nominal rigidities, can dramatically prolong the adjustment to monetary shocks; see Kimball (1995) and Jeanne (1998). Whether plausible real rigidities can generate the real exchange rate persistence in the data remains an open question for research.

Before rushing to embrace sticky price exchange rate models, however, note that alternative flexible-price models have some similar implications for real and nominal exchange rates to those just discussed. The next section explores this point.

III. Models with Separated Goods and Asset Markets

Even when goods prices and wages are perfectly flexible, lags in the transmission of monetary shocks from asset to goods markets can generate high nominal and real exchange rate variability, as well as correlations between nominal and real exchange rates similar to those usually seen in conditions of low to moderate inflation. Rotemberg (1985) first made this observation, but the recent emergence of explicitly stochastic models along the lines he proposed has allowed a more systematic study of the empirical implications of impediments to the flow of money and information between markets.[4]

A Basic Framework

A bare-bones framework for exploring exchange- and interest-rate implications of asset-market segmentation is provided by Grilli and Roubini (1992), who build closely on Lucas (1990).

In a variant of the framework, there are two countries, Home and Foreign, producing distinct perishable consumption goods. As a conveni-

---

[4] Similar effects can occur in random matching models where agents exchange national monies against each other and against commodities; see Head and Shi (1996). The problem with such models is that they abstract from the interest-bearing assets whose trade is thought to be central to exchange-rate determination in reality. Stockman (1988) showed how the possibility of capital or trade controls under a fixed exchange rate could dampen the variability of real exchange rates in a flexible price model. However, the empirical regularities noted in the last section apply even to such episodes as France's 1926 return to the gold standard, which would not itself have generated heightened expectations that stringent capital controls would be imposed; see De Grauwe, Janssens and Leliaert (1985). For a discussion of interwar capital controls, see Obstfeld and Taylor (1998).

ence in depicting equilibrium I will assume that residents in the two countries have identical preferences and have pooled their output risks, as in Lucas (1982), so that the representative Home and Foreign residents both own exactly half of the stochastic Home output process $\{Y_{Ht}\}_{t=0}^{\infty}$ and half of the stochastic Foreign output process $\{Y_{Ft}\}_{t=0}^{\infty}$. The further assumption that Home and Foreign residents start out with equal holdings of the Home and Foreign monies allows us to work in terms of a world representative household, that is assumed to maximize

$$U_0 = E_0 \left\{ \sum_{t=0}^{\infty} \beta^t u(c_{Ht}, c_{Ft}) \right\}, \qquad \beta \in (0, 1).$$

The complete menu of assets held and the assumed organization of asset and commodity trading are as follows: At the start of a period t the household output levels $y_{Ht} = \frac{1}{2}Y_{Ht}$ and $y_{Ft} = \frac{1}{2}Y_{Ft}$ are revealed and households hold domestic nominal balances money m_{Ht} and foreign nominal money balances m_{Ft}. Then one member of each (two-member) household takes $n_{Ht} \leq m_{Ht}$ currency units to the goods market, purchasing $c_{Ht} = n_{Ht}/p_{Ht}$ units of the domestic good and $c_{Ft} = n_{Ft}/p_{Ft}$ units of the foreign good, where p_{Ht} and p_{Ft} are the local-currency prices of the two goods, while simultaneously receiving $p_{Ht}y_{Ht}$ and $p_{Ft}y_{Ft}$ in money dividends that cannot be spent until period $t+1$.[5]

The household's second member takes $m_{Ht} - n_{Ht}$ and $m_{Ft} - n_{Ft}$ Home and Foreign currency units to an asset market, which operates contemporaneously with the goods market but has no communication with the latter. In the asset market, monies may be traded against each other at an exchange rate of e_t Home currency units per Foreign currency unit. Also, monies may be traded against government discount bonds denominated in the issuer's domestic currency. A bond is a promise to pay a single currency unit after a period. It is in the asset market that the model's other random shock is realized, the shock representing the supply of one-period bonds. If $M_{Ht} = 2m_{Ht}$ and $M_{Ft} = 2m_{Ft}$ are aggregate money supplies at the start of t, the two governments' bond issues are:

$$B_{Ht} = x_{Ht}M_{Ht}, \qquad B_{Ft} = x_{Ft}M_{Ft}.$$

By making money transfers, governments pay off bonds issued in period t at the start of period $t+1$, before households have split to visit the two markets. Thus, B_{Ht} and B_{Ft} represent gross rather than net bond issues — possibly a very large number relative to the money supply in countries such as Italy where much public debt is rolled over frequently. The date t

---

[5] Households cannot consume their own output. I assume that nominal interest rates always are positive, so that the cash-in-advance constraints $p_{Ht}c_{Ht} \leq n_{Ht}$ and $p_{Ft}c_{Ft} \leq n_{Ft}$ always bind at the individual level.

own-currency market prices of Home and Foreign bonds are q_{Ht} and q_{Ft}. When governments initially auction off bonds, each insists on trading its bond issue against its *own* currency, so that in equilibrium the conditions

$$B_{Ht} = x_{Ht}M_{Ht} = q_{Ht}(M_{Ht} - N_{Ht}),$$
$$B_{Ft} = x_{Ft}M_{Ft} = q_{Ft}(M_{Ft} - N_{Ft}),$$

(1)

must hold (where $N_{Ht} = 2n_{Ht}$ and $N_{Ft} = 2n_{Ft}$).

An agent already in the date t asset market and deciding bond purchases b_{Ht} and b_{Ft} faces the portfolio constraint $(m_{Ht} - n_{Ht}) + e_t(m_{Ft} - n_{Ft}) = q_{Ht}b_{Ht} + e_tq_{Ft}b_{Ft}$ and must be indifferent between allocating a marginal Home currency unit (say) to Home or Foreign government bonds. This result provides the "uncovered interest parity" condition for this model. Before households split up at the start of a period t, they are similarly indifferent between sending a marginal currency unit to the goods or asset market. The result is a pair of intertemporal Euler conditions, one for each currency. In equilibrium price levels are determined by

$$p_{Ht} = N_{Ht}/Y_{Ht}, \qquad p_{Ft} = N_{Ft}/Y_{Ft}.$$

Define $z_{Ht} = (m_{Ht} - n_{Ht})/m_{Ht}$ and $z_{Ft} = (m_{Ft} - n_{Ft})/m_{Ft}$ as the fractions of individual (in equilibrium, aggregate) money holdings devoted to security purchases. Equation (1) gives equilibrium bond prices as

$$q_{Ht} = \frac{z_{Ht}}{x_{Ht}}, \qquad q_{Ft} = \frac{z_{Ft}}{x_{Ft}}.$$

(2)

If all uncertainty is i.i.d., z_H and z_F will be time-invariant constants. To make my main points it suffices to describe the equilibrium in the special case $u(c_H, c_F) = \gamma \log c_H + (1 - \gamma) \log c_F$. Observe that individual consumption of Home goods satisfies (for all t)

$$c_{Ht} = \frac{n_{Ht}}{p_{Ht}} = \frac{(1 - z_H)m_{Ht}}{p_{Ht}}.$$

At the same time Home-money holdings at the start of period $t+1$ equal payments on domestic bonds b_{Ht} plus proceeds from the sale of last period's Home-generated output, $p_{Ht}y_{Ht}$:

$$m_{Ht+1} = b_{Ht} + p_{Ht}y_{Ht}.$$

Parallel relationships apply for Foreign-goods consumption and Foreign-money holdings.

According to eq. (2), the constancy of z_H and z_F imply that unanticipated bond issues will cause unanticipated increases in nominal interest rates (q_H is the inverse of $1 + i_H$, in the obvious notation, and similarly for Foreign).

There is no way, in the model, for financial market changes to feed contemporaneously into the goods market, so asset-market clearing requires that bond prices fluctuate more than they would in a Walrasian model.

Anticipated bond issues, however, will have no such effects. For example, suppose a government has been issuing bonds equal to 10 percent of its money supply. Suddenly it announces it will henceforth raise that figure to 20 percent, thereby withdrawing 20 percent of its money stock from circulation at the end of each period via the asset market. In that case people will simply double their allocation of currency to the bond market (relative to its prior path), causing the price level in the goods market to fall (relative to its prior path) in proportion to the additional end-of-period money-supply contraction. Bond prices are unaffected. The effect is the same as if the monetary contraction had occurred prior to the opening of the goods market.

Of central interest are the model's implications for the nominal exchange rate and the real exchange rate, the latter defined here in terms of GDP deflators, so as to correspond to the terms of trade. From the model's interest parity condition one derives the equilibrium nominal exchange rate with log utility as:

$$e_t = \frac{(1-\gamma)}{\gamma} \frac{z_H(1-z_H)}{z_F(1-z_F)} \frac{x_{Ft}}{x_{Ht}} \frac{M_{Ht+1}}{M_{Ft+1}}. \tag{3}$$

Given this last result, analysis of the *real* exchange rate is simplest if it is defined as

$$r_t = \frac{e_t p_{Ft+1}}{p_{Ht+1}} = \frac{(1-\gamma)}{\gamma} \frac{z_H}{z_F} \frac{x_{Ft}}{x_{Ht}} \frac{y_{Ht+1}}{y_{Ft+1}}, \tag{4}$$

that is, as the notional relative price of Home and Foreign goods evaluated at the most recent market exchange rate.[6]

Equations (3) and (4) show that the nominal and real exchange rates will be positively correlated because of the common multiplicative term x_{Ft}/x_{Ht}, which is absent in more common flexible-price models such as that of Lucas (1982). In essence, the relative shock x_{Ft}/x_{Ht} affects the nominal exchange rate but does not feed into the subsequent goods market, so it affects the real exchange rate as well. From an empirical point of view,

---

[6] "Real exchange rate" is a misnomer, since equation (4) actually describes the terms of trade. As observed above, however, the relevant empirical regularities applying to real exchange rates also characterize terms of trade to a significant degree. Furthermore, if nontraded goods were incorporated into the model, the patterns of real and nominal exchange rate behavior described in the next paragraph would emerge.

however, it is very unlikely that this model, interpreted literally, can explain the data. The bond-market shocks that drive exchange rates are, for most countries, simply too small to explain their variability, especially over very short periods. In addition, the model above does not generate the *persistent* real exchange rate movements we see in reality. Even if serially correlated output shocks are introduced, monetary shocks will not have the persistent effects on the real exchange rate that the data suggest. The results reported by Schlagenhauf and Wrase (1995) suggest that these problems cannot be remedied simply by introducing endogenous output and capital accumulation.[7]

Modeling Persistence in Exchange Rates

Alvarez and Atkeson (1997) advance a related model intended to over-come some of these empirical shortcomings. In their complete-contingent-claims setup households receive monetary transfers and output endowments at the start of a period. However, families are split up into "parents" and "children". Parents trade currencies and contingent bonds in the asset market, then sell endowments for money in the goods market. Children are shoppers who purchase consumption goods with currency gifts from their parents. Children's trips into the goods market have stochastic lengths, however, so that shoppers need not return home at the end of the day.

Why do monetary shocks affect real exchange rates in their model despite the fact that new money diffuses immediately into the goods market? Output prices are determined by the total monetary demand of those shoppers who have just received gifts from parents and those who have not; in contrast, only a fraction of existing money balances are traded in asset markets and monetary innovations thus have larger proportional effects on exchange rates than on price levels. Therefore nominal and real exchange rate movements are positively correlated once again.

Further, movements in real and nominal exchange rates can be quite persistent in Alvarez and Atkeson's model. Unlike in the Lucas–Grilli–Roubini setup, even *anticipated* monetary changes can have real effects. This logical implication of the model strikes me as quite unrealistic, although it is needed for the model to generate persistence in real and

---

[7] Christiano, Eichenbaum, and Evans (1997) compare a closed-economy flexible-price model of this *genre* with a sticky-price model, and find that neither is a satisfactory representation of U.S. data. They conjecture that greater attention to wage rigidities might help resolve the empirical anomalies they detect.

nominal exchange rates through persistent monetary growth. Shoppers stranded in the goods market do not come home when future monetary changes are announced, or come home more frequently when inflation is higher. Thus, even expected monetary changes have amplified effects on exchange rates compared to commodity prices. Persistent real excange rate movements result from persistent money-growth shocks.

Both the Grilli–Roubini model, see eqs. (3) and (4), and the Alvarez–Atkeson model imply that real and nominal exchange rate changes will become decoupled in conditions of very high inflation. But they do so for the wrong reason, in my judgment. In the Alvarez–Atkeson story, for example, "old" shoppers' money balances become a negligible fraction of the economy's total money holdings when inflation is extremely high, so exchange rates, like price levels, move roughly in proportion to the total money supply. In reality, however, financial-market structure and the interface between goods and asset markets is not invariant to the rate of inflation. As Keynes (1923) reported of the post-World War I Austrian hyperinflation:

> "In Vienna mushroom exchange banks have sprung up at every street corner, where you can change your krone into Zurich francs within a few minutes of receiving them, and so avoid the risk of loss during the time it will take you to reach your usual bank."

More recent examples abound; see Dornbusch and Reynoso (1993).[8] Innovation in individual market access (on-line portfolio management, etc.) should weaken the liquidity effects of money shocks if the models of this section capture the main forces at work. Evidence that this is so has yet to emerge.

A Role for Sterilized Intervention

Liquidity models such as that of Grilli and Roubini can imply a role for sterilized foreign exchange interventions, which are defined as interventions that do not alter the paths of national money supplies. Suppose the Home government (randomly) decides to accept Foreign currency in payment for some of its bond issue; it simultaneously uses this Foreign currency to purchase part of the Foreign government's bond issue. This operation does not alter money supplies on any date, assuming the Home

---

[8]One might hope to improve the models' empirical performance by endogenizing the frequency of contact between goods and asset markets. Romer (1987) illustrates the difficulties in carrying out this program.

government rebates to the private sector the next-period payments on its Foreign bond purchases that it receives from Foreign's government.[9]

How are asset prices affected? The Foreign-bond equilibrium condition in eq. (2) does not change, but because the Home government is allowing Foreign-currency holders directly to purchase some of its bonds, their price q_H rises, that is, i_H falls. This development makes Foreign-currency bonds incipiently more attractive. As market actors attempt to sell Home for Foreign currency in order to buy more Foreign bonds, Home's currency depreciates against Foreign's until both types of bond once again are equally attractive at the margin.

In practice, central banks use sterilized interventions to defend exchange rates when they do not wish their actions to impinge on monetary aggregates. The evidence that sterilized interventions affect asset prices, especially over the longer term, is mixed and difficult to interpret; see Obstfeld and Rogoff (1996, Chapter 8). But it has long been vaguely conjectured that asset-market frictions could give sterilized interventions some bite in the very short run. Here we see just such a short-run effect. Clearly, however, the model provides little support for the idea that central banks can systematically exploit sterilized intervention to attain policy objectives over any significant period of time. For understanding the short-run dynamics of the interactions between exchange markets and governments, however, more detailed attention to the micro-structure of money and exchange markets plainly is in order.

IV. Optimum Currency Areas

It is an article of faith among economists, more than a quantifiable fact, that allocative efficiency is enhanced by merging under a single currency two markets previously served by separate currencies with a flexible exchange rate. Relative prices become more predictable, currency conversion and calculation costs are avoided, the economic basis for trade becomes more transparent, and so on.

When nominal prices or wages are sticky, however, this gain in allocative efficiency comes at a price: asymmetrical shocks that alter employment unevenly in different parts of the currency area cannot be cushioned through nominal exchange rate adjustments, which shift aggregate demand among regions by quickly altering relative prices. An optimum currency area efficiently trades off the allocative gain from expanding the zone of exchange-rate stability against the increased vulnerability to local

---

[9] To maintain the Lucas (1982)-style perfectly-pooled real equilibrium, one has to assume that, *ex ante*, private agents pool claims on the currency rebates due to stochastic sterilized interventions.

economic shocks. Mundell (1961), who introduced the concept, building on earlier insights of Meade (1951), identified the optimal currency area as an area of factor mobility, one within which factors can avoid unemployment through migration. The concept was refined further by McKinnon (1963) and Kenen (1969).[10]

Optimum Currency Areas and Asset-Market Structure

The optimum currency argument has always been based on the tacit assumption that asset markets are incomplete, so that people cannot pool income risks. In a country is hit by an adverse demand shock, the resulting higher unemployment is likely to be distributed unevenly over the labor force: some lose their jobs entirely. An exchange-rate induced terms-of-trade deterioration eases unemployment via a real national income reduction with a much more uniform, and therefore less harsh, incidence. From this interpretation flows the importance of fiscal federalism, stressed by Ingram (1973) and others. Government redistribution partially replaces private risk pooling when asset markets are incomplete.

Under asymmetric information, problems of moral hazard and adverse selection tend to eliminate many forms of contingent contracting, for example, most forward sales of labor income. Clever incentive contracts sometimes can be devised so as to prompt truthful revelation of private information, but these tend to break down when agents can unravel their provisions through unobserved side transactions in asset markets. As illustrated in Obstfeld and Rogoff (1996, Chapter 6), noncontingent contracting will tend to predominate in these circumstances.

Financial liberalization within a currency area may be of limited help for another reason. Capital is much more footloose than labor, which, within the EU, is still generally highly immobile between countries (and sometimes within them). In these cases, capital-accoount liberalization of the type the EU has now achieved may actually worsen the optimum-currency-area dilemma. Countries hit by adverse shocks will see capital leave, adding to the woes of the workers who are left behind.

Currency unions may have a subtle additional cost; they affect how near incomplete asset markets can come to an efficient allocation of risks. Neumeyer (1998) has developed this point in some generality, but a simple

---

[10] See Bayoumi and Eichengreen (1996) for a recent survey of empirical work. An additional cost of currency union is the loss of discretion over seigniorage financing of the fiscal deficit. I will not take up that topic here, however. Stabilization questions are widely agreed to be more important.

example may be based on Lucas's (1982) model of international risk sharing with complete markets.[11]

Lucas's 1982 model is similar in its basic setup to the Grilli–Roubini liquidity model of Section III. However, there is no separate cash-in-advance constraint for securities purchases, only a constraint for goods purchases, and the timing of events is different. Information on endowments and money transfers is revealed at the start of the period, then money and securities are exchanged in an asset market, after which monies are traded for national outputs in goods markets.

Lucas models a perfectly pooled (complete-markets) allocation in which representative Home and Foreign households each own exactly half of the stochastic Home output process $\{Y_{Ht}\}_{t=0}^{\infty}$ and half of the stochastic Foreign output process $\{Y_{Ht}\}_{t=0}^{\infty}$. Consider the following incomplete-markets setup, however. The only assets traded are nominal bonds denominated in Home and Foreign currency, and the national money stocks M_H and M_F are constant. The representative Home resident holds a perpetuity issued by Foreign, which pays its owner $\frac{1}{2}M_F$ Foreign currency units at the start of each period, while symmetrically, the Foreign resident holds a perpetual claim to half Home's constant money stock, $\frac{1}{2}M_H$.

Interestingly, this allocation will be perpetutated over time, as it replicates Lucas's perfectly pooled equilibrium, in which each country own exactly half of the other's endowment process. Assuming positive nominal interest rates, the goods-market equilibrium conditions

$$Y_{Ht} = M_H/p_{Ht}, \ Y_{Ft} = M_F/p_{Ft},$$

imply that the Home household's endowment at the start of a period will be

$$(Y_{Ht} - \tfrac{1}{2}M_H/p_{Ht}, \tfrac{1}{2}M_F/p_{Ft}) = (\tfrac{1}{2}Y_{Ht}, \tfrac{1}{2}Y_{Ft}).$$

The Foreign household's endowment has the identical value. Each Home household, for example, uses the Home currency left over after paying interest to Foreigners to purchase domestic goods; its Foreign interest receipts exactly finance its imports.

Fixing the exchange rate, in this environment, would undermine the efficiency of the equilibrium by removing one asset. However, the conclu-

---

[11] Mundell (1973) was the first formally to tie the choice of exchange rate regime to its implications for risk allocation. His model, however, assumes that the only internationally traded asset is a noninterest-bearing reserve asset of fixed purchasing power — presumably "gold" — and that there can be no reserve flows under floating rates. Helpman and Razin (1982) further explored the question in models with more realistic (incomplete) asset markets.

sion that a fixed exchange rate reduces welfare is easily overturned once money-supply randomness is introduced, as Neumeyer (1998) points out. Monetary shocks contaminate the perfect sharing of output risks that noncontingent nominal contracts otherwise allow, and are likely to inhibit international asset trade, as in Bacchetta and van Wincoop (1997). Overall welfare therefore may rise, especially if the adoption of a fixed rate or common currency reduces monetary instability throughout the currency area. The argument complements traditional political-economy justifications of EMS or EMU based on importing the Bundesbank's low-inflation credibility; see Giavazzi and Pagano (1988), although in practice it remains to be seen how closely the planned European Central Bank will mirror German inflation aversion.

Allocative Gains from Currency Unification

Quantification and even theoretical modeling of the microeconomic efficiency gains from monetary union has proven very elusive. Perhaps the best known number is the Commission of the European Communities (1990) calculation that the savings from eliminating currency conversion costs alone could be as high as 0.4 percent of EU GDP. Interestingly, the European banks currently lamenting the foreign exchange business they will lose under EMU refer to the same gains consumers will reap as resources now devoted to prospectively redundant financial transactions are liberated for more productive uses.

Rodríguez Mendizábal (1996) analyzes a formal model of the transaction costs in a multicurrency system. Based on calibrating the model, his preferred upper-bound estimate for currency conversion costs is around 0.7 of EU GDP, somewhat above the European Commission's figure. In the spirit of Baumol and Tobin, all financial transactions in the model have a bank as counterparty and there is a fixed cost of a trip to the bank. But in the spirit of Lucas (1982), transactions in a given country require prior withdrawal of its currency from the bank. When transactions occur stochastically, individuals will not, as optimally occurs with perfect foresight, exhaust all their currency holdings at once. Thus extra trips to the bank will occur, producing an excessive cost from a multiple currency system, even under fixed exchange rates.

Economists also believe that use of a single currency within Europe will simplify the trading process. One model that potentially captures the effect is a random matching model of monetary exchange, along the lines of Head and Shi (1996). In such models international trade with a single currency may welfare-dominate an equilibrium in which many currencies are used because on average trades that lead to immediate consumption occur more often. This "thick market" effect offers a means of rationalizing the "network externalities" in money use posited by Dowd and Greenaway (1993). Unfortunately, the random matching monetary models are quite stylized and underestimate the ability of real financial markets to overcome the double-coincidence-of-wants problem through credit instruments.[12]

Another literature bearing on the question is the extensive empirical research seeking an effect of exchange-rate volatility on trade flows. This research is largely inconclusive; see Obstfeld (1995) for discussion. A newer tack is to look directly at international departures from the law of one price (LOOP) for tradable goods. Engel and Rogers (1995) find that the variability of LOOP deviations is systematically related to nominal exchange rate volatility. Obstfeld and Taylor (1997) use the same data set to estimate a model in which transport and other trade costs lead to a range of LOOP deviations within which arbitrage is unprofitable; cf. the "commodity points" suggested by Heckscher (1916). For all four tradable commodity groups they analyze, their trade-cost estimates have a strong, positive cross-sectional correlation (across location pairs) with nominal exchange rate volatility. The implication seems to be that exchange rate volatility indeed inhibits profitable trade flows, although more reliable inferences must await further modeling of international arbitrage and intraindustry trade under uncertainty.

One implication of the discussion is that small and very open countries may gain more than large ones from joining a currency union, as they trade more and therefore bear higher costs from exchange rate fluctuations. Small countries also gain less from macro policy sovereignty; see McKinnon (1963). The general stability of the United States currency union can be ascribed to high levels of inter-state trade, coupled with inter-state labor mobility and America's federal fiscal system. These favorable conditions are not reproduced to the same degree among European countries.

Political economy intrudes here as well. Unquestionably, floating exchange rates make it harder for governments to resist sectorial pressures for protection. In an EU context, floating rates are viewed as inimical to maintaining and extending the single market. Currency unification thus can have a substantial indirect microeconomic payoff to the extent that it discourages protectionism. Needless to say, this payoff, too, has eluded rigorous quantification.

---

[12] In a model with a potentially richer array of assets, Rey (1996) assumes a transaction technology incorporating a related thick market externality. For further discussion of externalities in models with non-Walrasian trading frictions, see Cooper's (1998) section on search models.

V. The Stability of Fixed Exchange Rates

In the run-up to EMU, core members will likely be defending existing or new EMS exchange parities, whereas countries aspiring to join after EMU is launched will target the euro as part of their entry requirement. In line with the Maastricht convergence criteria, "outs" will also be targeting low inflation and reduced levels of public deficits and debt. A major question is whether these transitional arrangements will run smoothly or be disrupted by speculative crises, as in 1992–93. Macroeconomic probity may be no guarantor of a smooth ride: a new generation of crisis models suggests that even sustainable currency pegs may be attacked and even broken.

The focus of these models is on the government's continuous comparison of the net benefits from changing the exchange rate versus defending it. Like a run on a bank, speculation against a currency creates objective economic conditions that make liability devaluation more likely.[13] As a result, even pegged exchange rates that could be sustained indefinitely in the absence of a speculative attack can succumb to adverse market sentiment. Underlying macroeconomic "fundamentals" are far from irrelevant to the outcome, however, for they determine the range of possible equilibria. Some currency pegs are unequivocally doomed by bad macroeconomic fundamentals — unemployment, real currency appreciation, government deficits, large foreign debts, and so on. For others, the fundamentals are so favorable that the exchange rate plainly is immune to speculative attack. But there is also a grey area in which multiple equilibria are possible, with seeming tranquility in exchange markets suddenly giving way to currency collapse.

A Prototype Model with Multiple Equilibria

A barebones model illustrates how the coordination problem of currency-market traders changes when changing macroeconomic fundamentals alter the degree of discomfort a government will suffer because of an attack.[14] The model contains three agents, a government that sells foreign reserves to fix its currency's exchange rate and two private holders of domestic currency who can continue holding it or sell it to the government for foreign currency. I have in mind an economy with many competitive money holders, of course, but the two-trader paradigm captures important features of more realistic cases.

---

[13] Cooper (1998) briefly touches on the theoretical literature on bank runs.
[14] This subsection's discussion draws on Obstfeld (1996).

The government commits a finite reserves stock, *R*, to defend the currency peg. This assumption need not reflect an inelastic lower limit to reserve holdings; more realistically, alternative reserve "limits" reflect differing degrees of commitment to the exchange rate's defense. The tenacity with which the exchange rate is defended can depend on a variety of developments in the domestic economy, as in the fully-articulated models to be reviewed below. For now the government's payoffs are not modeled explicitly.

The size of the committed reserve stock defines the payoffs in the one-shot noncooperative game that the two private traders play. A first game, shown in normal form in Figure 4a, is the High Reserve game. Committed government reserves, *R*, are 20 and each trader has domestic money

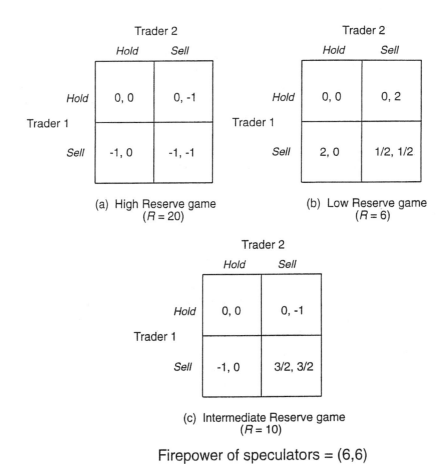

(a) High Reserve game
($R = 20$)

(b) Low Reserve game
($R = 6$)

(c) Intermediate Reserve game
($R = 10$)

Firepower of speculators = (6,6)

Fig. 4.

resources of 6 which can be sold to the government for reserves ("Sell"), or held ("Hold"). (Think of these resources as a measure of the strength of market opinion, as well as of the extent of leverage, the amount of speculative "firepower".) To sell, thereby taking a position against the current rate, traders bear a cost of 1. but even if both sell their resources of 6 to the government, its reserves remain at 8 and allow it to maintain the fixed exchange rate. So a trader who speculates receives a payoff of -1, regardless of what the other one does, while one who holds gets 0. Speculation thus is a strictly dominated strategy. The sole Nash equilibrium is the northwest corner: the currency peg necessarily survives.

The game in Figure 4b is the Low Reserve game. Committed reserves $R = 6$, meaning that either trader alone can take out the currency peg.[15] Suppose that in the event of giving up its peg the government devalues by 50 percent. A trader who has sold *all* his domestic currency has a capital gain (in domestic currency terms) of 3, for a net gain of 2 after paying the transaction cost. If both traders sell, however, each gets half the government reserves and earns only $\frac{3}{2} - 1 = \frac{1}{2}$. (Assume that in a successful attack, a trader's gains are proportional to his initial domestic currency holdings.) Now, holding is a strictly dominated strategy; so the unique Nash equilibrium is the southwest corner, implying a collapse of the exchange rate.

Figure 4c shows the Intermediate Reserve game, which is the most interesting case. Here $R = 10$, so neither trader alone can run the government's reserves although both can if they sell together. The payoff structure is derived as follows. Either trader acting alone fails in an attack, bearing the cost -1 while the player who holds earns 0. But if both attack, each gains $\frac{5}{2} - 1 = \frac{3}{2}$. There are now two Nash equilibria. In the first, shown in the southeast corner, both traders sell and the currency peg falls. But if neither trader believes the other will attack, the Nash equilibrium in the northwest corner results and the currency peg survives. In this game the attack equilibrium has a self-fulfilling element because the exchange rate collapses if attacked, but survives otherwise. The intermediate state of fundamentals (government reserves) makes a collapse possible, but not an economic necessity.[16]

A fairly robust prediction of this setup, noted in a different model by Jeanne (1995), is that the health of fundamentals determines the existence and multiplicity of attack equilibria. In the simplest Krugman (1979)

---

[15] The assumption here that either player can unilaterally cause a collapse is simply a crude device for making collapse inevitable, as in Krugman's (1979) original model.

[16] Experimental evidence, in e.g. Cooper *et al.* (1994), suggests that if the structure of the game is indeed as in Figure 4c, speculators may not coordinate on the equilibrium that maximizes their joint profits.

model, fundamentals are either consistent with long-run fixity of the exchange rate or are not. Here the same is true for extreme values of fundamentals, but there is also a large middle ground over which fundamentals are neither so strong as to make a successful attack impossible, nor so weak as to make it inevitable.

The Role of Government Objectives

The literature contains more detailed accounts of crises that explicitly model the government's objectives; see Obstfeld (1996) for a brief survey. Many mechanisms have been discussed. Labor union expectations of devaluation may translate into higher wage demands, real appreciation, and unemployment. In such circumstances, the government is more likely to be pushed into realignment by an adverse shock. The process is clearly circular, since heightened devaluation expectations themselves make devaluation more likely, given the government's objectives. Nominal public debt provides another channel for self-fulfilling crisis, since high domestic nominal interest rates may worsen the public finances to the point where devaluation appears the optimal (or only) way out for the government. In many experiences a weak banking system has proven the Achilles' heel of an otherwise sustainable exchange rate policy, as rising interest rates induced governments to step in and essentially backstop bank solvency with official reserves; see e.g. Kaminsky and Reinhart (1995).

In these models, governments ratify market expectations through accommodative devaluation and monetary expansion. Yet, Eichengreen, Rose, and Wyplosz (1995, p. 283) find, for a panel of industrial-country crisis episodes, that "there is little evidence that speculative attacks, whether self-fulfilling or not, typically prompt governments to ease fiscal and monetary policies". Some authors, for example Flood and Marion (1996), take this as evidence against the idea that crisis-induced realignments reflect official accommodation of market pressures.[17] A more accurate interpretation of the data, to my mind, is that there is substantial heterogeneity in country experiences and circumstances that is not well captured by Eichengreen, Rose, and Wyplosz's averages over a rather widely dispersed sample. The experiences of Britain and Italy after the 1992–93 crises offer examples of post-devaluation monetary expansion. In addition, devaluation alone can be expansionary.

---

[17] Flood and Marion also present an interesting model in which the authorities can sterilize so as to avoid monetary expansion after a devaluation.

Narrowing the Range of Equilibria

In an important contribution, Morris and Shin (1997) show how the presence of uncertainty can render the attack outcome the *unique* outcome in speculation games with uncertainty. In essence, their point is this: if it isn't too costly to take a position against a currency and if it there is a good chance other speculators believe the peg to be unsustainable, then it is prudent to speculate yourself even if you know the peg to be conditionally viable. This result can eliminate the multiplicity of equilibria, but it is hardly good news for fixed exchange rates, as it implies that pegs that could survive absent speculation will necessarily be attacked.

Consider the following static Bayesian game. The central bank's reserves are $R = 10$. There are again two traders. Each is independently endowed with "firepower" of 6 or 10; but traders don't observe the endowments of others. Thus, it is never common knowledge that the exchange parity is not unconditionally unsustainable. If Trader 1 has 6, he sees the contingent payoffs shown in Figures 5a and 5b.

Let π be the common probability of a trader having 10. Suppose Trader 2's strategy is

$$\sigma^2(6) = \text{sell}, \qquad \sigma^2(10) = \text{sell}.$$

In that case Trader 1's expected profit from a strategy with $\sigma^1(6) = \text{sell}$ is $(1-\pi)\frac{3}{2}+\pi\frac{7}{8}>0$, whereas that from $\sigma^1(6) = \text{hold}$ is 0. Of course, $\sigma^1(10) = \text{sell}$ also is a best response to the foregoing strategy of Trader 2. There thus is one equilibrium in which everyone always sells, regardless of information.

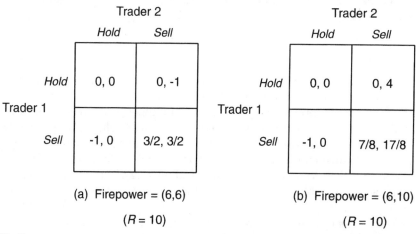

(a) Firepower = (6,6)

(R = 10)

(b) Firepower = (6,10)

(R = 10)

Fig. 5.

What if Trader 2's strategy instead is

$\sigma^2(6) = $ hold, $\sigma^2(10) = $ sell?

Now Trader 1's expected profit from $\sigma^1(6) = $ sell is $(1-\pi)(-1)+\pi\frac{7}{8}$ whereas his expected profit from $\sigma^1(6) = $ hold equals 0. Thus, strategy $(\sigma(6), \sigma(10)) = $ (hold, sell) is a best response to itself if and only if

$$(1-\pi)(-1)+\pi\tfrac{7}{8}\leq 0 \Leftrightarrow \pi\leq\tfrac{8}{15}.$$

For $\pi\leq\frac{8}{15}$, there therefore are *two* pure-strategy equilibria,

$(\sigma(6), \sigma(10)) = $ (hold, sell)

and

$(\sigma(6), \sigma(10)) = $ (sell, sell),

in a parallel with the Intermediate Reserve game of Figure 4c.

If $\pi>\frac{8}{15}$, however, $\sigma^1(6) = $ sell always is better so the second equilibrium above, the attack equilibrium, is the *only* one. Introducing a high enough probability that other traders will defeat the central bank and reap all the profits on their own eliminates the possibility that the traders, both finding themselves endowed with 6, find it optimal not to mount an attack. Uniqueness could also be guaranteed, of course, by making the cost of speculation (here -1) sufficiently low.

It is an important task for research, one fraught with consequences for exchange-rate policy, to understand the factors that generate crises and determine their timing. Some research will focus on the microdynamics of asset markets, as might be fruitful also for understanding sterilized interventions and other tactics governments employ in their defenses of exchange rates. This literature is in its infancy, but surely will mature in the years ahead.

VI. Conclusion

The theoretical and empirical progress in open-economy macroeconomics in recent years has led to new ways of thinking about the economic costs and benefits of a project like EMU. Unfortunately, a reliable quantitative analysis of costs and benefits in specific cases remains elusive. In particular, our current theoretical basis for evaluating the microeconomic efficiency gains from currency unification is much too slim. For this reason, observers like the Swedish commission on EMU, Calmfors *et al.* (1997), viewed early entry as inadvisable, at least under the current circumstances of high unemployment.

At this juncture, the most persuasive arguments for EMU remain those based on political-economy considerations. Currency misalignments could promote protectionist sentiment and undermine the single market. By taking the issue away, EMU can promote further economic integration. Furthermore, EMU can help establish and maintain a broad zone of monetary and possibly fiscal stability. Finally, if the politically practical alternative to EMU is fixed exchange rates bedevilled by credibility problems and capital controls, some form of currency union might be preferable. Unfortunately, the laudable goals could be thwarted by popular backlash and disintegration if EMU ultimately is seen as a cause of slow growth and unemployment.

References

Alvarez, F. and Atkeson, A.: Money and exchange rates in the Grossman–Weiss–Rotemberg model. *Journal of Monetary Economics 40*, 619–640, Dec. 1997.

Bacchetta, P. and van Wincoop, E.: Trade in nominal assets and net international capital flows. DP 1569, Centre for Economic Policy Research, Feb. 1997.

Bayoumi, T. and Eichengreen, B.: Operationalizing the theory of optimum currency areas. DP 1484, Centre for Economic Policy Research, Oct. 1996.

Calmfors, L. et al.: *EMU: A Swedish Perspective*. Kluwer, Dordrecht, 1997.

Chari, V. V., Kehoe, P. J. and McGrattan, E.: Monetary shocks and real exchange rates in sticky price models of international business cycles. Research Department Staff Report 223, Federal Reserve Bank of Minneapolis, Dec. 1996.

Christiano, L. J., Eichenbaum, M. and Evans, C. L.: Sticky price and limited particiation models of money: A comparison. *European Economic Review*, forthcoming, 1997.

Clarida, R. and Gali, J.: Sources of real exchange-rate fluctuations: How important are nominal shocks? *Carnegie-Rochester Conference Series on Public Policy 41*, 1–56, 1994.

Commission of the European Communities: One market, one money. *European Economy 44*, special issue, Oct. 1990.

Cooper, R.: Business cycle models: Theory and policy implications. *Scandinavian Journal of Economics 100*, this issue, 1998.

Cooper, R. et al.: Alternative solutions for resolving coordination problems: Experimental evidence on forward induction and preplay communication. In J. W. Friedman (ed.), *Problems of Coordination in Economic Activity*, Kluwer, Boston, 129–146, 1994.

De Grauwe, P., Janssens, M. and Leliaert, H.: *Real Exchange-rate Variability from 1920 to 1926 and 1973 to 1982*. Princeton Studies in International Finance 56, 1985.

Dornbusch, R. and Reynoso, A.: Financial factors in economic development. In R. Dornbusch (ed.), *Policymaking in the Open Economy: Concepts and Case Studies in Economic Performance*, Oxford University Press, Oxford, 64–89, 1993.

Dowd, K. and Greenaway, D.: Currency competition, network externalities and switching costs: Towards an alternative view of optimum currency areas. *Economic Journal 103*, 1180–1189, Sept. 1993.

Eichengreen, B.: *Golden Fetters*. Oxford University Press, London, 1992.

Eichengreen, B., Rose, A. K. and Wyplosz, C.: Exchange market mayhem: The antecedents and aftermath of speculative attacks. *Economic Policy 21*, 251–312, Oct. 1995.

Engel, C. and Rogers, J. H.: Regional patterns in the law of one price: The roles of geography vs. currencies. NBER WP 5395, Dec. 1995.

Flood, R. P. and Marion, N. P.: Speculative attacks: Fundamentals and self-fulfilling prophecies. Mimeo, International Monetary Fund and Dartmouth College, Aug. 1996.

Giavazzi, F. and Pagano, M.: The advantage of tying one's hands: EMS discipline and central bank credibility. *European Economic Review 32*, 1055–1082, June 1988.

Grilli, V. and Roubini, N.: Liquidity and exchange rates. *Journal of International Economics 32*, 339–352, May 1992.

Head, A. and Shi, S.: Search, inflation, and exchange rates. Mimeo, Queen's University, Sept. 1996.

Heckscher, E. F.: Växelkursens grundval vid pappersmyntfot (The basis of the exchange rate under the paper standard). *Ekonomisk Tidskrift 18*, 309–312, Oct. 1916.

Helpman, E. and Razin, A.: A comparison of exchange rate regimes in the presence of imperfect capital markets. *International Economic Review 23*, 365–388, June 1982.

Ingram, J. C.: *The Case for European Monetary Integration*. Princeton Essays in International Finance 98, April 1973.

Jeanne, O.: Models of currency crises: A tentative synthesis. Mimeo, ENPC-CERAS, Paris, 1995.

Jeanne, O.: Generating real persistent effects of monetary shocks: How much nominal rigidity do we really need? *European Economic Review*, forthcoming, 1998.

Kaminsky, G. L. and Reinhart, C. M.: The twin crises: The causes of banking and balance of payments problems. Mimeo, Board of Governors of the Federal Reserve System and International Monetary Fund, Nov. 1995.

Kenen, P. B.: The theory of optimum currency areas: An eclectic view. In R. A. Mundell and A. K. Swoboda (eds.), *Monetary Problems of the International Economy*, 41–60, University of Chicago Press, Chicago, 1969.

Keynes, J. M. (1923): *A Tract on Monetary Reform*. The Collected Writings of John Maynard Keynes, vol. IV. St. Martin's Press, London, 1971.

Kimball, M. S.: The quantitative analytics of the basic neomonetarist model. *Journal of Money, Credit, and Banking 27*, part 2, 1241–1277, Nov. 1995.

Kollmann, R.: The exchange rate in a dynamic-optimizing current account model with nominal rigidities: A quantitative investigation. Mimeo, Université de Montréal, June 1996.

Krugman, P. R.: A model of balance of payments crises. *Journal of Money, Credit and Banking 11*, 311–325, Aug. 1979.

Krugman, P. R.: What do we need to know about the international monetary system? In P. B. Kenen (ed.), *Understanding Interdependence: The Macroeconomics of the Open Economy*, Princeton University Press, Princeton, 1995.

Leiderman, L. and Bufman, G.: Searching for nominal anchors in shock-prone economies in the 1990s: Inflation targets and exchange rate bands. Mimeo, Berglas School of Economics, Tel-Aviv University, Nov. 1995.

Lucas, R. E., Jr.: Interest rates and currency prices in a two-country world. *Journal of Monetary Economics 10*, 335–360, Nov. 1982.

Lucas, R. E., Jr.: Liquidity and interest rates. *Journal of Economic Theory 50*, 237–264, April 1990.

McKinnon, R. I.: Optimum currency areas. *American Economic Review 53*, 717–725, Sept. 1963.

Meade, J. E.: *The Balance of Payments*. Oxford University Press, London, 1951.

Morris, S. and Shin, H. S.: Unique equilibrium in a model of self-fulfilling currency attacks. DP 1687, Centre for Economic Policy Research, Aug. 1997.

Mundell, R. A.: A theory of optimum currency areas. *American Economic Review 51*, 657–675, Sept. 1961.

Mundell, R. A.: Uncommon arguments for common currencies. In H. G. Johnson and A. K. Swoboda (eds.), *The Economics of Common Currencies*, Harvard University Press, Cambridge, MA, 114–132, 1973.

Mussa, M.: A model of exchange rate dynamics. *Journal of Political Economy 90*, 74–104, Feb. 1982.

Mussa, M.: Nominal exchange rate regimes and the behavior of real exchange rates: Evidence and implications. *Carnegie-Rochester Conference Series on Public Policy 25*, 117–213, 1986.

Neumeyer, P. A.: Currencies and the allocation of risk: The welfare effects of a monetary union. *American Economic Review*, forthcoming, 1998.

Obstfeld, M.: International currency experience: New lessons and lessons relearned. *Brookings Papers on Economic Activity*, 1, 119–220, 1995.

Obstfeld, M.: Models of currency crises with self-fulfilling features. *European Economic Review 40*, 1037–1048, April 1996.

Obstfeld, M. and Rogoff, K.: *Foundations of International Macroeconomics*. MIT Press, Cambridge, MA, 1996.

Obstfeld, M. and Taylor, A. M.: Nonlinear aspects of goods-market arbitrage and adjustment: Heckscher's commodity points revisited. *Journal of the Japanese and International Economies 11*, 441–479, Dec. 1997.

Obstfeld, M. and Taylor, A. M.: The Great Depression as a watershed: International capital mobility over the long run. In M. D. Bordo, C. Goldin, and E. N. White (eds.), *The Defining Moment: The Great Depression and the American Economy in the Twentieth Century*. University of Chicago Press, Chicago, 1998.

Rey, H.: International trade and currency exchange. Mimeo, London School of Economics, Mar. 1996.

Rodríguez Mendizábal, H.: Monetary union and the transaction cost savings of a single currency. Mimeo, University of Chicago, Jan. 1996.

Rogoff, K.: The purchasing power parity puzzle. *Journal of Economic Literature 34*, 647–668, June 1996.

Romer, D.: The monetary transmission mechanism in a general equilibrium version of the Baumol–Tobin model. *Journal of Monetary Economics 20*, 105–122, 1987.

Rotemberg, J. J.: Money and the terms of trade. *Journal of International Economics 19*, 141–160, Aug. 1985.

Schlagenhauf, D. E. and Wrase, J. M.: Liquidity and real activity in a simple open economy model. *Journal of Monetary Economics 35*, 431–461, June 1995.

Stockman, A. C.: Real exchange-rate variability under pegged and floating nominal exchange-rate systems: An equilibrium theory. *Carnegie-Rochester Conference Series on Public Policy 29*, 259–294, 1988.

Scand. J. Economics 100(1), 277–283, 1998

Comment on M. Obstfeld, "Open-Economy Macroeconomics: Developments in Theory and Policy"

*Patrick J. Kehoe**

University of Pennsylvania, Philadelphia, PA 19104 and Federal Reserve Bank, Minneapolis, MN 55480, USA

Introduction

Obstfeld has done a masterful job of laying out the recent developments in open-economy macroeconomics. There is an underlying tone to the paper, however, that I find disturbing. In various parts of his paper he comments on which features of models he finds realistic and which he finds unrealistic, as if that is particularly relevant for judging the models. My view of economics, especially quantitative economics, is diametrically opposed to Obstfeld's view. All models are abstractions. As I see it, the goal of quantitative economics is to use abstract, highly stylized, and therefore highly unrealistic models to capture the essence of an idea and then to use numbers to put some bounds on the potential magnitudes of the resulting effects. The interesting task of applied economists is to decide which features of the world to abstract from and which to include. A guiding principle is that all the features of an actual economy that are not quantitatively essential to the point at hand should be abstracted from. When this principle is not followed the driving forces of the model get confounded with some inessential, but possibly complicated, details. Indeed, the defining feature of failure in a quantitative exercise is that it is impossible to tell which features of the model are essential for which quantitative results.

In my comments I will be manifestly unfair to the overall extremely high quality of the paper and pick on several comments Obstfeld made about realism. I then indulge myself by doing exactly what I argued a good modeler should not, which is make my own comments about realism. I go on to argue that, notwithstanding its lack of realism, the existing quantitative work in the area is informative because it isolates what is needed to

*I am grateful to the NSF and to the Ronald S. Lauder Foundation for research support. The views expressed herein are those of the author and not necessarily those of the Federal Reserve Bank of Minneapolis or the Federal Reserve System.

generate volatile and persistent exchange rates. Finally, I ask how much evidence is there really for the whole premise of the paper, namely, that during the post-Bretton Woods era monetary shocks can account for most of the observed movements in real exchange rates.

On the Realism of Anticipated Money Having Real Effects

In discussing models with segmented goods and asset markets, Obstfeld begins with a simple model of Grilli and Roubini in which currency and asset markets are separated from goods markets for only one period. As he notes, such a model can generate movements in exchange rates for at most one period. He then turns to an elaboration of this model by Alvarez and Atkeson, in which, for each agent, currency and asset markets are separated for many periods. As he notes, this model can generate persistent movements in real exchange rates. He argues that an implication of the model which is quite unrealistic is that anticipated money has real effects. If you think about how the model works for a minute or two, it is obvious that unless anticipated money has large real effects, the model has no hope of generating the type of persistence in real exchange rates that we see in the data. In fact, unless anticipated money has real effects, it cannot generate persistence for more than one period. So, in these models, generating persistent real exchange rate movements is intricately linked to anticipated money having real effects.

I find it odd that when Obstfeld discusses the sticky price models he does not make the same point. If the stickiness lasts only one period, then only unanticipated money shocks have real effects. But then the model can generate movements in exchange rates for only one period. For the model to generate persistence of the type we see in the data, prices have to be sticky for three years. But this persistence, of course, is all coming from the real effects of anticipated money shocks. To see this consider a producer who has just set his price for three years on, say, the morning of January 1, and that afternoon there is a money shock. The producer obviously anticipates the higher money supply for the next three years, but there are real effects because the producer cannot change his price. Thus, just as in the segmented markets model, getting persistent effects from monetary shocks goes hand in hand with having real effects from anticipated shocks.

In fact, as far as I know, there is no model which can generate quantitatively relevant amounts of persistence in real exchange rates from monetary shocks without simultaneously having real effects of anticipated monetary shocks. Indeed, I think this is one of the key messages of the recent literature that Obstfeld surveys. Thus, as a quantitative economist, I suggest that Obstfeld either start buying into the idea that anticipated money has real effects or give up the idea that real exchange rates are driven by monetary shocks.

On the Realism of Incomplete Markets

In discussing various models of sticky prices, Obstfeld argues that exogenously incomplete market models, in which agents can save in a very limited set of securities, local currency and uncontingent nominal bonds, are more realistic than complete market models. I find this argument both strange on the face of it and strange for someone familiar with principles of economic modelling to make.

On the face of it, I find it strange to argue that agents have very limited means of insuring themselves against aggregate risk at the level of a country. While I am writing this comment my most recent Vanguard statement has arrived in the mail asking me which of nearly a hundred different stock and bond funds I want to invest in. A minimum wage worker on my floor has received a similar statement, and we have a nice chat about the various pluses and minuses of one global fund versus another. So at a very practical level it is not so obvious to me what Obstfeld is talking about.

As an economic modeler, I also find this a strange argument. First, we know from a large literature in finance that with standard assumptions on preferences, it takes only a small number of assets to effectively complete the markets against aggregate risk at the level of a country. Second, in the kind of models Obstfeld is talking about, Chari, Kehoe and McGrattan (1996) have shown that the quantitative difference between complete markets and incomplete markets is of the same magnitude as the roundoff error. Third, in the name of simplicity and clarity we abstract from all features of the situation we are modelling except for those which are absolutely critical to the point we are trying to make. Often, it is difficult to decide which aspects of an economy to include and which ones not to. Here, however, we have what in common parlance is called a no brainer: incomplete markets in these models are exactly the kind of feature that should be abstracted from.

So far I have discussed one model in which one type of incomplete market is essentially irrelevant. I want to conjecture that in a whole class of models many types of incomplete markets will be irrelevant. Imagine two-country models in which all agents have unfettered access to at least two assets: uncontingent nominal bonds, like T-bills, denominated in both currencies. For incomplete markets to have a big effect it must be that fluctuations in nominal prices result in large wealth redistributions from one set of agents to another. For example, suppose that American consumers have huge debts denominated in dollars and that the Japanese are holding these claims. Then if the dollar depreciates sharply and prices are such that the purchasing power of dollars falls sharply, then there is a large wealth redistribution from the Americans to the Japanese. If this scenario actually happened in the models, then clearly incomplete markets could have a big effect. However, it typically does not happen. If this scenario had nontrivial probability in a model with maximizing agents, then the Americans would self-insure by, say, holding half of their debt in the yen-denominated debt and thus insulating themselves from the wealth redistribution. In the model described above we made a more extreme assumption on incomplete assets: namely, that both the Americans and the Japanese could hold only one asset, dollar-denominated T-bills. Even there, we could not get big wealth effects because agents optimally chose to keep their debts at moderate levels.

Of course, I am not arguing that abstracting from incomplete markets is inessential in all models. Rather, I am arguing that in this class of models, the type of exogenously specified incompleteness that Obstfeld seems to prefer serves to do little but complicate the model. In other contexts, I have argued that endogenous incomplete markets can greatly improve the predictions of international business cycle models.

On the Realism of Sticky Prices

As I have argued above we should not judge models on their realism, rather we should judge them on their usefulness in capturing a simple story for organizing and interpreting the data. Nevertheless, since Obstfeld indulged himself in off-the-cuff impressions of realism, bear with me as I do the same.

It seems that Obstfeld's favorite explanation of real exchange rate movements is a sticky price model. As I mentioned above, to generate anywhere near the persistence in real exchange rates that we see in the data we need output prices to be sticky for at least a couple of years. If I just think about my personal expenditures on goods, I am hard pressed to find a significant fraction of goods that do not change prices every couple of weeks, let alone every three years. For example, I buy airline tickets all the time, and their prices change week to week. I went shopping for a car recently, and the price in December was a fair bit different than the price in November. I also do the grocery shopping for our family, and I see enormous variation in prices. When he is forming his opinions about the realism of sticky prices, I hope Obstfeld is getting to the grocery store more than President Bush does.

Another type of stickiness we often hear about is sticky wages. Even Keynesian economists have given up on this because models with them typically imply highly countercyclical real wages, which we do not see in the data. Moreover, in most jobs there are well-understood implicit contracts about the amount of effort and often the amount of time a worker supplies over the course of a business cycle. In such a circumstance, even if the compensation does not vary, that is not necessarily evidence that wages are sticky in the way they are typically modelled.

I do not judge these sticky price models on their realism. I find the work in this area informative because it isolates the key features of the model that are necessary to generate observed volatility and persistence in real exchange rates. These features are extremely long price stickiness (on the order of three years), high risk aversion (a coefficient of relative risk aversion of about 7) and preferences which are separable between consumption and leisure. If we drop any of these three features the model cannot come close to the relevant statistics in the data.

On the Realism of Separated Goods and Currency Markets

Let me indulge myself further and make some off-the-cuff remarks about the other class of models that Obstfeld seems to favor, namely, those with separated markets. In these models agents commit a certain amount of money to home and foreign currency before the current money shock and then use it to purchase home and foreign goods in the goods market subject to cash-in-advance constraints. After, say, a positive shock to the home money supply, there is an incentive for an agent in the goods market to take some of his foreign money, convert it to home money and buy more of the home good. In essence, there is an incentive for an agent to find a local currency exchange and shift his money. Now, in the data we often see movements in real exchange rates on the order of 50% that last for several years. In the model, agents wander around for years unable to find currency exchanges. On my last 20 trips to Europe, however, I could find a currency exchange every 15 minutes or so. This feature of the model is patently unrealistic.

When I think about this aspect of the model, I am not worried that it is unrealistic, rather I am just not sure what friction it is trying to capture in an abstract way. It is certainly not about rigidity in portfolios, since I am not talking about the incentive to cash in bonds to be used as money; rather it is rigidity in currency holdings. I am in favor of using abstract models and simplifying assumptions, but this particular assumption leaves me a little puzzled. If we drop it, the persistent real effects of money disappear.

Nevertheless, I find this literature quite informative in that it isolates what is needed in this class of models to generate real exchange rates that are as volatile and persistent as those in the data. Basically, markets need to be extremely segmented: for each agent, the goods markets need to be segmented from asset markets for several years and goods markets need to be segmented from currency markets for several years.

Now that I have indulged myself with flights of reality judging, let me turn to a deeper issue.

Is it Obvious that Real Exchange Rates are Driven by Money?

The underlying presumption of Obstfeld's discussion of empirical regularities and the underlying motivation for the models he discusses seem to be that monetary policy accounts for most of the short to medium term movements in real and nominal exchange rates. I will argue that when we restrict attention to floating exchange rate regimes, there is currently no reliable evidence for this presumption. (There is evidence that across fixed and floating exchange rate regimes there are systematic differences in real exchange rates. Of course, across such regimes there are a whole host of differences, such as implicit current account targeting and different direct and subtle forms of capital controls either observed or incipient. So, in general, the across-regime evidence is not that clean.) I am interested in attempts that try to determine, within a given floating exchange rate regime, what fraction of the movements in real exchange rates come from money shocks. There is remarkably little systematic work that even attempts to provide such a breakdown.

The only systematic approach I have seen that attempts this breakdown is the decomposition of variance in structural VARs. I will argue that standard theory suggests these decompositions are uninterpretable. More generally, structural VARs are often peddled as a way to elicit the dynamic response of the economy to a monetary policy shock and as such are useful in evaluating alternative theories. I will argue that they are not useful. Interpretation of reduced-form equations requires identifying restrictions. Standard theoretical models, such as the sticky price models discussed above, imply their own VARs with very precise identifying restrictions, from the cross-equation implications, that typically contradict the identifying assumptions made in the "structural" VARs. Thus for a researcher guided by a standard theoretical model, the so-called monetary policy innovations are just some mongrel of all the shocks in the economy, like taste shocks, fiscal policy shocks, technology shocks, and maybe even sunspots. For such a researcher, the impulse responses from these structural VARs are not only not useful as data summary devices; they are basically uninterpretable. (The only way the theoretical models I know can be made consistent with the exclusion restrictions in VARs is to make strange timing assumptions in the theory. Of course, for anyone interested in models that do not satisfy these strange assumptions the VAR evidence is useless.)

It is worthwhile noting that even for the subset of economists who buy into the identifying assumptions of VARs, the results are not supportive of the view that much of the movements in real exchange rates come from money shocks. In Eichenbaum and Evans (1993, Table II) the percentage of forecast error variance of real and nominal exchange rates attributable to monetary shocks across countries ranges from a low of 8% to a high of 14%. Given the large standard errors on these numbers, the VARs suggest that perhaps almost none of the movements in exchange rates is attributable to monetary shocks. If researchers running the VAR used an information set for the monetary authorities that included other standard variables which monetary authorities observe, I think I could drop the "perhaps" in the previous sentence.

References

Chari, V. V., Kehoe, P. J. and McGrattan, E.: Monetary shocks and real exchange rates in sticky price models of international business cycles. Research Department Staff Report 223, Federal Reserve Bank of Minneapolis, 1996.

Eichenbaum, M. and Evans, C.: Some empirical evidence on the effects of monetary policy shocks on exchange rates. NBER WP 4271, 1993.

Scand. J. Economics 100(1), 285–288, 1998

Comment on M. Obstfeld, "Open-Economy Macroeconomics: Developments in Theory and Policy"

Asbjørn Rødseth *

University of Oslo, N-0317 Oslo, Norway

In Part II, Obstfeld documents the well-known facts that the variability of both real and nominal exchange rates is related to changes in nominal exchange rate regimes, and that under floating exchange rates there is near-perfect correlation between real and nominal exchange rates in the short run. Both these facts are readily explained if we assume short-run nominal price or wage rigidity. However, many economists seem to have strong prejudices against nominal rigidities, and hence, Part III is devoted to a discussion of alternative explanations based on some kind of separation and information lag between asset and goods markets.

Obstfeld's main message in Part III is that the alternative explanations are not convincing, since they do not explain the persistence of real exchange rates. The problem is familiar from Lucas' attempt at explaining the business cycle by information lags. It is difficult to see how delays in the dissemination of information about aggregate monetary shocks can have real effects beyond the very short run.

Obstfeld's main model in Part III can probably be refined to produce more variance in the nominal exchange rate and more covariance between the nominal and the real rate. In the model, monetary shocks have two opposing effects on the present exchange rate e_t. Consider a positive shock to x_{Ht}, which means an increased supply of home bonds in period t. This raises the domestic interest rate in period t. It also raises the expected supply of domestic money in period $t+1$, and thus raises the expected value of e_{t+1}. The first effect is towards appreciation now, the second effect towards depreciation now. The net effect of x_{Ht} on e_t can thus be small. This is confirmed if we rewrite (3) by inserting for future money supplies. We then get

$$e_t = \frac{1-\gamma}{\gamma} \frac{z_H(1-z_H)}{z_F(1-z_F)} \frac{x_{Ft}}{x_{Ht}} \frac{(1-z_H+x_{Ht})}{(1-z_F+x_{Ft})} \frac{M_{Ht}}{M_{Ft}}$$

where we can see clearly how the x's have two opposing effects. The variables z_H and z_F measure the value of the stocks of bonds relative to the flows of goods. If the basic period of the model (equal to the information lag) is short, z_H and z_F are likely to be close to one. Then the two opposing effects of the monetary shocks on e_t tend to cancel. In the next period there will be a stronger effect on the exchange rate, but then the agents have had time to talk, and monetary policy ceases to have effect on real variables.

One route to stronger immediate effects on the exchange rate may be to widen the menu of assets, and thus open the possibility for different monetary policies. Whether this research strategy is worth pursuing can be questioned, however.

Some economists seem to say that we should avoid models with nominal rigidity because they lack proper "microfoundations". The demand is for models with optimizing agents and market clearing. However, these are purely formal, methodological requirements, and the only philosophical underpinning for them seems to be a desire for unity in economic modelling. A more sensible requirement would be for "empirical microfoundations": macro models should be broadly consistent with what we know about economic behaviour and economic structure at the micro level. Simplifications must be allowed to make models tractable, but the main institutional and behavioural assumptions should have their counterparts in observed phenomena at the micro level. In this sense it can be questioned whether Obstfeld's model in Part III (and the other models discussed there) has proper microfoundations.

In Obstfeld's model, each household makes a final allocation of domestic currency for the purchase of domestic goods and foreign currency for the purchase of foreign goods before the period's news from financial markets is known. In real life, who commits cash in advance for imports and spends the same amount irrespective of the price? Is it not so that the bulk of international trade is based on credit? Most tradable goods are storable and there are shipping lags. Does this not induce importers to exhibit more forward-looking behaviour at the moment of buying than just spending a pre-committed amount of foreign currency? All money that is taken to the asset market must in the end be used to buy bonds in the same currency, even if interest rates may be negative. Bond prices are equal to a constant times the ratio between last period's money supply and this period's bond supply, simply because a certain fraction of the money supply is always used for buying bonds in the same currency.

The point I wish to make is that in order to satisfy the poorly justified demand for methodological microfoundations, one is willing to go very far in neglecting the better justified demand for empirical microfoundations. We should be less dogmatic about methodology. Considering the facts in Part II, it should not be necessary to make particular excuses for models with nominal rigidities.

In Part IV, Obstfeld gives a brief, but interesting, review of some of the literature on monetary union in Europe. There is a potential gain from monetary union which neither he, nor the scientific literature in general, has given much attention. To many observers there seems to be a lot of "noise" in foreign exchange markets. Investors seem to behave in changing and rather erratic ways. They may be highly rational, but still entertain different expectations, because they rely on different models and theories for prediction. Forecasting exchange rates is such a complex problem that agents have to simplify and focus on a few factors which they consider the most important at the moment. The focus changes over time. Forecasters are sometimes told to look at "fundamentals", but at the deepest level the fundamental value of paper money is zero, and the fundamental exchange rate between two paper monies is indeterminate. It all depends on beliefs.

In these circumstances it is quite possible for exchange rate behaviour to be rather erratic and "noisy". There may be a significant gain from getting rid of this noise, but a gain which probably escapes all serious attempts at quantification.

Part V is a brief review of the literature on speculative attacks on fixed exchange rates. A central concept in the prototype model is the "fire-power" of speculators. Speculators get firepower both from owning a currency and from being able to borrow it. In most cases the total creditworthiness of speculators must be an order of magnitude greater than the foreign exchange reserves. The focus on the relative size of "firepower" versus reserves may therefore not be the most interesting.

Whether a speculative attack will be an economic success for the speculators depends on what the defending government does both before and after the attack. Perhaps there should be more focus on the policy after an attack. The usual defence against a speculative attack is a combination of intervention and high interest rates. The first fails because reserves are less than "firepower", the second may be counterproductive if interest rates are set too high. Everybody understands that interest rates cannot be kept too high for long. High interest rates may produce a debt crisis, which may in itself be a reason for devaluing. After an eventual devaluation, interest rates are brought down and reserves are rebuilt by buying back foreign currency.

However, the defence can choose another strategy. Keep the economy in shape by avoiding extremely high interest rates. Make a tactical withdrawal by letting the exchange rate float at an earlier stage. Postpone some of the intervention until after the exchange rate has moved a few percent. Keep interest rates moderately high and keep the old parity as a target for the future while the exchange rate is floating. Do not buy back foreign currency. Speculators are usually going for short-term profits, which means they want to get out of their speculative positions soon. The exchange rate is then likely to move back. With some patience this strategy may bring the exchange rate back to the old parity and inflict a loss on the speculators. This will have a preventive effect on future speculation.

The method is not foolproof. Its efficacy depends on expectations which the government has no direct control over, and fiscal policy must be consistent with a return to parity.

Most speculative attacks have happened when there are good economic reasons for devaluing, and governments have not been too keen on restoring the old parities. However, as the number of speculative attacks has multiplied, and the attacks are more often directed against countries with less reason to devalue, we should also expect to see a different kind of defence.

Scand. J. Economics 100(1), 289–324, 1998

The Demand for Broad Money in the United Kingdom, 1878–1993*

Neil R. Ericsson

Federal Reserve Board, Washington, DC 20551, USA

David F. Hendry

Nuffield College, Oxford OX1 1NF, England

Kevin M. Prestwich

American Management Systems, Fairfax, VA 22033, USA

Abstract

Using annual data from Friedman and Schwartz (1982), Hendry and Ericsson (1991a) developed an empirical model of the demand for broad money in the United Kingdom over 1878–1975. We update that model over 1976–1993, accounting for changed data definitions and clarifying the concept of constancy. With appropriate measures of opportunity cost and credit deregulation, the model's parameters are empirically constant over the extended sample, which was economically turbulent. Policy implications follow for parameter nonconstancy and predictive failure, causation between money and prices, monetary targeting, deregulation and financial innovation, and the effect of policy on economic agents' behavior.

I. Introduction

We are delighted to contribute to a volume celebrating the centenary of the *Scandinavian Journal of Economics*, and we offer our birthday greetings to a journal that has played a distinguished role in the development of our science over the last century. As befits such an occasion, this paper

*The views expressed here are solely the responsibility of the authors and should not be interpreted as reflecting those of the Board of Governors of the Federal Reserve System or other members of its staff. The first author gratefully acknowledges the generous hospitality of Norges Bank, where he revised some of the material herein. The second author gratefully acknowledges financial support from the U.K. Economic and Social Research Council under grant R000234954. We wish to thank Chris Allsopp, Torben Andersen, Peter Hammond, Svend Hylleberg, Neva Kerbeshian, Jaime Marquez, Karl Moene, John Muellbauer, Timo Teräsvirta, a referee, the participants at the *SJE*'s symposium, and workshop participants at the Oxford Institute of Economics and Statistics and the University of California at San Diego for helpful discussions and comments; and Clifford Attfield, David Demery, and Nigel Duck for compiling the data in Attfield, Demery, and Duck (1995). All numerical results were obtained using PcGive Professional Versions 8.10 and 9.00; see Doornik and Hendry (1994), Doornik and Hendry (1996), and Hendry and Doornik (1996).

reconsiders a perennial controversy with important policy implications — the demand for money — using a long historical data record for the United Kingdom.

This re-assessment emphasizes the intertwining of empirical modeling, econometric methodology, and conceptual issues when evaluating econometric models over additional observations. Hendry and Ericsson (1991a) developed a model of U.K. money demand on data spanning 1878–1975. In the current paper, we extend that model to include nearly two decades of new data for 1976–1993, and, in so doing, clarify the concept of parameter constancy. Lengthening the sample expands the number of alternative measures of both credit derestrictions and the opportunity cost of holding money. Thus, we test for parameter constancy in models using different measures of those concepts. Mechanistic updates of these measures result in models with predictive failure. However, for coherent updates, the model's short-run and long-run properties remain virtually unchanged over the unusually long forecast period of 18 years, despite substantial financial innovation in the economy and major changes in monetary control rules.

Sections II, III, and V focus on the empirical aspects, and Section IV on the methodological and conceptual developments. The empirical, methodological, and conceptual contributions all have implications for inferences about economic policy, and all help in understanding those implications. Section V discusses several such implications, including the role of parameter nonconstancy and predictive failure, the direction of causation between money and prices, monetary targeting, deregulation and financial innovation, the Lucas critique, the role of expectations in economic agents' decisions, and the effect of policy on economic agents' behavior. The paper's results also have ramifications for the modeling and analysis of other sectors of the U.K. economy and of sectors of other countries' economies.

In somewhat greater detail, the structure of the paper is as follows. Section II briefly reviews the economic theory of money demand and defines and describes the data series. Section III records the estimated model in Hendry and Ericsson (1991a) and notes its nonconstancy if the model is extended mechanistically over the new data. Section IV considers how to evaluate and update empirical models over samples involving major changes to the economy. Specifically, for the forecast period 1976–1993, economic extensions of the empirical model are required for the changing measurement of money, for the associated changes in the opportunity cost of holding money, and for financial innovation and deregulation. Data measurement, the opportunity cost, and financial innovation and deregulation each have implications for parameter constancy. Section V extends the economics of the model in Hendry and Ericsson (1991a) to incorporate these issues, and it tests for and shows the constancy of the model's parameters. This section also considers identification and policy implications. Section VI concludes. Ericsson, Hendry and Prestwich (1997) document the data in detail and compare the performance of the annual model with other models, including with models based on Friedman and Schwartz's phase-average data.

II. Economic Theory and Data Description

This section provides the backdrop for the subsequent sections. After sketching the standard theory underlying empirical models of money demand, we describe the data modeled and characterize the data's basic properties.

Economic Theories of Money Demand

The theoretical and empirical study of the demand for money in the United Kingdom has an impressive history, matching the extensive time series now available on money and its main determinants; see Jevons (1884) [reprinted in part as Hendry and Morgan (1995, Chapter 6)], Marshall (1926), Keynes (1930), and Hawtrey (1938) *inter alia* for earlier contributions. More recently, the literature on money demand has seen an explosion in the modeling of numerous monetary aggregates, both for the United Kingdom and for other countries. Goldfeld and Sichel (1990) extensively review that more recent theoretical and empirical work.

As discussed in the papers cited above, and elsewhere, money may be demanded in a modern economy for at least two reasons: as an inventory to smooth differences between income and expenditure streams, and as one among several assets in a portfolio. Both demands lead to a long-run specification in which nominal money demanded (M^d) depends on the price level (P), a scale variable (I), inflation ($\dot{p}$), and a vector ($\mathbf{R}$) of rates of returns on various assets:

$$M^d = g(P, I, \dot{p}, \mathbf{R}). \tag{1}$$

The function $g(\cdot)$ is assumed to be unit homogeneous in P, increasing in I, decreasing in both inflation and those elements of $\mathbf{R}$ associated with assets excluded from money (M), and increasing in those elements of $\mathbf{R}$ for assets included in M. The opportunity cost is determined through $\mathbf{R}$ and is a focus of Section IV. See Cagan (1956) on the inclusion of $\dot{p}$ in $g(\cdot)$.

Commonly, (1) is specified in log-linear form, albeit with interest rates entering either in logs or in levels:

$$m^d - p = \mu_0 + \mu_1 i + \mu_2 \dot{p} + \mu_3 R^{\text{own}} + \mu_4 R^{\text{out}}. \tag{2}$$

Capital letters denote both the generic name and the level, logs are in lowercase, and (somewhat symbolically) R^{own} and R^{out} denote the own and outside rates of interest. The coefficients $\mu_0, \ldots, \mu_4$ are an intercept, the income elasticity, and the semi-elasticities on inflation, the own interest rate, and the outside interest rate. Anticipated signs of the coefficients are $\mu_1 > 0$, $\mu_2 < 0$, $\mu_3 > 0$, and $\mu_4 < 0$.

Data Description

We now define the data and present some descriptive statistics. Both graphs and simple time-series regressions help characterize the data's properties, which should be considered in empirical modeling.

The basic data series are annual values of the broad money stock (M), real net national income (I), the corresponding deflator (P), short-term and long-term nominal interest rates (RS and $R\ell$), and high-powered money (H), all for the United Kingdom. Data from 1871 to 1975 are from Friedman and Schwartz (1982). Attfield, Demery and Duck (1995) extended those series over 1976–1993, constructing them from a variety of sources and splicing together several alternative definitions of money. These measures of money as such are discussed in Section IV. The variables M and H are in £ million; I is in £ million for 1929; $P = 1.00$ in 1929; and RS and $R\ell$ are fractions.

Some constructed variables are also of interest. First, under the quantity theory of money, the income elasticity is unity [$\mu_1 = 1$ in (2)], so a key derived variable is velocity V, constructed as $(I \cdot P)/M$. Second, there are dummy variables. Retaining the notation in Hendry and Ericsson (1991a), the variables D_1 and D_3 are zero-one dummies for World Wars I and II, and D_4 is a zero-one dummy for 1971–1975. The latter aims to capture the deregulation of the banking sector with the introduction of Competition and Credit Control in 1971. A similar period of deregulation occurs in 1986–1989; see Section IV below. As a proxy for both episodes of deregulation, the dummy D_c is unity for 1971–1975 and 1986–1989, and zero otherwise. See Friedman and Schwartz (1982), Topping and Bishop (1989), Hendry and Ericsson (1991a), Attfield, Demery and Duck (1995), and Ericsson, Hendry and Prestwich (1997) for details on these data and on the additional data discussed below.

Before examining the data, we introduce a few more conventions. Uppercase delta (Δ) is the difference operator.[1] "Levels" often means the

---

[1] The difference operator Δ is defined as $(1 - L)$, where the lag operator L shifts a variable one period into the past. Hence, for x_t (a variable x at time t), $Lx_t = x_{t-1}$ and so $\Delta x_t = x_t - x_{t-1}$. More generally, $\Delta_j^i x_t = (1 - L^j)^i x_t$ for positive integers i and j. If i or j is not explicit, it is taken to be unity.

logarithm of the levels, and the context clarifies this. Figures typically appear as 2 × 2 panels of graphs, with each graph labeled by a suffix *a, b, c,* or *d,* as follows: [^a_c ^b_d]. Single and double asterisks (* and **) adjacent to values of statistics denote significance at the 5% and 1% levels.

Figure 1 shows the full-sample time series of (m, p), $(m - p, i)$, (RS, v), and $(\Delta m, \Delta p)$ as a 2 × 2 panel, with the variables adjusted for their means in the first two graphs and for their means and ranges in the third graph. Figure 1a emphasizes the huge changes in money and prices over the century. Noting that the graph is in logs (for ease of display), the actual level of money moves from £492.4 million in 1871 to £291,173 million in 1993, an increase of almost 600-*fold.* Over the same period, prices rise about 55-fold, from 0.579 to 31.38. Thus, a pound sterling in 1993 is equivalent in purchasing power to just over 4d (approximately 2 new pence) at the beginning of the sample. From Figure 1b, real money increases 10.9-fold over the sample, closely matching the 9.2-fold increase in real national income. To characterize adequately such massive growth and change in money is a serious challenge, particularly in a parsimonious constant model.

As Figure 1b also shows, real money grows most rapidly over the last two decades, notwithstanding the two world wars elsewhere in the sample and despite the U.K. government's attempt at monetary control over much of

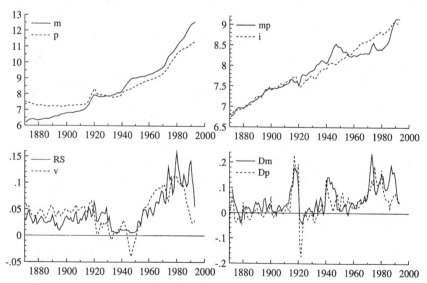

Fig. 1. Nominal money and prices (m, p), real money and real income $(m - p, i)$, interest rates and velocity (RS, v), and money growth and inflation $(\Delta m, \Delta p)$.

the 1980s. Correspondingly, velocity falls sharply to levels prevalent in the last century; see Figure 1c. Even relative to the previous century, large changes have occurred over the last two decades.

Figure 1d plots the inflation rate and the growth rate of nominal money. These series move relatively closely overall. There are four notable departures: 1920–1922, when prices fall by 25% but nominal money by only 5%; World War II and the early 1970s, when money growth greatly exceeds the rate of inflation; and 1985–1990, when money growth is about 17% with inflation of 6%.

Univariate autoregressive models can help characterize the order of integration of time series for use in subsequent cointegration analysis. Specifically, the augmented Dickey-Fuller (ADF) statistic t_{ADF} can be used to test whether a series is integrated of order d [or I(d)], where an I(d) series requires differencing d times to remove all its unit roots; see Dickey and Fuller (1981). Table 1 records the ADF statistics over the sample 1875–1993 for the key variables. Each ADF statistic is reported for the shortest lag length obtainable (commencing from 2 lags) without dropping a lagged difference significant at the 5% level.

The hypothesis of a unit root cannot be rejected for any variable in levels, whereas it is strongly rejected for all variables in differences, consistent with the visual evidence that the differences repeatedly return to their means over the sample. Despite their smooth and trending appearance, m and p appear to be I(1) rather than I(2). The smoothness in m and p may be associated with the main regime shifts over the sample, such as wars and financial innovations. If so, a non-negligible part of their observed variation may be due to non-stationarities arising from structural change. Thus, given their univariate nature and the absence of tests for congruency, these ADF (and related) statistics should not be regarded as definitive.

The I(1)-ness of m and p contrasts with evidence in Johansen (1992), who finds money and prices in the United Kingdom to be I(2). These discrepant results have several potential explanations. First, the data differ and so need not have the same order of integration. Johansen's data are M1 and the implicit price deflator for total final expenditure, whereas our data are M2 (recently, M3 and M4) and the implicit price deflator for net national income. Second, the testing procedures differ, with potentially different size and power properties. Johansen tests for integration by a system-based procedure, whereas the ADF statistics in Table 1 are univariate. Third, and relatedly, both measures of money and prices display regime shifts, which are liable to affect the properties of the test procedures; see Figure 1d and Johansen (1992, Figure 2). Fourth, the order of integration need not be an inherent property of data. For instance, the order might alter over time, due to changes in government policy or economic innovation. Subsample values of first-order augmented Dickey-

Fuller statistics provide evidence on both the third and fourth issues. For the change in a given variable, the corresponding recursive values of t_{ADF} should decline monotonically over time if the original variable is I(1), or remain relatively flat if the original variable is I(2). For each measure of money and of prices, the recursive values of t_{ADF} do neither, but rather increase sharply over some periods and decrease sharply over others, where the precise datings of the movements depend on the series and dataset. Fifth, the samples differ. Johansen's data are quarterly over 1964–1989, our data are annual over 1875–1993, and the characteristics of the economy vary over the respective sample periods.

Table 1. *ADF Statistics and Related Calculations*

Variable	t_{ADF}	$\hat{\rho}$	$\hat{\sigma}$	Lag	t_{lag}	t_{lag}-prob (%)	F-prob (%)
m	-0.44	0.997	0.0263	2	-4.58	0.0	—
p	-1.29	0.990	0.0396	1	9.47	0.0	16.7
i	-2.67	0.913	0.0313	1	3.54	0.1	88.8
$m-p$	-2.78	0.934	0.0356	1	7.23	0.0	6.2
v	-2.35	0.949	0.0428	1	6.05	0.0	52.7
RS	-2.28	0.897	0.0124	2	-3.59	0.0	—
$R\ell$	-2.35	0.936	0.0059	1	3.60	0.0	5.9
RN^{a}	-1.66	0.925	0.0099	2	-4.39	0.0	—
$\hat{u}$	-5.17^{**}	0.695	0.0901	1	3.84	0.0	8.4
$\bar{u}$	-3.30	0.790	0.0696	2	-3.16	0.2	—
Δm	-5.18^{**}	0.725	0.0262	1	5.01	0.0	41.9
Δp	-4.87^{**}	0.658	0.0397	0	—	—	29.0
Δi	-7.24^{**}	0.042	0.0316	2	2.36	2.0	—
$\Delta(m-p)$	-6.72^{**}	0.408	0.0358	1	2.62	1.0	15.7
Δv	-6.58^{**}	0.463	0.0436	0	—	—	22.5
ΔRS	-10.22^{**}	-0.244	0.0126	1	4.26	0.0	5.3
$\Delta R\ell$	-7.61^{**}	0.139	0.0059	1	2.29	2.4	6.3
ΔRN^{a}	-11.34^{**}	-0.269	0.0100	1	5.08	0.0	28.1
$\Delta\hat{u}$	-8.33^{**}	-0.369	0.0928	2	2.33	2.2	—
$\Delta\bar{u}$	-9.24^{**}	-0.420	0.0714	2	2.16	3.3	—

Notes:
1. Second-order ADF regressions were initially estimated and, in an iterative sequence, the longest lag was repeatedly dropped until its t-ratio was at least two in absolute value. For each variable examined, the columns report the ADF statistic on this simplified regression (t_{ADF}), the estimated coefficient on the lagged level that is being tested for a unit value ($\hat{\rho}$), the estimated equation standard error ($\hat{\sigma}$), the lag length of the ADF regression (lag), the t-statistic on the longest lag of the final regression (t_{lag}), its tail probability (t_{lag}-prob), and the tail probability of the F-statistic for the lags dropped (F-prob). Sections III and V define $\hat{u}$ and $\bar{u}$.
2. All of the ADF regressions include both an intercept and a linear trend. MacKinnon's (1991) approximate finite-sample critical values for the corresponding ADF statistic are -3.45 (5%) and -4.04 (1%), except for $\hat{u}$, $\bar{u}$, $\Delta\hat{u}$, and $\Delta\bar{u}$, for which the critical values are -3.86 (5%) and -4.46 (1%). The sample is 1875–1993 ($T = 119$) in all cases. Rejection of the null hypothesis of a unit root is denoted by * and ** for the 5% and 1% levels.

III. Previous Estimates and a Mechanistic Extension

We now turn to the initial annual model in Hendry and Ericsson (1991a) and their alternative model on a slightly different sample. Both models use the annual data as compiled by Friedman and Schwartz (1982), which end in 1975. We also evaluate a simple mechanistic extension of Hendry and Ericsson's model over the sample 1976–1993 and find strong evidence of parameter nonconstancy. However, the way in which a model is extended over a new sample bears directly on its statistical performance on that sample, leading to economic extensions of empirical models (Section IV) and a re-evaluation of the model in Hendry and Ericsson (1991a) on the new data (Section V).

The Annual Models in Hendry and Ericsson (1991a)

Economic theory offers little guidance in modeling the behavior of money out of equilibrium, beyond saying that adjustments to "desired" levels of money holdings are likely to take time, due to adjustment costs. In that light, Hendry and Ericsson (1991a) developed a dynamic equilibrium correction model (EqCM) of broad money M, allowing the economic theory above to define the long-run equilibrium while determining short-run dynamics from the data.[2] That EqCM is:

$$\Delta(m-p)_t = 0.45\,\Delta(m-p)_{t-1} - 0.10\,\Delta^2(m-p)_{t-2} - 0.60\,\Delta p_t$$
$$[0.07] \qquad\qquad [0.04] \qquad\qquad [0.07]$$

$$+\,0.39\,\Delta p_{t-1} - 0.021\,\Delta rs_t - 0.062\,\Delta_2 r\ell_t$$
$$[0.07] \qquad [0.006] \qquad [0.023]$$

$$-\,2.54\,(\hat{u}_{t-1}-0.2)\hat{u}^2_{t-1} + 0.005 + 3.7\,(D_1+D_3)_t \qquad (3)$$
$$[0.67] \qquad\qquad\qquad [0.002]\;[0.7]$$

$T = 93\,[1878–1970] \quad R^2 = 0.87 \quad \hat{\sigma} = 1.424\% \quad dw = 1.82$

$AR\!: F(2, 82) = 1.39 \quad ARCH\!: F(1, 82) = 1.51 \quad Normality\!: \chi^2(2) = 1.9$

$RESET\!: F(1, 83) = 0.41 \quad Hetero\!: F(15, 68) = 0.87$

$Form\!: F(43, 40) = 0.81 \quad Jt = 1.18 \quad Var = 0.09.$

Here and below, t is the annual time subscript; T is the number of annual observations; R^2 is the squared multiple correlation coefficient; $\hat{\sigma}$ is the standard deviation of the residuals, expressed as a percentage of real money and adjusted for degrees of freedom; and the coefficient on the war

---

[2]Although Hendry and Ericsson (1991a) called the model in (3) below an error correction model, technically speaking it is an equilibrium correction model. See Hendry (1995, p. 213) for a discussion of the distinction between the two.

dummies $(D_1 + D_3)$ has been scaled up 100-fold so that it is interpretable as a percentage. OLS standard errors are in parentheses ($\cdot$), whereas heteroscedasticity-consistent standard errors are in square brackets [$\cdot$]; see White (1980), Nicholls and Pagan (1983), Messer and White (1984), and MacKinnon and White (1985) on the latter. Equation (3) also includes diagnostic statistics for testing against various alternative hypotheses: residual autocorrelation (*dw* and *AR*), autoregressive conditional heteroscedasticity (*ARCH*), skewness and excess kurtosis (*Normality*), RESET (*RESET*), heteroscedasticity (*Hetero*), heteroscedasticity quadratic in the regressors (alternatively, functional form mis-specification) (*Form*), and joint parameter nonconstancy and variance nonconstancy (*Jt* and *Var*).[3,4] The asymptotic null distribution is designated by $\chi^2(\cdot)$ or $F(\cdot,\cdot)$, the degrees of freedom fill the parentheses, and (for *AR* and *ARCH*) the lag order is the first degree of freedom.

The derived variable $\hat{u}$ in (3) is the equilibrium correction residual from the static Engle–Granger regression over 1873–1970:

$$(m - p - i)_t = -0.310 - 7.00RS_t \tag{4}$$

$T = 98\,[1873–1970] \quad R^2 = 0.56 \quad \hat{\sigma} = 10.86\% \quad dw = 0.33 \quad t_{ADF} = -2.77;$

see Engle and Granger (1987). Based on Escribano (1985), $\hat{u}$ enters (3) nonlinearly.

Equation (3) appears reasonably well specified within sample, given the diagnostic statistics above and additional results in Hendry and Ericsson (1991a). In particular, Hendry and Ericsson (1991a) provide graphical evidence that (3) is empirically constant, using recursive least squares.

However, (3) as specified is nonconstant over the period 1971–1975, following the introduction of Competition and Credit Control regulations (CCC). Hendry and Ericsson (1991a) expand (3) to account for CCC by including the dummy D_4, both by itself and interactively with Δrs. Estimated over 1878–1975, the resulting model is close to (3) for comparable coefficients:

---

[3]For derivations of the test statistics, see Godfrey (1978), Engle (1982), Doornik and Hansen (1994), Ramsey (1969), White (1980) (for both *Hetero* and *Form*), and Hansen (1992) (for both *Jt* and *Var*). For additional discussion and for their implementation, see Hendry and Doornik (1996).

[4]Due to increased numerical accuracy in recent versions of PcGive, some coefficients and test statistics in (3), (4), and (5) differ slightly from those reported in the equivalent equations in Hendry and Ericsson (1991a). See Doornik and Hendry (1992, Appendix C) and Hendry and Doornik (1996, Appendix A2) for details on the specific improvements in accuracy, noting that the results in Hendry and Ericsson (1991a) were produced with PcGive version 6.0/6.01. Also, the heteroscedasticity-consistent standard errors in Hendry and Ericsson (1991a) are those from White (1980), whereas the ones reported herein are the jackknife version from MacKinnon and White (1985).

$$\Delta(m-p)_t = 0.47\,\Delta(m-p)_{t-1} - 0.11\,\Delta^2(m-p)_{t-2} - 0.59\,\Delta p_t$$
$$\quad\;\;[0.06]\qquad\qquad\;\;[0.04]\qquad\qquad\;\;[0.06]$$

$$+\,0.41\,\Delta p_{t-1} - 0.017\,\Delta rs_t - 0.078\,\Delta_2 r\ell_t$$
$$\quad[0.07]\qquad\;[0.008]\qquad\;[0.026]$$

$$-\,1.15\,(\hat{u}_{t-1} - 0.2)\,\hat{u}^2_{t-1} + 0.007 + 3.4\,(D_1 + D_3)_t$$
$$\quad[1.46]\qquad\qquad\qquad\;\;[0.003]\;[0.8]$$

$$+\,7.1\,D_{4t} + 0.090\,D_{4t}\,\Delta rs_t \qquad\qquad\qquad\qquad (5)$$
$$\quad[1.8]\qquad[0.046]$$

$T = 98\,[1878\text{–}1975]\quad R^2 = 0.88\quad \hat{\sigma} = 1.478\%\quad dw = 1.89$

$AR\colon F(2,\,85) = 1.50\quad ARCH\colon F(1,\,85) = 1.43\quad Normality\colon \chi^2(2) = 4.2$

$RESET\colon F(1,\,86) = 0.03\quad Hetero\colon F(18,\,68) = 0.43$

$Form\colon F(48,\,38) = 0.97\quad Jt = 1.22\quad Var = 0.05.$

As with $(D_1 + D_3)$, the coefficient on D_4 (and on D_c, below) has been scaled up 100-fold — when it enters the equation as D_4 (or as D_c) alone. The coefficient on $D_{4t}\Delta rs_t$ is *not* rescaled, so as to maintain units comparable to those of the coefficient on Δrs_t. Figure 2 shows the fitted and actual values, scaled residuals (scaled to be in units of $\hat{\sigma}$), residual correlogram, and residual histogram and estimated density for (5). The model appears congruent within this sample against the available information.

Predictive Failure of a Mechanistic Extension of the Model

In evaluating a model over a new sample, a common approach updates the model mechanistically, simply "plugging in" the new data into the existing equation; see Attfield, Demery and Duck (1995). For (5) and the data described in Section II, the results are as follows over the 18 years of new data:

$$\Delta(m-p)_t = 0.54\,\Delta(m-p)_{t-1} - 0.11\,\Delta^2(m-p)_{t-2} - 0.63\,\Delta p_t$$
$$\quad\;\;[0.07]\qquad\qquad\;\;[0.05]\qquad\qquad\;\;[0.09]$$

$$+\,0.47\,\Delta p_{t-1} - 0.008\,\Delta rs_t - 0.089\,\Delta_2 r\ell_t$$
$$\quad[0.08]\qquad\;[0.007]\qquad\;[0.026]$$

$$-\,0.056\,(\hat{u}_{t-1} - 0.2)\,\hat{u}^2_{t-1} + 0.009 + 3.1\,(D_1 + D_3)_t$$
$$\quad[0.072]\qquad\qquad\qquad\;\;[0.002]\;[0.7]$$

$$+\,5.0\,D_{ct} + 0.126\,D_{4t}\,\Delta rs_t \qquad\qquad\qquad\qquad (6)$$
$$\quad[1.4]\qquad[0.059]$$

$T = 116\,[1878\text{–}1993]\quad R^2 = 0.82\quad \hat{\sigma} = 1.931\%\quad dw = 1.48$

$AR\colon F(2,\,103) = 4.32^*\quad ARCH\colon F(1,\,103) = 0.01$

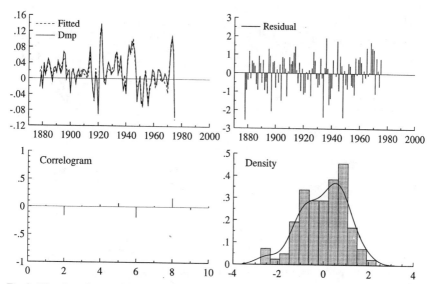

Fig. 2. Fitted and actual values of $\Delta(m-p)_t$ from (5), and the corresponding scaled residuals, residual correlogram, and residual histogram and estimated density.

Normality: $\chi^2(2) = 4.2$ *RESET*: $F(1, 104) = 0.92$

Hetero: $F(18, 86) = 3.74^{**}$ *Form*: $F(52, 52) = 2.83^{**}$

Chow: $F(18, 87) = 5.13^{**}$ $Jt = 2.58$ $Var = 0.86^{**}$.

Despite the benefit of using D_c (the extended dummy for credit loosening), (6) appears nonconstant. The Chow (1960) predictive-failure statistic (*Chow*) strongly rejects constancy; Hansen's statistic *Var* likewise rejects constancy; and *Jt* nearly rejects at the 90% critical value, even though it has 12 degrees of freedom. Several residual diagnostic tests also reject, and the equilibrium correction term has become insignificant.

Predictive failure is extensive and not isolated to one or two observations. Figure 3 demonstrates this failure through the fitted, actual, and forecast values for $\Delta(m-p)_t$, their cross-plots, the equation's residuals, and the equation's forecasts (with ± 2 standard error bars) compared with actual outcomes. Both numerically and statistically, the model's forecast performance is dramatically worse than its in-sample behavior.

IV. Economic Extensions of Empirical Models

Mechanical extensions of an empirical model, such as (6), can mislead because of their simplistic approach to updating. Rather, changing

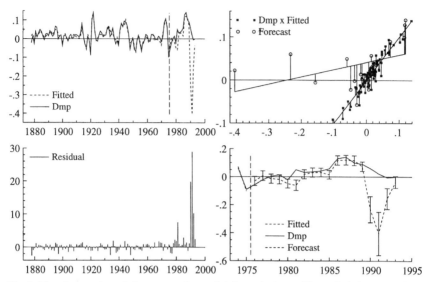

Fig. 3. Fitted, actual, and forecast values of $\Delta(m-p)$, from (5), and their cross-plots, corresponding scaled residuals, and forecasts with ± 2 standard error bars.

environments may require economic adaptation of a model. To that end, this section considers four issues: (i) how the adopted measure of money changes when extending the data series; (ii) the consequent effects on the opportunity cost of holding the new measure of money; (iii) the effect of financial innovation and financial deregulation on both the original measure of money and the new measure; and (iv) statistical implications for a model's constancy over an extended sample with financial innovation and changed data definitions and opportunity costs.

Measures of Money

Here, we review some difficulties in measuring money, and then focus on the specific statistical measures used herein. Difficulties include vagueness in the concept of money itself, the effects of financial innovation on measurement of a consistent series, and changing definitions of observed series. The measurement of money leads directly to the calculation of its opportunity cost.

The concept of money is imprecise and ambiguous, and has been so for decades. In their evidence to the U.K. Royal Commission on the Values of Gold and Silver, Marshall and Edgeworth cited important changes contributing to these difficulties: the newly introduced checkbook, more rapid transfers between bank accounts in different locations due to the telegraph, and bimetallism itself through the respective quantities and prices of gold and silver. The first and third factors affected the definition of money itself, and all three factors allowed economization in the transactions medium. Later work has emphasized the changing importance of portfolio considerations versus liquidity.

Also, the very form of the transactions medium has changed greatly, becoming interest bearing (for the most part) towards the end of the sample. While cash may not have changed much, its substitutes have. Checks have fallen from favor relative to credit cards, and recently debit card transactions have grown rapidly. The recorded measures of money also have changed over the period, especially the coverage of the most cited measures — M0, M1, M2, M3, and M4.[5] In particular, building societies (akin to savings and loans associations) have grown rapidly, offering close substitutes for commercial-bank liabilities, and with some building societies converting their legal status to commercial banks from 1989 onwards. Hendry and Ericsson (1991a, pp. 32–34) highlighted such reservations on the measurement and interpretation of *M*.

These difficulties and their consequences are apparent in the series for money used herein. Both Friedman and Schwartz (1982) and Attfield, Demery and Duck (1995) were faced with incomplete series on any measure of broad money over their samples. The measure M2 ("old definition") exists through 1971; M3 from 1963 through 1987; and M4 (adjusted for slight definitional breaks) from 1982 through 1993. To create their annual money series, Friedman and Schwartz (1982, p. 114) spliced M3 onto M2, multiplying M3 by approximately 0.996 to match the value of M2 in 1968 and using that rescaled M3 from 1969 through 1975. To extend the data through 1993, Attfield, Demery and Duck (1995, Data Appendix)

---

[5]The key measures of money discussed herein are high-powered money, M0, M1, M2, M3, and M4, which are ordered (more or less) from the narrowest measure to the broadest measure. These measures are defined in brief below; details appear in Ericsson, Hendry and Prestwich (1997). High-powered money *H* is the sum of "currency outside banks, currency held by banks, bankers' deposits, special deposits, and private deposits at the Bank of England"; cf. Friedman and Schwartz (1982, p. 137). Attfield, Demery and Duck (1995) spliced together *H* and the monetary base M0, which is notes and coins in circulation outside the Bank of England plus banks' operational deposits with the Bank of England. The measure M1 is notes and coins in circulation with the public plus sight bank deposits (i.e., current accounts or, equivalently, checking accounts). If interest-bearing sight deposits are excluded from M1, the resulting measure is non-interest-bearing M1 (NIB M1). The measure of M2 in Friedman and Schwartz (1982, pp. 134–135) is total M1 plus deposit accounts (time deposits) at deposit banks and discount houses. The measure M3 is M2 plus all other bank deposits. The deposits in M3 are of U.K. residents only; those in M1 and M2 are of private sector residents only and sterling-denominated. The measure M4 is the sterling-denominated component of M3 plus (essentially) private sector holdings of building societies' shares, deposits, and sterling certificates of deposit.

similarly spliced M4 onto M3 in 1987, with M4 multiplied by approximately 0.545. Attfield, Demery, and Duck also spliced M0 onto Friedman and Schwartz's measure of high-powered money H in 1975, with M0 being multiplied by approximately 1.27.

The statistical magnitudes of the splicings for M are apparent from Figure 4, which plots the logs of M [as from Friedman and Schwartz (1982)], rescaled M3, and rescaled M4 (Figure 4a); the logs of Friedman and Schwartz's M and the unrescaled M3 and M4 (Figure 4b); the growth rates of the three measures (Figure 4c); and logs of the ratios of the series for periods with overlapping observations (Figure 4d). The first splice in M appears minor in nature. The second, by contrast, markedly broadens the definition of money, with M4 being 1.83 times M3 in 1987, the date of the second splicing. The non-M3 component of M4 (dominated by building society deposits) is almost entirely interest-bearing, so the implicit opportunity cost on the spliced money series is nearly halved, leading to the discussion in the next subsection.

The Opportunity Cost of Holding Money

Because older series such as M2 and M3 and some of their components are not published for the latter part of the sample, construction of a "consistent" series is infeasible, so modelers are left with little option other than

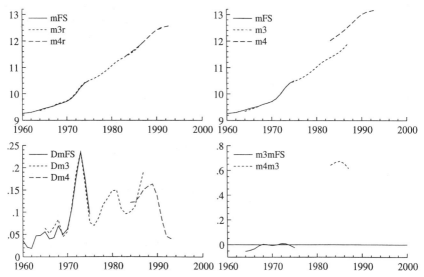

Fig. 4. Logs of rescaled money, logs of unrescaled money, growth rates of unrescaled money, and logs of the ratios of unrescaled money for overlapping periods.

splicing series together. However, splicing may alter the implied opportunity cost of holding the (measured) money, with the second splice being of primary concern because of the numerical magnitudes involved. The choice of measured opportunity cost in turn can dramatically affect the performance of empirical models of money demand. Thus, this subsection re-examines existing measures of the opportunity cost. They prove inadequate, so we develop a modified measure of the opportunity cost, which is key to the empirical constancy of (5) when the data are extended through 1993.

Friedman and Schwartz (1982) and Hendry and Ericsson (1991a) propose two different measures of the opportunity cost for M. Hendry and Ericsson (1991a) use the short-term interest rate RS as the primary opportunity cost of holding money, as in (3), (4), and (5) above. Friedman and Schwartz (1982) advocate using a fraction of RS, denoted by RN and calculated as $(H/M)RS$. This alternative measure assumes that all components of M except for high-powered money H earn interest at the (outside) short-term rate RS. Three issues bear on the choice between RS and RN and on the suitability of either as an opportunity cost: the ratio H/M, the relationship between the actual own rate and RS, and the measures of H and M for calculating RN.

First, if H/M is nearly constant, empirical results should be relatively unaffected by the choice between RS and RN, aside from a scale factor on the estimated coefficient. For Friedman and Schwartz's sample period, H/M varies almost exclusively within the narrow range $[0.22, 0.28]$. As Hendry and Ericsson (1991a, p. 32, footnote 26) note, their annual models are little affected by those choices of interest rate.

Second, if the relationship between RS and the own rate of interest changes, neither RS nor RN may be good proxies for the actual opportunity cost. Hendry and Ericsson (1991a) expressed this concern, particularly because the behavior of the own interest rate did change at the end of Friedman and Schwartz's sample.

> A potential explanation ..., consistent with the earlier evidence and economic analysis, is presaged by Klovland's (1987) result for pre-1914 data that the *own* interest rate on broad money is an important omitted variable from the present information set. ... Over much of the sample, U.K. commercial banks acted like a cartel with administered (and generally low) deposit interest rates; this situation changed after 1970 due to the competition regulations [i.e., CCC]. Thus, own interest rates rose rapidly, altering the historical differentials and inducing predictive failure in models that excluded that variable. (p. 32)

Third, constructed RN may use either spliced or unspliced high-powered money and broad money. In Friedman and Schwartz's framework, proper measurement of RN requires the unspliced data, even while the modeled money series is spliced. By way of explanation, note that the second splice itself sharply decreases the percentage of (spliced) money not bearing interest. That percentage is measured by the ratio of unspliced high-powered money to unspliced broad money. To distinguish between measures using spliced and unspliced series, H and M denote spliced series, whereas H^a and M^a denote actual values (superscript a for actual). Specifically, H^a and M^a are not rescaled for the definitional changes in 1975 (for H) and 1987 (for M). Correspondingly, RN denotes $(H/M)RS$ (as above) with spliced series, and RN^a denotes $(H^a/M^a)RS$.

Figure 5 shows the time series of H^a/M^a and H/M. The ratio H^a/M^a changes little over the period prior to 1970, but falls sharply and rapidly to near zero over 1971–1993. The two largest drops in H^a/M^a occur from redefinitions: in 1976, when H switches from high-powered money to M0, with a rescaling of 0.787; and in 1988, when M switches from M3 to M4, with a rescaling of 1.83. These effects play an important role in explaining the mis-predictions of the mechanically updated annual model (6), as shown in Section V. The ratio H/M equals H^a/M^a through 1975, with H/M increasing over 1976–1978 while H^a/M^a declines. The ratio H/M then falls throughout the remainder of the sample, with its differential relative to H^a/M^a widening after 1987. Differences in the empirical consequences from using RS, RN, and RN^a are thus most likely to be detectable on the recent data.

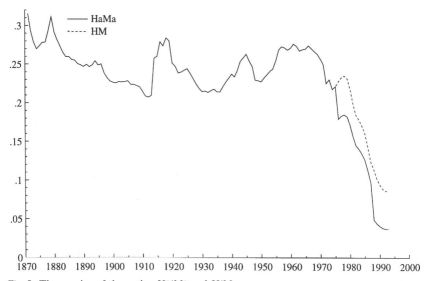

Fig. 5. Time series of the ratios H^a/M^a and H/M.

Financial Innovation and Financial Deregulation

The last century has witnessed considerable financial innovation. Examples early in the sample include the telegraph, the checkbook, and building societies. More recent examples include interest-bearing sight deposits, credit cards, and cash machines. All have combined to alter the financial scene radically. In particular, they have changed the role of money as an asset in portfolios, as a source of liquidity, and as the main component of the transactions medium.

Financial deregulation has played a pivotal role as well, both by allowing some forms of financial innovation to occur and by allowing rates of return on existing assets to be determined in a more competitive atmosphere. This subsection considers three key deregulations affecting the latter part of the sample: Competition and Credit Control, the allowance of interest-bearing sight deposits, and a 1986 Act of Parliament. Later on, we discuss how to account for innovation and deregulation in the model.

As the quote above notes, in 1971 Competition and Credit Control deregulated the commercial banking sector, abolishing the earlier cartel arrangements. CCC reduced credit rationing and led to an otherwise unexplained increase in money holdings, which Hendry and Ericsson (1991a) modeled using the dummy variable D_4. For earlier attempts at accounting for this change, see Hacche (1974), Hendry and Mizon (1978), and Lubrano, Pierse and Richard (1986) *inter alia*.

Financial deregulation in 1984 permitted retail sight deposits (checking accounts) to bear interest. The opportunity cost of holding narrow money fell substantially, and the demand for (e.g.) M1 increased correspondingly, as shown in Hendry and Ericsson (1991b). The increase in M1 is large, e.g., 129% in nominal M1 (86% in real M1) between 1984Q3 and 1989Q2.

During 1986–1989, additional financial deregulation loosened credit rationing, particularly for building societies, following the U.K. Parliament's 1986 Building Societies Act. See Muellbauer (1994) for a discussion of the Act's large effects on consumers' expenditure. Given the similarities between the deregulations of the 1970s and the 1980s, the dummy D_c includes both episodes.

Constancy

As Judd and Scadding (1982) document, constancy is a critical and often elusive feature of empirical money-demand equations. Indeed, the historical review in Hendry (1996) shows that constancy has long been regarded as a fundamental requirement for empirical modeling generally, since models with no constancies cannot be used for forecasting, analyzing economic policy, or testing economic theories. Equally, model evaluation is central to any progressive research strategy: retrospective evaluations are particularly valuable for learning about the evolution of the economy and how to improve the performance of existing empirical models.

This subsection thus analyzes statistical implications for a model's constancy over an extended sample with financial innovation and changed data definitions and opportunity costs. To do so, it helps to formalize the concept of constancy for econometric equations fitted to time series. Briefly, suppose a parameter θ indexes a stochastic process: by definition, θ is constant across realizations of that process. Even so, θ may vary over time, perhaps depending on other stochastic processes. If θ has the same value throughout the period $\mathcal{T}$, then θ is constant over that period. A model is constant over $\mathcal{T}$ if all of its parameters are constant over $\mathcal{T}$; see Hendry (1995, pp. 32, 355). Hendry (1996) highlights important ambiguities for constancy concerning parameterization and model formulation. By drawing on and expanding that analysis, we illustrate some of the subtleties involved through five examples with a simple conditional linear model.

Constancy of a model depends upon how the model is formulated and upon how its variables are updated for extended samples. In particular, constancy may depend upon inclusion in the model of data that are zero over the initial sample. Five forms of a simple conditional linear model aid in discussing this and related aspects of constancy:

Initial model $\qquad\qquad y_t = \theta'z_t + \varepsilon_t \qquad\qquad t = 1,\ldots,T_1 \qquad\qquad$ (7)

Isolikelihood model $\qquad y_t = \theta'z_t + \delta'w_t + \varepsilon_t \qquad t = 1,\ldots,T \qquad\qquad$ (8)

Expanded model $\qquad\quad y_t = \theta'z_t + \gamma'Qw_t + \varepsilon_t \qquad\qquad\qquad$ (9)

Reparameterized model $\;\; y_t = \theta'(z_t + AQw_t) + (\gamma' - \theta'A)Qw_t + \varepsilon_t \qquad$ (10)

Translated model $\qquad\quad y_t = \theta'(z_t + A^*Qw_t) + \varepsilon_t$

$$= \theta'z_t^* + \varepsilon_t. \qquad\qquad\qquad\qquad (11)$$

In the *initial model* (7), the variable y_t depends linearly on k variables z_t with coefficient vector θ and error ε_t over the initial sample $[1, T_1]$. Here and elsewhere, a prime $'$ transposes a vector or matrix. In the remaining four models, the data period is extended to include K more observations $[T_1 + 1, T]$. In the second or *isolikelihood model* (8), the initial model is extended to include K variables w_t that are zero over $[1, T_1]$, linearly independent over $[T_1 + 1, T]$, and with an arbitrary coefficient vector δ. This second model has the same likelihood value as the initial model (7).

The variables w_t might enter the isolikelihood model as some subset of K nonsingular linear combinations of w_t — e.g., as Qw_t, for some known full-rank matrix Q. If w_t does so, this generates the *expanded model* (9), where Qw_t has some coefficient vector γ. The expanded model always can be rewritten as the *reparameterized model* (10), which depends upon some linear combination $(I:A)$ of $(z_t:Qw_t)$ with coefficient θ, and upon Qw_t itself. Finally, a specific linear combination of $(z_t:Qw_t)$ may exist $[(I:A^*)$, say] such that the reparameterized model depends on that linear combination alone and not additionally on Qw_t *per se*. If such a linear combination exists, the resulting *translated model* is (11), so-called because z_t has been translated into z_t^* ($=z_t+A^*Qw_t$) over the extended sample. Thus, the expanded and reparameterized models provide a bridge from the initial and isolikelihood models to the translated model. Five examples help clarify the interpretation of these models.

Example 1: The Chow statistic for testing predictive failure. The initial model (7) and the isolikelihood model (8) are the basis of Chow's (1960) statistic for testing predictive failure. Without loss of generality, suppose that w_t is a set of zero-one impulse dummies: specifically, K dummies for the K observations in $[T_1+1, T]$. By construction, the coefficient vector θ on z_t remains unchanged as the sample and model expand from (7) to (8); and (7) and (8) are identical over the initial subsample. The F-statistic testing that $\delta = 0$ is simply the Chow statistic for predictive failure; see Salkever (1976). That is, the Chow statistic tests whether or not extending the sample requires extending the model relative to the initial measurements $\{y_t, z_t\}$.

If $\delta = 0$, lengthening the sample does not require any extension of the model. This is the "purest" form of model constancy. Conversely, for any initial model (7), θ is always unchanged over the extended sample $[1, T]$, provided the model is expanded by the K dummies w_t with arbitrary weights δ. This constancy of θ is trivial in that constancy holds by construction.

Example 2: A reduced set of additional variables. The expanded model (9) provides a testably simpler representation of the isolikelihood model (8). Suitable choice of Q in (9) can generate any time series over $[T_1+1, T]$. For Q of rank less than K, only certain linear combinations of w_t are relevant over the extended sample, thus simplifying or reducing (8) to (9). For instance, (5) above extends (3) by 5 observations but uses only 2 additional variables to do so: D_{4t} and $D_{4t} \cdot \Delta rs_t$.

Example 3: The measurement of money. Earlier, we discussed how the measurement of money alters over the sample. That is, y_t is translated into some new variable y_t^*, much as z_t is translated into z_t^* above. Equation (9), with known γ and Q, includes translations of y as a special case, with $y_t^* = y_t - \gamma'Qw_t$. For translated z, though, A (and A^*) and Q generally are known, whereas γ is estimated.

Example 4: Financial innovation and interest rate spreads. Achieving a translated model requires both a reduction from w_t to Qw_t to achieve (9), and the restriction that $\gamma' = \theta'A$ to obtain (11). The empirical modeling of U.K. M1 in Hendry and Ericsson (1991b) and Hendry (1996) illustrates such simplifications.

Specifically, suppose $T_1 \approx 1984$, y is nominal M1 in the United Kingdom, z is the Local Authority 3-month deposit rate R^{LA} (the outside rate for M1), Qw is the interest rate on sight deposits R^{SD} (the own rate of M1), and other variables in the relationship are ignored for ease of exposition. Hendry and Ericsson (1991b) and Hendry (1996) demonstrate the constancy through 1984 of a pre-existing model for U.K. M1, where that model includes R^{LA} but not R^{SD}. Over 1985–1989, that model fails miserably on Chow's statistic. By construction, and trivially, the original parameters of that model are constant if a dummy is added for each observation in the forecast period, giving (8). More interestingly, the initial model remains constant if just R^{SD} is added to it. That is, the expanded model (9) is such that $Qw_t = R_t^{SD}$. Finally, $\gamma = -\theta$ is a statistically acceptable restriction, implying that the interest rate differential $R^{LA} - R^{SD}$ is a suitable translation of the original variable R^{LA}, resulting in (11) with $A^* = -1$. Importantly, the translated model has the same parameter as the initial model: only the measurement of the data changes, and that, only for the extended portion of the sample.

Constancy is an operational concept for both the expanded and translated models. Both are testably constant over the whole sample period, i.e., relative to the isolikelihood model. Furthermore, the corresponding tests are interpretable as encompassing tests of the additional information in the forecast period.

Economically, the introduction of interest-bearing sight deposits requires redefining the opportunity cost of holding transactions money. Initially, the opportunity cost is the outside interest rate R^{LA}. Once sight deposits begin earning interest, the opportunity cost becomes the differential with the own rate, i.e., $R^{LA} - R^{SD}$. Equally, the opportunity cost is the differential $R^{LA} - R^{SD}$ for the full sample, and that measure is observationally equivalent to the outside rate R^{LA} over the initial subsample. Similar examples arise for numerous other countries. In particular, see Baba, Hendry and Starr (1992) for the United States and Ericsson and Sharma (1996) for Greece.

Example 5: The measurement of opportunity cost. Sections III and V empirically analyze a similar issue in the measurement of the opportunity cost for the annual data on broad money demand. The current example sets up the algebra of constancy for that analysis.

Suppose $T_1 = 1975$; y is nominal broad money m; z is the short-term interest rate RS, which is the interest rate in (4); Qw is $(1 - H^a/M^a)RS$, which is the own rate on M proposed above and based on Friedman and Schwartz (1982); and $A^* = -1$. For ease of presentation, other variables in the relationship are ignored (as in Example 4), and B is defined as the term $(1-H^a/M^a)$ in the proposed own rate. Because this example is central to Sections III and V, and because it is somewhat more complicated than Example 4, the five model representations are written explicitly:

Initial model	$m_t = \theta RS_t + \varepsilon_t$	$t = 1, \ldots, T_1$	(12)

Isolikelihood model $m_t = \theta RS_t + \delta' w_t + \varepsilon_t$ $t = 1, \ldots, T$ (13)

Expanded model $m_t = \theta RS_t + \gamma B_t RS_t + \varepsilon_t$ (14)

Reparameterized model $m_t = \theta (RS_t + A \cdot B_t RS_t) + (\gamma - \theta A) B_t RS_t + \varepsilon_t$ (15)

Translated model $m_t = \theta (RS_t - B_t RS_t) + \varepsilon_t$

$$= \theta RN_t^a + \varepsilon_t. \qquad (16)$$

Hendry and Ericsson (1991a) demonstrate the constancy through 1975 of the initial model (12), which is (5) in conjunction with (4). Using the Chow statistic implied by (13), we showed that this initial model is nonconstant on the sample extended through 1993. However, model translation recovers constancy. Section V shows that the coefficients in the initial model remain constant if two variables are translated: RS into RN^a, as from (12) to (16); and D_4 into D_c, which follows from a similar model path. Paralleling Example 4, the translated model (16) has parameters equivalent to those in the initial model (12): only the measurement of the data changes.

Because $B_t RS_t$ is actually nonzero over the whole sample and not just over $[T_1 + 1, T]$, the empirical basis for this example is slightly more complicated than that given in (12)–(16). The ratio H^a/M^a is nearly constant through 1975 (Figure 5), so RS and RN^a are virtually indistinguishable over that period, aside from a scale factor (see Figure 6b below). The parameter θ in the initial model (12) is thus the coefficient on the opportunity cost RN^a ($= RS \cdot H^a/M^a$), multiplied by the (near constant) value of H^a/M^a over that subsample. As H^a/M^a falls in the late 1970s and the 1980s, the measure of opportunity cost RN^a accounts for that fall, as in (16). With RS alone, the model breaks down. Mis-measurement of RN^a by RN also can induce predictive failure because H^a/M^a and H/M behave differently over the last two decades of data; see Figure 5.

General Remarks

This subsection considers several related issues: time-varying coefficient models, the consequences of nonsingular reparameterizations and data transformations, tests of constancy, data redefinitions, and Divisia indexes.

First, constant models can have time-varying coefficients, provided a deeper set of constant parameters characterizes the data generation process. Examples include the structural time-series models in Harvey (1981) and Harvey and Shephard (1993), random-coefficients models, and the smooth transition dynamic models in Teräsvirta and Anderson (1992) and Granger and Teräsvirta (1993). Example 5 above also falls into this category, in that $\theta(1-B_t)$ in (16) varies over time even though θ does not. Thus, the existence of constancy may depend on whether raw coefficients or underlying parameters are evaluated.

Second, since one-to-one transformations of parameters are also valid parameters, zero can be the population value for some parameters in an equivalent representation. Consequently, the definition of model constancy above allows for an expanded model, provided that the *existing* parameters stay constant. Relatedly, there is often a choice between nearly equivalent variables at various stages of empirical modeling, with subsequent data clarifying which variables actually determine a sustainable relationship. Example 5 illustrates this point with RS and RN^a.

Third, no tests could exist in-sample (i.e., using only information up to T_1) for whether an empirical model will manifest predictive failure out of sample. An in-sample test correctly indicating the failure of the initial model would incorrectly indicate the failure of a (constant) translated model, as the initial model is identical to the translated model in-sample. Consequently, predictive failure is uniquely a post-sample problem, requiring change somewhere to induce change elsewhere. Hence, models should not be selected on the basis of their forecast performance unless their sole purpose is forecasting. Clements and Hendry (1996) show that forecasting models can be robustified against important forms of predictive failure by intercept corrections or differencing; see also Hendry and Mizon (1996).

Fourth, previous experience with updating models of money demand and of consumers' expenditure has revealed many pitfalls, including redefinitions of variables, large changes in measurements between data revision vintages, and important structural changes; see Hendry and Ericsson (1991b) and Hendry (1994) respectively for examples. In the present context, many measures of money exist, their definitions and coverages have altered over time, and the principal measure in Friedman and Schwartz (1982) (namely M2) ceased to be the appropriate one for the United Kingdom and was replaced by M3 and then by M4. The measure M4 (but not M2 or M3) includes the liabilities of building societies and seems the most appealing as a measure of broad money; see Hendry and Ericsson (1991a, Data Appendix). These changes in measured money require adaptations elsewhere in the model. This section has focused on the most obvious adaptation, that for the measured opportunity cost of money itself. Coherent measurement of the opportunity cost (and of data generally) is contextual rather than absolute, in that the measurement may differ depending upon the economic relationship being modeled.

Fifth, to address issues such as deregulation and financial innovation, some researchers have sought to develop better indices of money, weighting money's components by their "liquidity". In Divisia indices, for example, the liquidity of a component of money is inversely related to the corresponding rate of return; see Diewert (1976), Barnett (1980), and la Cour (1996). We do not follow this route because Divisia indexes *per se* seem unlikely to resolve the changes that occurred. For instance, the relevant rates of return were controlled over some subsamples and deregulated over others. A Divisia approach implies (implausibly) that liquidity suddenly changes when interest rates move upon deregulation, even when the quantities of an aggregate's components and the characteristics of those components (other than their rates of return) remain unchanged. Furthermore, mortgage rationing was prevalent over most of the 20th century in the United Kingdom, with building societies offering high interest rates on their (highly liquid) deposit and share accounts; see Anderson and Hendry (1984) and Muellbauer (1997).

V. An Economic Extension of the Annual Model

This section re-analyzes the annual model (5) over the extended sample. With the statistical measures of opportunity cost and deregulation adjusted to reflect the economic concepts that they attempt to capture, the annual model's coefficients remain constant over the two decades of the forecast period. We examine long-run properties first and the dynamic equilibrium correction model subsequently, as in Hendry and Ericsson (1991a). We then turn to the identification of the model as a money demand equation and to the model's policy implications.

Constancy of an Economic Extension of the Model

In the annual model (5) with (4), the measure of opportunity cost is RS and so does not incorporate the definitional and institutional changes described in Section IV, which occur primarily after 1975. To address these changes, RS is replaced by RN^a, which leaves the estimates in (5) and (4) virtually unaffected. To show the value of model translation, (4) and (5) are each estimated with RN^a rather than RS, first over their initial sample and then over the extended sample. For ease of comparison between coefficients on RS and RN^a, RN^a is divided by 0.25, the approximate mean of H^a/M^a for the sample 1878–1975.[6] This subsection finishes by estimating the economic extensions of (4) and (5) jointly by nonlinear least squares.

Using RN^a rather than RS to measure the opportunity cost, the Engle-Granger regression (4) becomes:

$$(m-p-i)_t = -0.318 - 6.67RN_t^a \tag{17}$$

$$T = 98[1873-1970] \quad R^2 = 0.59 \quad \hat{\sigma} = 10.57\% \quad dw = 0.31 \quad t_{ADF} = -2.77,$$

which mirrors the results in (4).[7] The residuals from (17) provide the equilibrium correction term $\tilde{u}_t$, which proxies for long-run excess demand and replaces the residual $\hat{u}_t$ from (4). Figure 6a plots the two residuals ($\hat{u}_t$ and $\tilde{u}_t$) through 1970. Figure 6b plots the corresponding measures of opportunity cost (RS and RN^a) over the same period. The differences between the old and new measures are minor in both graphs. Figures 6c and 6d plot the same series on the new sample: both of these graphs show

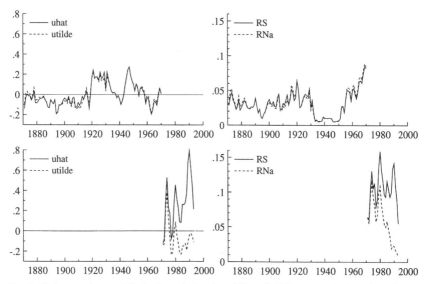

Fig. 6. Cointegration residuals $\hat{u}$ and $\tilde{u}$ using RS and RN^a respectively, plotted over subsamples, and the corresponding values for RS and RN^a.

---

[6]Because the data here are annual rather than (e.g.) quarterly, we have not attempted to adjust RN^a for agents' learning of financial innovations; cf. Hendry and Ericsson (1991b) and Baba, Hendry and Starr (1992).

[7]To parallel the approach in Hendry and Ericsson (1991a), this section presents Engle-Granger regressions rather than (say) the cointegration analysis in Johansen (1995) based on vector autoregressions. We intend to report such an analysis at a later date for the complete system of money, prices, income, and interest rates. A subsystem analysis appears in Ericsson and Irons (1995b).

marked differences between the old and new measures, as implied by H^a/M^a in Figure 5.

The translated model is (17) estimated over the full sample:

$$(m-p-i)_t = -0.344 - 6.30RN_t^a \tag{18}$$

$$T = 121[1873-1993] \quad R^2 = 0.63 \quad \hat{\sigma} = 11.73\% \quad dw = 0.42$$

$$t_{ADF} = -4.68^{**}.$$

Equation (18)'s coefficients and fit hardly differ from those of (4) and (17), and the additional data more clearly confirm cointegration.

Following Hendry and Ericsson (1991a), regression residuals from either (17) or (18) could enter as the equilibrium correction term in the dynamic equation. Equation (17) has the advantage that its sample pre-dates the forecast period. Conversely, assuming that the relation does cointegrate, (18) should be more precisely estimated than (17). In practice, the choice makes little difference, and (17) is used below.

With RN^a as the opportunity cost measure in the cointegrating relation, the sample to 1973 delivers the following re-estimated dynamic model, paralleling (5):

$$\Delta(m-p)_t = 0.46\,\Delta(m-p)_{t-1} - 0.10\,\Delta^2(m-p)_{t-2} - 0.59\,\Delta p_t$$
$$ [0.07] \phantom{\Delta(m-p)_{t-1}} [0.04] \phantom{\Delta^2(m-p)_{t-2}} [0.07]$$

$$+ 0.40\,\Delta p_{t-1} - 0.021\,\Delta rn_t^a - 0.064\,\Delta_2 r\ell_t$$
$$ [0.07] \phantom{\Delta p_{t-1}} [0.006] [0.022]$$

$$- 2.83\,(\tilde{u}_{t-1} - 0.2)\tilde{u}_{t-1}^2 + 0.004 + 3.7\,(D_1 + D_3)_t$$
$$ [0.62] \phantom{(\tilde{u}_{t-1} - 0.2)\tilde{u}} [0.002]\ [0.7]$$

$$+ 6.4 D_{4t} + 0.094 D_{4t}\Delta rs_t \tag{19}$$
$$ [1.6] \phantom{D_{4t}} [0.078]$$

$$T = 96[1878-1973] \quad R^2 = 0.88 \quad \hat{\sigma} = 1.406\% \quad dw = 1.89$$

$$AR: F(2, 83) = 1.14 \quad ARCH: F(1, 83) = 1.40$$

$$Normality: \chi^2(2) = 0.7 \quad RESET: F(1, 84) = 0.42$$

$$Hetero: F(18, 66) = 0.67 \quad Form: F(46, 38) = 0.74$$

$$Jt = 1.26 \quad Var = 0.08,$$

where $\tilde{u}$ is from (17). The switch from RS to RN^a leaves the coefficients and $\hat{\sigma}$ in (19) virtually unaltered relative to those in (3) and (5).[8]

---

[8]Similar estimates result for the sample period extended through 1975 or truncated at 1970, the latter for the model without the two terms involving D_4; see Figure 8. We chose 1973 as the end point because it allows a minimal sample consistent with estimating the impact of CCC.

Estimation of (19) over the sample through 1993 obtains:

$$\Delta(m-p)_t = 0.48\,\Delta(m-p)_{t-1} - 0.10\,\Delta^2(m-p)_{t-2} - 0.62\,\Delta p_t$$
$$\qquad [0.07] \qquad\qquad [0.04] \qquad\qquad\quad [0.07]$$

$$+\,0.40\,\Delta p_{t-1} - 0.020\,\Delta rn_t^a - 0.041\,\Delta_2 r\ell_t$$
$$\quad [0.07] \qquad\quad [0.006] \qquad\quad [0.019]$$

$$-\,2.26\,(\bar{u}_{t-1} - 0.2)\bar{u}_{t-1}^2 + 0.004 + 3.9\,(D_1 + D_3)_t$$
$$\quad [0.46] \qquad\qquad\qquad [0.002]\ [0.6]$$

$$+\,5.2\,D_{ct} + 0.100\,D_{4t}\,\Delta rs_t \qquad\qquad\qquad (20)$$
$$\quad [1.0] \qquad [0.042]$$

$T = 116\,[1878\text{–}1993] \quad R^2 = 0.87 \quad \hat{\sigma} = 1.622\% \quad dw = 1.68$

$AR\!: F(2,\,103) = 3.72^* \quad ARCH\!: F(1,\,103) = 0.02$

$Normality\!: \chi^2(2) = 0.0 \quad RESET\!: F(1,\,104) = 1.35$

$Hetero\!: F(18,\,86) = 0.90 \quad Form\!: F(52,\,52) = 0.95$

$Jt = 1.93 \quad Var = 0.82^{**},$

where the deregulation dummy D_4 has been extended as D_c when entering by itself. In this translated model, the coefficients are virtually unaltered from the initial model (19), although $\hat{\sigma}$ has increased by about 15%. Correspondingly, Jt is insignificant, whereas Var rejects. Consistent with this evidence, the covariance statistic for testing constancy of the coefficients over 1974–1993 yields $F(10,\,95) = 1.31$, whereas the Chow predictive-failure statistic is $F(20,\,85) = 2.73^{**}$. The latter has power to detect changes in equation error variances as well as in regression coefficients. An outlier in 1981 is primarily responsible for this rejection. Equally, rejection by the predictive-failure and Var tests reflects their high power to detect numerically modest changes in $\hat{\sigma}$. The long sample and the high variance of the data relative to that of the equation error are the proximate reasons for that high power.

Figures 7 and 8 summarize additional information on the performance of (19) and (20). Figure 7 graphs descriptive statistics for model (19): fitted, actual, and forecast values, plotted as time series and cross-plotted; the corresponding residuals; and the forecast and actual values, with ± 2 standard error bars for the forecasts. Figure 7 for (19) parallels Figure 3 for (5). The dissimilar consequences of mechanistic and economic extensions of a model are apparent from comparison of Figure 3 and Figure 7, keeping in mind their markedly different scales. Figure 8 graphs the recursively estimated coefficients and plus-or-minus twice their recursively estimated standard errors (first nine panels), the 1-step residuals and $0 \pm 2\hat{\sigma}_t$, the 1-step Chow statistics normalized by their one-off 1% critical values,

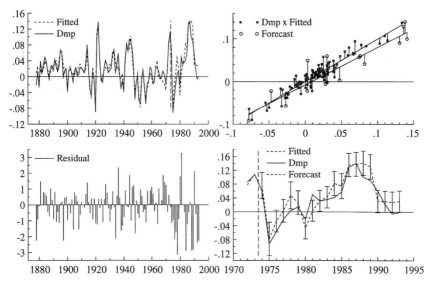

Fig. 7. Fitted, actual, and forecast values of $\Delta(m-p)_t$ from (19), and their cross-plots, corresponding scaled residuals, and forecasts with ± 2 standard error bars.

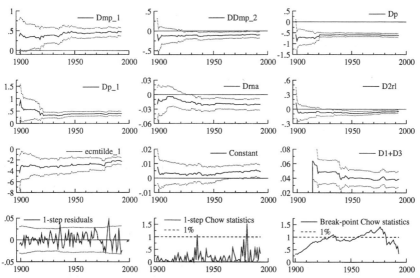

Fig. 8. Recursive estimates for the first nine coefficients in (20), and the corresponding 1-step residuals, 1-step Chow statistics, and break-point Chow statistics.

and the break-point Chow statistics likewise normalized, all for (20).[9] From all of these graphs, the translated model (20) performs well over this turbulent period for the U.K. economy.

Equations (17) and (20) are together a single model, even though they are estimated sequentially. If (17) and (20) were estimated jointly, their coefficients would differ from those reported above, both because the dynamics in (20) would affect the estimates in (17) and because $\bar{u}_t$ enters (20) nonlinearly. Joint estimation of the long-run and short-run parameters by nonlinear least squares obtains:

$$\Delta(m-p)_t = 0.49\,\Delta(m-p)_{t-1} - 0.10\,\Delta^2(m-p)_{t-2} - 0.62\,\Delta p_t$$
$$(0.06)(0.04)(0.04)$$

$$+0.41\,\Delta p_{t-1} - 0.020\,\Delta m_t^a - 0.040\,\Delta_2 r\ell_t$$
$$(0.05)(0.006)(0.016)$$

$$-2.13\,(\bar{u}_{t-1} - 0.13)\,\bar{u}_{t-1}^2 + 0.005 + 3.7\,(D_1 + D_3)_t$$
$$(0.48)(0.11)(0.002)\,(0.6)$$

$$+5.4\,D_{ct} + 0.090\,D_{4t}\,\Delta rs_t \tag{21}$$
$$(0.7)(0.028)$$

$T = 116\,[1878\text{–}1993]\quad R^2 = 0.87\quad \hat{\sigma} = 1.620\%\quad dw = 1.77$

$AR\colon F(2, 100) = 2.80\quad ARCH\colon F(1, 100) = 0.06$

$Normality\colon \chi^2(2) = 0.1\quad Hetero\colon F(21, 80) = 0.85,$

where the equilibrium correction residual $\bar{u}_t$ is now:

$$\bar{u}_t = (m-p-i)_t - (-0.302 - 6.89 RN_t^a). \tag{22}$$
$$(0.043)\,(0.39)$$

The coefficients in (21) and (22) are little changed from those in (20) and (17), although the "interwar equilibrium departure" in the nonlinear equilibrium correction term is somewhat lower than previously, now being estimated at $+13\%$ relative to the remainder of the period. No residual diagnostics are significant. Overall, the equilibrium correction model appears constant and well-specified on over a century of data, and the model confirms a nonlinear feedback reaction; see Escribano (1996).

Hendry and Ericsson (1991a) emphasized the role of constancy in their modeling approach.

> Parameter constancy is at the heart of model design from both statistical and economic perspectives. Since economic systems are far from being constant and the coefficients of derived ("nonstructural" or "reduced form")

---

[9] Recursively estimated coefficients for D_{ct} and $D_{4t}\,\Delta rs_t$ are not displayed, given those variables' brief, transitory nature. Both sequences of Chow statistics are of the predictive-failure, rather than covariance, form.

equations may change when any of the underlying parameters or data correlations change, it is important to identify empirical models that have reasonably constant parameters, which remain interpretable when change occurs.
(p. 21)

Change in government policy rules is one obvious source of such change,
and invariance of the estimated equation's coefficients to changes in policy
rules is central to calculating the economic effects of those changes
properly. From Section IV, parameter constancy is compatible with (and
may even require) economic extensions of the data and model. With the
economic extensions for the opportunity cost of money and the proxy for
deregulation, the EqCM in Hendry and Ericsson (1991a) remains constant
over the additional two decades of data. Coherent rather than mechanical
extensions are critical for obtaining that constancy.

Identification of Money Demand

The estimated relation, (17) plus (20), is interpreted as a money demand
function for three reasons. First, being a conditional model, the parameterization of the demand function is unique. That conditional model
arises from factorizing the joint distribution of money, prices, income, and
interest rates into a (conditional) distribution for money conditional on
prices, income, and interest rates, and a marginal distribution for prices,
income, and interest rates. Given that factorization, the parameterization
of the distribution of money is unique. Second, from institutional knowledge, the supply equation in the United Kingdom is an interest rate policy
function, and it shifted substantially as economic policy regimes changed
over the sample. Specific regimes include the Gold Standard and the policy
of low interest rates during the interwar period. Consequently, any
combination of the shifting supply function with the demand equation
would be nonconstant, yet the estimated demand function is constant. In
effect, these shifts in the supply function (over-)identify the demand function in the sense of the Cowles Commission. Third, the estimated coefficients have sensible interpretations as demand responses, but they are
problematic in a policy reaction function. In particular, if the estimated
equation is viewed as an inverted policy reaction function, it is difficult to
understand why — or how — the Bank of England might seek to control
the differential between the outside interest rate and the own interest
rate.

The dummies for wars and credit deregulation complicate the issue of
identification, as they might represent either supply perturbations or
changed (unmodeled) conditions in money demand. The risks of wartime
might induce additional money demand relative to usual opportunity costs,
with the model implying a 3.9% increase in demand. Conversely, exigen-

cies of financing war may have led to excessive printing of money. The equality of the coefficient across the two wars is more consistent with the former interpretation, given the changes induced by Keynes (1940), but is hardly definitive proof. Similarly, the proxy for deregulation could capture a shift in either demand or supply. Interpretation as a demand shift again seems preferable. Supporting evidence includes "round-tripping" (borrowing from a commercial bank to relend the money in the market at a higher rate) and withdrawal of housing equity (borrowing extra on a mortgage and redepositing some when the after-tax liquidity cost is low); see Green (1987) and Patterson (1993).

Policy Implications

Policy implications fall into (at least) three distinct categories, each involving a pair of related concepts: constancy and prediction, causation and endogeneity, and expectations and the Lucas (1976) critique. See Banerjee, Hendry and Mizon (1996) for a general discussion.

First, parameter nonconstancy and predictive failure need not be germane to the policy under analysis if, for instance, the parameter nonconstancy or predictive failure arises from data mis-measurement. As shown above, mechanistic extension of a model can result in parameter nonconstancy and predictive failure, whereas economic extension of the same model can obtain constant parameters. So, parameter nonconstancy and predictive failure in themselves are not sufficient cause for discounting a model; see Hendry and Mizon (1996). Equally, econometric models may fit better than they forecast, simply because the proper economic extension is unknown *ex ante*. Predictive failure reflects a change somewhere in the structure of the economic process during the forecast period. Conversely, models do not suffer predictive failure unless such change occurs.

That said, existing econometric models may provide information on the effects of future structural change. For example, in (20), the effect of the two World Wars on money demand is partialed out by using the dummy variables D_1 and D_3. Their coefficients are statistically insignificantly different from each other, so the effect on money demand from the First World War could predict in large measure the effect from the Second World War. A parallel result holds for the two major episodes of credit derationing, where both episodes have similar percentage effects on money demand.

Second, for the empirical models above, specific policy issues center on the direction of causation between money and prices. Does money growth cause inflation; or is it the converse, with inflation being responsible for increased money holdings? While causation cannot be wholly resolved from a single-equation study, Hendry and Ericsson (1991a) and Ericsson and Irons (1995a, 1995b) demonstrate super exogeneity of prices and interest rates in (3) and the non-invertibility of that conditional model; see also Engle and Hendry (1993). Those results carry over to (20). The evidence on super exogeneity and non-invertibility is consistent with a constant demand equation in which money is endogenously determined by private sector decisions, with policy determining the outside interest rate to which agents react.

Targeting the stock of an endogenous money stock could be problematic, especially if the demand for money depended on an interest rate spread or if the induced higher volatility in short-term interest rates increased the risk premium on long-term interest rates; see Sprenkle and Miller (1980) and Baba, Hendry and Starr (1992). Both the Bank of England and the Federal Reserve Board targeted various monetary aggregates during the late 1970s and early 1980s. Both experienced difficulties in achieving the set targets, and both eventually abandoned monetary targeting. In testimony to the Joint Economic Committee of the U.S. Congress, Paul Volcker (1982), the then Chairman of the Board of Governors of the Federal Reserve System, is particularly explicit about those difficulties.

> As you are aware, the current job of developing and implementing monetary policy has been complicated by regulatory decisions as well as by recent developments in the economy and in our financial markets. We have as a consequence (1) made some technical modification in our operating procedures to cope with obvious distortions [due to the introduction of interest-bearing checking accounts] in some of the monetary data, particularly M1, and (2) accommodated growth in the various monetary aggregates at rates somewhat above the targeted ranges. The first of those decisions was essentially technical. The latter decision is entirely consistent with the view I expressed in testifying before the Banking Committees in July [1982] that the Federal Open Market Committee would tolerate "growth somewhat above the targeted ranges ... for a time in circumstances in which it appeared that precautionary or liquidity motivations, during a period of economic uncertainty and turbulence, were leading to stronger than anticipated demands for money." (p. 747)

Deregulation and financial innovation can affect monetary growth rates, so interpretation of the latter must account for the former. In particular, from the early 1980s onward in both the United Kingdom and the United States, the large increases in real money might have simply reflected portfolio adjustments due to changed interest rate differentials. Or, they might have induced higher inflation in the future. These two alternatives suggest very different responses on the part of the central bank. Considerable evidence supports the interpretation of a portfolio shift, including the model (20) itself, the models for M1 in Hendry and Ericsson (1991b) and Baba, Hendry and Starr (1992), the historical track record of the Bank of

England and the Federal Reserve Board, and the actual low inflation rates in both countries during the late 1980s and the 1990s.

Third, super exogeneity rules out the role of model-based expectations in (20), in which case the Lucas critique is not empirically germane. *Data-based* predictors are allowable, so equilibrium correction models such as (20) can have a forward-looking interpretation; see Hendry and Ericsson (1991b). Specifically, current and lagged inflation enter (20) as approximately $-0.3(\Delta p_t + \Delta^2 p_t)$, where $\Delta p_t + \Delta^2 p_t$ is a natural predictor of next period's inflation. Flemming (1976, Chapter 7) proposes similar functions for forming expectations about inflation.

Even when super exogeneity holds, policy can and (in general) does affect agent behavior. It does so through the variables entering the conditional model, albeit not through the parameters of that model. Government policy might well affect inflation and interest rates, and so the demand for money. However, under super exogeneity, the precise mechanism that the government adopts for such a policy does not affect agent behavior, except insofar as the mechanism affects actual outcomes.

VI. Conclusions

This paper develops a framework for economic extensions of empirical models, and it applies that framework to the dynamic model of broad money demand in Hendry and Ericsson (1991a). The analysis clarifies the importance of coherently measured time series when building and evaluating empirical models. It also reflects the progressive nature of empirical research. Econometric equations are not one-off laws cast in stone, but are flexible tools for understanding the economy and for helping guide both policy and forecasting; see Pagan (1987).

Empirically, the broadening of measured money and the concurrent financial innovations required a measure of the opportunity cost that reflects those changes. Consequently, a measure was developed that depends on the proportion of non-interest-bearing money. With that measure, the cointegrating vector remains constant over the extended sample, which is nearly 20% longer than the initially available dataset. The coefficients in the dynamic model itself are also virtually unchanged for the extended sample, once the new measure of opportunity cost is incorporated and the dummy for deregulation is extended to account for the 1986 Building Societies Act. Even so, the dynamic equation's error variance does increase over the extended sample. That increase may reflect effects from interest rate volatility similar to the effects on U.S. M1 from the risk of capital loss induced by volatile long-term interest rates; see Baba, Hendry and Starr (1992).

The model's degree of empirical constancy seems reasonable, especially in light of the very large changes over the last 120 years in the variables' magnitudes, in the underlying economic structure, and in the financial system. Nevertheless, several developments could improve the model's fit in the most recent period and thereby improve its constancy. First, a more consistent series for money might be constructed, allowing for the liabilities of building societies throughout. Second, the measure of opportunity cost also could be improved. Specifically, the effects of interest-rate volatility and learning adjustment could be modeled with higher frequency data and then mapped to annual values; and series on the own rate could be gathered. Third, the indicator (dummy) variables require more study. They are endogenously chosen to remove nonconstancies and may reflect non-modeled factors, such as data measurement errors, structural changes, and omitted transitions. Equally, war, financial innovation, and deregulation have complex effects on the economy, typically generating the most perturbed and informative data of the sample. Finally, econometrics has progressed during the model's forecast period. Methods for estimating nonlinear equilibrium correction models are now available, as are techniques for estimating transition effects; see Escribano (1996) and Granger and Teräsvirta (1993) respectively. Also, the technology of multivariate cointegration analysis is bound to yield additional insights if the marginal models can be developed as congruent relations.

References

Anderson, G. J. and Hendry, D. F.: An econometric model of United Kingdom building societies. *Oxford Bulletin of Economics and Statistics* *46* (3), 185–210, 1984.

Attfield, C. L. F., Demery, D. and Duck, N. W.: Estimating the UK demand for money function: A test of two approaches. Mimeo, Department of Economics, University of Bristol, Bristol, England, Nov. 1995.

Baba, Y., Hendry, D. F. and Starr, R. M.: The demand for M1 in the U.S.A., 1960–1988. *Review of Economic Studies 59* (1), 25–61, 1992.

Banerjee, A., Hendry, D. F. and Mizon, G. E.: The econometric analysis of economic policy. *Oxford Bulletin of Economics and Statistics 58* (4), 573–600, 1996.

Barnett, W. A.: Economic monetary aggregates: An application of index number and aggregation theory. *Journal of Econometrics 14* (1), 11–48, 1980.

Cagan, P.: The monetary dynamics of hyperinflation. Ch. 2. In M. Friedman (ed.), *Studies in the Quantity Theory of Money*, University of Chicago Press, Chicago, 25–117, 1956.

Chow, G. C.: Tests of equality between sets of coefficients in two linear regressions. *Econometrica 28* (3), 591–605, 1960.

Clements, M. P. and Hendry, D. F.: Intercept corrections and structural change. *Journal of Applied Econometrics 11* (5), 475–494, 1996.

la Cour, L. F.: The problem of measuring 'money': Results from an analysis of Divisia monetary aggregates for Denmark. Mimeo, Institute of Statistics, University of Copenhagen, Copenhagen, Denmark, Mar. 1996.

Dickey, D. A. and Fuller, W. A.: Likelihood ratio statistics for autoregressive time series with a unit root. *Econometrica 49* (4), 1057–1072, 1981.

Diewert, W. E.: Exact and superlative index numbers. *Journal of Econometrics 4* (2), 115–145, 1976.

Doornik, J. A. and Hansen, H.: An omnibus test for univariate and multivariate normality. Discussion paper no. W4&91, Nuffield College, Oxford, England, Nov. 1994.

Doornik, J. A. and Hendry, D. F.: *PcGive Version 7: An Interactive Econometric Modelling System.* Institute of Economics and Statistics, University of Oxford, Oxford, England, 1992.

Doornik, J. A. and Hendry, D. F.: *PcGive 8.0: An Interactive Econometric Modelling System.* International Thomson Publishing, London, 1994.

Doornik, J. A. and Hendry, D. F.: *GiveWin: An Interface to Empirical Modelling.* International Thomson Business Press, London, 1996.

Engle, R. F.: Autoregressive conditional heteroscedasticity with estimates of the variance of United Kingdom inflation. *Econometrica 50* (4), 987–1007, 1982.

Engle, R. F. and Granger, C. W. J.: Co-integration and error correction: Representation, estimation, and testing. *Econometrica 55* (2), 251–276, 1987.

Engle, R. F. and Hendry, D. F.: Testing super exogeneity and invariance in regression models. *Journal of Econometrics 56* (1/2), 119–139, 1993.

Ericsson, N. R., Hendry, D. F. and Prestwich, K. M.: Friedman and Schwartz (1982) revisited: Assessing annual and phase-average models of money demand for the United Kingdom. Mimeo, Board of Governors of the Federal Reserve System, Washington, D.C., Nov. 1997; forthcoming in *Empirical Economics*.

Ericsson, N. R. and Irons, J. S.: Book review of *Applied Econometric Techniques* by Keith Cuthbertson, Stephen G. Hall, and Mark P. Taylor. *Econometric Reviews 14* (1), 121–133, 1995a.

Ericsson, N. R. and Irons, J. S.: The Lucas critique in practice: Theory without measurement. Ch. 8. In K. D. Hoover (ed.), *Macroeconometrics: Developments, Tensions and Prospects*, Kluwer Academic Publishers, Boston, Massachusetts, 263–312, 1995b.

Ericsson, N. R. and Sharma, S.: Broad money demand and financial liberalization in Greece. International Finance discussion paper no. 559, Board of Governors of the Federal Reserve System, Washington, D.C., July 1996; forthcoming in *Empirical Economics*.

Escribano, A.: Non-linear ‘error-correction: The case of money demand in the U.K. (1878–1970). Mimeo, University of California at San Diego, La Jolla, California, Dec. 1985.

Escribano, A.: Nonlinear error correction: The case of money demand in the U.K. (1878–1970). Mimeo, Department of Statistics and Econometrics, Universidad Carlos III de Madrid, Madrid, Spain, July 1996.

Flemming, J. S.: *Inflation.* Oxford University Press, Oxford, 1976.

Friedman, M. and Schwartz, A. J.: *Monetary Trends in the United States and the United Kingdom: Their Relation to Income, Prices, and Interest Rates, 1867–1975.* University of Chicago Press, Chicago, 1982.

Godfrey, L. G.: Testing against general autoregressive and moving average error models when the regressors include lagged dependent variables. *Econometrica 46* (6), 1293–1301, 1978.

Goldfeld, S. M. and Sichel, D. E.: The demand for money. Ch. 8. In B. M. Friedman and F. H. Hahn (eds.), *Handbook of Monetary Economics*, Vol. 1, North-Holland, Amsterdam, 299–356, 1990.

Granger, C. W. J. and Teräsvirta, T.: *Modelling Nonlinear Economic Relationships.* Oxford University Press, Oxford, 1993.

Green, C. J.: Money market arbitrage and commercial banks' base rate adjustments in the

United Kingdom. *Bulletin of Economic Research 39* (4), 273–296, 1987.

Hacche, G.: The demand for money in the United Kingdom: Experience since 1971. *Bank of England Quarterly Bulletin 14* (3), 284–305, 1974.

Hansen, B. E.: Testing for parameter instability in linear models. *Journal of Policy Modeling 14* (4), 517–533, 1992.

Harvey, A. C.: *Time Series Models*. Philip Allan, Oxford, 1981.

Harvey, A. C. and Shephard, N.: Structural time series models. Ch. 10. In G. S. Maddala, C. R. Rao and H. D. Vinod (eds.), *Handbook of Statistics*, Vol. 11, North-Holland, Amsterdam, 261–302, 1993.

Hawtrey, R. G.: *A Century of Bank Rate*. Longmans, Green and Company, London, 1938.

Hendry, D. F.: HUS revisited. *Oxford Review of Economic Policy 10* (2), 86–106, 1994.

Hendry, D. F.: *Dynamic Econometrics*. Oxford University Press, Oxford, 1995.

Hendry, D. F.: On the constancy of time-series econometric equations. *Economic and Social Review 27* (5), 401–422, 1996.

Hendry, D. F. and Doornik, J. A.: *Empirical Econometric Modelling Using PcGive 9.0 for Windows*. International Thomson Business Press, London, 1996.

Hendry, D. F. and Ericsson, N. R.: An econometric analysis of U.K. money demand in *Monetary Trends in the United States and the United Kingdom* by Milton Friedman and Anna J. Schwartz. *American Economic Review 81* (1), 8–38, 1991a.

Hendry, D. F. and Ericsson, N. R.: Modeling the demand for narrow money in the United Kingdom and the United States. *European Economic Review 35* (4), 833–881, 1991b.

Hendry, D. F. and Mizon, G. E.: Serial correlation as a convenient simplification, not a nuisance: A comment on a study of the demand for money by the Bank of England. *Economic Journal 88* (351), 549–563, 1978.

Hendry, D. F. and Mizon, G. E.: Selecting econometric models for policy analysis by forecast accuracy. Mimeo, Nuffield College, Oxford, England, 1996.

Hendry, D. F. and Morgan, M. S. (eds.): *The Foundations of Econometric Analysis*. Cambridge University Press, Cambridge, 1995.

Jevons, W. S.: *Investigations in Currency and Finance*. Macmillan, London, 1884.

Johansen, S.: Testing weak exogeneity and the order of cointegration in UK money demand data. *Journal of Policy Modeling 14* (3), 313–334, 1992.

Johansen, S.: *Likelihood-based Inference in Cointegrated Vector Autoregressive Models*. Oxford University Press, Oxford, 1995.

Judd, J. P. and Scadding, J. L.: The search for a stable money demand function: A survey of the post-1973 literature. *Journal of Economic Literature 20* (3), 993–1023, 1982.

Keynes, J. M.: *A Treatise on Money*. Macmillan, London, 1930.

Keynes, J. M.: *How to Pay for the War: A Radical Plan for the Chancellor of the Exchequer*. Harcourt, Brace and Company, New York, 1940.

Klovland, J. T.: The demand for money in the United Kingdom, 1875–1913. *Oxford Bulletin of Economics and Statistics 49* (3), 251–271, 1987.

Lubrano, M., Pierse, R. G. and Richard, J.-F.: Stability of a U.K. money demand equation: A Bayesian approach to testing exogeneity. *Review of Economic Studies 53* (4), 603–634, 1986.

Lucas, Jr., R. E.: Econometric policy evaluation: A critique. In K. Brunner and A. H. Meltzer (eds.), *Carnegie-Rochester Conference Series on Public Policy: The Phillips Curve and Labor Markets*, Vol. 1, *Journal of Monetary Economics*, Supplement, 19–46, 1976.

MacKinnon, J. G.: Critical values for cointegration tests. Ch. 13. In R. F. Engle and C. W. J. Granger (eds.), *Long-run Economic Relationships: Readings in Cointegration*, Oxford University Press, Oxford, 267–276, 1991.

MacKinnon, J. G. and White, H.: Some heteroskedasticity-consistent covariance matrix estimators with improved finite sample properties. *Journal of Econometrics 29* (3),

305–325, 1985.

Marshall, A.: *Official Papers*. Macmillan, London, 1926.

Messer, K. and White, H.: A note on computing the heteroskedasticity consistent covariance matrix using instrumental variable techniques. *Oxford Bulletin of Economics and Statistics 46* (2), 181–184, 1984.

Muellbauer, J. N. J.: The assessment: Consumer expenditure. *Oxford Review of Economic Policy 10* (2), 1–41, 1994.

Muellbauer, J. N. J.: Measuring financial liberalization in the UK mortgage market. Mimeo, Nuffield College, Oxford, England, Mar. 1997.

Nicholls, D. F. and Pagan, A. R.: Heteroscedasticity in models with lagged dependent variables. *Econometrica 51* (4), 1233–1242, 1983.

Pagan, A. R.: Three econometric methodologies: A critical appraisal. *Journal of Economic Surveys 1* (1), 3–24, 1987.

Patterson, K. D.: The impact of credit constraints, interest rates and housing equity withdrawal on the intertemporal pattern of consumption — A diagrammatic analysis. *Scottish Journal of Political Economy 40* (4), 391–407, 1993.

Ramsey, J. B.: Tests for specification errors in classical linear least-squares regression analysis. *Journal of the Royal Statistical Society, Series B 31* (2), 350–371, 1969.

Salkever, D. S.: The use of dummy variables to compute predictions, prediction errors, and confidence intervals. *Journal of Econometrics 4* (4), 393–397, 1976.

Sprenkle, C. M. and Miller, M. H.: The precautionary demand for narrow and broad money. *Economica 47* (188), 407–421, 1980.

Teräsvirta, T. and Anderson, H. M.: Characterizing nonlinearities in business cycles using smooth transition autoregressive models. *Journal of Applied Econometrics 7* (Supplement), S119–S136, 1992.

Topping, S. L. and Bishop, S. L.: Breaks in monetary series. Discussion paper no. 23, Technical Series, Bank of England, London, England, Feb. 1989.

Volcker, P. A.: Statements to Congress. *Federal Reserve Bulletin 68* (12), 747–753, 1982.

White, H.: A heteroskedasticity-consistent covariance matrix estimator and a direct test for heteroskedasticity. *Econometrica 48* (4), 817–838, 1980.

Scand. J. Economics 100(1), 325–328, 1998

Comment on N. R. Ericsson, D. F. Hendry and K. M. Prestwich, "The Demand for Broad Money in the United Kingdom, 1878–1993"

Timo Teräsvirta
Stockholm School of Economics, S-113 83 Stockholm, Sweden

In the Eighteenth Annual Lecture of the Scottish Economic Society, one of the authors of the present paper reprinted a verse[1] by D. H. Robinson with the title "The Non-Econometrician's Lament"; see Hendry (1983). Because of this I think that he and perhaps the other authors as well would feel comfortable if I recycle parts of the verse in this, not just annual but even centennial, occasion. I should hasten to add, however, that the present paper makes excellent reading even for non-econometricians. Everybody should be fascinated, or intrigued, or both, by the fact that while monetary policies come and go, the UK money demand function, at least if slightly modified for new definitions of money, remains unchanged and has done so for more than a century. I begin by quoting D. H. Robinson:

> *"As soon as I could safely toddle*
> *My parents handed me a* Model[2]
> *My brisk and energetic pater*
> *Provided the accelerator.*
> *My mother, which may sound funny,*
> *Used one to control my demand for money."*[3]

As this makes clear, the topic of the paper is that of characterizing money demand in the U.K. over a long time period with a single econometric equation. Next I would like to discuss some details:

> *"And every week I had from her*
> *A lovely new* parameter..."*

The single most important claim in the paper is that the authors' money demand equation has constant parameters. This remains true even after

---

[1] Dated September 3, 1952; first published in Lundberg (1955).
[2] Italics here and later added by Hendry (1983).
[3] With an apology to D. H. Robinson. The original verse had to be modified slightly to meet the present needs.

extension of the estimation period 1878–1975 in Hendry and Ericsson (1991a) to 1993. Suppose that I extend the period even further and assign a new impulse dummy to each of these new observations. Then, as the authors point out, I obtain a model whose parameter estimates are identical to those for the original period. But has the model itself (the parameters) remained constant? This example highlights the role of dummy variables in considering constancy. Any parameter change may be hidden from sight by a sufficient number of dummies. Engle and Hendry (1993) mention the idea of testing invariance using a model whose parameters may stabilize only after adding dummy variables to it. Note that dummy variables introduced to deal with "unusual events" also imply strong assumptions about the dynamics of the process to be modelled (the dynamics are assumed not to be affected by these events). In this paper, dummy variables are used for the two World War periods and two periods of financial deregulation. Nevertheless, the *same* dummy variable works for both periods in both cases. The dummy variables are thus applied with restraint and care, which gives credibility to the claim of parameter constancy.

A situation in which time-varying parameters may be a rule rather than an exception arises when seasonal data is modelled with the help of seasonal dummy variables. These frequently do not have constant coefficients. Nevertheless, all the other parameters may be constant. The slow institutional change in seasonal patterns should then be parametrized separately, which may lead to nonlinear specifications. Teräsvirta (1998) provides a recent example of how this may be done in practice. The problem is not present here since the series are annual.

> "...With optimistic expectations
> I started on my explorations...
>
> Alas! I knew how it would end:
> I've mixed the cycle and the trend..."

It appears from the paper that all variables in the model are integrated of order one, $I(1)$. The money stock and the price deflator might be taken to be $I(2)$, but the authors argue that "despite their smooth and trending appearance" they appear to be $I(1)$. It does seem to me that the $I(2)$-ness may be a rather elusive concept in practice. The test results often change with the observation period. On the other hand, an incorrect order of integration is likely to be discovered at the evaluation stage when the estimated model is subjected to a battery of misspecification tests. Thus I regard the $I(1)$ assumption as a sound and realistic starting point as far as this exceptionally long data set is concerned.

"I wander glumly through the house
As though I were exogenous..."

Long series not only mean more information but also more problems. Exogeneity is one of them. The authors assume weak exogeneity of the right-hand side variables in their equations for the parameters of interest (the corresponding regression coefficients) and even argue in favor of super exogeneity which is important for policy analysis. It may be, however, that weak exogeneity becomes time-varying when the period considered is sufficiently long. This possibility has not been discussed very much in the literature, but see Richard (1980). It might be interesting to extend the alternative to the null of weak exogeneity in statistical tests to contain, in addition to lack of weak exogeneity, time-varying weak exogeneity as well. This could perhaps be done in the smooth transition regression ("deeper parameter") framework by introducing time as a transition variable in a suitable fashion.

"...And fear that, growing daily skinnier,
I have at length become non-linear..."

Consider the term

$$(\bar{u}_{t-1} - 0.2)\bar{u}_{t-1}^2$$

in equation (19) or its counterpart in equation (20) of the paper. This represents the nonlinear error correction which the authors discuss in the paper. On the other hand, the squared term may also be viewed as a first-order Taylor approximation to the transition function $1 - \exp\{-\gamma \bar{u}_{t-1}^2\}$ around $\gamma = 0$ in an exponential smooth transition regression (STR) model. Nonlinearities in this U.K. money demand function could indeed be investigated in the STR framework; see Granger and Teräsvirta (1993) and Teräsvirta (1998). That could be done more generally than the above example indicates by beginning with assumptions of the possible nonlinear structure that are less specific than those made here. It appears from the paper that this alternative is not unknown to the authors either. Some work is in progress in this direction.

The authors may feel that their outstanding contribution should have deserved a more creative and less random discussion. D. H. Robinson provides the necessary excuse:

"...My thoughts are sadly inelastic,
My acts incurably stochastic."

References

Engle, R. F. and Hendry, D. F.: Testing super exogeneity and invariance in regression models. *Journal of Econometrics 56*, 119–139, 1993.

Granger, C. W. J. and Teräsvirta, T.: *Modelling Nonlinear Economic Relationships.* Oxford University Press, Oxford, 1993.

Hendry, D. F.: Econometric modelling: The "consumption function" in retrospect. *Scottish Journal of Political Economy 30*, 193–220, 1983.

Hendry, D. F. and Ericsson, N. R.: An econometric analysis of U.K. money demand in *Monetary Trends in the United States and the United Kingdom* by Milton Friedman and Anna J. Schwartz. *American Economic Review 81*, 8–38, 1991.

Lundberg, E. (ed.): *The Business Cycle in the Post-war World.* Macmillan, London, 1955.

Richard, J.-F.: Models with several regimes and changes in exogeneity. *Review of Economic Studies 47*, 1–20, 1980.

Teräsvirta, T.: Modeling economic relationships with smooth transition regressions. In A. Ullah and D. E. A. Giles (eds.), *Handbook of Applied Economic Statistics*, 507–552, Dekker, New York, 1998.

Scand. J. Economics 100(1), 329–334, 1998

Comment on N. R. Ericsson, D. F. Hendry and K. M. Prestwich, "The Demand for Broad Money in the United Kingdom, 1878–1993"

Svend Hylleberg
University of Aarhus, DK-8000 Aarhus C, Denmark

The paper by Ericsson, Hendry and Prestwich (EHP) is a report on an empirical analysis of the demand for money in the UK over the period 1878 to 1993.

In spite of the very long period with a vast number of institutional changes and tremendous changes in the degree of openness of the economy, the authors are able to find an econometric model with underlying constant parameters. This somewhat surprising result is obtained through a redefinition of variables based on the opportunity cost of holding money, use of nonlinear formulations, and use of dummy variables.

The period is divided into two subperiods: one running from 1878 to 1973 and the other from 1878 to 1993. It is shown that the differences between the parameter values in the two estimated models are negligible.

The actual model has a nonlinear equilibrium correction term which seems quite interesting. The cointegrating relation for the period 1878 to 1973 is (EHP equation 17):

$$\tilde{u}_t = (m - i - p)_t + 0.318 + 6.67 RN_t \tag{1}$$

and the equilibrium correction term (EHP equation 19) is:

$$z_t = (\tilde{u}_t - 0.2)\tilde{u}_t^2 \tag{2}$$

lagged one period and with a coefficient estimate of -2.83. (2) implies that $z_t > 0$ for $\tilde{u}_t > 0.2$, $z_t < 0$ for $\tilde{u}_t < 0.2$, while $z_t = 0$ for $\tilde{u}_t = 0.0, 0.2$.

Applying (2) it is seen that

$$\frac{\partial z_t}{\partial \tilde{u}_t} = 3\tilde{u}_t(\tilde{u}_t - 0.133) \tag{3}$$

---

*Thanks to Neil Ericsson for correcting an error in an earlier version of my comment and for lending me the data. The computations were made using PcGive version 9; see Hendry and Doornik (1996).

Here

$$
\frac{\partial z_t}{\partial \bar{u}_t} \begin{cases} >0 \text{ for } \bar{u}_t > 0.133 \\ = 0 \text{ for } \bar{u}_t = 0.133 \\ <0 \quad \text{for } 0 < \bar{u}_t < 0.133 \\ = 0 \text{ for } \bar{u}_t = 0 \\ >0 \text{ for } 0 > \bar{u}_t \end{cases}
$$

As $\partial z_t/\partial RN_t = [\partial z_t/\partial \bar{u}_t] \ [\partial \bar{u}_t/\partial RN_t]$ where $\partial \bar{u}_t/\partial RN_t = 6.67$ the sign of $\partial z_t/\partial RN_t$ is easily derived from the sign of $\partial z_t/\partial \bar{u}_t$. A graph of $\partial z_t/\partial \bar{u}_t$ is shown in Figure 1, with the dots indicating the value of the derivative at the estimated values of $\bar{u}_t$.

It is seen that the nonlinear form of the error correction term is substantiated by the data as the "observations" are distributed over all the relevant areas of $\bar{u}_t$. However, the plots of the function for the subperiods indicate that the "observations" for the period until 1919 all lie on the left arm of the parabola, while the "observations" for the period 1920–1946 lie at the bottom of the parabola on both arms.

In the period after the Second World War, 1947–1993, the "observations" lie along the whole curve, but especially on the left arm.

This change in the equilibrium correction mechanism is even more visible from the cross plots of z_t and $\bar{u}_t$ in Figure 2. It is seen that the vast majority of the values of $\bar{u}_t$ are below 0.2 and the z values are therefore nonpositive. This is especially the case for the first subperiod where most of the "observations" on $\bar{u}_t$ are negative and a few between zero and 0.2. Consequently, the equilibrium correction to the next years $(m-p)$, i.e., $-2.83 z$ are all positive or zero but also quite small. In the second subperiod the equilibrium correction is also small but both negative and positive, while the last subperiod exhibits much larger corrections. The biggest positive value of $\bar{u}_t$ is the 1974 value of 0.38 with a corresponding value of z equal to 0.026 and the smallest values of $\bar{u}_t$ are the 1977, 1983 and 1984 values of -0.24, -0.22 and 0.23, respectively, with the corresponding z values of -0.025, -0.020 and -0.23.

From these observations it is seen that the nonlinear form of the equilibrium correction term is determined mainly through the later years, and not from the period before the First World War.

I would like to mention two other points. The first is concerned with the Dickey–Fuller test for unit roots. These are computed by PcGive and a standard routine in this very nice piece of software, is applied.

However, it is now well known in the literature that the size and power of such unit root tests depend critically on the white noise of the errors and the applied lag augmentation which must be the most parsimonious with

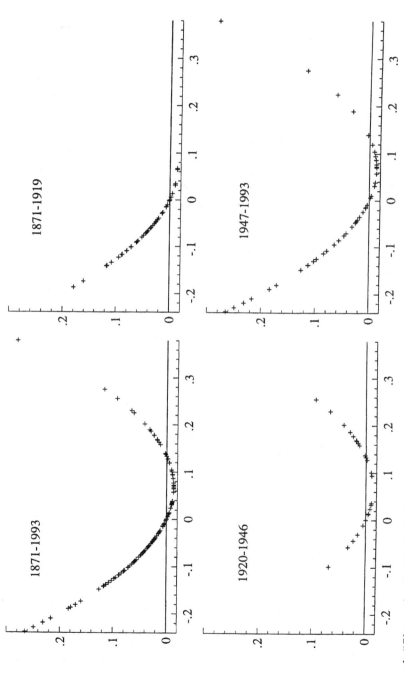

Fig. 1. "Observations" of the derivative $\partial z_t / \partial \bar{u}_t$ graphed against $\bar{u}_t$ for the period 1871–1993, and for the subperiods 1871–1919, 1920–1946 and 1946–1993

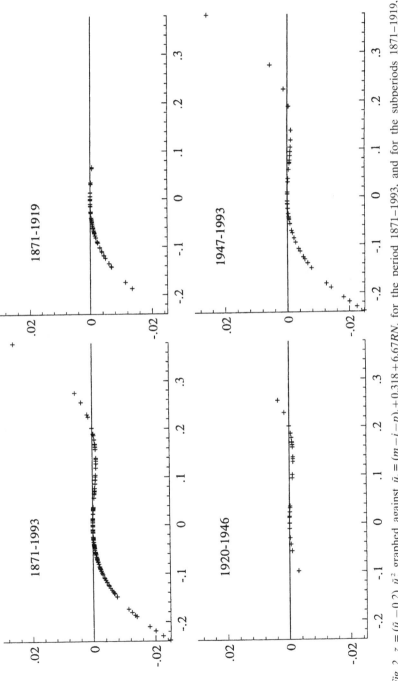

Fig. 2. $z_t = (\bar{u}_t, -0.2)$ $\bar{u}_t^2$ graphed against $\bar{u}_t = (m-i-p)_t + 0.318 + 6.67RN_t$ for the period 1871–1993, and for the subperiods 1871–1919, 1920–1946 and 1946–1993

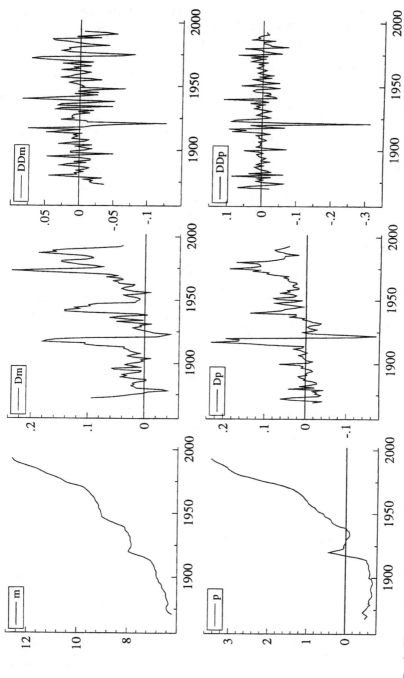

Fig. 3. Time series plots of m_t and p_t denoted by m and p and their first and second differences denoted by Dm, Dp, DDm and DDp, respectively

respect to the number of parameters in the lag augmentation. Hence, it may be very important to allow for holes in the lag distribution, a feature not available in the standard PcGive routine. Consequently, it is advisable to apply the standard regression routines of PcGive in constructing the Dickey–Fuller tests. Of course, if only short lags are necessary, as seem to be the case here, the actual results of EHP would probably not be improved much by doing this.

Figure 3 shows the smooth nature of m_t and p_t, which could indicate that these series are $I(2)$. A proper procedure for testing such a hypothesis, see Dickey and Pantula (1987), is to do a sequence of auxiliary regressions starting with a regression of the second-order differenced series, i.e., $(x_t - x_{t-1}) - (x_{t-1} - x_{t-2}) = \Delta^2 x_t$ on Δx_{t-1}, dererministic terms like an intercept and a trend and the appropriate number of lags of $\Delta^2 x_t$ in order to make the errors white noise. The t value on the coefficient to Δx_{t-1} is then used to test the hypothesis of $I(2)$ against that of $I(1)$ in the Dickey–Fuller distribution. If the null of $I(2)$ cannot be rejected, the procedure is stopped. If the null is rejected a new auxiliary regression is done with $\Delta^2 x_t$ on Δx_{t-1} and x_{t-1}, deterministic terms and lagged values of $\Delta^2 x_t$. The test of $I(1)$ against $I(0)$ is then performed by applying the t value to the coefficient to x_{t-1} in the Dickey–Fuller distribution. For both m_t and p_t the result of such a testing procedure showed that both series are $I(1)$, thereby supporting the results in the article (EHP).

Second, it is also argued that a one-equation approach and not a multi-variate VAR approach is applied to parallel earlier analysis of the UK demand for money. The interesting problem addressed in the report is whether it is possible to find an econometric model for U.K. money demand having constant parameters throughout a period of more than one hundred years. Whether to use a one-equation approach or a multivariate approach is only a matter of degree and it can and should be properly tested. I would have preferred to see such an analysis applied here and not later as promised by the authors.

In conclusion, I want to congratulate the authors for an interesting and stimulating report, which shows that it is possible to apply proper econometric modelling in addressing an important economic question.

References

Dickey, D. and Pantula, S. P.: Determining the order of differencing in autoregressive processes. *Journal of Business and Economic Statistics 5*, 45–461, 1987.

Hendry, D. F. and Doornik, J. A.: *Empirical Econometric Modelling Using PcGive for Windows*. International Thomson Business Press, London, 1996.

Scand. J. of Economics 100(1), 335–357, 1998

Limits to Institutional Reforms

Thráinn Eggertsson*

University of Iceland, IS-101 Reykjavik, Iceland and Max Planck Institute for Research into Economic Systems, D-07745 Jena, Germany

Abstract

The essay draws on the theory of (macro)economic policy, as it has evolved, to discuss implicit policy determinism in the new economics of institutions. The extension of rational-choice methods to new levels of analysis, such as micropolitics, macropolitics, political macroeconomics, and microfoundations of cooperation, has apparently reduced the policy choice set and diminished the role of experts. All outcomes reflect constrained maximization by rational agents. The essay argues, however, that scarcity of knowledge leads to incomplete and variable policy models, and that competition among policy models creates a role for experts in social change.

I. The Dilemma

The new economics of institutions, which employs economic, political, and sociological variables to study economic systems, hints at policy determinism. The brave new world of endogenous politicians, bureaucrats, and social structures appears to give few degrees of freedom and little room for choice to reformers who attempt to steer economic systems onto a new path. A passage in a review essay by Leif Johansen (1979) well illustrates the quandary that is my concern. Johansen was reviewing the report of an official committee in the United Kingdom that had been appointed to examine whether application of optimal control techniques to macro-economic planning might improve the overall performance of the British economy. Johansen felt that the Committee on Policy Optimization was "almost apologetic" about past performance of British policymakers, and made the following observation ([1979] 1987, p. 569):

> One might so to speak ask what degrees of freedom the Committee has assumed for the comparison of possible alternatives. If all sorts of constraints referring not only to the strictly economic aspects, but to problems of infor-mation, political pressures etc. are introduced, then one might end up with a sort of overall social theory in which the government is endogenous rather

* I was Visiting Fellow at Hoover Institution, Stanford University, when I wrote this essay, and I thank my colleagues at the institute for their support. In revising the paper, I received helpful comments from participants at a Hoover workshop and at the *SJE* 100th Anniversary Symposium. Of the many people who have helped me, I thank, in particular, Avner Ben-Ner, Tone Ognedal, the two editors of this journal, an unknown referee, and Uwe Siegmund.

than an autonomous decision-maker, and there will not be much point in discussing hypothetically what would have been the outcome if the government had behaved differently. On the other hand, one may consider the government as a rather free decision-maker with a wide scope for choice between alternatives.

The new literature on institutions lies closer to the deterministic end of Johansen's scale than the free choice one, as Avinish Dixit (1996, p. 2) confirms in his survey of "transaction-costs politics". Dixit rejects the common argument that economists have a duty to make "sound" economic judgments and leave political considerations to others. "This argument appears to assume that economic and political aspects are additively separable in their effects — that one can analyze each separately and then find the total effect by adding together the two calculations. But that is not in general true", says Dixit (1996, p. 150).[1]

In this essay, I am concerned with limits to institutional reforms, and the theory of institutional policy. To organize my thoughts I have in this and previous essays drawn inspiration from the theory of economic policy and macroeconomic planning, which for more than half a century has perfected the fine art of manipulating economic systems; see Eggertsson (1997a, 1997b). The new institutionalism, so far, has spent most of its energy explaining social outcomes, both analyzing the effects of alternative institutional arrangements and attempting to explain institutional change. In these theories, the forces driving institutional change may reflect individual optimization, new political balance, or evolution and selection in the context of particular political and economic institutions, but the literature seldom offers lessons for government policy, except perhaps implicitly.

Section II draws lessons from the theory of (macro)economic policy which, in the postwar period, has gradually reduced the role of reformers and set rather narrow limits to reforms. Section III counters the centrifugal forces of the new institutionalism by suggesting a specific research agenda for the economics of institutions. Section IV finds evidence of policy determinism in four areas of recent research associated with the new institutionalism. And, finally, Section V argues that incomplete knowledge (or bounded rationality) reduces determinism in institutional policy and creates a role for experts.

---

[1] Notwithstanding Dixit's dictum, many economists still argue for partial analysis of the social system, with the economy treated in isolation from other sectors. Lucas (1986, p. 405) states "that the problem of controlling inflation has been 'successfully solved' in a scientific sense." Lucas then adds a footnote for skeptics, which reads: "Obviously, few societies have solved the problem of inflation in a political sense. I do not see this fact as qualifying my claim in the text, any more than I would view the current popularity of 'creationism' as qualifying the scientific status of the theory of evolution."

II. Experts and Degrees of Freedom: Lessons from Macroeconomic Planning

Experts and the Old Theory of Economic Policy

The classic targets and instruments approach to economic policy modeled the economic system in isolation from the political system and assumed, at least implicitly, that policymakers enjoyed a relatively broad range of choices.[2] Johansen (1977, pp. 55–64) provides an excellent compact summary of the traditional view.[3] Johansen's formulation accords with Arrow's (1956, p. 44) four components of any decision problem: (1) an objective function, $W = W(x)$; (2) a set of available policy instruments, A; (3) a *policy model* which specifies empirical relations, $x = f(a, z)$, where outcomes, x, depend on policy measures, a, and exogenous factors, z; and (4) computational methods for finding policy instruments that maximize the objective function. X_z is the set of possible outcomes given prevailing exogenous factors, z, and the goal of public policy is to apply policy measures, a^*, that generate the outcome, x^* which maximizes the social welfare function, $W^* = W(x^*)$. In this world of planning, the role of economists or "analytical experts" formally involves specifying the policy model and computing the optimal solution, whereas $W = W(x)$ reflects preferences of the policy authority.[4]

In the classical theory of economic policy, the dichotomy of economics and politics shows up in Frisch's distinction between *selection analysis* and *implementation*, and in Tinbergen's notion of the *optimal economic system*. Frisch defines selection analysis as the task of finding optimal outcomes,

---

[2] The old theory of economic policy emerged in large measure from the work of Ragnar Frisch and Jan Tinbergen, who were influenced by (and contributed to) Keynesian macroeconomics. Frisch pioneered models designed explicitly for planning and policy purposes, but published relatively little of this material internationally; see Johansen (1977, p. 22). Tinbergen's (1952) *On the Theory of Economic Policy* recognizes his debt to Frisch's work on decision models.

[3] In his own work, Johansen (1977) goes beyond the traditional planning mode and incorporates team theory, games, and the effects of pressure groups.

[4] The pioneers realized that the real world is murky and the roles of politicians and experts often overlap; see Johansen (1977, pp. 104–109). For instance, Frisch was concerned that analytical experts might find it difficult to establish $W(x)$ in a form usable for the decision problem. Johansen ([1974] 1987, pp. 542–544) reports that, in contemplating this problem, Frisch identified six different approaches to acquiring information about the policy preference function: (1) the decision-makers directly specify their decision functions; (2) experts interview decision-makers; (3) experts conduct imaginary interviews; (4) experts draw inference about preferences from planning documents; (5) experts rely on revealed preferences of policymakers from observed behavior. Frisch also recognized that politicians might hesitate to reveal their preferences, either for strategic reasons or because they were uncertain about elements of the planning process.

W^*, in a world free from political constraints.[5] Political constraints often interfere with implementation and place W^* out of bounds. If W' represents the highest value of W that social realities permit, then $(W^* - W')$ measures the cost of political constraints in terms of the social welfare function. Similarly, Tinbergen (1952, 1959) recognizes that social and political forces often support suboptimal economic systems. He refers to policy aimed at reforming the economic system as *qualitative policy* and distinguishes it from *quantitative policy* which leaves basic structures intact. Tinbergen believed in a long-run propensity for policymakers to optimize over all known institutional arrangements, and this belief contributed to his famous notion of worldwide *convergence* of economic systems toward a common basic structure. Johansen (1977, pp. 147–148) makes a distinction between *minor* and *basic* qualitative policy measures.[6] Basic qualitative policy implies radical change in power structures, "which will generally not be contemplated by any central authority under the prevailing power structure"; see Johansen (1977, p. 148).

Rational-Expectations Macroeconomics and Private Policy Models

The Keynesian-inspired classical policy theory assumed that quantitative policy measures would not change the relationship between instruments and targets in the policy model, $x = f(a, z)$. The rational expectations revolution permanently changed this perspective by recognizing that economic agents have an incentive to ease the burden of new constraints imposed by a policy authority, and these responses can change the structure of $x = f(a, z)$; see Lucas (1976, 1990).

In its pure form, the rational expectations paradigm makes rather extreme assumptions about the information environment of economic agents. Representative economic agents base their decisions on a correct model of the macroeconomy, and they also know how the policy authority reacts when desired values for target variables differ from their actual values. The interaction between private and public policy models in the world of rational expectations significantly reduces the set of outcomes, X, that are available to the policymakers. For instance, demand management no longer can systematically move the economy below the natural rate of

---

[5] Reported in Johansen ([1974] 1987, pp. 227–233). Johansen ([1974] 1987, p. 227) tells us that Frisch first made the distinction between selection analysis and implementation in a University of Oslo Memorandum in 1944.

[6] Minor qualitative measures in the sense of Johansen have some correspondence with Lucas's (1990) notion of *regime change*, in contrast with policy action within a regime.

unemployment, except by random measures which take economic agents by surprise, but such measures have little or no practical use as policy.

Bounded-Rationality Macroeconomics, and Policy Models as Dependent Variables

The relative strength of rational expectations macroeconomics lies in explaining how systems operate when relevant agents have adjusted to coherent rules and expectations, and share a common understanding of their environment. Theorists building their models must decide in advance how much their agents should know, what they do NOT know, and how they learn; see Sargent (1993, p. 165).[7] In rational expectations macroeconomics, as Sargent (1993, p. 21) points out, representative economic agents are endowed with more knowledge than their creator, the model builder. The economist or econometrician must estimate and infer information about policy models, which these procedures assume the agents already know.

When economists try to understand a social system, they formulate a theory, collect data, and test the theory against their data, and, therefore, Sargent (1993, p. 23) sees rational expectations equilibrium as prevailing when the agents have solved their scientific problem of establishing appropriate policy models. A regime change involves a shift of policy models, but economics lacks a generally recognized theory of the dynamic path between two regimes. One solution, suggested by Sargent (1993), is to model social agents as behaving like economists and scientists when they acquire new knowledge, but Sargent recognizes that relatively little is known of how scientists learn about the world, although, of course, their statistical estimation techniques (such as classical or Bayesian econometrics) are known.

Lessons for Institutional Policy

What can a theory of institutional policy learn from half a century of theorizing about the process of macroeconomic intervention? In my view,

---

[7] The behavior of governments that in the 1960s and early 1970s attempted to exploit the Phillips curve and trade unemployment for inflation, or vice versa, is puzzling in the context of rational expectations economics. A strand in the literature assumes that, during this episode, private economic agents were endowed with a correct policy model of the economy, whereas the policy model of the government was based on erroneous economic theory; see Sargent (1993, p. 160) and footnote 12 below.

each stage in the evolution of macroeconomic planning teaches an important lesson, and I list several such lessons below.

Classical macroeconomic planning teaches the theory of institutional policy two lessons: (1) the importance of clearly establishing the preference function of the policy authority, and (2) the importance of identifying both the set of policy instruments, A, available to the policy authority, and the policy model, $x = f(x, z)$. Political macroeconomics, a close relation of the economics of institutions and a flourishing new field, has learned these lessons well, as would be expected from the field's proximity to macroeconomics; see Alesina (1988, 1995).[8] Political macroeconomics adds political outcomes, g, to the policy preference function, which now becomes $W = G(g, x)$, sometimes with economic outcomes playing little or no role independently of political outcomes.[9] Other branches of the new institutionalism are frequently not concerned with the practice of government policy, and do not directly identify effective instruments of policy.

The idea that *individual policy models* affect the outcome of policy is the main message of rational expectations macroeconomics to institutional policy. In a social system, equilibrium is associated with perceptions of the environment which are embodied in individual policy models. The ability of private agents to model their environments, including the decision rules of governments, limits choices in public policy. Some contributors to the new institutional literature have implicitly recognized that the process of institutional change is frequently marked by clashes of private and public policy models (in addition to conflicts of interest). Steven Cheung's (1975, 1976) investigation of rent control in Hong Kong is noteworthy in this context.

Finally, bounded-rationality macroeconomics draws attention to the quality of public and private policy models and to the role of learning in updating these models. Substantial institutional change requires that various agents adapt new policy models. It is logical, therefore, for institutional policy (and experts) to be concerned with influencing policy models, which may now become *intermediate targets* in the transformation process. Usually the economics of institutions frames information problems as arising from lack of data (due to measurement costs) or from an inability

---

[8] Alesina (1995, p. 145) lists the following topics as an example of recent work in political macroeconomics (my quotations are selective): "political business cycles, the politics of the government budget, the political economy of growth, the politics of inflation and stabilization policies, problems of external debt and capital flight in less developed countries, the effect of ... different electoral systems on economic policy, the performance of coalition and minority governments relative to single party governments .. "

[9] Political macroeconomics has primarily examined quantitative policy, but also to some extent minor qualitative policy, in Johansen's definition.

to process data rapidly, but not as resulting from ignorance of what data to collect and how to interpret them.

Figure 1 summarizes the discussion so far by extending a diagram due to Johansen (1977, p. 58) to incorporate political constraints and rational expectations. This figure shows how rational expectations, r, reduce the choice set from X_z in the classical (Keynesian) policy model to $X_{z,r}$ in a model with private counterpolicy. In addition, political economy suggests that the political process puts certain outcomes, p, off limits, which in *Figure 1* further limits choices to the set $X_{z,r,p}$. Finally, Figure 1 recognizes that economic outcomes, x, have valued political consequences, g. If economic outcomes are still preferred in themselves, the policy preference function now becomes $W = G(x, g)$, and $g = g(x)$, which limits the ability of economists and other experts to influence the goals of public policy.

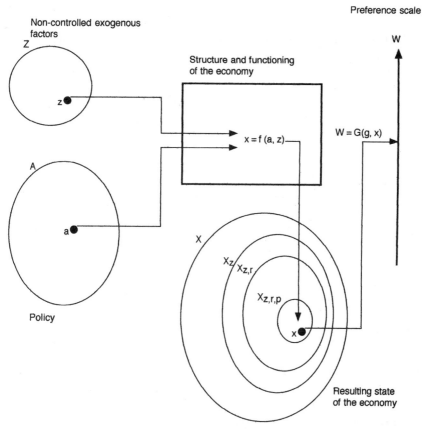

Fig. 1. The policy process; based on Johansen (1977, p. 58)

The story changes substantially when we introduce bounded rationality and the related concept of incomplete and variable policy models. The introduction of new models of complex social systems has some of the features and appeal of technological change. Experts are sometimes listened to when they appear to have made important discoveries (there is/there is not an exploitable Phillips curve); furthermore, uncertainty about the true nature of policy models creates scope for various forms of persuasion.

III. What is the Domain of the New Institutional Economics?

The New Economics of Institutions

The new economics of institutions is a somewhat undisciplined discipline with a fuzzy domain. The field is concerned with economic systems, and usually defines institutions as binding rules or systematic rule-directed behavior; see Calvert (1995a), North (1990a), Ostrom (1986) and Schotter (1981). The emphasis on rules links the economics of institutions with the economics of property rights and the economics of law; see Alchian (1977), Barzel (1989), Demsetz (1988), Furubotn and Pejovich (1972), Cooter (1997) and Posner (1992). As social systems are usually hierarchical, the literature distinguishes various levels of authority, such as constitutional rules, collective-choice rules, and operational rules, both in society at large and within organizations; see Buchanan (1990), Kieser and Ostrom (1982), Voigt (1996) and Gifford (1991). Rules create institutional environments for organizations, and the new economics of institutions and the new economics of organizations overlap substantially; see Williamson (1985). Both fields are preoccupied with information problems, transaction costs, and the implications of soft budget constraints and insecure control of resources; see Barzel (1989), Libecap (1989) and North (1994).

Recent concern with information in mainstream economics, especially in industrial organization, has further blurred the distinct status of the economics of institutions; see Milgrom and Roberts (1992) and Werin and Wijkander (1992). In addition to links to various branches of economics, the new economics of institutions has ties to various other branches of social science. As governments create and enforce rules, the fields of political science and public administration contribute to the study of institutions; see Schiavo-Campo (1994), Alt and Shepsle (1990), Banks and Hanushek (1995) and Mueller (1989). Cooperation and effective rules have not only political and legal foundations but also social ones, which opens yet another line of investigation; see Greif (1993, 1994), Hechter *et al.* (1992) and Putnam (1994). Studies of microfoundations of institutions often rely on game theory, and, moreover, some scholars now question whether the traditional economic model of man is rich enough to deal with questions at this level of analysis; see Calvert (1995a, 1995b) and Denzau and North (1994).

The Domain of the New Institutional Economics

Although the new economics of institutions benefits from cooperating with various related disciplines, the field needs a clear agenda and a reason for being which is sometimes lost in the rush to create a new research program. Before suggesting two important roles that seem natural for institutional economics, let me first examine how the new institutionalism might view Frisch's selection analysis and the related problem of reaching Tinbergen's optimal regime, which I mention in Section II. Conceptually, the problem has three components, which all test human knowledge to the limit. To simplify the discussion, I assume that the policy preference function gives priority to economic growth.

The first issue concerns the growth potential of qualitatively different economic systems. In particular, the reformer would have to explore the potential of quantitative policies in different social structures, which calls for evaluation of policy models, $f_j(a, z)$, for all (known) economic systems — for all j's, which are elements of the set J. The evaluation involves operational characteristics, such as how growth is affected by monetary and fiscal policy, import substitution, and industrial policy.

The second issue bears on what political and social foundations regime $f_j(a, z)$ requires to display the characteristics of a well-functioning system of type j — what social arrangements are needed for supporting necessary cooperation, coordination, and communication in a system of type j.

The third question pertains to dynamics. If a reformer wants to transform regime $f_j(a, z)$ into regime $f^*(a, z)$, then what does the best path between the two look like? This third issue partly corresponds to Frisch's implementation phase of the planning process, but it goes deeper than what we usually mean by political wheeling and dealing. One level is concerned with macroeconomic issues of sequencing, when all reform measures cannot be undertaken at once; see McKinnon (1991). Will the introduction of X (free international capital flows) before Y exists (mature domestic market for securities) destabilize the system? But, at another level, the reformer must ask how sequencing interacts with politics, see e.g. Dewatriport and Roland (1995), and, at a third level, whether fundamental social structures need and can be adapted so as to be consistent with the desired economic system. Imagine that a country, which is to be reformed, is a *collectivist* society, to use Greif's (1994) concepts, and also imagine that the target policy regime, $f^*(a, z)$, only functions properly in *individualist* societies. How then does one transform the existing social structure into the desired one?[10]

The reader probably agrees that full-scale selection analysis would keep a representative social scientist busy for a while, but I now turn to the two roles that I see for the economics of institutions in social science. The comparative advantage of the field is in two areas. The first role has some correspondence with applied fields like public administration and business administration. In a world where scholarly work is divided into narrow subdisciplines, social science requires an interdisciplinary field to coordinate research into the links between institutions (binding rules) and economic results, because these links are facilitated by various political, social, and economic factors. By identifying the links, along with relevant transmission mechanisms and interactions, the economics of institutions defines a joint research program, puzzles and problems, to which the various disciplines contribute.

The second role of the economics of institutions relates to analytical tools. When social science is not able to provide methods appropriate for analyzing important research puzzles which emerge in the economics of institutions, institutionalists must attempt to design new tools and, in that endeavor, possibly seek inspiration in unrelated fields, even in biology and cognitive science.

Coase's (1937) famous study of the nature of the firm fits well with the research program that I have described. In his essay, Coase first identifies a research question relevant to the study of economic systems: why are there firms in a market economy, and what limits their size? And then, in an attempt to answer his question, Coase introduces a new analytical concept, the relative cost of using markets and firms to allocate resources, an insight that gradually evolved into the transaction-cost approach. Similarly, our knowledge of institutional change would be advanced if we understood more about the formation and evolution of policy models, both in government and among private agents.

IV. Impressions of Policy Determinism in the New Economics of Institutions

The extension of rational-choice methods to new levels of analysis has had similar consequences for the economics of institutions as it has had for macroeconomics by reducing the set of policy choices. In the study of economic growth, the institutional approach looks for various economic,

---

[10] Reformers might also want to take up the research question of Marx and Schumpeter, and consider the long-term stability of $f*(a, z)$ as well as and examine whether internal dynamics eventually are likely to destroy the system.

political, and social explanations of why inputs, investments, and new technology are not forthcoming or why their allocation is wasteful. These studies usually attempt to demonstrate how social and historical factors constrain agents, and how economic outcomes are the aggregate result of rational individual behavior. Explanations of economic outcomes in terms of optimizing behavior at all levels by economic, political, and social agents do not leave much room for reforms. It is not obvious how an independent expert could switch an economic system from one Nash equilibrium to another. Examples from four strands of the literature — micropolitics, macropolitics, political macroeconomics, and microfoundations — illustrate my point.

Micropolitics

Micropolitical theories of stagnation emphasize how costly information and political institutions empower special interests to pressure governments to transfer wealth to these groups. The transfers often have the attributes of negative-sum games. Olson (1965, 1982) made pioneering contributions in this area, and a vast literature has emerged under various names, such as the theory of rent seeking and the economics of regulation; see Becker (1983); Buchanan *et al.* (1980), Stigler (1971) and Tollison (1982).

Micropolitical theories of stagnation make it clear that nations must somehow escape their negative-sum games and neutralize special interests, if the nations are to enjoy more rapid economic growth. These theories, however, do not show us, in their own terms, how such changes can be brought about: what agents have the incentive to take the necessary measures, and why the agents have not already taken these measures. Micropolitical explanations usually attribute relief from special interest pressure to exogenous factors, such as wars which fragment interest groups, to the balance of power between conflicting interests, or to the small size of polities (which may induce interest groups to internalize their external effects); see Olson (1982).

Macropolitics

The pressure group literature presents the state as a passive playing ground for special interests. Political science and political economy have recently rediscovered the state as an enterprising agent with an agenda of its own; see Almond (1988). To strengthen their hold on power, rulers and political leaders in both democratic and autocratic states form coalitions of supporters and design regulations to create new client groups; see Bates (1990). Bates' (1981) study of tropical Africa is a prime example of macropolitical analysis which explains economic decline in terms of coalition politics. Similarly, Weingast (1994) uses the term *political risk* to explain the common failure of political leaders to find support and secure cooperation for policies of economic growth. Reforms often require clear-cut removal of special privileges from traditional supporters of the state, whereas the benefits and the identity of beneficiaries are uncertain; see Fernandez and Rodrik (1991). When the identity of those who benefit is obvious, governments find it difficult to assure groups outside their current coalition of supporters that these outsiders will share in the benefits from reforms. For instance, African farmers may not want to risk their assets and adopt advanced agricultural techniques, because the farmers do not believe government promises of full world market prices for future output. The government is unable to make a credible commitment to the farmers, and the farmers are adverse to political risk; see Weingast (1994, p. 12)

If techniques for making credible commitments are generally known, the failure to commit to institutional reforms must be due to coalition politics and exogenous historical circumstances. When circumstances allow rational leaders to build coalitions for supporting strong economic growth, we expect them to do so, otherwise not.

Political Macroeconomics

Economists are fairly uniform in condemning various aspects of macro-economic policy as it is practiced in many parts of the world. The condemned policy may involve an over-valued exchange rate, import substitution, excessive supply of money, or credit rationing; see Krueger (1994). Political macroeconomics has abandoned the view that such policy reflects economic ignorance; see Alesina (1995). Increasingly, economists now explain the pursuit of macroeconomic policies of decline as rational behavior in a particular political context, which puts their explanations in one or both of the two previous categories.

Microfoundations

In the new institutional economics, the subfield of microfoundations studies the social foundations of economic systems, whereas traditional microeconomics examines incentives and outcomes inherent in particular systems. Obviously, the two fields are intimately related and both share an interest in the relationship between production efficiency and transaction efficiency; see Greif (1995). A general propensity in a population to honor the social system for assigning and transferring control of resources reduces uncertainty about effective ownership and releases productive forces.

The critical research question in microfoundations concerns how effect-ively rules are enforced. In exchange, rules are enforced by a trading partner, by oneself, and by some third party (fellow members of one's community, government agents), see North (1990a). The enforcement mechanisms involve not only naked force but conventions, norms, and reputation effects. Most scholars agree that sole reliance on detection and punishment with the help of the police and the courts would make trans-actions exceedingly costly and only permit limited specialization and exchange. The literature has recently given much attention to binding norms that emerge in repeated games in which the players care about the future. Repeated play, however, does not guarantee satisfactory outcomes because iterated games tend to have multiple equilibria, both inefficient and efficient. Many studies solve this theoretical problem by appealing to exogenous social structures that shape the game by acting as focal points and thus guide the process to an efficient equilibrium. These focal points are sometimes ideas or shared beliefs, c.f. Weingast (1995), culture, cf. Kreps (1990), ethnic networks, cf. Landa (1994) and Greif (1995) or ideol-ogy, cf. Hinich and Munger (1992) and Bawn (1996).

Rational-choice social science is reluctant to recognize personal ethics and internalized norms as exogenous variables, and, moreover, social science does not offer any generally accepted theory of preference forma-tion. Few reliable studies exist which examine whether governments are able, as a matter of policy, to directly dictate norms and focal points, and thus create desired mass behavior.[11] If such manipulations were possible, one may add, norms would become equivalent to laws, which leads us back into the realm of political economy. Governments would select norms to meet demands of powerful pressure groups or to create and maintain coalitions of supporters.

V. How Incomplete Knowledge Increases Degrees of Freedom in Institutional Reforms

Competing Policy Models

What conclusions can we draw about limits to institutional reforms and the role of experts in social change? The literature that I sketch in Section IV obviously carries a valid message: there are often formidable political and social limits to reforms; sometimes greater obstacles than we care to admit. My main point in this essay, however, is that the literature often fails to

---

[11] Governments can legislate self-enforcing coordination devices, such as standards; see Sugden (1989). Even then, standard-specific investments can create opposition to new stand-ards; see Kiwit (1995).

recognize that scarcity of knowledge leads to incomplete and variable policy models, and competing policy models create a role for experts in social change. My point is not unique. Dixit (1996, p. 30), who emphasizes limits to reforms, states that "one should admit there are some degrees of freedom for policy making at almost all times, more at some times than others". Dixit (1996, p. 30) sees "economic policy making ... [as] a dynamic game, whose conditions are uncertain and changing ... " and, "in this view of the policy process the degrees of freedom mostly consist of opportunities to make various strategic moves." Witt (1992, p. 121) endogenizes the role of the public choice theorist by drawing on theories of cognition, and sets out an "evolutionary, individualistically founded interpretation' of this process of persuasion.

Social systems are complex phenomena, which we only partly understand. As North (1990b) emphasizes, agents often interpret their environment with the help of incomplete or incorrect models, and, furthermore, as they test the models with new information, the tests do not necessarily lead to satisfactory revisions.[12] Therefore, policy authorities usually rely on models that are incomplete, and even within government conflicting policy models compete. Experts can affect institutional change by influencing the models of those who control government policy.

In principle, scholars can influence institutional reforms either by affecting basic preference for social order and the policy preference function, $W = G(g, x)$, or they can attempt to improve $x = f(a, z)$ and (ideally) show the authorities how to use old and new instruments to reach their goals more effectively. I am concerned here with the latter alternative where social scientists are like natural scientists who make new technology available to industry, except that the quality of social science theories is relatively uncertain. Therefore, social scientists, more than natural scientists, must select moments when the authorities are receptive to change.

Although the idea of uncertain truths may disturb committed scholars, the literature is awash in conflicting scholarly policy models, as is well illustrated in a somewhat adventurous study by Fratianni and Pattison (1976). They searched published and unpublished documents of the OECD to uncover the model "that is used [by the organization] in the formulation of hypotheses for testing as well as for policy making;' (p. 78). Fratianni and Pattison, monetarists of the Brunner-Meltzer persuasion, conclude that advice by the OECD was dominated by a British–Keynesian

---

[12] Sargent (1993, pp. 160–165) provides a fascinating summary of studies by Sims (1988) and Chung (1990), where they model a private sector which knows its rational expectations economics, and an "irrational" government which does not and erroneously believes in an exploitable Phillips curve. Chung (1990) estimates a model of the government's learning process using data for the United States.

approach to stabilization policy. In a comment on their study, Bent Hansen (1976), who partly faults their findings and methodology, agrees with the authors that the OECD Department of Economics and Statistics was dominated in its thinking by British Keynesianism and "was always firmly anchored in British institutions and tended to think that a policy that is good in Britain must be good for any other country;" (p. 142) And reflecting on the OECD Committee on Fiscal Policy, with which he had been associated, Hansen (1976, p. 152) states that: "It would hardly be wrong in this instance to characterize the OECD as an overseas missionary post for British Keynesianism trying to form continental European budgetary policies."[13]

Life and Death of Policy Models

Modern economic history provides many examples of countries switching their policy regimes for the whole economy or for individual sectors, sometimes with such changes correlated across regions. Siegmund (1997) gives empirical evidence of waves of nationalization and privatization in the period 1900–1995 in Europe and select Asian and Latin American countries. To an outsider, it may look as if the state occasionally changes its mind; see Eggertsson (1997b).

A major switch in government policy need not imply that new policy models have emerged.[14] Cycles of privatization and nationalization, for instance, can reflect political cycles and different economic interests of alternative political coalitions. Also, decisions to nationalize and privatize may reflect pure public finance considerations; under certain circumstances the privatization of state enterprises may be the cheapest source of government revenue; see Rosa (1993; 1997).[15]

---

[13] To this Hansen (1976, p. 152) adds the following footnote: 'I recall once having seen an internal OECD document where France and Germany were called 'overseas countries'!" For recent examples of divergent models in development policy, see Rodrik (1996).

[14] Fratianni and Pattison (1976) are of two minds as to why the OECD peddled British Keynesianism rather than Brunner-Meltzer monetarism. On the one hand, they suggest that the OECD leadership was genuinely committed to the Keynesian view, but, on the other hand, they hint at falsification of preferences, cf. Kuran (1995), or — more accurately — falsification of policy models. The latter conclusion is derived from analysis which assumes that the internal policy preference function for the OECD emphasizes self-preservation. In particular, the authors find that the OECD is inclined toward eclecticism and avoids falsifiable hypotheses, which they interpret as a strategy of self-preservation; see Fratianni and Pattison (1976, pp. 122–124). Therefore, a switch by the OECD to a new regime of policy recommendations may simply reflect an update of a strategy for self-preservation in response to changes in the political environment of the organization.

[15] Rosa (1993) tests a public finance model of nationalization and privatization on data from nine West European countries and finds some statistical support for his thesis.

Explanations of structural changes which rely on the financial circumstances of the state or changing political equilibria do not give experts much scope to influence the fundamental thrust of policy. But it is unreasonable to claim that people's ideas about the nature of social and economic systems are stationary and that the median policy model does not move.[16] Witt (1992, p. 121) is right when he states that in the social process of creating and shaping knowledge "the normative political economist has to play a role, among many other voices and influences, and it is probably a role similar to that of prophets, preachers, and propagandists in earlier times." If the median policy model does move, we must ask what factors account for such volatility. Below I discuss how social dynamics affect the popularity of policy models.

Cognitive science and psychology have studied extensively how people model social issues, and important work has been undertaken in applied fields, especially in political psychology.[17] For our purpose it is enough to state the general finding that agents respond to scarce resources — scarce information, knowledge, brain power, and time — by economizing and using shortcuts (schematic models) when they model social systems. Empirical evidence of simple schematic policy models is found, for instance, in DeNardo's (1995) fascinating empirical study of how Americans modeled deterrence in the nuclear age. The study looks for qualitative differences in models and beliefs of everyday people (novices), and experts (corporate managers in the aerospace and the defense industry, professional defense analysts, senior government officials, and academic specialists). Although he detects differences between novices and experts — the latter group, for instance, thinks more abstractly and knows more about weapons' systems — DeNardo (1995, p. 240) concludes that: "Experts rely on the same heuristic rules of thumb that novices use, and

---

[16] In the years before the Second World War, a faction of the British Conservative Party, with which Harold Macmillan (later prime minister) was associated, competed with, and sometimes outdid, the Labor Party in demands for nationalization and central control of the economy; see Macmillan (1938), Singleton (1995) and Eggertsson (1997b.)

[17] DeNardo (1995) provides an excellent recent survey of the cognitive and psychological approach to social policy models, particularly of applications in political psychology. DeNardo recognizes that formal theorists are uncomfortable with the incompleteness of the models or belief systems that this literature reveals. Converse's (1964) study of belief systems in mass publics is a seminal contribution, which for decades has framed the debate about political belief systems. Converse emphasizes frequent lack of systematic thinking, but recent theorists have brought some order to his world by introducing schematic models which, according to DeNardo (1995, p. 81), "give local coherence to people's thinking without necessarily providing a globally integrated world view. ... Schemas are mental prototypes, images, metaphors, 'scripts', or categories that provide a frame of reference against which experience is compared and interpreted". An interesting application of schema theory is found in Larson (1985).

they combine them in the same intuitive, understandardized, unprogrammed way."

Agents, who use simple schematic policy models in a world of bewildering social complexity, do not properly understand institutional arrangements or how to interpret economic outcomes. When social systems repeatedly, or on a large scale, produce unexpected disagreeable results, which the agents cannot interpret in terms of their models, they often respond (not unlike scientists) by seeking alternative solutions. Alexander Gerschenkron's (1962) grand theme, the relative backwardness hypothesis, partly emphasizes the introduction of powerful ideologies to justify industrialization, which implies rejection of previous policy models. The Great Depression, the collapse of the Soviet system, economic success in Southeast Asia, economic collapse in Africa are indicators that signaled revisions of policy models and created demand for expert advice on institutional reforms.

When knowledge is scarce, those who launch institutional regimes usually do not anticipate the nature and complexity of all the dimensions that require control or the economic and political reactions and interactions that new measures unleash. In terms of policy preference functions, the dynamic path of regimes can be either increasingly satisfactory or increasingly unsatisfactory; see Krueger (1994). Sometimes the sequence of interactions involves only a specific policy authority and a subset of economic agents. Such is the case in Cheung's (1975, 1976) analysis of how agents on the Hong Kong housing market discovered and invented new margins of evasion, which the authorities then proceeded to close until learning-by-doing had established a relatively satisfactory regime.

In general, the literature on regulation provides ample empirical examples of dynamic paths, increasingly costly negative-sum games, and policy reversals. Interesting cases at the micro level include Victor's (1994) study of the airline industry in the United States, Krueger's (1990) account of institutional dynamics in the US sugar program, and Higg's (1982) analysis of technical regress in the salmon industry of the US Pacific Northwest. At the macro level, Krueger (1978) and Bhagwati (1978) provide pioneering analyses of the institutional dynamics of foreign trade regimes, and Lindbeck's (1994, 1995) analysis of the cumulative path of the Swedish welfare regime combines macro and micro perspectives, and considers complex revisions of private policy models by various types of players.

Using the Degrees of Freedom

I have argued that scarce knowledge and incomplete policy models create a role for independent experts when systems crash. Uncertain dynamics of institutional regimes, moreover, give rise to demand for expert advice on incremental reforms. What type of advice, then, would new institutionalists give, if they were asked? I conclude by briefly outlining three theoretical issues in the literature that have obvious implications for institutional policy. These issues are: techniques for reducing political risk; prescriptions for effective vertical distribution of control; and formulas for initiating paths of micro-level cooperation.

Techniques for reducing political risk. Political risk arises when governments are unable to make credible commitment to particular policies of reforms and fail to form necessary coalitions of supporters for introducing and sustaining the measures. The theory of institutional reforms faces a major challenge in trying to improve our knowledge of mechanisms for reducing political risk. One approach to the problem is to study successful commitment mechanisms in history. Recent studies of federalist competition among government units, e.g. Weingast (1993, 1995) and V. Ostrom (1987), or corporatist organization of private interests in their financial relations with the state, e.g. Root (1989) aim in the right direction.

Prescription for effective vertical distribution of control. Emphasis in the economics of institutions on problems of enforcement, incomplete policy models, and incremental refinement of institutional regimes through learning-by-doing suggests that the vertical distribution of control within a social hierarchy is a critical issue in designing efficient institutions; see Williamson (1985). Although high-level authorities may have an advantage in coordination, their information problems generally tend to be relatively difficult. The new institutionalism already offers some insight into the nature of effective governance structures. Theoretical and empirical studies by E. Ostrom (1990) and Ostrom *et al.* (1994) on the organization of common-pool resources illustrate my point. Ostrom and colleagues show the conditions which are necessary for control by local users to be effective, and how local groups often have a relative advantage in monitoring and fine-tuning governance systems and in protecting resources against dissipation.

Formulas for initiating paths of increasing micro-level cooperation. There is considerable agreement among the new institutionalists that norms supportive of cooperation are required for facilitating extensive impersonal exchange, but little is known of how informal norms and personal ethics complement formal laws and regulations. Even less is known of how to generate appropriate norm-driven behavior. A case in point is the problem of understanding what factors give Japanese industrial organization its distinctive and desirable operational character, and how these features could be imported to the West. Milgrom and Roberts (1994), for instance, find that the Japanese system consists of a set of factors, which cannot be separated, if the system is to work properly. In governments' attempts to create microfoundations for growth, perhaps ideologies, ethnic networks or deep social beliefs had best be left alone, and formal rules be designed to take advantage of and draw support from existing norms and beliefs. The new institutionalists could contribute to better understanding of interactions between government instruments and various exogenous social variables. This is precisely what Cooter (1996) has done in a study which shows how efficient new laws can be achieved by grounding them on existing norms or, in effect, by publicly enforcing (desirable) norms.

References

Alchian, A. A.: *Economic Forces at Work*. Liberty Press, Indianapolis, 1977.

Alesina, A.: Elections, party structure, and the economy. In J. S. Banks and E. A. Hanushek (eds.), *Modern Political Economy. Old Topics, New Directions*. Cambridge University Press, Cambridge, 145–170, 1995.

Alesina, A.: Macroeconomics and politics. In S. Fischer (ed.), *NBER Macroeconomic Annual*, MIT Press, Cambridge, MA, 13–52, 1988.

Almond, G. A.: The return to the state. *American Political Science Review 82*; reprinted in G. A. Almond: *A Discipline Divided. Schools and Sects in Political Science*, Sage, Newbury Park, CA, 189–218, 1990.

Alt, J. E. and Shepsle, K. A. (eds.): *Perspectives on Positive Political Economy*. Cambridge University Press, Cambridge, 1990.

Arrow, K. J.: Statistics and economic policy. *Econometrica 25*, 523–531, 1956; reprinted in K. J. Arrow: *Collected Papers 4: The Economics of Information*. Harvard University Press, Cambridge, MA, 1984.

Banks, J. S. and Hanushek, E. A.: *Modern Political Economy. Old Topics, New Directions*. Cambridge University Press, Cambridge, 1995.

Barzel, Y.: *Economic Analysis of Property Rights*. Cambridge University Press, Cambridge, 1989.

Bates, R.: *Markets and States in Tropical Africa*. University of California Press, Berkeley, 1981.

Bates, R.: Macropolitical economy in the field of development. In J. Alt and K. Shepsle (eds.): *Perspectives on Positive Political Economy*, 31–54, 1990.

Bawn, K.: Constructing "US": Coalition politics as the foundation of ideology, identity and empathy. WP, Department of Political Science, University of California, Los Angeles, 1996.

Becker, G. S.: A theory of competition among pressure groups for political influence. *Quarterly Journal of Economics 98*, 371–400, 1983.

Bhagwati, J. D.: *Foreign Trade Regimes and Economic Development: Anatomy and Consequences of Exchange Control Regimes*. Ballinger, Cambridge, 1978.

Buchanan, J. M.: The domain of constitutional economics. *Constitutional Political Economy 1*, 1–18, 1990.

Buchanan, J. M. *et al*. (eds). *Toward a Theory of the Rent Seeking Society*. Texas A&M University, College Station, 1980.

Calvert, R. L.: The rational choice theory of social institutions. Coordination, cooperation, and communication. In J. S. Banks and E. A. Hanushek (eds.), *Modern Political Economy. Old Topics, New Directions.* Cambridge University Press, Cambridge, 1995a.

Calvert, R. L.: Rational factors, equilibrium, and social institutions. In J. Knight and I. Sened (eds.), *Explaining Social Institutions*, University of Michigan Press, Ann Arbor, 1995b.

Cheung, S. N. S.: Roofs or stars: The stated intents and actual effects of rent ordinance. *Economic Inquiry 13*, 1–21, 1975.

Cheung, S. N.S.: Rent control and housing reconstruction: The postwar experience of prewar premises in Hong Kong. *Journal of Law and Economics 17*, 27-53, 1976.

Chung, H.: Did policy makers really believe in the Phillips curve? An econometric test. Ph.D. dissertation, University of Minnesota, 1990.

Coase, R. H.: The nature of the firm. *Economica 4*, 386–405, 1937.

Converse, P. E.: The nature of belief systems in mass publics. In D. Apter (ed.), *Ideology and Discontent*. Free Press, New York, 1964.

Cooter, R. D.: Decentralized law for a complex economy: The structural approach to adjudicating the new law merchant. *University of Pennsylvania Law Review 144*, 1643–1696, 1996.

Cooter, R. D. and Ulen, Thomas. *Law and Economics*, 2nd ed. Addison-Wesley, New York, 1997.

Demsetz, H.: *The Organization of Economic Activity* (2 vols.) Basil Blackwell, Oxford, 1988.

DeNardo, J.: *The Amateur Strategist. Intuitive Deterrence Theories and the Politics of the Nuclear Arms Race*. Cambridge University Press, Cambridge, 1995.

Denzau, A. T. and North, D. C.: Shared mental models: Ideologies and institutions. *Kyklos 47*, 3–31, 1994.

Dewatriport, M. and Roland, G.: The design of reform packages under uncertainty. *American Economic Review 85*, 1207–1223, 1995

Dixit, A. K.: *The Making of Economic Policy. A Transaction-Cost Politics*. The MIT Press, Cambridge, 1996.

Eggertsson, T.: The old theory of economic policy and the new institutionalism. *World Development 18*: 1187–204, 1997a.

Eggertsson, T.: When the state changes its mind. Discontinuity in government control of economic activity. In H. Giersch (ed.), *Privatization at the Turn of the Century*. Springer, Berlin, 1997b.

Fernandez, R. and Rorik, D.: Resistance to reform. *American Economic Review 91*: 1146-55, 1991.

Fratianni, M., and Pattison, J. C. The economics of the OECD. In K. Brunner and A. Meltzer (eds.), *Institutions, Policies and Economic Performance*. North-Holland, Amsterdam, 75–140, 1976.

Furubotn, E. G. and Pejovich, S.: Property rights and economic theory: A survey of recent literature. *Journal of Economic Literature 10*, December: 1137–1162, 1972.

Gerschenkron, Alexander: *Economic Backwardness in Historical Perspective*. Harvard University Press, Cambridge, MA, 1962.

Gifford, A.: A constitutional interpretation of the firm. *Public Choice 68*, 91–106, 1991.

Greif, A.: Contract enforceability and economic institutions in early trade: The Maghribi traders' coalition. *American Economic Review 83*, 833–850, 1993.

Greif, A.. Cultural beliefs and the organization of society: A historical and theoretical reflection on collectivist and individualist societies. *Journal of Political Economy 102*, 912–950, 1994.

Greif, A.: Institutional structure and economic development: Economic history and the new institutionalism. WP, Department of Economics, Stanford University, 1995.

Hansen, B.: The economics of the OECD: A comment. In K. Brunner and A. H. Meltzer (eds.), *Institutions, Policies and Economic Performance*. North-Holland, Amsterdam, 141–153, 1976.

Hechter, M., Opp, K.-D. and Wippler, R.: *Social Institutions: Their Emergence, Maintenance, and Effects*. Aldine de Gruyter, New York, 1990.

Higgs, R.: Legally induced technical regress in the Washington state salmon fishery. *Research in Law and Economics 7*, 55–86, 1982; reprinted in L. Alston, T. Eggertsson and D. C. North (eds.), *Empirical Studies in Institutional Change*, Cambridge University Press, Cambridge, 1996.

Hinich, M. and Munger, M.: A spatial theory of ideology. *Journal of Theoretical Politics 4*, 5–30, 1992.

Johansen, L.: *Lectures on Macroeconomic Planning. I. General Aspects*. North-Holland, Amsterdam, 1977.

Johansen, L.: Establishing preference functions for macroeconomic decision models. Some observations on Ragnar Frisch's contributions. *European Economic Review 5*, 1974; reprinted in F. Førsund (ed.), *Collected Works of Leif Johansen, II*, North-Holland, Amsterdam, 541–566, 1987.

Johansen, L.: The report of the Committee of Policy Optimization — UK. *Journal of Economic Dynamics and Control 1*, 1979; reprinted in F. R. Førsund (ed.), *Collected Works of Leif Johansen II*, North-Holland, Amsterdam, 567–576, 1987.

Kieser, L. and Ostrom, E.: The three worlds of action: A meta-theoretical synthesis of institutional approaches. In E. Ostrom (ed.), *Strategies of Political Inquiry*, Sage Publications, Beverly Hills, 1982.

Kiwit, D.: Path-dependence in technological and institutional change — Some criticisms and suggestions. WP, Max Planck Institute, Jena, 1995.

Kreps, D.: Corporate culture and economic theory. In J. Alt and K. Shepsle (eds.), *Perspectives on Positive Political Theory*, Cambridge University Press, Cambridge, 1990.

Krueger, A. O.: *Foreign Trade Regimes and Economic Development: Liberalization Attempts and Consequences*. Ballinger, Cambridge, 1978.

Krueger, A. O.: The political economy of controls: American sugar. In M. Scott and D. Lal (eds.), *Public Policy and Development: Essays in Honour of Ian Little*, Oxford University Press, Oxford, 1990.

Krueger, A. O.: *Political Economy of Policy Reform in Developing Countries*. MIT Press, Cambridge, MA, 1994.

Kuran, T.: *Private Truths, Public Lies. The Social Consequences of Preference Falsification*. Harvard University Press, Cambridge, MA, 1995.

Landa, J. T.: *Trust, Ethnicity, and Identity: Beyond the New Institutional Economics of Ethnic Trading Networks, Contract Law, and Gift-Exchange*. University of Michigan Press, Ann Arbor, 1994.

Larson, D. W.: *Origins of Containment: A Psychological Explanation*. Princeton University Press, Princeton, 1985.

Libecap, G. D.: *Contracting for Property Rights*. Cambridge University Press, Cambridge, 1989.

Lindbeck, A.: Overshooting, reform and retreat of the welfare state. *De Economist 142*, 1–19, 1994.

Lindbeck, A.: Welfare state disincentives with endogenous habits and norms. *Scandinavian Journal of Economics 97*, 477–494, 1995.

Lucas, R. E., Jr.: Econometric policy evaluation: A critique. In Karl Brunner and Allen H. Meltzer (eds.). *The Phillips Curve and Labor Markets*, North-Holland, Amsterdam, 1976.

Lucas, R. E., Jr.: Adaptive behavior and economic theory. *Journal of Business 59*, 401–426, 1986.

Lucas, R. E., Jr.: Supply-side economics: An analytical review. *Oxford Economic Papers 42*, 293–316, 1990.

Macmillan H.: *The Middle Way: A Study in the Problem of Economic and Social Progress in a Free and Democratic Society.* Macmillan, London, 1938.

McKinnon, R.: *The Order of Economic Liberalization.* Johns Hopkins University Press, Baltimore, 1991.

Milgrom, P. and Roberts, J.: *Economics, Organization and Management.* Prentice Hall, Englewood Cliffs, 1992.

Milgrom, P. and Roberts, J.: Complementarities and systems: Understanding Japanese economic organization. *Estudios Económicos 9*, 3–41, 1994.

Mueller, D. C.: *Public Choice II.* Cambridge University Press, Cambridge, 1989.

North, D. C.: *Institutions, Institutional Change, and Economic Performance.* Cambridge University Press, Cambridge, 1990a.

North, D. C.: A transaction cost theory of politics. *Journal of Theoretical Politics 2*, 355–367, 1990b.

North, D. C.: Economic performance through time. *American Economic Review 84*, 359–368, 1994.

North, D. C. and Weingast, B. R.: Constitutions and commitment: The evolution of institutions governing public choice in seventeenth-century England. *Journal of Economic History 49*, 803–832, 1989. Reprinted in L. J. Alston, T. Eggertsson and D. C. North (eds.), *Empirical Studies in Institutional Change*, Cambridge University Press, Cambridge, 1996.

Olson, M.: The *Logic of Collective Action.* Harvard University Press, Cambridge, MA, 1965.

Olson, M.: *The Rise and Decline of Nations: Economic Growth, Stagflation, and Social Rigidities.* Yale University Press, New Haven, 1982.

Ostrom, E.: An agenda for the study of institutions. *Public Choice 48*, 3–25, 1986.

Ostrom, E.: *Governing the Commons: The Evolution of Institutions for Collective Action.* Cambridge University Press, Cambridge, 1990.

Ostrom, E.: Gardner, R. and J. Walker: *Rules Games, and Common Pool Resources.* University of Michigan Press, Ann Arbor, 1994.

Ostrom, V. *The Theory of a Compound Republic.* University of Nebraska Press, Lincoln, 1987.

Posner, R. A.: *Economic Analysis of Law*, 4nd ed. Little Brown, Boston, 1992.

Putnam, R. D.: *Making Democracy Work.* Princeton University Press, Princeton, 1994.

Rodrik, D.: Understanding economic policy reform. *Journal of Economic Literature 34*, 9–41, 1996.

Root, H.: Tying the king's hands: Credible commitments and royal fiscal policy during the old regime. *Rationality and Society 1*, 240–258, 1989.

Rosa, J.-J.: Nationalization, privatization, and the allocation of financial property rights. *Public Choice 75*, 317–337, 1993.

Rosa, J.-J.: Public choice aspects of privatization policies: Driving forces and obstacles. In H. Giersch (ed.), *Privatization at the Turn of the Century*, Springer, Berlin, 1997.

Sargent, T. J.: *Bounded Rationality Macroeconomics.* Oxford University Press, Oxford, 1993.

Schiavo-Campo, S. (ed.): *Institutional Change and the Public Sector in Eastern Europe and the Former Soviet Union.* World Bank, Washington, DC, 1994.

Schotter, A.: *The Economic Theory of Social Institutions.* Cambridge University Press, Cambridge, 1981.

Siegmund, U.: Are there nationalization–privatization cycles? A theoretical survey and first empirical evidence. WP 757. Institute of Economics, Kiel, 1996.

Sims, C. A.: Projecting policy effects with statistical models. *Revista de Analisis Economico 3*,

3–20, 1988.

Singleton, J.: Labour, the conservatives and nationalization. In R. Millward, and J. Singleton (eds.), *The Political Economy of Nationalization in Britain 1920–1950,* Cambridge University Press, Cambridge, 1995.

Stigler, G. J.: The economic theory of regulation. *Bell Journal of Economics and Management Science* 2, 3–21, 1971.

Sugden, R.: Spontaneous order. *Journal of Economic Perspectives 3,* 85–97, 1989.

Tinbergen, J.: The theory of the optimum regime. In his *Selected Papers,* North-Holland, Amsterdam, 1959.

Tinbergen, J.: *On the Theory of Economic Policy.* North-Holland, Amsterdam, 1952.

Tollison, R. D.: Rent seeking: A survey. *Kyklos 35,* 575–602, 1982.

Vietor, R. H. K.: Contrived competition: Economic regulation and deregulation, 1920s–1980s. *Business History 36,* 1–32, 1994.

Voigt, S.: Positive constitutional economics — A survey. *Public Choice 90,* 11–53, 1997.

Weingast, B. R.: Constitutions as governance structures: The political foundations of secure markets. *Journal of Institutional and Theoretical Economics 149,* 286–311, 1993.

Weingast, B. R.: The political impediment to economic reform: Political risk and enduring gridlock. WP, Hoover Institution, Stanford University, 1994.

Weingast, B. R.: The economic role of political institutions: Market preserving federalism. *Journal of Law, Economics and Organization 7:* 1–31, 1995a.

Weingast, B. R.: A rational choice perspective on the role of ideas: Shared belief systems and state sovereignty in international cooperation. *Politics and Society 23,* 449–464, 1995b.

Werin, L. and Wijkander, H. (eds.): *Contract Economics.* Basil Blackwell, Oxford, 1992.

Williamson, O. S. *The Economic Institutions of Capitalism. Firms, Markets, Relational Contracting.* Free Press, Boston, 1985.

Witt, U.: The endogenous public choice theorist. *Public Choice 73,* 117–129, 1992.

Scand. J. Economics 100(1), 359–363, 1998

Comment on T. Eggertsson, "Limits to Institutional Reforms"

Avner Ben-Ner

University of Minnesota, Minneapolis, MN 55455, USA

Louis Putterman

Brown University, Providence, RI 02912, USA

Values, Institutions and Economics

Much of economics can be seen as an elaboration of Adam Smith's celebrated remark that "[i]t is not from the benevolence of the butcher, the brewer, or the baker that we expect our dinner, but from their regard to their own interest." It is sometimes suggested, however, that self-interest can be relied upon to generate want-satisfying economic activity only if a proper institutional environment is in place, and that such an environment cannot itself rest only on self-interest in its narrowest sense. Without respect for others' rights and for law and property, without some prospect of integrity and trust in exchange relations, the costs of many economic transactions would become prohibitive.

The relationship between the economic and the moral orders of society remains remarkably underexplored, however, with economists generally preferring either to assume that moral considerations affect behavior only in rare instances,[1] or to leave its investigation to other disciplines. Even institutional economics, a field that one might expect to show an interest in such issues, appears by and large to overlook them, if Eggertsson's survey article is any guide. By convention, economists take preferences as given, and ask what economic institutions will maximize social well-being, defined as a function of those preferences. The possibility that institutions, including markets, firms, families, and schools, are as much a basis of preference formation as they are a reaction to given preferences, is left out of most accounts.[2] To the extent that preferences might themselves be objects of

---

[1] Attempts to model rule obedience as strictly self-interested responses to incentives — for instance, investments in reputation, desire to avoid penalties, etc. — can indeed go a long way, and their importance is by no means denied by us. We simply come down on the side that they are far from being the whole story.

[2] This is not to say that there have not been some notable exceptions, such as Knight (1922). Unfortunately, space limitations prevent us from providing extensive citations here; see, however, our 1998 paper and edited volume.

choice — we would prefer people to be trustworthy rather than deceitful, for example — and that institutions shape preferences, we could as easily turn the neoclassical procedure around and ask: what is the optimal set of institutions from the standpoint of the preferences that it generates?

It can be argued that this and related questions are not only important, but that they deserve a major place on the agenda of research in economics. However, economists cannot address them without certain modifications to their prevailing assumptions about human nature.[3] In particular, the abstraction of *homo economicus* assumes away any possibility for social preferences, since it posits objectives defined over own consumption and leisure only. Confronted with the fact that human beings invest considerable resources into attempts to "mold character" and "shape the values" of their offspring, the standard approach is at an impasse: either it must conclude that people are not after all rational (for they squander resources in a futile attempt to change hopelessly selfish individualists) or it must concede that they are not after all exclusively selfish (for they can, unlike *homo economicus*, be made responsive to moral signals). Only when rationality and self-interest are broadened to make room for preferences extended over domains of social process and the well-being of others can the strengths of the economic approach be expanded to a domain of values.

Economists often resist an extended conception of preferences because exploring what can be explained on the basis of rationality and self-interest has been at the core of the neoclassical research program, and because opening the preference function up to moral concerns or sympathies strikes many as *ad hoc* and antithetical to intellectual rigor. From another standpoint, however, it is the *homo economicus* assumption that is *ad hoc*. One might expect, that is, that a science that begins its analysis with a depiction of human preferences would begin with human beings as they have emerged from organic evolution. But extant models of evolution provide no grounds for predicting exclusively self-interested individuals. Evolution, after all, must have selected in us those propensities that are favorable to the survival of our genetic material. Since the raw material on which evolution worked in the case of our species was that of an animal whose young were dependent upon older individuals over the course of a lengthy maturation process, and for which banding and social cohesion were requisites of survival through tens of thousands of formative generations, strict individualism would almost certainly have been selected against. Not only is there abundant empirical evidence for the maternal

---

[3] See Aaron (1994), who argues that critical social issues such as crime and drug abuse have important economic facets, yet cannot be understood by economists without a willingness to look at values.

and broader kin altruism that evolutionary theorists predict on the basis of inclusive fitness theory, but the evidence now emerging suggests that people are predisposed to offer cooperation or reciprocity to those inter-acting likewise with them in an ongoing manner, and that they react on often "irrational" punitive impulses, linked to deep-seated emotions, when they feel their trust to have been betrayed.[4]

An economics of preference formation could begin with the biological predispositions shaped by selection pressures and then ask how the incentives provided by specific human environments mold those predispositions into realized preferences. In the language of biology, the innate predispositions belong to the human *genotype*, but environment and genes together determine preferences, which belong to the *phenotype*. We are innately predisposed, for instance, to care deeply about how we are perceived by others. But what specific preferences this gives rise to — e.g., *whose* judgments matter most to us, and *by what criteria* we expect them to judge us — depend on the structure of our social interactions and on the expectations and standards that have been inculcated in those others by the environments that have impacted on them. The relevant standards, or in other words the values that are fostered by a given culture or subculture, must presumably bear some congruence with universal genetic predispositions (such as our concerns with our personal survival and our capacities for empathy). But these values would also have passed tests imposed by *social* evolutionary pressures, as well, perhaps, as the test of reflection; see Sen (1998).[5]

Incentives geared to self-interest, and those that appeal to our senses of fairness, sympathy, entitlement, and so forth, interact in complex ways. Far from imagining a selfish nature and a moral nature operating in separate spheres and mainly at cross-purposes, we find it noteworthy that appeals to self-interest lie at the heart of much value-oriented socialization. While reasoning and appeals to fairness are also used, in many cultures parents encourage children to emulate favored moral models in part by using rewards or penalties based upon the children's interests, whether for affection and approval, or for toys and favorite activities. Successful organizations are also notable for reinforcing cooperative and loyal behavior by rewarding it both with social status and esteem and with long-run material pay-offs. Yet, while value-driven behaviors by definition entail sacrifice of *some* short-run satisfactions, in those cases in which these are offset by

---

[4] Again, details and references must be suppressed. For a brief introductory discussion of the relevant literature, see our 1997 paper.

[5] The large human brain, unique among animals, provides the capacity to contemplate and assess the results of genetic and social evolution, and even to conceive of purposeful interventions to affect these values.

long-run benefits in ways that can be relied upon, then not only may the individual become capable of foregoing the satisfactions in question out of a longer-term but selfish calculus; she may also develop a taste for moral behavior such that the requisite choices become their own rewards. This illustrates how rewards to self-interest can promote the formation and add to the strength of other- and process-regarding preferences.

Elsewhere, we have sketched out examples to illustrate how a cognizance of the influences of institutions on value formation and an understanding of the effects of values on institutional performance may play constructive roles in economic analysis; see Ben-Ner and Putterman (1998). We discuss the dual role of families as self-interested economic and emotional alliances of individuals and as investors in forms of socialization that can generate positive externalities to society at large. With economic and other incentives towards family continuity and cohesion waning, policy-makers might weigh carefully any tax and social insurance measures that erode those incentives further, unless substitute mechanisms for rearing healthy citizens can be found. In the workplace, loyalty and team work may be engendered by organizations willing to meet the moral expectations of employees, while a culture of self-seeking and confrontation may cause employees to withhold all effort not promptly rewarded, necessitating increased supervision and putting modes of production requiring joint problem-solving and employee initiative out of an organization's reach. In the realm of social insurance, rich societies might wish to provide a "safety net" to members falling into economic hardship, but the generosity of such programs may come into question as increasing numbers find it acceptable to abuse proffered benefits, a phenomenon that may snowball as the belief that "everybody does it" becomes widespread. A better understanding of the mechanisms giving rise to a sense of shame that deters program abuse could play a major role in making adequate social insurance programs sustainable.[6] Such understudied examples only begin to hint at the role that a fuller understanding of the formation of values, of the role of economic and other institutions in that process, and of the impacts of the extant value stock on institutional performance, might play in a future economics of institutions.

References

Aaron, H.: Public policy, values, and consciousness. *Journal of Economic Perspectives 8*, 3–21, 1994.

---

[6] As before, this is not to assert the absence of notable exceptions, such as Akerlof's (1982) well-known work on 'gift exchange' and work by Lindbeck (1995) and others on norms and welfare states.

Akerlof, G.: Labor contracts as partial gift exchange. *Quarterly Journal of Economics 97*, 43–69, 1982.

Ben-Ner, A. and Putterman, L.: *Homo economicus* meets "the moral animal": On some implications of evolutionary psychology. Mimeo, University of Minnesota, 1997.

Ben-Ner, A. and Putterman, L.: Values and institutions in economic analysis. In A. Ben-Ner and L. Putterman (eds.), *Economics, Values and Organization*, Cambridge University Press, New York, 1998.

Knight, F. H.: The ethics of competition. *Quarterly Journal of Economics 36*, 454–81, 1922.

Lindbeck, A.: Hazardous welfare state dynamics. *American Economic Review (Papers and Proceedings) 85*, 9–15, 1995.

Sen, A. K.: Foreword. In A. Ben-Ner and L. Putterman (eds.), *Economics, Values and Organization*, Cambridge University Press, New York, 1998.

Scand. J. Economics 100(1), 364–366, 1998

Comment on T. Eggertsson, "Limits to Institutional Reforms"

Tone Ognedal

University of Oslo, N-0317 Oslo, Norway

Institutional Reforms and Distributional Concerns

Eggertsson provides an interesting overview of the theory of institutional policy. In particular, he emphasizes how social change and institutional reforms become constrained when policies are endogenous. Referring to the works of Fernandez and Rodrik (1991) and Olson (1965 and 1982), Eggertsson concludes that lack of a policy to compensate those who lose from a reform may explain failures to implement reforms even though a majority would gain. This may be so in some cases. However, reforms are also blocked when they can be implemented as Pareto improvements and the policy to do so is both feasible and known. If Eggertsson's view is right, one should think that access to more flexible redistribution schemes would facilitate reforms. I will argue that it is not lack of feasible compensation schemes that is the most serious obstacle to reform efforts. On the contrary, when the gains from a reform can be redistributed in many ways, the fight between different groups to obtain the distribution most favourable to them can easily block the reform.

A simple example can illustrate how the conflict over distribution of the gains from a reform can block reforms even though losers can be compensated. A parliament discusses a reform, with a net gain normalized to 1. Each of the three parties, A, B and C, has one-third of the votes and wants to maximize the income of their voters. All decisions are made by majority rule. The parties can form coalitions at no costs. Let us first assume that (i) any redistribution of the gain from the reform is admissible and costless, and that (ii) any representative has the right to submit a proposal for how to distribute the gains from the reform. With assumption (i) it is always possible to propose an implementation of the reform that makes everybody better off. However, no majority of two parties will be satisfied with less than what they can obtain by forming a coalition which, with the assumptions above, is the entire gain. There is obviously no equilibrium distribution in this so-called "voting-over-a-dollar" game, since it is impossible to give the entire gain to all majority coalitions. For any distribution proposed, there is always a majority that can do better by submitting an alternative proposal. Since each proposal is blocked by a counterproposal, no agreement is reached on implementing the reform. It is not lack of available compensation policies that limits reforms in this example, but the possibility of any majority to costlessly propose the implementation it prefers.

To prevent perpetual disputes over any reform or other decision that has distributional consequences, it may be necessary to restrict the right to make proposals or the type of redistributions that can be proposed. Delegation of power is one such restriction. For some decisions, the agenda setter may be given the exclusive right to make proposals, and the other representatives can only accept or reject. Persson, Roland and Tabellini (1997) analyse public finance decisions in legislatures with this decision structure. In other cases, counterproposals are possible but the type of feasible proposals is constrained. Legislatures often delegate the responsibility to work out the full reform proposal to an agenda setter, for example the government. The benefit of the agenda setter is access to the resources and expertise of the ministries, which facilitates finding the most efficient way to obtain a certain distribution of the gain from the reform. Since those who make counterproposals do not have access to the resources of the government, they may easily end up with inferior suggestions for redistributions. Hence, a majority of the representatives can suggest a distribution that gives them a larger share of the gains than the government reform proposal, but with a lower total gain. Below, I demonstrate how constraints on the feasible counterproposals may make it possible to reach an agreement on the reform.

Let us assume that while the government can redistribute the gain from a reform at no costs, redistributions proposed by the representatives reduce the total gain to be shared. The outcome of a reform with no redistribution is the vector $r = (r_A, r_B, r_C)$, determined by the endowments of the different groups. Let R_S denote the total gain to a majority S under a reform with no redistribution, i.e., $R_{AB} = r_A + r_B$ and so on. If any coalition can distribute income among its members at no costs, no majority S will accept a lower total income than R_S, since that is what they can get by forming a coalition and propose r. Since any redistribution of the gains from the reform will leave some majority with less than R_S, it follows that such proposals would be blocked by a counterproposal from the majority who prefers r. Hence, either there will be a reform with no redistribution, or no reform at all. If any majority can obtain a higher total income than R_S by submitting its own counterproposal, it will block the reform proposal r from the government. This counterproposal will in turn be blocked by a proposal from the majority who prefers r. Hence, the reform will only be accepted if no majority can obtain more than R_S.

What limits reforms in this example is the possibility of some majority coalition to obtain more for its members by some redistribution of the gains from the reform than what they are offered in the government proposal. Two implications are immediate. First, holding the reform outcome *r* constant, restrictions on the opportunities to work out efficient counterproposals may facilitate reforms. For example, in the extreme case where the only alternative to accepting the government proposal is to reject it, any reform that leaves no majority with a loss will be accepted. Hence, the democratic ideal of encouraging competition over policy proposals may have to be constrained by the requirement of a workable decision structure. Second, what matters is not whether a majority gains from a reform but whether any majority loses. With the "accept or reject" policy, for example, a reform with a total gain equal to 1 and the distribution $(2, 1, -2)$ will not be implemented even if only C loses. The reason is that a coalition of B and C loses -1 and is therefore better off by voting against the reform. Group C can simply "bribe" B into voting against the reform and still be better off.

If transfers within coalitions are costless, as assumed above, there can never be an agreement to redistribute the gains from the reform. In many cases, transfers within coalitions are costly since they have to be implemented via the same type of redistribution policies as used for redistributions between coalitions. Hence, for every dollar group C transfers to group B to obtain support against the reform, B may receive only a fraction. If this is the case, it can be shown that reforms with redistribution of the gain may be an equilibrium outcome, that is, no majority coalition can propose an alternative that is preferred by all its members; see Ognedal (1997). The reason is that those who would prefer a reform with no redistribution may find it too costly to "bribe" other parties to form a coalition against the government proposal when transfers within coalitions are costly.

To sum up, a legislature may fail to reach an agreement on a reform because it is too easy to propose feasible compensation schemes. Delegating the power to formulate reform proposals and restricting the admissible counterproposals may facilitate reforms, but may also constrain the representatives' possibility of influencing the distributional implications of the reform. Hence, there may be a tradeoff between the limits to reforms and the limits to democratic decision-making.

References

Fernandez, R. and Rodrik, D.: Resistance to reform: Status quo bias in the presence of individual-specific uncertainty. *American Economic Review 81*, 1146-1155, 1991.

Ognedal, T.: Reforms and redistribution. WP, University of Oslo, 1997.

Olson, M.: *The Logic of Collective Action*. Harvard University Press, Cambridge, MA, 1965.

Olson, M.: *The Rise and Decline of Nations: Economic Growth, Stagflation and Social Rigidities*. Yale University Press, New Haven, CT, 1982.

Persson, T., Roland, G. and Tabellini, G.: Towards micropolitical foundations of public finance. WP, University of Stockholm, 1997.

Scand. J. of Economics 100(1), 367–394, 1998

The Political Economy of Fiscal Consolidations

Roberto Perotti*

Columbia University, New York, NY 10027, USA

Abstract

In the context of recent research in political economy, this paper addresses the policy problem of fiscal consolidation in terms of three types of issues: i) the macroeconomic effects of alternative strategies to consolidate; ii) the institutional setups conducive to a consolidation; and iii) the best strategy for implementing a consolidation in order to maximize its political feasibility. One methodological feature of this survey is an emphasis on policy feasibility. One methodological feature of this survey is an emphasis on policy issues in order to bridge the gap between the level of abstraction of politico-economic models of fiscal policy and the issues faced by a policymaker when attempting a fiscal consolidation.

I. Introduction

Most of the recent research in political economy can be summarized as an attempt to explain why the aggregation of preferences of decision-makers often leads to outcomes that are widely regarded as inefficient on purely economic grounds. Foremost among these inefficiencies, many economists would argue, are the spending and deficit patterns of most industrial democracies, especially after the oil shocks. In fact, the need for fiscal consolidation is currently the single most important policy problem faced by policymakers in many, perhaps most, OECD countries.

This paper asks what insights with some policy relevance the recent research has to offer on the issue of budget deficit reductions. If I were a policymaker who is trying to carry out a fiscal consolidation, I believe that, roughly speaking, I would welcome suggestions on three types of issues. First, what are the macroeconomic effects of alternative strategies to consolidate? Second, what institutional setups are more conducive to a consolidation? Third, what is the best strategy for implementing a consolidation in order to maximize its political feasibility? Of these questions, only the last two are politico-economic in nature. But they cannot be given a relevant and realistic answer without also addressing the first question.

The structure of the paper reflects the three policy questions posed above. In the first part, Section II, I review theoretical explanations and the

---

*I thank my discussants, Assar Lindbeck and Michael Wallerstein, and an anonymous referee for comments.

empirical evidence on two key macro aspects of consolidations, which have only recently have been the object of investigation in academic circles: the link between the composition of consolidations and their persistence, and the link between the initial conditions under which consolidations take place and their macroeconomic effects. The postwar experience of OECD countries strongly suggests that consolidations implemented by reducing certain types of expenditures are much more persistent than those achieved by increasing taxes. There also seems to be interesting evidence that, when a consolidation is carried out in situations of fiscal stress (for example, a high debt/GDP ratio or large deficit), it might not have the recessionary effects posited by many standard macroeconomic theories. I argue that these two empirical regularities, if confirmed, are of primary importance for our understanding of the political economy of fiscal consolidations.

In the second part, Sections III to VI, I survey the theory and evidence on the link between the institutional setup and the fiscal outcome, in particular the ability of a government to carry out a fiscal consolidation. The notion of institutional setup can be interpreted in different ways: it can refer to the bargaining between parties within the government or within the legislature, to the formal process of preparation, discussion, approval and implementation of the budget, or to the bargaining between government and interest groups in society at large. A common element to all these interpretations is the notion that a more fragmented decision-making process — whether voting or bargaining or any other aggregation mechanism — leads to an inability to agree on "efficient' policies and, specifically, to an inability to agree on significant consolidations. It is interesting to note at the outset that this preoccupation with excessive fragmentation has informed much of the recent spate of reforms of the budget process in several countries.

In the third part, Section VII, I investigate the third question posed above, namely the strategy for maximizing the political acceptability of a reform, given the institutional setup where the policymaker operates. While there is a substantial body of (mainly theoretical) research on the optimal speed and comprehensiveness of trade and market reform in the presence of political constraints, I argue that this research is rarely applicable to the case of a fiscal consolidation. Moreover, the analysis of individual episodes of consolidation does not provide much guidance, since for each type of strategy it is easy to cite cases of success and failure. However, the· specific details of these episodes might have been the key to the outcome, and we do not yet know much, on a comparative basis, about these details to reach strong conclusions. Thus, I conclude with a number of open issues that are, in my view, of crucial importance for a deeper understanding of the political economy of fiscal consolidations.

Methodologically, the first feature of this survey is its strong emphasis on policy issues. This emphasis is purely a matter of taste, of course, and therefore I offer no apology for it. I do offer a justification, however trite and routine it might sound: the large discrepancy between the level of abstraction of existing politico-economic models of fiscal policy and the issues typically faced by a policymaker when attempting a fiscal consolidation.

The second methodological feature is an emphasis on the composition of the budget, and it follows directly from the first. Whether we like it or not, it is impossible to conduct a meaningful analysis of policy issues without getting into the details of contemporary budgets. As I argue below, not only the macroeconomic effects, but also the decision-making process of the various budget items differ widely from each other. Hence, a meaningful and relevant investigation of the three questions posed above requires going beyond the budget deficit as the sole indicator of fiscal policy, by considering explicitly the individual components of expenditure and revenues.

These methodological features also differentiate this paper from two other recent surveys on the political economy of fiscal policy, Alesina and Perotti (1995a) and Alesina and Perotti (1996), and from two more general surveys on the political economy of reforms, Rodrik (1996) and Tommasi and Velasco (1996). In addition, the present paper is much more selective than its predecessors, both because I focus on a more specific topic — fiscal consolidations — and because I limit the discussion to relatively few recent papers with strong empirical and policy links.

II. Macroeconomics and Composition of Fiscal Consolidations

As argued in the introduction, a realistic investigation of the political economy of fiscal consolidations should be based on an equally realistic investigation of the effects of alternative consolidation strategies. Other things equal — in particular, holding constant the size of the cut in the deficit — policymakers prefer a consolidation that is long-lasting and minimizes disruption of the economy, since both features contribute to minimize the political costs and maximize political acceptability. A growing body of recent research can help shed light on exactly these two features.

Persistence

First, are there ways of ensuring that a consolidation is long-lasting? Alesina and Perotti (1995b) and (1997a) show that the key is the composition of the adjustment. In a sample of 20 OECD countries between 1960 and 1992, we consider all episodes of large consolidations, defined as reductions in the cyclically adjusted primary deficit by at least 1.5% of GDP. We define these large consolidations as successful if, after three years, the debt/GDP ratio has decreased by at least 5%.

The results are rather striking. Of all the 66 episodes[1] of large consolidations that we consider, the 14 successful ones are those that relied mainly on cuts in expenditure, and specifically in transfers and in the government wage bill. The unsuccessful ones are those that relied mainly on tax increases or cuts in investment. The difference is large: on average, in the successful episodes, expenditure fell by 2.19% of GDP, and only by 0.49% in the unsuccessful ones; moreover, in successful episodes, transfers and the wage bill fell by an average of 0.54% and 0.58% of GDP, respectively, while the corresponding figures in unsuccessful episodes were 0.02% and 0.07% of GDP. On the revenue side, taxes increased by only 0.44% of GDP in successful episodes, and by 1.28% in unsuccessful ones; most of the latter increase was in labor taxes. Importantly, the average size of the reduction in the deficit was similar in the two types of consolidations: 2.74% and 2.18% of GDP, respectively. Thus, the composition, rather than the size, seems to be the key determinant of the success of a consolidation.

These results are remarkably robust, both to changes in the definitions of consolidations (for instance, a multi-year definition rather than a one-year definition), of success (for instance, different cut-off points for the fall in the debt/GDP ratio), of the horizon (for instance, two years rather than three years after the consolidation) and of the methodology used to cyclically adjust the deficit. A broadly similar picture, although with non-trivial disagreements on individual aspects, emerges from Coeur et al. (1996), Heylen (1997), IMF (1996), and OECD (1996a), using different methodologies, samples, and definitions.

The exact interpretation of these results, however, is less clear-cut. Roughly speaking, there are two classes of possible explanations. First, cuts in wage government consumption and in transfers can start a virtuous cycle that makes the economy more competitive. Particularly in highly unionized and very open countries (most of the countries in the sample), a cut in wage government consumption causes a fall in the demand for labor, while a cut in transfers reduces the alternative income available to union members, respectively; both effects reduce the bargaining power of the

---

[1] The specific numbers presented here are taken from Alesina and Perotti (1995b). The numbers in Alesina and Perotti (1997a) are very similar, although obtained with slightly different methodologies.

unions, thus increasing the competitiveness of the tradeable sector.[2] Heylen (1997) also finds that successful consolidations were more likely in countries with low unemployment persistence. In the unsuccessful consolidations, which rely mostly on higher labor and indirect taxes, exactly the opposite occurs, as unions increase their wage demand to shift the burden of higher taxes. Some tentative support for this interpretation is provided in Alesina and Perotti (1997a), where we show that successful consolidations were associated with large reductions in unit labor costs relative to trade partners and in interest rates, while nothing comparable occurred during unsuccessful consolidations. There is similar evidence in OECD (1996a), which emphasizes in particular that successful fiscal consolidations were associated with improvements in the current account.

A second interpretation is that cuts in the wage bill and transfers are politically more costly. Hence, *ex post* they are more persistent exactly because only strong governments can and want to implement them. These two interpretations are not necessarily mutually exclusive: cuts in the wage bill and transfers might be more politically costly exactly because they reduce the bargaining power of organized labor. However, at this stage it is difficult to discriminate between these two explanations.

Whatever its precise interpretation, this evidence on the different persistence of alternative types of consolidations is potentially crucial for an understanding of the political economy of consolidations. Taken at face value, it suggests that policymakers cannot avoid the tradeoff between persistence and popularity: to achieve a lasting consolidation, intervening on what is universally acknowledged to be the easiest budget items — government investment or indirect taxes — will not do; it seems that hard choices cannot be avoided.

Or can they? A second recent development in the macroeconomics of fiscal consolidations suggests that, sometimes, a decisive fiscal consolidation could have large economic and political payoffs.

The Expansionary Effects of Consolidations

The idea that fiscal consolidations are necessarily recessionary was first challenged in an important paper by Giavazzi and Pagano (1990), who showed how the large consolidations in Ireland in 1987–89 and in Denmark in 1983–86 were associated with large consumption and invest-

---

[2] On a sample of 19 OECD countries over the 1960–94 period, Lane and Perotti (1997) show that wage government consumption is strongly negatively associated with profitability and positively with unit labor costs. This relationship is particularly strong when the exchange rate is flexible, because in this case an increase in wage government consumption also causes an appreciation of the exchange rate, in addition to its labor market effects.

ment booms. This outcome contrasts strongly with the prediction of most standard textbook models, and of forecasters at the time.

There are basically two types of explanations for such "expansionary effects of consolidations". First, a consolidation causes a fall in interest rates, which increases the market value of assets held by households. If the ensuing positive wealth effect on consumption is stronger than the negative demand effect of a consolidation, a consumption boom can result. In addition, the fall in interest rates can stimulate investment directly and, indirectly, through an accelerator mechanism. A second, very different explanation is that a consolidation now eliminates the need for a stronger, more disruptive consolidation in the future; hence, the present discounted value of disposable income accruing to the private sector is revised *upward*, which leads to an increase in private consumption. This "expectational" effect of a consolidation has been modeled by Bertola and Drazen (1993) for expenditure-based consolidations and by Blanchard (1990) and Sutherland (1995) for tax-based consolidations. Perotti (1997) develops a framework where both expenditure cuts and tax increases can be associated with higher consumption; however, the mechanism does not rely on large discontinuities in the size and effects of future expected fiscal policy, but only on the existence of distortionary taxation and of a group of liquidity constrained individuals, along with a standard incentive for policymakers to postpone taxation whenever the probability of non-reelection is positive.

Some recent work has been devoted to gathering more systematic empirical evidence on these "expansionary fiscal consolidations", using panels of OECD countries between 1960 and the early 1990's. Giavazzi and Pagano (1996) show that small and less persistent changes in government consumption have the usual, "keynesian" positive association with changes in private consumption; however, large and more persistent changes display the opposite, negative association. Similar, but far weaker results hold for changes in transfers and, with the opposite sign, of taxation.

We do not expect fiscal consolidations *always* to be expansionary. In fact, both classes of explanations of the expansionary effects of consolidations apply best to situations of "fiscal stress", i.e. when the debt/GDP ratio is high or growing fast. The first explanation, because in this case the fall in the interest rate is high and it also affects a large stock of nominal public debt[3]; the second explanation, because only in this case is the threat of a future, more disruptive consolidation likely to be important.

---

[3] Of course, in this case one must assume that Ricardian equivalence does not hold.

In principle it is possible to test for the role of initial conditions directly. In Perotti (1997), I divide the sample into normal periods and periods of fiscal stress, defined as a high rate of accumulation of debt. In addition, because the "expansionary effects of consolidations" work through a wealth effect, with rational forward-looking individuals, consumption should react only to unanticipated changes in fiscal policy and interest rates, not to their anticipated components. I measure the unanticipated component of changes in government consumption and taxes using country-specific VAR's. Indeed, as suggested by the theory, in the usual sample of 20 OECD countries over the period 1960–94, unanticipated changes in government consumption have the usual positive correlation with private consumption during normal times, but a significantly smaller, and often negative, correlation with private consumption in years of fiscal stress. There is much less evidence of an expansionary effect of unanticipated increases in taxation during bad times.

Overall, this evidence suggests that the most persistent type of consolidation, far from being the surest way to electoral defeat as the conventional wisdom holds, might be politically rewarding precisely when it is most needed. Ultimately, this is an empirical question, above which we know very little. Alesina, Perotti and Tavares (1997) show that large consolidations, and those mostly based on public wages and transfers, are not conducive to electoral defeat or a change in government more frequently than average; if anything, the opposite seems to be true.

III. Fragmentation

Even though consolidations may be less disruptive events than conventional wisdom holds, they invariably contain measures that hurt some specific groups. In a democracy, these measures might have to be negotiated with these groups or their representatives; even if they are not, they can be still generate substantial and sometimes disruptive opposition within the country.

Hence the importance of the second question set out in the introduction: whether consolidations are politically easier to carry out under certain institutional arrangements. In view of the evidence on the preceding question, a related question is whether certain institutional arrangements are more amenable to controlling expenditure on the wage bill and on transfers.

One key theme running through the theoretical literature and the policy discussion, and the one around which I organize my discussion, can be termed "fragmentation of fiscal decision-making". Roughly speaking, it is the notion that modern democracies are inherently prone to fiscal indiscipline because each group in a majority can lay claim to some expenditure, but internalizes only partially the costs and distortions of the associated taxes. Hence, expenditures and deficits tend to be larger than those a central planner would set. Moreover, the larger the number of groups that have a say in fiscal decision-making, the less each will internalize the costs of expenditure, and the larger the deviation form the "optimal" path of fiscal policy.

At the risk of some oversimplification, this basic intuition lends itself to three types of interpretations. The first focuses mainly on the informal political process within the government or the parliament, leading to a certain fiscal policy. It emphasizes the process of bargaining and negotiations between parties in the government coalition or in parliament. Hence, this notion can be called "political fragmentation". The second interpretation focuses on the formal process leading to the adoption of a certain budget. It emphasizes the role of individual players participating in the budget process, like the finance minister, the spending minister, and their relative power. Hence, this notion can be called "procedural fragmentation". The third interpretation emphasizes the bargaining on fiscal policy between the government and different interest groups, and the power of the latter to influence the government's decision-making process. This notion is difficult to formalize, nor has it been the object of a systematic empirical investigation. However, even a cursory look at the recent experience of many OECD countries shows that this notion is of foremost importance in the policy debate. For lack of a better name, I call this "social fragmentation". In the next three sections, I review the theory and evidence on each of these three notions of fragmentation.

IV. Political Fragmentation

Theory

Fragmentation across decision-makers. Perhaps the earliest, and certainly the classical, formulation of the notion of political fragmentation is in Weingast, Shepsle and Johnson (1981) (WSJ) and in Shepsle and Weingast (1981). The key intuition is simple. Because of basic constitutional principles, taxation is in general diffuse, while expenditure can be more easily targeted towards specific groups, which can be defined in terms of their social, geographical, occupational, or other characteristics. Hence, each group (or its representatives) fully internalizes the benefits of any expenditure targeted to that group; however, it internalizes only a small fraction of the revenue costs of the expenditure, and more generally of the distortionary costs it imposes on the whole economy. Of course, this is not the end of the story, because a mechanism is also needed by which a majority of policymakers agree on some positive expenditure. Once such a mechanism is provided, the basic intuition is simple and seemingly robust: the larger the number of players involved in the decision about fiscal policy — i.e., the more "fragmented" the decision-making process is — the less these players internalize the costs of expenditure. It follows that a more fragmented decision-making process leads to a larger total expenditure.

In a sense, this logic applies even more forcefully to the *executive* decision-making process on fiscal policy. By their nature, ministers and parties cater to the interests of different groups, hence the same problem of lack of internalization of all revenue costs exists; in fact, the logic of the model applies even if these interests are not geographically located, as in the case of transfers. For instance, if a party or minister has a disproportionate share of the poor and the elderly in its constituency, it will internalize very little of the revenue costs of increased transfers.

From the point of view of the topic of this paper, a limit of this approach is that it is static, and therefore it cannot explain the effects of fragmentation on the deficit, but only on total expenditure. Velasco (1997) perhaps comes closest to a dynamic version of the WSJ approach. Here too the key mechanism is a "common pool" problem, except that now each group regards the whole of government assets — including the present discounted value of all future taxes — as common property. If a group moderates its expenditure demands and hence "saves" more tax revenues for the future, its perceived rate of return on these budget savings is less than the social rate of return, because in a non-cooperative equilibrium the other groups will appropriate much of these savings. Hence, there are powerful incentives to anticipate expenditure relative to what a central planner would do, and given the path of taxes, higher expenditure at the beginning also means larger deficits.

A common element to both the WSJ and the Velasco approach is that the expenditure bias (in the former case) and the deficit bias (in the latter case) are endogenous.[4] A second class of models rationalizes deficits as due to the inability to adjust to exogenous shocks. This approach is typified by the well-known "war of attrition" model of Alesina and Drazen (1991). Here deficits arise as each of two groups tries to wear out its opponent in order to make it bear most of the burden of the adjustment to a shock. This theoretical insight of the Alesina and Drazen model turns out to be quite important for the topic of this survey, although it was not the main motiva-

---

[4] Perotti (1996) presents a model where both expenditure and the deficit are endogenous. The model, however, is meant to capture mainly the 'populist experiences' of developing countries. Larger deficits and expenditure result when the distribution of income and preferences is highly skewed and the average income is low.

tion of the paper. As we will see, there is some support for the plausible notion that institutions and political factors are important determinants of the ability of governments to carry out fiscal consolidations and, in general, to react to large shocks.

Although these models make considerable progress by adopting an explicitly dynamic framework, the price they have to pay is that the link between fragmentation and budget outcomes becomes less clear. In Velasco (1997), the relationship between the number of groups and the deficit is highly dependent on the functional form of the utility function. In a slightly different model still based on the dynamic common pool problem, Lane and Tornell (1996) show that, as the number of groups with a say on fiscal policy increases from one to two, the response of fiscal policy to shocks becomes more profligate because of the mechanism illustrated above. But as the number increases further, redistribution in response to shocks falls, basically because of increased competition among groups.[5] On the other hand, Spolaore (1993) shows that, in an extended version of the Alesina and Drazen approach, larger coalitions respond to negative shocks with larger deficits.

Fragmentation over Time

A second class of models — including Tabellini and Alesina (1990) and Persson and Svensson (1989) — emphasizes the role of fragmentation of decision-makers *over time*. Suppose that at each point in time a single policymaker is in charge of fiscal policy. Suppose also that there is uncertainty about the identity and therefore preferences of the future policymaker in charge of fiscal policy. Because of risk aversion, the current policymaker has an incentive to run a deficit in order to constrain the actions of the future policymaker.[6]

Note that, like in the Velasco model, here also the rate of return on budget savings is lower than the social one. Still, the empirical implications of the Tabellini-Alesina approach are very different. The root of the problem is now the instability of governments over time, and the polarization of preferences between governments that alternate in office. These concepts have very different empirical counterparts than the concept of fragmentation across policymakers. Precisely to assess the relevance of

---

[5] This result is reminiscent of the logic of Olson (1982) and Calmfors and Driffill (1988). I will come back to these results later.
[6] More recently, Lizzeri (1996) presents a model of deficit and transfers with many policy-makers based on a similar logic.

these alternative approaches, I now turn to the empirical research they have spurred.

Empirical Evidence

Roubini and Sachs (1989a, 1989b) were the first to investigate the relationship between fragmentation and fiscal outcomes. They construct an index of political fragmentation, encompassing in ascending order of fragmentation single-party majority governments, coalition governments, and minority governments; in a panel of 14 OECD countries in the period 1960–85, this index correlates well with the size of the deficit, after controlling for standard economic determinants like inflation, growth and unemployment. Subsequently, Edin and Ohlsson (1991) showed that, if different coefficients are allowed for each of the types of government in the Roubini and Sachs index, all their results are explained by minority governments: among majority governments, there is practically no difference in the average fiscal performance of single-party and coalition governments. These results would suggest that the problem is not so much fragmentation within the government, but the inherent weakness of minority governments, which by their nature are in a difficult position *vis-à-vis* parliament. De Haan and Sturm (1994) argue that not even this last finding is robust; Grilli, Masciandaro and Tabellini (1989) also find little evidence that coalition or minority government are systematically associated with larger deficits. They also show that a more immediate measure of the fragmentation of *legislative* policymaking, the probability that two lawmakers taken at random belong to two different parties, works much better as a determinant of deficits, and that countries with proportional electoral systems have accumulated, on average, much larger public debts than countries with electoral systems that reduce the fragmentation of parliamentary representation. Hallerberg and von Hagen (1997a) find similar results in a panel of European countries.

Regarding the notion of fragmentation over time, Grilli, Masciandaro and Tabellini (1989) find that higher instability, as measured by the average rate of government turnover, is indeed significantly associated with higher average deficits in cross sections. Yet, the theoretical arguments on fragmentation over time suggest that what matters is the probability that a given government will be followed by a government with very different preferences. This concept would be measured by the probability of *major* government changes, rather than the probability of *any* government change. Only the latter definition, however, is statistically significant in explaining government deficits.

As can be seen, the evidence on the effects of fragmentation on the deficit is rather inconclusive. One problem is that the interpretation of these contrasting results is made slightly difficult by the fact that these studies use different measures of the deficit and are based on very different samples. A second problem is that, by their nature, many of these studies are based on largely subjective measures of the characteristics of governments and legislatures; the resulting differences in classifying governments along measures of fragmentations make it difficult to compare their statistical results.

In Kontopoulos and Perotti (1997), we use two objective variables, the number of spending ministers ("cabinet size") and the number of parties in the coalition ("coalition size") in addition to the Roubini and Sachs variable. In a sample of 20 OECD countries over the entire period 1960–94, when political fragmentation is measured along the majority/coalition/minority breakdown, we too find that only minority governments are associated with larger deficits. By disaggregating the deficit into expenditure and revenues, we find that the reason for the higher deficits is lower taxes, not higher expenditure; this is consistent with the notion that minority governments are politically weaker and therefore less able to increase taxes. Of the other two variables, cabinet size is an important and robust determinant of deficits and expenditure in the decade following the first oil shock, while coalition size is an important determinant in the last decade.

These results are consistent with the following interpretation: the 1970s and early 1980s were a decade of oil shocks common to all countries in the sample; the task of fiscal policymakers was more or less clear to all — contain the growth of expenditure as much as possible. In this situation, it was important to minimize the number of decision centers that could exert demands on the budget within the government. By contrast, for many countries, the last decade was a period of attempted consolidations; the decision to consolidate must "come from the top", and requires political cohesion. This interpretation is supported by the fact that "ideology" is an important determinant of deficits in the last decade, but not before. In the last ten years, more conservative governments do exhibit a lower rate of growth of the deficit; in addition, this effect works through the two budget items that one would indeed expect to be most closely influenced by ideological factors, transfers and wage government consumption.

The effects of cabinets and coalition size on fiscal outcomes also tend to be stronger in periods of low growth, lending some support to the notion that institutions and political conditions are particularly important in "difficult" times. Another piece of evidence suggests that political fragmentation is important when hard choices have to be made. Alesina and Perotti (1995c) show that there is virtually no difference in the probability that single-party majority governments and coalition governments engage in a very loose fiscal policy (an increase in the cyclically adjusted deficit by at least 1.5% of GDP) or in a large consolidation (a cut in the cyclically adjusted deficit by at least 1.5% of GDP). However, 35% of the large consolidations implemented by single-party majority governments were successful, while only 8.7% of those carried out by coalition governments were successful.

If verified further, these results might be of a certain policy relevance. They suggest that countries with persistent fiscal problems should contemplate adopting a first-past-the-post system to reduce the number of parties represented in parliament and in the government. The usual objection to this proposal is that electoral systems are often fixed in the constitution and in general deeply rooted in the tradition of a country. But the results above do indicate that an easier route might exist in the short run. Cabinet size seems to have the strongest association with fiscal outcomes; at the same time, and unlike the electoral system, it is usually not fixed in the constitution, and indeed it often does vary widely over time within a country.

V. Procedural Fragmentation

Theory

A more recent strand of literature can be interpreted as applying the notion of fragmentation to the formal organization of the process whereby the budget is proposed, approved, and implemented. This second interpretation is different from the first because, although the parliament must ultimately give the final approval, in matters of budget a government typically has considerable power of initiative and of agenda setting. Hence, quite independently of the characteristics of government and parliament, the structure of the budget process within the government is an important determinant of the fiscal outcome.

For the purposes of this survey it is possible to identify three aspects of the fragmentation of the budget process. The first aspect is how diffuse the responsibility is at the various stages of preparation, negotiation within the government, presentation to parliament, and implementation of the budget. In all countries, the final budget must be formally approved by the whole cabinet before it is submitted to parliament; but in some countries, some or all of these functions are strongly concentrated in the hands of the finance minister or a small government committee. At the other extreme, these functions may be fulfilled by the cabinet as a whole. The reason why this notion of fragmentation is important is reminiscent of the concept of political fragmentation: a finance minister or a small subcommittee with large powers in the budget process can better internalize the costs of the overall budget. In fact, from the point of view of modeling, at the existing level of abstraction much of the theory on political fragmentation could be applied, with a change of labels, to this aspect of the budget process.

A second notion of procedural fragmentation, with a long history in the literature on the budget process, refers to the method of arriving at the final budget; see e.g. Premchand (1983). Suppose that the identity and number of decision-makers in the process are given, i.e., suppose that the previous concept of procedural fragmentation is held constant. Conceptually, one can imagine two different ways to arrive at the final budget. At one extreme (often termed "top-down approach"), the total budget is decided first, and the allocations to individual ministries or programs second. At the other extreme ("bottom-up approach"), the total budget is determined simply as the sum of individual allocations. Here again, it could be argued that the first method is likely to lead to a smaller budget because, in some sense, it should be easier to take into account the overall constraint when setting the total budget first.

A well-known result by Ferejohn and Krehbiel (1987), however, shows that in general this is not necessarily the case. The reason is that in both methods the number and identity of decision-makers remain constant; by backward induction, when setting the total budget first, decision-makers will take into account the likely allocations in the second stage. There is no reason why the common pool problem should be resolved by setting the total budget first. In fact, the total size of the budget in the two methods depends only on the distribution of preferences among decision-makers.

The result would be different if the identity of the agent or agents involved in setting the initial total budget were different from that of the agents deciding its allocation.[7] According to the first notion of procedural fragmentation discussed above, fiscal discipline is likely to be enhanced if the overall budget were set initially by, say, the finance minister or a small subcommittee.[8]

The theoretical literature often overlooks the distinction between deficit and expenditure bias. In fact, spending limits have rarely appeared in the theoretical discussion, in sharp contrast to the long-standing and often heated debate on balanced-budget rules. And there are good reasons for this difference. There is no agreement, and there will never be any, on what the appropriate level of government expenditure is. More importantly, it is difficult even to think about a realistic model providing a plausible framework for determining the optimal level of expenditure. By contrast, zero is

---

[7] See Hallerberg and von Hagen (1997b) for a formalization of this argument.

[8] This seems to be the motivation of some recent proposals to make the budget process more conducive to fiscal consolidations. von Hagen and Harden (1994) and Eichengreen and von Hagen (1995) have proposed constituting an independent body, the National Debt Council (NDC), composed of individuals appointed for relatively long terms, with the task of setting a binding ceiling on the budget deficit at the beginning of each budget cycle. Eichengreen, Hausmann and von Hagen (1996) discuss the applicability of such an independent body, with enhanced powers, to Latin America.

a natural and, under some assumptions, easily defensible target for the deficit. Interestingly, we will see that, in practice, spending limits have played a much larger role than deficit targets in most recent episodes of fiscal consolidation.

A third notion of procedural fragmentation refers to the relative power of the government and the parliament in budget matters. A more centralized budget process within the government might not be very useful if the parliament can ultimately decide everything. Hence, more agenda-setting power for the government and less ability for the parliament to amend the budget proposals of the government are likely to result in more responsible fiscal policy. These aspects have been investigated in a series of important papers beginning with Baron and Ferejohn (1989) and Baron (1991). However, in this literature, the focus is typically on the classic bargaining problem of splitting a given pie; hence, it is difficult to apply it to the type of problems studied here. In addition, the specific focus on the committee system of the US Congress also makes it difficult to generalize it. Nevertheless, the main insight of the importance of the agenda-setting amendment powers matters for the study of fiscal consolidations.

Empirical Evidence and Recent Experience

The first systematic cross-country statistical study of the effects of procedural fragmentation on fiscal outcomes is von Hagen (1992), who considers 12 members of the European Community over the period 1981–90. von Hagen constructs an aggregate index of the characteristics of the budget process, which includes among its components indices of fragmentation but also other indicators, like the degree of transparency of the budget and the degree of flexibility at the implementation phase. In cross sections, this index correlates well with fiscal performance: on average, an increase in the index by 10 points leads to a long-term increase in the deficit by 1.9% of GDP. These numbers are extremely — perhaps excessively — large, when considering that the difference between the largest value (80, for Ireland) and the lowest value (20, for Luxembourg) is 60 points.[9] Alesina *et al.* (1995) find qualitatively similar results for Latin America, using pooled yearly data for 20 countries over the period 1980–92.[10]

---

[9] Curiously, Luxembourg has the lowest value on this index, but it is the only country that would meet all the fiscal criteria of the Maastricht Treaty.

[10] A different strand of literature, including Alt and Lowry (1994), Bohn and Inman (1995), Poterba (1994), and von Hagen (1991), has studied the effects of different budget procedures on the fiscal outcome of US states. The focus of this literature has been mainly on the efficacy of balanced budget rules to curb deficits, however, rather than on the notion of fragmentation. Moreover, the scope for an autonomous fiscal policy, the composition of the budget,

These studies use aggregate indices that combine different features of the budget process, some relating to fragmentation, and some to other aspects. von Hagen and Harden (1994) argue that, among countries which have achieved fiscal discipline, some combined a top-down approach with a relatively weak position of the finance minister in the budget process, others combined a bottom-up approach with a strong position of the finance minister. Hallerberg and von Hagen (1997a) and Kontopoulos and Perotti (1997) also find some evidence that variables capturing the degree of centralization of the budget process and the existence of spending targets tend to have a significant coefficient in panel regressions explaining the change in the deficit or expenditure. A caveat with these types of regressions is that the budget process exhibits very little or no variation over time within each country.

Recent years have witnessed a great deal of much needed research on the effects of budget procedures. Yet, we have to be aware that, because of the many institutional aspects and unwritten rules that define the budget process, procedural fragmentation is even more difficult to define and measure than political fragmentation. In particular, I believe we do not have strong empirical evidence proving that budget procedures have *macroeconomic* significance in the long run. Perhaps one can adventure two partial conclusions. First, whatever the empirical evidence, the theoretical arguments for more centralization in the initial phases of the budget process seem compelling. Second, an appropriate budget process might be instrumental in effectively implementing a fiscal consolidation, although the decision to start the latter is probably an independent factor.

Be as it may, it is important to note that in recent years several countries have substantially reformed their budget process, at the same time as they embarked on a program of fiscal consolidations. Some, like Belgium, Spain, the U.K., and New Zealand, actually changed their budget laws to considerable extents. An important feature of the first three reforms was that they aimed at incorporating decisions on revenues and expenditures, which were previously separate, in the same budget. This was done with the goal of making explicit the connection between the two sides of the budget, and therefore to increase the degree of internalization of the revenue costs of expenditure. Many other countries modified their budget procedures in less formal ways, but always in the direction of a less fragmented process. For instance, all of the six countries considered in a study by the General Accounting Office (1994) on fiscal consolidations, except Mexico, adopted some form of top-down approach; interestingly, in all of these countries it

and the goals of fiscal policy, are very different between US states and the typical OECD government. As a consequence, the fiscal policy problems faced by US states are much more limited than those faced by sovereign countries.

took the form of limits on the level or the rate of growth of spending, rather than on the deficit. These limits were particularly stringent in the U.K., and less so in Canada, Germany, Australia, and Japan. As a result of recent changes, spending limits are now used, besides the U.K., in all Scandinavian countries except Sweden; see OECD (1996b). Thus, although as we have seen the theory predicts that a top-down approach is not necessarily conducive to more fiscal discipline, in practice most countries seem to have made this association. The main reason could be that, in practice, a top-down approach is combined with more centralization and internalization of the process.[11]

It is obviously difficult to assess the effects, if there were any, of these reforms, because of the practical impossibility to partial out all other concurrent events with an impact on the budget. For instance, in many countries these reforms coincided with the mild recessions of the early 1990s, which caused a *ceteris paribus* increase in the deficit. It would also be easy to list cases where procedural reforms turned out to be irrelevant for the fiscal outcome. An example is Canada, where the spending limits were set so generously that they turned out not to be binding; see Government Accounting Office (1994). Another is the U.S., where the Gramm–Rudman–Hollings Act was never seriously considered. In addition, perhaps the best-known and more radical of all recent budget reforms, by New Zealand, was based not on any deficit or spending limit, but only on enhanced accountability and transparency. But the undeniable fact is that so many governments felt the need for budget reform and implemented it precisely in the direction of more centralization.

VI. Social Fragmentation

OECD countries differ substantially in the strength of organized groups outside parliament and government, and in their ability to influence and participate in the fiscal decision-making process. A third notion of fragmentation therefore captures the extent to which the government and parliament must compromise with outside interest groups when deciding on fiscal policy. This notion is important precisely because the two most important items in a successful consolidation, government wages and transfers, are those that are likely to affect the interests of powerful organized groups the most.

Yet, because it is so difficult to define, this notion of fragmentation has not received much attention in the literature. Becker (1983) and Lindbeck (1985) were the first to formalize the process whereby multiple interest

---

[11] However, as shown above, von Hagen and Harden (1994) argue that the two dimensions are indeed independent.

groups extract rents from the government budget. A second strand of research that can shed light on this aspect is the literature on "corporatism", which has been developed in the last 15 years, mainly by Scandinavian scholars; see Calmfors (1993) and Scarpetta (1996) for excellent surveys. The basic idea is that the presence of organized interests groups is most distortionary when there are relatively few of them. If interest groups are numerous and dispersed, they have little rent-seeking power and the equilibrium outcome is relatively efficient. At the other extreme, a very large, encompassing group can internalize the distortionary consequences of its rent-seeking behavior; although for different reasons, in this case as well the outcome tends to be relatively efficient. The most inefficient outcome is likely to arise when there are few large groups, because they are powerful enough to impose large distortions, but not large enough to internalize them. In a more specific application, Calmfors and Driffill (1988) show that unemployment rates during the 1970s and early 1980s were highest in countries with powerful, industry level unions. In corporatist countries, where a large umbrella organization of unions negotiates the wage with the entrepreneurs' counterpart and the government, the average unemployment rate has been lower.[12]

The involvement of governments in labor market negotiations suggests that fiscal policy might play a large role in explaining these findings. Indeed, Summers, Gruber and Vergara (1993) argue that in corporatist countries, unions internalize the link between labor taxation and higher transfers, which make labor taxes less distortionary in corporatist countries. Exploring this logic one step further, Alesina and Perotti (1997b) show that, empirically, labor and social security taxes cause smaller increases in unit labor costs in corporatist countries than in countries with intermediate levels of centralization of labor negotiations.

This evidence could suggest that fiscal consolidations are easier to implement in countries where institutions are in place that ensure a large degree of consultation between the government and the other parties involved. This is far from obvious. Under this type of institutional arrangement, it is unlikely that a fiscal consolidation will fall exactly on the items that, as we have seen, are most important for its success: wage government expenditure and transfers. For instance, in corporatist countries, fiscal policy is typically a bargaining chip in tripartite agreements. Rosen (1995) has argued that government employment in Sweden has been used exactly to absorb unemployment. As we have seen, the smaller effects of labor taxes on unit labor costs can be explained by the participation of the government in labor market negotiations. This is supported by a large

---

[12] Like all empirical findings, this too has been disputed, sometimes hotly so; see Scarpetta (1996) for the latest update on this debate.

amount of anecdotal evidence. To take a specific example, in 1975–76 in Sweden, there was a sharp increase in social security contributions; according to Flanagan, Soskice and Ulman (1983), the centralized system of negotiations "might explain why the contractual increases were not even greater than they were: the wage agreement was reached on the understanding that social security payments would subsequently be increased, and the government felt obliged to honor this commitment — *as indeed it had done on similar occasions in the past*" (p. 325, emphasis added).[13]

VII. Optimal Consolidation Strategy

In this section, I study the third key question set out in the introduction: what is the optimal strategy for consolidating, given the constraint that it must be politically feasible? Of course, many aspects of a consolidation have a bearing on its political feasibility. Here, I want to focus on three particularly important and general aspects.

First, how much effort should a government spend on mustering consensus around a fiscal consolidation? Second, should the consolidation be comprehensive, or focused on a few items, and should it be fast, or gradual? Third, is its probability of success likely to be greatly enhanced by other concurrent reforms, and how?

Consensus

This is just the normative side of the positive question analyzed in Section VI. Even a cursory view to the recent experience suggests that a key preliminary question facing governments that attempt a consolidation is: negotiate or not negotiate? As we have seen, part of the answer depends on the institutional characteristics of the country. But much of it is a matter of choice.

Historically, fiscal policymaking by consensus has been adopted by countries like Austria, Australia, Belgium, Italy, and Sweden. The problem with this strategy is obvious, and has already been pointed out: it is unlikely to succeed in pushing through exactly those measures that, as we have seen, are crucial to make a fiscal consolidation long-lasting. This is especially true because, in all the countries that have adopted this strategy, among the largest and better organized counterparts of the government are public sector unions. On the other hand, it would be easy to point to the example of Ireland in 1987–89, where the most dramatic fiscal consolidation of all was implemented with a large degree of consultation with public sector unions. In fact, part of the explanation for the success of this consolidation

---

[13] Since then, there has been a move towards more decentralization in most corporatist countries, but the system still remains more centralized than in most other countries.

is precisely that labor taxes were used as a means of exchange: the government refrained from increasing labor taxes and obtained wage moderation from public and private sector unions; see Alesina and Perotti (1997a) on this point.

The advantage of the alternative strategy is that a government serious about its fiscal consolidation can push it through without having to risk watering it down. Here also there are examples of success and failure. The Thatcher government consolidation can be counted among the former; the Juppé government attempt is the most recent, and highly visible, example of the latter.

These two episodes also remind us that the notion of a "strong" government being able to push through a fiscal consolidation against all interest groups is easy to rationalize, but only *ex post*. The Thatcher government was nearly brought down by its policies, and the Chirac administration started its mandate with very high levels of popular approval.

Here, even more so than on the other issues, we are unlikely to ever come up with conclusive answers and with a recipe that can be applied to all situations. Too much depends on the institutional details, on the politics of the moment, and, ultimately, on a good dose of luck. Still, the debate could be more informed if we had a piece of information that, I believe, we are still largely missing: the effects of fiscal consolidations on income distribution. Unfortunately, because of lack of data in the foreseeable future, we are unlikely to ever have reliable, systematic evidence on this aspect.

Comprehensiveness and Speed

A fiscal consolidation is, in some respects, similar to a policy reform: as we have seen, it often involves reforming the budget process, and in the most decisive and successful cases it might involve changing the government's employment policies and the structure of transfer programs. One might therefore be tempted to apply the tools and insights of the literature on the political economy of reforms to fiscal consolidations. As emphasized in two excellent recent surveys by Tommasi and Velasco (1996) and Rodrik (1996), much of the literature on the political economy of reform can be interpreted in light of the two criteria of the speed (how fast should a given distortion been removed?) and comprehensiveness (how many distortions should be removed?) of reforms. However, most of the literature has focused on the reform of the trade and capital flow regime in developing countries, and on problems of transition to a market economy in former communist countries. Some of the issues involved also apply to the problem of fiscal consolidation; but in many respects fiscal consolidations pose problems that are not immediately interpretable in terms of the existing theories on trade and market reforms.

To illustrate this point, it is useful to start from theoretical arguments pro and against gradualism, and pro and against comprehensiveness. I focus here on two such theories, because they are fairly typical and highlight well the contrast with the kinds of problems that are more likely to be encountered during fiscal consolidations.

Martinelli and Tommasi (1993) construct a model where strong groups have veto power at each stage of the reform process. If a group benefits from the partial reform more than from the full reform, it will block further progress once the partial reform is in place. Knowing this, a different group might veto even the first, partial reform. Thus, a fast, comprehensive reform might be the only way to overcome political opposition to a partial reform. At the other extreme, Dewatripont and Roland (1995) argue that gradualism might be the only way to gather enough initial support to start the reform process. Suppose the payoffs of reform are uncertain, and partial reform is dominated by both the status quo and full reform; then if the partial reform is successful, individuals will favor completing the reform in order not to lose the benefits of the partial reform. A different argument is found in Dewatripont and Roland (1992). A policymaker can convince a majority today to accept a reform by threatening a reform that will be even more detrimental to a large part of today's majority. This mechanism is rational because the future reform, if proposed by the government, will receive the support of a majority of individuals. Thus, gradualism — a sequence of such offers and associated threats — allows the government to implement deeper reforms, that would not be accepted if proposed all at once.

The arguments in Martinelli and Tommasi (1993) and in Dewatripont and Roland (1992, 1995) depend critically on the structure of payoffs from partial and full reform. It is doubtful whether governments have and, especially, use this type of information in such a sophisticated way. The mechanism in Dewatripont and Roland (1992) has one interesting aspect: it is conceivable that governments might play one group against another to ensure some support for a fiscal consolidation. To do so, however, a government must have strong agenda-setting powers and a sufficiently long horizon, exactly the two features it might lack if it has to negotiate support with other groups. In addition, this argument, with small variations, can just as easily be turned into an argument *against* gradualism. If the idea is that in the absence of a fiscal consolidation "something worse will come", it can be argued that this might make a sweeping fiscal consolidation more acceptable. A formalization of this idea is, for instance, in Drazen and Grilli (1993), who show that in times of crisis it might be easier for a government to push through a reform.

The main point is that, when it comes to fiscal policy, issues of speed and comprehensiveness take very different, and very specific, forms. First, should consolidations be across-the-board, or program-specific? Second, should targeting be used extensively as a fast way to reduce transfers? Third, should certain groups be compensated explicitly through the fiscal system? On all three issues, the remarkable fact is the extent to which the recent practice of many governments has departed from what would be, I believe, the advice of a majority of economists.

The debate on "rules vs. discretion" suggests that an across-the-board reduction in expenditures might be a way to cut the Gordian knot of fiscal consolidations and eliminate the incentives for endless bargaining and vetoing. In practice, however, this strategy is difficult to implement. The original 1985 Gramm–Rudman–Hollings Act, later abandoned, is the best illustration of these difficulties. Precisely in order to avoid drawn-out negotiations, it prescribed an across-the-board cut in case the yearly target expenditures were not achieved. However, it explicitly excluded social security and other programs — summing to 60% of all government expenditure — from this provision, because their inclusion would have been regarded as somewhat "unjust" by most, and impossible to implement. This, of course, put all the burden of the consolidation on the remaining 40% of expenditures, which made it practically impossible to enforce the Act and quickly led to its abandonment. Hence, in practice, across-the-board strategies are likely to be time inconsistent, as strong pressure might develop to spare programs considered too important to be cut automatically.

A variant of the previous problem is whether targeting should be used as a means of fiscal consolidation.[14] As is well known, on efficiency grounds, targeting is widely regarded as a distortionary way to provide insurance and redistribute income. A workfare requirement can partly reduce these problems in the presence of information asymmetries between the government and the target population, as shown in a recent series of papers by Besley (1990) and Besley and Coate (1992, 1995).

In contrast to these theoretical results, it is remarkable how all governments that have gone in the direction of an explicit reform of the welfare state have made targeting one of their workhorses. In what is admittedly a rather extreme example so far, Australia in the mid-1980s means tested unemployment and family benefits, and even old-age pensions. By contrast, workfare has been virtually ignored everywhere (with the very recent exception of U.S. welfare reform), because of its administrative costs and its mixed results, at best, in several experiments around the

---

[14] For a more extensive discussion of this and other related issues, see Lindbeck (1994) and Lindbeck *et al.* (1993).

world. Other theoretical ways to increase the efficiency of redistribution while achieving more effective targeting, like the negative income tax, have also been almost universally ignored because of their budgetary costs.

These experiences contain an important message: despite its efficiency problems, targeting is likely to be a key ingredient of the political accept-ability of welfare state reforms, for two reasons: it can be sold as a fair way to reform the welfare state, and by its nature, is a politically inexpensive way to create support. But most of all, it is a fast way to achieve those initial results that might be crucial for the success of a consolidation.

The case of Australia also illustrates the third fiscal aspect of compre-hensiveness and reforms: the net benefits of the bottom three deciles of the population were increased between 1984 and 1989, even while the govern-ment was engaging in a fiscal consolidation, to a substantial extent involv-ing government transfers. Compensation to the poorest segments of the population can obviously be an important ingredient of the political acceptability of a reform. It remains to be seen, however, whether it is compatible with the goal of a decisive reduction in transfers. Conceivably, this might be the case only if compensation to the poorest is accompanied by extensive targeting to neutralize its fiscal costs without jeopardizing the perception of its equity. We have virtually no theory or evidence on this important point. Yet, it does demonstrate once more the fundamental role of seemingly mundane details in a relevant discussion of the political economy of fiscal policy; for an informed discussion of many of these details, see Lindbeck (1994).

Optimal Sequencing

Conceptually, there are two key aspects of the issue of optimal sequencing: does a certain reform enhance the effectiveness of a fiscal consolidation? If yes, should it be implemented before, after, or concurrently with the fiscal consolidation?

Theoretically, there is almost no end to the list of reforms that could complement a fiscal consolidation. Moreover, as Dewatripont and Roland (1995) have shown, complementarity is not necessarily an argument for implementing all complementary reforms at once: as we have seen, a gradual implementation of reforms can enhance their political support, even when they are complementary.

But once again, it is difficult to apply these theoretical models to the problems of sequencing that a typical policymaker is likely to encounter. Here, I focus on two reforms that arise most naturally from the discussion so far.

Most OECD countries entered the 1980s with tax systems that were widely regarded as antiquated and inefficient: certain marginal tax rates were finally recognized as way too high by any standard, and tax bases were often capriciously selective. Under these conditions, a tax reform seems to be a natural complement of a fiscal consolidation; at the same time it is likely to be politically rewarding, because it can be sold as enhancing the equity of the system.

The main problem with this seemingly no-lose strategy was quickly perceived by all governments: initially, tax reforms cause a fall in tax revenues.[15]. This is particularly worrisome, of course, when the government is also engaged in a fiscal consolidation aimed at reducing the deficit. In fact, in the 1980s many governments — like the Haughey government in Ireland and the Kohl government in Germany — explicitly made a reduction in expenditure a precondition for tax reform. Critics of this strategy argue that it could lead to macroeconomic instability; see e.g. Lindbeck (1994).

The second key reform that arises naturally in the context of fiscal consolidations is labor market reform. There are at least three reasons for this. As we have seen, all three key ingredients of fiscal consolidations — wage government consumption, transfers, and labor taxes — feed directly into labor costs, and the mechanism by which this occurs depends crucially on the structure of labor markets. Second, we have also seen that the institutional framework of labor market negotiations affects the determination of fiscal policy: certain types of labor market negotiations impose more demands on the budget than others. Third, effective and long-lasting cuts in wage government consumption cannot be achieved without changing labor market regulations.

Of course, changing labor market institutions is a very thorny political issue, particularly in times of high unemployment, because it almost unavoidably leads to confrontations with powerful unions. Tackling fiscal policy and labor markets at the same time might prove too much for any government, as the experience of the Juppé government has made abundantly clear. Yet, I believe that this is perhaps *the* key issue currently faced by most governments contemplating a fiscal consolidation.

VIII. What Have We Learnt?

A skeptic might answer: not much. All the research surveyed here — it could be argued — stresses once more that theory is one thing, practice is another, and "the two shall never meet". Many inefficiencies are evident to almost everyone with a minimum of common sense; everyone understands that they exist because they benefit some specific group with some political

---

[15] This was the case, for instance, even in a highly successful case of tax reform like the Swedish one: see Lindbeck *et al.* (1993).

weight; and policymakers do what they can to correct them, given the political constraints. Positive models merely tell us why things go a certain way; normative models are often too stylized to be of any practical guidance at the right moment. We have all heard economists turned policymakers say "how can anyone — including myself at one time — believe in these models?" The litmus test of all this, the argument might go on, is that economists in government are often observationally equivalent, to the average citizen at least, to the policymakers they once criticized.

We should not dismiss this position too lightly. Excessive, and implausible, theorizing is the skeleton in the closet of macroeconomists: even those who do not practice it dare not criticize it. And as I have tried to show, governments often had no choice but to embark on a fiscal consolidation with little or no regard for the prescriptions of mainstream economic theory. A round table discussion of a paper by Dornbusch on the Irish situation concluded as follows: " ... The gravity of the Irish situation came as a surprise to some panel members. They showed concern about the apparent lack of solutions to the current problems. It was suggested that one realistic policy could be to raise corporate and land taxes. A moratorium on the debt might also be considered ... " [Dornbusch (1989, p. 207)]. As it happened, the Irish government was simultaneously engaged in a drastic consolidation, which in the three years between 1987 and 1989 led to a cut in total outlays by 10% of GDP, at the same time as it *reduced* current taxes by 3.2% of GDP. Interestingly, a cut in expenditure was *never* suggested in the panel discussion as a possible remedy to the fiscal crisis.

On the other hand, I believe that the empirical evidence and the recent experience of many countries do provide three important and relevant messages. First, fiscal consolidations are not just a question of reducing the deficit; how it is reduced is relevant. The second conclusion descends directly from the first: because of the importance of transfers, government employment, and labor taxes in fiscal consolidations, the interaction of fiscal policy with labor market institutions is crucial to the implementation and success of a consolidation. Third, when all is said and done there is probably no defense against a government that is determined to run an irresponsible fiscal policy: balanced budget rules can be easily circumvented, and there are no prison terms for finance ministers who exceed spending limits. But properly designed procedural institutions can be very important in enhancing the ability and effectiveness of a government to implement a fiscal consolidation.

References

Alesina, A. and Drazen, A.: Why are stabilizations delayed? *American Economic Review 81*, 1170–1188, Dec. 1991.

Alesina, A., Housemann, R., Hommes, R. and Stein, E.: Budget institutions and fiscal performance in Latin America. OCE WP, Paris, 1995.

Alesina, A. and Perotti, R.: The political economy of budget deficits. *IMF Staff Papers*, March, 1995a.

Alesina, A. and Perotti, R.: Fiscal expansions and fiscal adjustments in OECD countries. *Economic Policy*, no. 21, Oct. 1995b.

Alesina, A. and Perotti, R.: Fiscal expansions and fiscal adjustments in OECD countries. NBER WP 5214, 1995c.

Alesina, A. and Perotti, R.: Budget deficits and budget institutions. NBER WP, 1996.

Alesina, A. and Perotti, R.: Fiscal adjustments in OECD countries: Composition and macroeconomic effects. *IMF Staff Papers*, 1997a.

Alesina, A. and Perotti, R.: The welfare state and competitiveness. *American Economic Review 87*, 920–939, Dec. 1997b.

Alesina, R., Perotti, R. and Tavares, J.: The political economy of fiscal adjustments. Mimeo, Harvard University, 1997.

Alt, J. and Lowry, R. C.: Divided government and budget deficits: evidence from the states. *American Political Science Review 88*, 811–828, 1994.

Baron, D. P.: Majoritarian incentives, pork barrel programs, and procedural control. *American Journal of Political Science 35* (1), 57–90, 1991.

Baron, D. P. and Ferejohn, J. A.: Bargaining in legislature. *American Political Science Review 83* (4), 1181–1206, 1989.

Becker, G.: A theory of competition among pressure groups for influence. *Quarterly Journal of Economics 48*, 371–400, 1983.

Bertola, G. and Drazen, A.: Trigger points and budget cuts: Explaining the effects of fiscal austerity. *American Economic Review 83* (1), 1170–1188, 1993.

Besley, T.: Means testing versus universal provision in poverty alleviation programmes. *Economica 57*, 119–129, 1990.

Besley, T. and Coate, S.: The design of income maintenance programs. *Review of Economic Studies 62*, 187–221, 1995.

Besley, T. and Coate, S.: Workfare vs. welfare: Incentive arguments for work requirements in poverty-alleviation programs. *American Economic Review 82*, 249–261, 1992.

Blanchard, O.: Comments on Giavazzi and Pagano. In O. Blanchard and S. Fischer (eds.), *NBER Macroeconomics Annual 1990*, MIT Press, Cambridge, MA, 110–117, 1990.

Bohn, H. and Inman, R. P.: Constitutional limitations and public deficits: Evidence from the U.S. states. Mimeo, place??, 1996.

Calmfors, L.: Centralization of wage bargaining and macroeconomic performance: A survey. Institute for International Economic Studies, SP 536, Stockholm, 1993.

Calmfors, L. and Driffill, J.: Bargaining structure, corporatism and macroeconomic performance. *Economic Policy 6*, 13–62, 1988.

Coeur, P., Dubois, E., Mahfouz, S. and Pisani-Ferry, J.: The costs of fiscal adjustments revisited. Mimeo, CEPII, Paris, 1996.

de Haan, J. and Sturm, J. E.: Political and institutional determinants of fiscal policy in the European Community. *Public Choice 80*, 157–172, 1994.

Dewatripont, M. and Roland, G.: Economic reform and dynamic political constraints. *Review of Economic Studies 59*, 703–730, 1992.

Dewatripont, M. and Roland, G.: The design of reform packages under uncertainty. *American Economic Review 85* (5), 1207–1223, 1995.

Dornbusch, R.: Credibility, debt, and unemployment: Ireland's failed stabilization. *Economic Policy 8*, 173–210, 1989.

Drazen, A. and Grilli, V.: The benefits of crises for economic reforms. *American Economic Review 83* (3), 598–607, 1993.

Edin, P. and Ohlsson, H.: Political determinants of budget deficits: Coalition effects versus minority effects. *European Economic Review 35*, 1597–1603, 1991.

Eichengreen, B., Hausmann, R. and von Hagen, J.: Reforming budgetary institutions in Latin America: The case for a national fiscal council. OCE WP, Paris, 1995.

Eichengreen, B. and von Hagen, J.: Fiscal restrictions and monetary union: rationales, reservations, and reforms. *Empirica 23* (1), 3–23, 1996.

Ferejohn, J. A. and Krehbiel, K.: The budget process and the size of the budget. *American Journal of Political Science 31* (1), 169–193, 1987.

Flanagan, R. J., Soskice, D. W. and Ulman, L.: *Unionism, Economic Stabilization, and Income Policies: The European Experience.* Brookings Institution, Washington, DC, 1983.

General Accounting Office (1994): *Deficit Reduction: Experiences of Other Nations.* Washington, DC, 1994.

Giavazzi, F. and Pagano, M.: Can severe fiscal adjustments be expansionary? In O. Blanchard and S. Fischer (eds.), *NBER Macroeconomics Annual*, MIT Press, Cambridge, MA, 75–110, 1990.

Giavazzi, F. and Pagano, M.: Non-Keynesian effects of fiscal policy changes: International evidence and the Swedish experience. *Swedish Economic Policy Review 3* (1), 67–103, 1996.

Grilli, V., Masciandaro, D. and Tabellini, G.: Political and monetary institutions and public financial policies in the industrial countries. *Economic Policy 13*, 341–392, 1991.

Hallerberg, M. and von Hagen, J.: Electoral institutions, cabinet negotiations, and budget deficits within the European Union. CEPR WP 1555, 1997a.

Hallerberg, M. and von Hagen, J.: Sequencing and the size of the budget: A reconsideration. CEPR WP 1589, 1997b.

Heylen, F.: A contribution to the empirical analysis of the effects of fiscal consolidations: Explanations of failure in Europe in the 1990s. University of Gent WP 97/32, 1997.

International Monetary Fund: *World Economic Outlook*, June, 1996.

Kontopoulos, Y. and Perotti, R.: Fragmented fiscal policy. Mimeo, Columbia University, 1997.

Lane, P. and Perotti, R.: The importance of the composition of fiscal policy: Evidence from different exchange rate regimes. Mimeo, Columbia University, 1997.

Lane, P. and Tornell, A.: Power, growth and the voracity effect. *Journal of Economic Growth 1* (2), June, 213–241, 1996.

Lindbeck, A.: Redistribution policy and expansion of the public sector. *Journal of Public Economics 28*, 23–44, 1985.

Lindbeck, A.: Overshooting, reform, and retreat of the welfare state. *De Economist 142* (1), 1–19, 1994.

Lindbeck, A., Molander, P., Persson, T., Petersson, O., Sandmo, A., Swedenborg, B. and Thygesen, N.: Turning Sweden around. *Economic Policy*, vol. ??, pp. ??, Oct. 1993.

Lizzeri, A.: Budget deficits and redistributive politics. Mimeo, Princeton University, 1996.

Martinelli,C. and Tommasi, M.: Sequencing of economic reforms in the presence of political constraints. IRIS Report 100, University of Maryland, 1993.

Olson, M.: *The Rise and Decline of Nations.* Yale University Press, New Haven, CT, 1982.

Organization for Economic Cooperation and Development: *The Control and Management of Government Expenditure.* Paris, 1987.

Organization for Economic Cooperation and Development: *Economic Outlook.* Paris, June, 1996a.

Organization for Economic Cooperation and Development: Managing structural deficit reduction. Occasional Paper in Public Management No. 11, Paris, 1996b.

Perotti, R.: Redistribution and non-consumption smoothing in an open economy. *Review of Economic Studies 63* (3), H11–13, 1996.

Perotti, R.: Fiscal policy when things are going badly. Mimeo, Columbia University, 1997.

Persson, T. and Svensson, L. E. O.: Why a stubborn conservative would run a deficit: Policy with time inconsistent preferences. *Quarterly Journal of Economics 104*, 325–345, 1989.

Poterba, J.: State responses to fiscal crises: The effects of budgetary institutions and politics. *Journal of Political Economy 102*, 799–821, 1994.

Premchand, A.: *Government Budgeting and Expenditure Controls: Theory and Practice.* IMF, Washington, DC, 1983.

Rodrik, D.: Understanding economic policy reform. *Journal of Economic Literature 34* (1), 9–41, 1996.

Rosen, S.: Public employment, taxes and the welfare state in Sweden. NBER WP 5003, Jan. 1995.

Roubini, N. and Sachs, J. D.: Political and economic determinants of budget deficits in the industrial democracies. *European Economic Review 33*, 903–938, 1989a.

Roubini, N. and Sachs, J. D.: Government spending and budget deficits in the industrialized countries. *Economic Policy 8*, 99–132, 1989b.

Scarpetta, S.: Assessing the role of labor market policies and institutional settings on unemployment: A cross-country study. *OECD Economic Studies*, No. 26, 43–98, 1996.

Shepsle, K. and Weingast, B.: Political preferences for the pork barrel: A generalization. *American Journal of Political Science 25* (1), 96–111, 1981.

Spolaore, E.: Policy making systems and economic efficiency: Coalition governments versus majority governments. Mimeo, ECARE, Brussels, 1993.

Summers, L., Gruber, J. and Vergara, R.: Taxation and structure of labor markets: The case of corporatism. *Quarterly Journal of Economics 108* (2), 385–412, 1993.

Sutherland, A.: Fiscal crises and aggregate demand: Can high public debt reverse the effects of fiscal policy? CEPR DP 1246, 1995.

Tabellini, G. and Alesina, A.: Voting on the budget deficit. *American Economic Review 80*, 37–49, 1990.

Tommasi, M. and Velasco, A.: Where are we in the political economy of reform? C. V. Starr Center for Applied Economics, RR 95-20, 1995.

United States General Accounting Office: *Deficit Reductions: Experience of Other Nations*, Washington, DC, 1994.

Velasco, A.: The common property approach to fiscal policy. Mimeo, New York University, 1997.

von Hagen, J.: A note on the effectiveness of formal fiscal restraints. *Journal of Public Economics 44*, 199–211, 1991.

von Hagen, J.: Budgeting procedures and fiscal performance in the European Communities. *Economic Papers 96*, Oct. 1992.

von Hagen, J. and Harden. I. J.: National budget processes and fiscal performance. *European Economy Reports and Studies 3*, 311–408, 1994.

Weingast, B., Shepsle, K. and Johnson, C.: The political economy of benefits and costs: A neoclassical approach to redistributive politics. *Journal of Political Economy 89*, 642–664, Aug. 1981.

Scand. J. Economics 100(1), 395–398, 1998

Comment on R. Perotti, "The Political Economy of Fiscal Consolidations"

Michael Wallerstein

Northwestern University, Evanston, IL 60208-1006, USA

Perotti's paper is a thoughtful and comprehensive review of an interesting literature on a politically salient topic: the political economy of deficit spending. Perotti states a high standard of evaluation when he asks: "[W]hat insights with some policy relevance the recent research has to offer on the issue of budget deficit reductions". After reading Perotti's survey, I find myself agreeing with Perotti's imaginary skeptic who answers "not much".

The research surveyed by Perotti suffers, in my view, from two major difficulties. The first is the absence of an explicit model or even a clear view of the economic effects of deficit spending. The second is the fragility of both theoretical or empirical models of one particular policy choice that ignore the existence of multiple alternative policy configurations that are close substitutes. I discuss each in turn.

In the literature surveyed in his paper, it is unclear why budget deficits are a problem worth worrying about. The problem is clearly evident when Perotti writes that "zero is a natural and, under some circumstances, easily defensible target for the deficit" without seeing the need to provide any further discussion, as if there were a consensus in economics that the optimal budget deficit is zero. In the United States, most economists seem united in their belief that forcing the government to balance the budget every year with a constitutional amendment is a bad idea. Even the more moderate position that the budget ought to be balanced on average over the business cycle is debatable. A government that is receiving a large income from the sale of a nonrenewable resource, as in Norway, should probably run a budget surplus. Many would argue that government investment is appropriately financed by government borrowing. American states that have a balanced budget requirement exclude capital expenditures from the budget, which means that state-level budgets are not balanced in practice.

The issue that needs to be made explicit is why deficit spending is a problem, except in those circumstances where the debt is growing at an unsustainable rate. In fact, Perotti's discussion implicitly points to two different problems that might be associated with budget deficits. Some of his discussion suggests that the real issue is the composition of government spending. We can all think of areas where the government spends too much and areas where the government spends too little. At other times, the real issue seems to be labor costs that are too high to sustain or regain full employment. But if the composition of government spending or labor costs are the real problem, why not address these problems directly? In this context, it is notable that Perotti never mentions the real economic issue that, in my view, underlies the discussion of the deficit in the United States: the low rate of savings. Again, if the low aggregate level of savings is the real issue, then we ought to be discussing how to raise savings rather than focusing only on government saving or dissaving.

Thus, Perotti's first conclusion that how the deficit is reduced is relevant indicates that the real problem is not the deficit at all but the composition of government spending, a problem that is independent of whether spending is financed by taxation or borrowing. Similarly, when Perotti concludes that the interaction of fiscal policy and wage-setting institutions is critical, this signifies that the real issue that needs to be addressed is the cost of labor. In both cases, the discussion could be improved if we changed the focus from deficit spending to the underlying economic problem that may or may not require a fiscal policy response.

Another problem mentioned by Perotti is the inability to adjust to an unexpected increase in the costs of inputs or a decline in productivity. When an economy is hit by a negative, temporary shock, however, is precisely when the optimal response entails a temporary increase in the deficit. In this context, there is a danger that the deficit will be too small as well as a danger that the deficit will be too large. As Spolaore's (1993) model illustrates, an institutional structure that allows a government to react decisively to a negative shock will produce too much response if the government is able to respond to the negative shock in a way that primarily hurts the constituents of the opposition. The optimal institutional structure for responding to unexpected shocks is unlikely to be one that allows the government to act without consulting the opposition, nor one that allows the opposition to block government action forever. In this matter, an interior solution is probably better than either corner solution.

Of course, if we restrict our attention to cases of an unsustainable increase in the deficit, then we have clear cases where the deficit per se is the problem. It is not clear, however, that we can learn anything useful about the politics of turning around an unsustainable policy from a data set that is composed mostly of country-year observations in which the current fiscal policy is not on an unsustainable course. The very fact that the current policy is unsustainable must affect the politics of deciding what should be done.

The second major difficulty with the literature surveyed by Perotti is the loose connection between characteristics of the political institutions and any particular policy outcome such as deficit spending. Let me discuss this issue with a particular example. On a scale of legislative fragmentation, the United States ought to score lower than any country in Western Europe. Of course, there are only two parties in the US Congress and the median number of parties in parliament in Western Europe is probably around six. But to look only at the number of parties is misleading. In fact, what we call parties in the United States are loose coalitions of individuals who may or may not vote together. If we look at behavioral measures, such as the propensity of legislators to vote together in a sequence of votes on different issues, we find that there is less unity inside each American party than there is between parties in the same government in Western Europe. In other words, coalition governments in Europe act more like a single party in a behavioral sense than do either Democratic or Republican legislators in the United States; see Diermeier and Feddersen (1996).

Given that the US legislature is more fragmented than legislatures in Western Europe, the models cited by Perotti would predict that the United States would be especially prone to policies with concentrated benefits and diffuse costs. I think the prediction is accurate, even though the United States has a lower budget deficit than any country in Europe other than Norway. As an illustration, consider the list of proposals for changes in fiscal policy made in the 1996 presidential campaign in the United States. Clinton proposed new tax breaks for families with children ($500 tax credit per child), families with children in college (college tuition tax credit or tax deduction) and home buyers and sellers (removal of capital gains tax on sale of homes and elimination of withdrawal penalties from tax-free savings accounts for home purchases). Dole proposed much the same package, with lower tax relief for families with children in college and more tax relief for families with significant stock portfolios. The ideal of a simple tax system in which the tax base is as wide as possible in order to keep the tax rate as low as possible that was pursued briefly during the Reagan administration is rapidly receding.

As a general statement, the argument that a fragmented legislature produces policy that favors narrow groups is probably empirically correct. However, the American example indicates that there need be little empirical correlation between policies that favor narrow groups and deficit spending. In my opinion, the primary cost of the many loopholes in the US tax system is not the deficit, currently close to zero, nor the average tax rate, much lower than in most of Western Europe, but the lack of sufficient government spending on a variety of programs from investment in infrastructure to the alleviation of poverty.

The number of dimensions of policy choice is vast. We are forced to restrict our attention to a few dimensions at a time, often only one, regardless of whether we are doing theoretical modelling or econometric estimation. The danger, however, is obvious. It is easy to forget that our results may not survive when we expand the number of choices in our model to more closely approximate the choice set that policymakers and institutional designers actually face.

References

Diermeier, D.and Feddersen, T. J.: Voting cohesion in presidential and parliamentary legislatures. Unpublished paper, Graduate School of Business, Stanford University and J. L. Kellogg Graduate School of Management, Northwestern University, 1996.

Spolaore, E.: Policy making systems and economic efficiency: Coalition governments versus majority governments. Unpublished paper, ECARE, Brussels, 1993.

Scand. J. Economics 100(1), 399–404, 1998

Comment on R. Perotti, "The Political Economy of Fiscal Consolidations"

Assar Lindbeck

IIES, Stockholm University, S-106 91 Stockholm, Sweden

Roberto Perotti has written an excellent survey of the literature on the political economy of fiscal consolidation — a literature to which he has made important contributions himself. I will confine my comments to a few issues in Perotti's paper on which I may have something to add.

A first question is how to explain the emergence and continuations of large budget deficits — or, more specifically, deficits that do not simply reflect a specific stage of the business cycle. A traditional, and quite reasonable, explanation is tax-smoothing behavior: politicians or voters (or both) may consciously spread out over time the costs of particularly high public-sector spending or low tax revenues when this situation is assumed to be temporary, though more long-lasting than deficits during ordinary recessions. The fact that large deficits have regularly emerged during periods of war and abrupt rearmament is consistent with this hypothesis. The hypothesis is also consistent with the emergence of large deficits in the mid-1970s in connection with the unexpected fall in GDP growth and the equally unexpected rise in unemployment — assuming (realistically) that it took quite a long time to realize that these changes were not temporary phenomena.

We would then have identified a case where a positive theory of political behavior follows directly from a normative theory of government — the theory of tax smoothing in public finance (assuming concave utility functions). An alternative positive theory of the emergence of (non-cyclical) budget deficits is that decision-makers simply underestimate either the consequences of expenditure and tax decisions for the budget deficit, or the disadvantages of such deficits. In other words, politicians may underestimate the negative effects on the tax base by underestimating various long-run disincentive effects — an example of fiscal illusion. For instance, the negative effects on the national economy of increased government spending and higher tax rates may not have become pronounced until spending and taxes reached rather high levels, such as in the 1970s and 1980s. It may have taken considerable time to realize that such effects had in fact arisen. There may also be important delays in the disincentive effects, for instance because economic disincentives are constrained in the short and medium term by the influence on economic behavior of habits and social norms inherited from the past.

These explanations are hardly sufficient, however, to explain why the budget deficits that emerged in the mid-1970s and early 1980s continued for so long — in some countries for a quarter of a century. Most decision-makers must gradually have realized that the driving forces behind the deficits were not temporary. Theories of tax-smoothing behavior, fiscal illusion and delayed effects must therefore be amended.

One possibility is to assume irreversibilities in political processes. It is certainly difficult for politicians to cut benefits that were granted a long time ago — largely during the "golden age" of rapid economic growth and low unemployment in the 1950s and 1960s when generous benefit systems looked quite affordable. In particular, many individuals must find it difficult to adjust their behavior to a sudden deterioration in benefit systems on which they have to a considerable extent based their lives, including saving and private insurance policies. We may also speculate that individuals are more upset by losing an already existing benefit than by never having received it in the first place. Individuals may have acquired subjectively perceived property rights to their benefits. Formally, the utility function may be steeper to the left of the initial point than to the right, as suggested by Khaneman and Twersky's "prospect theory".

Politicians are, of course, tempted to adjust their behavior to circumstances like these. This is probably an important reason why it is difficult for politicians to remove a budget deficit fast by expenditure cuts, perhaps by tax hikes as well, since they would then disrupt individual planning to a considerable extent.

Personally, I find these simple explanations of the emergence and persistence of budget deficits — and hence also the delays in budget consolidation — more compelling than the more sublime theories on this issue reviewed in Perotti's paper. There is, of course, also a possibility that politicians and voters (or both) consciously try to shift the costs of increased government spending to future generations, i.e., to individuals without voting rights today — even when a deficit is not believed to be the result of a temporary shock. This is simply an application of the median voter theory. (In the hypothetical "population" consisting of both today's voters and voters living tomorrow, the median voter is likely to be a person living today.)

Most of Perotti's paper does not, however, deal with explanations of the emergence and persistence of budget deficits but rather with alternative strategies for removing them, as well as with the degree to which the success of such policies depends on alternative institutional arrangements. The most impressive result of empirical research in this field is perhaps that budget consolidations seem to have been more sustainable in countries which cut expenditures than in countries which raised taxes. It is still an open question how robust these results will turn out to be. The studies suffer from the same problem as other cross-country studies of complex issues (such as regression studies of the determinants of economic growth): excluded variables may not be orthogonal to the included explanatory variables. For instance, governments that cut spending may differ from governments that raise taxes in many relevant aspects that are not considered in these studies.

Perotti emphasizes that the political feasibility and sustainability of a budget consolidation are also likely to depend on its macroeconomic consequences. In particular, a budget consolidation may be easier and more sustainable if it has, in fact, expansionary rather than restrictive effects on the national economy. Many economists and politicians have, as we know, recently argued that such an "anti-Keynesian" result may actually emerge when the government debt, or the deficits, are initially very large. I will add one point on this heatedly debated issue, namely the consequences of budget consolidations for the *uncertainty* among firms and households. One conceivable effect of a budget consolidation during a period of "financial stress" is that lingering doubts may recede among lenders regarding the ability of the government to service its debt without initiating a new round of inflation; this should induce lenders to require lower interest rates. Another mechanism may be less uncertainty among households about their future entitlements in the social security system; this may induce consumers to reduce their financial saving, which would have short-term expansionary effects on aggregate demand. It is tempting to refer to recent experiences in Finland and Sweden on these issues. Uncertainty seems to have increased dramatically in the early 1990s in connection with a drastic rise in the budget deficit. This may help explain the dramatic increase in both interest rates and the private financial saving rate at that time. It is often also believed, quite realistically I think, that the subsequent fall in interest rates and the household saving rate, is related to budget consolidation in the mid-1990s.

The choice between comprehensive and gradual reforms is another important issue dealt with by Perotti. To my mind, the basic dilemma is the following. A comprehensive strategy would rely on a policy package to avoid creating a number of new problems; in particular, such a policy would consider various interdependencies and complementarities in economic, social and political systems. Such a comprehensive strategy would be natural for a social planner trying to maximize some static social welfare function. It is often also argued that a comprehensive reform may make it easier to share the burden of budget consolidation among voters. Moreover, with a "package approach" each voter may not only be a loser in some dimensions but also a winner in other dimensions. It is often asserted that both these circumstances help make budget consolidation politically more acceptable to the electorate.

Gradualism, hence a sequence of partial reforms, will over time create a number of new problems, partly by revealing other weaknesses in economic, social and political systems. To a well-informed social planner who wants to maximize a static social utility function, this looks like a drawback. It is possible to look at the issue differently, however, in the context of the political feasibility of reforms. As partial reforms reveal new problems for politicians and the general public, political support may gradually build up to solve these problems. This argument resembles Hirschman's theory of the advantages of "unbalanced growth", by which new tensions in the economic system are gradually created and resolved during such a growth process.

For instance, the deregulation of capital markets in Sweden in the mid-1980s demonstrated to both a large number of politicians and the general public that high marginal tax rates, against which individuals can deduct interest payments, tend to stimulate individuals to build up debt, which could overheat the national economy. An isolated deregulation of the capital market may, therefore, subsequently increase the political support for reduced marginal tax rates, which seems to have happened in Sweden. A deregulation of capital and product markets may also create severe adjustment problems in the labor market, which may increase the political support for subsequent labor market reforms, as in New Zealand in the late 1980s and early 1990s.

Hence, the choice between comprehensive and gradual reforms is a very delicate one. Whether one strategy will turn out to be more successful than another may very well also depend on the personalities and abilities of specific political leaders. This means that "political artists" like Douglas in New Zealand and Thatcher in the UK can have a great impact on the outcome — not to mention the importance of good or bad luck. This makes life difficult, though interesting, for scholars trying to make robust generalizations in the field of political economy.

Another interesting part of Perotti's paper is his discussion of the importance of institutions for budget consolidation. The most robust result in this field is perhaps that minority governments have greater difficulties in consolidating the government budget than majority governments. Asserted advantages of "top-down" budget processes, relative to "bottom-up" mechanisms, seem to have less support in systematic empirical studies, though the view is well established among profound observers of the political process as well as among many decision-makers. My only comment on this issue is that restraining effects on aggregate government spending of "top-down" budget processes do not necessarily require that aggregate spending ceilings are set by others than those taking subsequent disaggregate spending decisions. A recursive decision-making process — with total spending decided first and individual items decided later — may restrain aggregate spending even if the same agents decide on both levels. An official announcement about the total spending level (a commitment mechanism) may restrain politicians' subsequent decisions about specific expenditure items, in the same way as individuals in their private lives often restrain their own detailed decisions in everyday life by an announcement of a fixed behavior rule, such as " I have stopped smoking". In other words, it may be possible to discipline one's own short-term temptation ("my inferior self") by announcing formally and solemnly one's own long-term preferences ("my better self").

Perotti also discusses complications of budget consolidations due to "social fragmentation". The problem has perhaps been accentuated over the years in some countries, as organizations originally founded to serve their members professionally have increasingly devoted their resources to lobbying for various favors from the government, i.e., from the taxpayers. Metaphorically, some organized interest groups may be said to have moved from being largely Putman-type organizations, vitalizing civil society, to rent-seeking organizations as described by Gordon Tullock, Anne Krueger and Mancur Olson.

A rather widespread advice on this issue is to advocate highly central-ized, "encompassing" organizations, i.e., organizations asserted to inter-nalize a large part of the effects of their own actions. A "corporatist" version of the argument is that the government should make contracts with such organizations to solve difficult political problems, including budget consolidation. Perotti expresses some reservations about this idea. I want to underline such skepticism. The fact that large and highly centralized organizations may be able to internalize much of the effects of their actions is not necessarily advantageous for society at large. Such organizations may, in fact, function as powerful "veto gates" for important reforms, including cuts in government spending. More generally, such organizations may be able to impose decisions on society at large, reflecting the ideology and interests of these organizations and their leaders, rather than values among voters in general. Large, centralized and encompassing organiza-tions may, therefore, often be a great *disadvantage* to society at large.

More specifically, the leaders of such organizations are not elected by *all* adult individuals in society. If the organizations are highly influential on government polices, their members will, in fact, have two votes each in politics — one in the general election and one within the organization. The situation is different if members' influence within the organization itself is very weak, for instance because of the lack of open and vigorous competi-tion between subgroups of members when leaders are elected, in contrast to competition between political parties in representative democracy. But then it is the leaders of the organizations who gain strong direct political influence on politics without being elected in efficiently operating general elections.

The political powers of large, centralized and encompassing organizations are derived partly from their powers to disrupt the macroeconomy, which puts them in a blackmail position towards the government. For instance, Swedish labor union leaders have used their powers in the labor market to enhance their powers in society at large by obtaining both labor-market legislation in their favor and cash grants from the government. The most obvious case is perhaps the creation in the early 1980s of so-called "wage earners" funds", designed to take over the bulk of the ownership of corporations in Sweden with the help of taxes paid by the firms themselves. The basic idea was that union representatives, via these funds, would seize ownership control of all (or most) Swedish corporations.

Such possibilities of blackmail on the part of strong organizations are, or course, a problem not only in the case of "mass organizations" — such as labor unions and organizations of farmers or homeowners — but also in the case of large corporations with close ties to politicians, or with strong bargaining positions *vis-à-vis* the government. Southeast Asia provides examples.

"Corporatist" agreements between the government and large encompassing organizations — social pacts — may very well help solve serious problems in specific situations, including an acute need for budget consolidation. My point is that such agreements may be associated with severe long-term risks for society at large. In particular, the government may be imprisoned by these organizations: "Faustian contracts" are not only tempting but also dangerous. Thus, even if "social fragmentation" may complicate policies designed to consolidate the government budget, or to solve other problems, agreements with large and highly centralized organizations may very well result in even more serious problems for society at large in a long-term perspective.